Backup: DO NOT READ WITHOUT PERMISSION 2012/10

Daniel Pickford-Gordon

Backup: DO NOT READ WITHOUT PERMISSION 2012/10 © 2012 Daniel Pickford-Gordon

ISBN 978-0-9561601-1-9

All rights reserved. No part of this publication may be reproduced, stored in a retrieval system, or transmitted, in any form or by any means, electronic, mechanical, photocopying, recording or otherwise, without the prior permission of the publisher.

Contents

Routines
Help
Topix
Letter To Nicholas Clegg 2: Part Of
Human Female Sexual
Correctness And Incorrectness
Health
Natural Science Identities
Possessions

ROUTINE CORRECTNESS AND INCORRECTNESS
FATHERS
Physical and mental pain has only been proven to exist at and above the bony fish class. Significant suffering only exists within humanity. Only humanity behaves incorrectly. What i feel can only be experienced by a human being. Only a very small number of human beings have had the experience that i've had. Only a very small number of species of organism have harmed a copy of themselves. Only an extremely small number of species of organism have intentionally harmed a copy of themselves.
MOTHERS
Physical and mental pain has only been proven to exist at and above the bony fish class. Significant suffering only exists within humanity. Only humanity behaves incorrectly. What i feel can only be experienced by a human being. Only a very small number of human beings have had the experience that i've had. Only in a very small number of species of organism has the mother harmed one or more of her offspring. Only in an extremely small number of species of organism has the mother intentionally harmed one or more of her offspring.
THE GROUND
The area of ground "infected" is very tiny compared to the whole in the United Kingdom, and to the Earth. The incorrecter/incorrectess hasn't changed what he or she has walked on, or if he or she has, then the change is tiny; if the incorrecter/incorrectess has changed what he or she has walked on, then the change perhaps, or probably, would have occurred anyway. Weather and climate have erased what the incorrecter/incorrectess has done. Much of it doesn't matter if i walk on the rock, on rocks, especially "lower" rocks, rocks that underlie, or lie under, other rocks, other rock. The area can be separated because area is a vertical thing as well as a horizontal thing; the volume, or "bubble" can be separated.

ROUTINE DAILY NOT "NATURAL SCIENCE VOLUME DAY"
Check Eyes 1 Right 1 Left: If One Or Both Eyes Close Then Close Eyes, And Repeat; If Both Eyes Don't Close, Proceed To 2.
Clothing Cover Bed Put On Full
Orange And Mango Juice Tropicana Drink
Orange And Mango Juice Tropicana Top Close 4 Times
Orange And Mango Juice Tropicana Top Stroke 4 Times
Orange And Mango Juice Tropicana Place In Refrigerator If It Contains Orange And Mango Juice
Spinach
Meat Ready Prepared 1/2
Tomato 1
Red Grapes 8
Peanut Bag KP Small, Some Of
Cereal Shreddies 750g And Milk
Chewing Gum

ROUTINE DAILY "NATURAL SCIENCE VOLUME DAY"
Check Eyes Preliminary 1 Right 1 Left: If Both Eyes Don't Close, Proceed To 2.
Check Eyes 1 Right, 1 Left, 1 Left, 1 Right
Look Out Of The Right Window In The Kitchen/Lounge Area
Move Lower Garment And Upper Garment To Bedroom
Shower
Breakfast, And Chewing Gum
Place On Bed This List
Place On Bed Bag Puma Black
Place On Bed Meal John West 2, Chocolate Bar Cadbury's Small 1, And Peanut Bag KP Small 1 In Tesco Bag 2
Place On Bed Water Bottle Small Buxton 1
Place On Bed Paper White 2
Place On Bed Pen Bic Medium Black 1
Place On Bed Scarf, Gloves, In Sainsbury's Bag
Place On Bed Long Sleeved Vest Blue (Thermal?)
Place On Bed Map Relevant Area In Sainsbury's Bag
Place On Bed Glasses In Glasses Case
Place On Bed Telephone Mobile Nokia 2610
Place On Bed Keys In Sainsbury's Bag
Move Clothing To Bedroom
Put On Clothing And Boots Brown With The First Rung Of Laces
Pack Bag Puma Black
Move This List To Chair Black

ROUTINE FOOD AND DRINK
DAY 1
Spinach 1
Potatoes 1
Meat 3 Including Trout/Salmon
Chicken Bernard Matthews 1
Ham Not Supermarket Brand 1/2
Milk Red Top 1/2

DAY 2
Spinach 1
Tomatoes 1
Red Grapes 1
Meat 4
King Prawns 1
Chicken Bernard Matthews 1
Ham Not Supermarket Brand 1/2
Milk Red Top 1/2
Juice Orange And Mango Tropicana 1
John West 1
John West 1

ROUTINE LOCKING DOOR FROM OUTSIDE AND ROUTINE LOCKING DOOR FROM OUTSIDE EXPLANATION
ROUTINE LOCKING DOOR FROM OUTSIDE
Lock Upper Lock
Move Finger(s)/Thumb Against Key In Upper Lock 4 Times
Press Upper Lock Bulge 4 Times
Lock Lower Lock
Move Finger(s)/Thumb Against Key In Lower Lock 4 Times

ROUTINE LOCKING DOOR FROM OUTSIDE EXPLANATION
It is unnecessary to Press Upper Lock Bulge 4 Times after Move Finger(s)/Thumb Against Key In Lower Lock 4 Times because, whether i succeeded with Move Finger(s)/Thumb Against Key In Lower Lock 4 Times or not, the result would still be the same, with no way of telling. If i failed with Move Finger(s)/Thumb Against Key In Upper Lock 4 Times, then the door would open into my home. However, once that process has been completed, the result of the door NOT opening into my home occurs with 100% certainty, regardless of whether i succeed with Move Finger(s)/Thumb Against Key In Lower Lock 4 Times or not.

ROUTINE LONG-TERM
ROUTINE MONTHLY
TUESDAY 1

Clothes Bed Old Put In Bags
Clothes Bed New Fasten To Bed Etcetera
SATURDAY 1

Human USA Internet Money Lloyds TSB 15/07/2012
Human USA Internet Money Paypal 15/07/2012
Human USA Internet Printings Lulu 15/07/2012
Human USA Internet Email 15/07/2012
Human USA Internet BookclubForum?
Human USA Internet Amazon.co.uk?
Human USA Internet Amazon.com?
SUNDAY 1
Human USA Internet Topix
TUESDAY 2
Hoover

ROUTINE MARCH, OCTOBER
Hair Head All Shaved

Oven Clean
Dishes Clean
Toilet Clean
Clothing Wash Oven Gloves
Clothing Wash Glasses Cloth

ROUTINE WEEKLY
DAY 1
Shower With/Without Shower Gel
Gymnasium £4.60
Routine Food And Drink
DAY 2
DAY 3
Shower With/Without Shower Gel
Lloyds TSB Folkestone Change 1 £20 => 1 £5 + 1 £2 + 10 £1 + 15 20p If Necessary
Clothing Wash If Necessary
DAY 4
Routine Food And Drink
DAY 5
Shower With Shower Gel
Clothing Underwear New Take Out
Natural Science Volumes
DAY 6
DAY 7

ROUTINE WHEN REQUIRED
CLEANING
Hoover Bag Empty
HEALTH
Hair Visage Shave
Hair Visage Epilate
Nails Cut
OBTAIN VARIOUS
Dettol Soap/Dettol Hand Gel 2
Shower Gel 1
Shampoo Wash And Go 1
Toothbrush Oral B Firm 1
Toothpaste Colgate 1
Mouthwash Listerine Zero Alcohol 2
Washing Powder(And Conditioner?) 1
Washing Up Liquid 1
Bicarbonate Of Soda 1
Artificial Washing Up Liquid Sponge 1
Steel Scourer 1
Toilet Cleaning Liquid 1
Toilet Clip 1, In The Toilet
OBTAIN FOOD AND DRINK
Water Small Buxton 2
Chewing Gum 4
Crackerbread 4
Ice Lolly 2
Cereal Shreddies 750g
Tinned Meat 1/2
Peanut Bag KP Small 2
Chocolate Bar Cadbury's Small 2
OBTAIN COMPUTER
Printer Paper 1
HP Photosmart 5510. HP 364 Ink Cartridges XL Colour 1 Each: 1 Each In The Printer
HP Photosmart 5510. HP 364 Ink Cartridge XL Black 2: 1 In The Printer, And 1 On The Shelf

HELP REMEMBER

EDWARD HUGHES
THE DROWNED WOMAN
[7 PARTS]
QUEST
[4 PARTS]
from THE LAST MIGRATION
So God died. And a new god
With narrowed eyes,
Carrying the Word reversed,
Gazed across the earth.

Which was cluttered with unbelievables.

HOWARD PHILLIPS LOVECRAFT
from THE QUEST OF IRANON
"....Toil without song is like a weary journey without an end. ...."
from THE HORROR AT RED HOOK
Policemen despair of order or reform, and seek rather to erect barriers protecting the outside world from the contagion.
from THE HORROR AT RED HOOK
More people enter Red Hook than leave it - or at least, than leave it by the landwardside - and those who are not loquacious are the likeliest to leave.
DESPAIR
[5 PARTS, 8 LINES PER PART]
THE ANCIENT TRACK
[2 PARTS, 24 LINES FOR PART 1, 20 LINES FOR PART 2]
ON THE CREATION OF NIGGERS
[8 LINES]
FRAGMENT ON WHITMAN
[18 LINES]
ON RELIGION
[32 LINES]

WILLIAM WORDSWORTH
3. COMPOSED AFTER A JOURNEY ACROSS THE HAMILTON HILLS, YORKSHIRE.
[SONNET, 14 LINES, 10 SYLLABLES PER LINE, RHYMING SCHEME ABBAACCADEFDFE]
4. follows on from COMPOSED AFTER A JOURNEY ACROSS THE HAMILTON HILLS, YORKSHIRE.
[SONNET, 14 LINES, 10 SYLLABLES PER LINE, RHYMING SCHEME ABBAACCADEDEDE]
SONNET, TO THOMAS CLARKSON, ON THE FINAL PASSING OF THE BILL FOR THE ABOLITION OF THE SLAVE TRADE, MARCH, 1807.
[SONNET, 14 LINES, 10 SYLLABLES PER LINE, RHYMING SCHEME ABBAACCADEEDFF]

Human USA Internet: Wikipedia

United Kingdom
News
Forums & PollsHuman USA Internet: W...

Real-Time News

Human USA Internet: Wikipedia

Posted in the United Kingdom Forum

Share

Read
Comments below
Add to my Tracker

More United Kingdom Discussions »

Comments

Showing posts1 - 1 of1

Pickford-Gordon

Since: Sep 09

232

London, UK

Reply »

Report Abuse

Judge it!

#1
1 hr ago

ROY ACUFF
http://en.wikipedia.org/wiki/Roy_Acuff
http://en.wikipedia.org/wiki/Talk:Roy_Acuff
http://en.wikipedia.org/w/index.php?title=Talk:Roy_Acuff&action=history

UNITED KINGDOM FORUM
List Of Posts http://www.topix.net/forum/world/united-kingdom/T367RKHF7P0991G1C

Tell me when this thread is updated:
(Registration is not required)

Add to my Tracker

Send me an email

Showing posts1 - 1 of1

incorrectness of collins, damian, 100% incorrect conservative/tory party

United Kingdom
News
Forums & PollsINCORRECTNESS OF COLL...

Real-Time News

incorrectness of collins, damian, 100% incorrect conservative/tory party

Posted in the United Kingdom Forum

Share

Read
9 Comments
Add to my Tracker

More United Kingdom Discussions »

Comments

Showing posts1 - 9 of9

Pickford-Gordon

Since: Sep 09

317

London, UK

Reply »

Report Abuse

Judge it!

#1
Mar 4, 2012

===========

INCORRECTNESS, OR CRIME, OF COLLINS, DAMIAN, 100% INCORRECT, OR ILLEGAL, CONSERVATIVE/TORY PARTY, MANAGER COUNTRY, MC,(CURRENTLY CALLED "MEMBER OF PARLIAMENT","MP") SHEPWAY
===========

SERIOUSLY DELAYED IF NOT BROKEN AGREEMENT
[Date]
The date is definitely between Sunday 06/02/2011, and Saturday 05/03/2011. My copy of the same letter, sent to an MP, is dated Sunday 06/02/2011, and I remember that I had met Damian Collins AFTER I had sent the letter to a number of other MPs. I was arrested(but not convicted. I will not discuss the issue right now.) on Monday 07/03/2011, and I KNOW that I didn't meet Damian Collins on a Saturday or a Sunday.
[Description]
1.
I met Damian Collins briefly: I handed him a copy of Letter To Nicholas Clegg 2, that I had placed in an envelope."Listen, I was really in a bad state when I wrote this. I haven't had a good life, you know." I was somewhat upset, against my will. I was in an incredibly weakened state, because of 1 or more things etcetera."I will read this letter and get back to you about it," said Damian Collins to me."Really?""Yes, but I'm REALLY busy at the moment, I've got this and that to do.""How will you contact me?""It'll be by post. I'll write back to you," said Damian Collins. I THINK that he added,"As soon as I am able to," but I'm not 100% certain about it. I think that I AM 85% certain that he said "As soon as I am able to," though."You'll definitely write back to me about it?" I asked Damian Collins."YES," he said firmly.
2.
Today is Sunday 04/03/2012, and he has NOT written to me AT ALL. Or if he has then I didn't receive the letter. It looks like it's exactly 1 year since then, or more than that.

Pickford-Gordon

Since: Sep 09

317

London, UK

Reply »

Report Abuse

Judge it!

#2
Apr 21, 2012

ATTEMPT TO BOOK A SURGERY MEETING WITH DAMIAN COLLINS
1.
1 DAY, MONDAY 12/03/2012-FRIDAY 16/03/2012. I shall give J.A. and Gordon, Damian Collins' 2 assistants, my own personal names: J.A. shall be called Human English F. Male I Can Assure You That That Wasn't Him, or HEFMICAYTTW'tH, and Gordon shall be called Human English F. Male This Is Your 1 Opportunity For Your MP To Ring You, or HEFMTIY1OFYMPTRY. I spoke to both HEFMICAYTTW'tH and HEFMTIY1OFYMPTRY on this day, after I had rung the bell. 1 of them said that the next surgery could be held here(Folkestone), in Hythe, or in Cheriton, or something like that. 1 or both of them said that they couldn't book me in for a surgery meeting with Damian Collins today because it was too early: it was not known where the surgery was going to be held. HEFMICAYTTW'tH said that I should come back from Wednesday of next week onwards for the purpose of booking a surgery meeting with Damian Collins.

ATTEMPT TO BOOK A SURGERY MEETING WITH DAMIAN COLLINS 2
1.
FRIDAY 23/03/2012 16:08. There was no answer when I rang the bell. I waited for at least 10 minutes after the bell was rung.

ATTEMPT TO BOOK A SURGERY MEETING WITH DAMIAN COLLINS 3
1.
1 DAY, MONDAY 26/03/2012 OR TUESDAY 27/03/2012. The time of the bell being rung was 10:08. No one came to the door. I waited 10, 15 minutes or so. 10, 15 minutes or so after 10:08 on this day HEFMICAYTTW'tH came to the door. "Sorry about that, I was at the other end of the room," he said. He said that he couldn't book a surgery meeting with Damian Collins for me for some reason or another. I think that he might have said that HEFMTIY1OFYMPTRY is the person who deals with surgery bookings. I asked what hours this office(this place) was open: HEFMICAYTTW'tH first said something like that there are no hours. Then, however, he said that the hours are 09:00-17:00.

ATTEMPT TO BOOK A SURGERY MEETING WITH DAMIAN COLLINS 4
1.
WEDNESDAY 28/03/2012. HEFMTIY1OFYMPTRY opened the door after I had rung the bell. "J. is out. J.A. deals with bookings," said HEFMTIY1OFYMPTRY, except he used, respectively, the first name and full name of HEFMICAYTTW'tH. HEFMTIY1OFYMPTRY said something like "Closed all day today". In any case I wrote down "Closed all day today," so he said something like that with 100% certainty. I think he said that this office was closed all day today. "I'm Gordon," said HEFMTIY1OFYMPTRY. "He's in tomorrow, J. is in tomorrow," said HEFMTIY1OFYMPTRY. "I'm just on my way out: I'm going to west Kent," said HEFMTIY1OFYMPTRY.

ATTEMPT TO BOOK A SURGERY MEETING WITH DAMIAN COLLINS 5
1.
THURSDAY 29/03/2012 15:19. I reached the door at 15:19. There was a sign on the door which said that(for the conservative party Shepway) "Office is unattended at the moment."

Pickford-Gordon

Since: Sep 09

317

London, UK

Reply »

Report Abuse

Judge it!

#3
Apr 21, 2012

ATTEMPT TO BOOK A SURGERY MEETING WITH DAMIAN COLLINS 6
1.
TUESDAY 03/04/2012. I rang the bell. I saw HEFMTIY1OFYMPTRY appear in the inner doorway more or less immediately after I had rung the bell: it was definitely him. I leaned back, waiting for him to open the door. The door didn't open. I looked again through the window. No one was there now. After a small number of seconds HEFMICAYTTW'tH appeared at the door. "Hello. Gordon's not here, he's in charge," said HEFMICAYTTW'tH. "He said that you dealt with the bookings," I said to him. He said no, Gordon deals with it. "You know I'm sure that I just saw Gordon appear in the doorway," I said to him, meaning the inner doorway. "I can assure you that that wasn't him: that was one of our volunteers." "He definitely had grey hair," I said to him. He said something like it was definitely not someone with grey hair. "Come back from next Tuesday onwards." "Gordon deals with it."

ATTEMPT TO BOOK A SURGERY MEETING WITH DAMIAN COLLINS 7
1.
WEDNESDAY 11/04/2012. I rang the bell and HEFMTIY1OFYMPTRY opened the door. "Now look here," he said. "The surgery's full for the rest of this week," he said to me. "Okay, I'll book for sometime next month then." "The surgery's full for the rest of the month," he replied. "Okay, well, next month then." "There are no diaries here," he replied. I was taking written notes. "Yes write that down: diaries, d-i-a-r-i-e-s: diaries," he went. It appeared that HEFMTIY1OFYMPTRY was mocking me. He was being highly aggressive and loud this whole time, and acted as though he was irritated with me: he was sort of acting as though he was going to move forward, to encourage me to move backwards and leave.
2.
"J. deals with the bookings," he said. "J. said that YOU deal with the bookings," I said to him. I said something like that. "That was last week and you know that," he said. The "you know that" is a sort of "verbal technique" used by certain people. "You're wasting my time, and quite frankly I'm wasting yours," he said. "If it's urgent then your mp will ring you." I said that I didn't want a phonecall: I wanted to book a surgery meeting with Damian Collins. "What problem do you have with your mp ringing you?" "You have 1 opportunity right now. This is your 1 opportunity for your mp to ring you. Will you take it or will you not take it?" After I said again that I didn't want a phonecall: that I wanted to book a surgery meeting with Damian Collins he said something like: "Right. Well if it's not urgent then that's all then." I said something like: "It IS urgent but I don't want my mp to contact me by telephone: I want to book a surgery meeting with Damian Collins." I think that he then repeated that the diaries were not here.

Pickford-Gordon

Since: Sep 09

317

London, UK

Reply »

Report Abuse

Judge it!

#4
Jun 10, 2012

ATTEMPT TO BOOK A SURGERY MEETING WITH DAMIAN COLLINS 3 2
2.
He might said that HEFMTIY1OFYMPTRY is the person who deals with surgery bookings. He then said: "Gordon's not in. His mother/aunt died." I can't remember which 1 he said, whether it was "mother" or "aunt".

TOPIX UNITED KINGDOM FORUM
List Of Posts http://www.topix.net/forum/world/united-kingdom/T367RKHF7P0991G1C

ATTEMPT TO BOOK A SURGERY MEETING WITH DAMIAN COLLINS 8
1.
WEDNESDAY 16/05/2012. I rang the bell 1, 2 minutes or so after 16:26. HEFMICAYTTW'tH, whose name, I had been told by HEFMTIY1OFYMPTRY, is James Alexander, opened the door. Me: "Hello. Er, is it Gordon who deals with the bookings, or...?" HEFMICAYTTW'tH: "Yes Gordon deals with it, Gordon's not here now. Ask Gordon when he comes back. Try tomorrow." Me: "I'm not sure if I have time tomorrow."

A BOOKING OF A SURGERY MEETING WITH DAMIAN COLLINS
1.
WEDNESDAY 30/05/2012. I rang the bell 1, 2 minutes or so after 16:32. HEFMTIY1OFYMPTRY opened the door. HEFMTIY1OFYMPTRY: "Okay. I don't have the diary." Me: "You don't have it?" "Come in," said HEFMTIY1OFYMPTRY. I came in and stood in the doorway. "I don't have the diary," he repeated. He was smiling as he said this. "The diary's in there isn't it?" I asked, with a slight tone in my voice, pointing to the room inside. "Right. WAIT THERE," commanded HEFMTIY1OFYMPTRY. He went into the room. After 5, 10 seconds or so HEFMICAYTTW'tH came out. HEFMICAYTTW'tH: "You DO know it's this Friday don't you? He starts at L. and then proceeds to N.R." Me: "Okay I'd like to book an appointment then. It's no problem for me to go there." HEFMICAYTTW'tH: "You know I think it'd be better if you come back tomorrow and (something or other)." Me: "No, I'll book now." HEFMICAYTTW'tH: "You know, it's funny, I think that the surgery's going to be held INSIDE Sainsbury's, in Hythe. It's INSIDE Sainsbury's." Me: "I'd like to book for N.R. Town Hall." HEFMICAYTTW'tH sighed and then said, tiredly: "ALright then. I have Four-Forty Five at N.R. Town Hall. Is that okay?" I think that, after having glanced at the diary paper, I saw that no one else had booked a Surgery Meeting with Damian Collins on that day. I think I saw that the sheet of paper looked very blank, very white.

Pickford-Gordon

Since: Sep 09

317

London, UK

Reply »

|
Report Abuse
|
Judge it!
|
#5
Sunday Jul 22

2012/06/01 FRIDAY
SURGERY MEETING WITH DAMIAN COLLINS
[START]
1.
The appointment time was 16:45. I entered N.R. Town Hall and saw HEFMICAYTTW'tH, Damian Collins, and a Human English F. Female, an older woman. The Human English F. Female remained in the initial room, with myself, Damian Collins, and HEFMICAYTTW'tH going to a different room. I shall refer to Damian Collins as Human English F. Male Private Company It's Theirs We Disagree, or HEFMPCI'sTWD. HEFMICAYTTW'tH appeared to be taking notes, or a transcript, of what was said....but i don't know, and perhaps doubt, whether he was actually doing that.
2.
HEFMPCI'sTWD: "Hello. I've been told that (there's an issue with you and) Sainsbury's. Is that correct?" He said something like that. Me: "Yes, well, my name is Daniel Pickford-Gordon, er, well you've got that written down haven't you? I've written down what i would like to occur with regard to this." I said something like that as i was looking in my bags for a number of items. Me: "I haven't been too well, i tried to commit suicide in May, er, May 2011, last year." I think that there was an expression of pity and/or sadness on HEFMPCI'sTWD's visage after i had said that, but i'm only 85% sure: it was a long time ago. HEFMPCI'sTWD was looking at the sheet of paper that i had handed him, which included the Sainsbury's F. Manager's first name. HEFMPCI'sTWD: "Do you know why you were banned from Sainsbury's?" Me: "He wouldn't even talk to me, he sent the Deputy Manager to talk to me. I've made a record of what happened. The Deputy Manager said that this girl had complained about me. I didn't do anything wrong." I had said something like that. HEFMPCI'sTWD: "I need to find out why you were banned first, and then we can decide if it's necessary to take it further. I will write to him." Me: "Couldn't you perhaps speak to him instead? I think that speaking is much better and easier, and since you're, you know, a political figure, he might agree then and there to let me back in, it saves time." HEFMPCI'sTWD: "A letter is more formal. If you have a letter it's a record, you can put it up there on the wall. It's a record. After that it's necessary to wait for him to write back." He said something like that. Me: "What if he doesn't write back? He's arrogant, he thinks that he can do whatever he wants." "He'll write back," said HEFMPCI'sTWD firmly and confidently. That was sort of a "He'll write back because if he doesn't there'll be serious consequences for him" phrase. Me: "Okay, i was wondering if perhaps you could tell me when you'll write to him?" HEFMPCI'sTWD: "I'll write to him this week." Me: "This week?" HEFMPCI'sTWD: "Yes, this week."
3.
Me: "The second issue is taking away the power of Managers to "ban" people". HEFMPCI'sTWD: "No i'm not doing that. These are private companies. It's theirs". There's nothing that the Prime Minister can do about that. There's nothing that can be done about it." Me: "Well i don't think that there IS such a thing as a private company." HEFMPCI'sTWD said a number of things in disagreement to that. Me: "Well, the thing is, i looked in the Oxford English Dictionary for the definitions of king and queen. And it says "ruler", "ultimate power". Now, the United Kingdom is a constitutional monarchy, which means that the power of the monarch has been transferred. The 650 mps have the power." As i said the phrase "Oxford English Dictionary", HEFMPCI'sTWD's expression changed into a "Yeah yeah", "Yes i know", "I know the game is up", "Here it comes" look, an expression like that.

Pickford-Gordon

Since: Sep 09

317

London, UK

Reply »

|
Report Abuse
|
Judge it!
|
#6
Sunday Jul 22

2012/06/01 FRIDAY
SURGERY MEETING WITH DAMIAN COLLINS
[MIDDLE]
+
HEFMPCI'sTWD: "It's theirs. These are private companies." Me: "I mean, you say that private companies are theirs'. Well, the thing about the country is that everything is connected. In order for things in THIS part of the country to keep going, things need to occur in OTHER parts of the country. They need electricity." HEFMPCI'sTWD: "Yes and we pay for that." As he said that he looked away from me. The pitch, or tone, of his voice had risen so that it was "higher" than normal, as he had said that sentence. His voice wobbled horribly as he said that sentence. He had said the sentence evasively. I sensed fear in his voice as he had said that sentence.
+
HEFMPCI'sTWD: "It's theirs. They pay for the land."
+
HEFMPCI'sTWD: "Well we disagree on/about that."
[END]
+
HEFMPCI'sTWD: "We have to finish now. I have another Surgery Meeting now."
+
HEFMPCI'sTWD: "I'll talk to him, I'll have a word with him."
+
HEFMPCI'sTWD: "I have (X) thousand constituents." X is a number.
+
HEFMPCI'sTWD: "That letter you gave me a long time ago: you asked me to pass it on to the Prime Minister didn't you?"
+
The Human English F. Female, the older woman, from the start, after Damian Collins had said something to me, nodded in agreement, and said "yeah".
+
I had said a large number of things during this Surgery Meeting that took apart the lie of "private companies", and the lie of "banning". HEFMPCI'sTWD, or Damian Collins, had been unable to provide any counter-arguments to the large number of points etcetera that i made that took apart the lie of "private companies" and the lie of "banning".

Pickford-Gordon

Since: Sep 09

317

London, UK

Reply »

Report Abuse

Judge it!

#7
Sunday Jul 22

2012/06/11 MONDAY(LETTER IS DATED THUS)
I have a signed letter dated 11 June 2012, which i received around that time-a short time after that date if i remember correctly- from HEFMPCI'sTWD, or Damian Collins. It says: "Dear Mr Pickford-Gordon, Thank you for coming to see me at my advice centre about the difficulties you have encountered; I was very sorry indeed to learn of this. I have raised your concerns with the store manager of Sainsbury's and will be back in touch as soon as I have received a response. Yours sincerely,(signature) DAMIAN COLLINS". The paper is custom-made for Damian Collins, and all other mps no doubt have equivalent versions. There's a picture of a "gate" at the top, and website details etcetera at the bottom.

Faloola Chong

Northwich, UK

Reply »

Report Abuse

Judge it!

#8
Wednesday Jul 25

i know right

i had exactly same problem

Pickford-Gordon

Since: Sep 09

317

London, UK

Reply »

Report Abuse

Judge it!

#9
31 min ago

2012/06/13 WEDNESDAY
ATTEMPT TO BOOK A SURGERY MEETING WITH DAMIAN COLLINS 9
After i had rung the bell, HEFMICAYTTW'tH opened the door. In response to me asking if i could book a Surgery Meeting for this Friday, HEFMICAYTTW'tH replied: "It's full this Friday." HEFMICAYTTW'tH also said: "Damian Collins said that you should write it down." After a period of time, HEFMICAYTTW'tH said: "There are people on the phone: i have to go."

Tell me when this thread is updated:
(Registration is not required)

Add to my Tracker

Send me an email

Showing posts 1 - 9 of 9

List Of Posts

United Kingdom
News
Forums & PollsList Of Posts - Topix

Real-Time News

List Of Posts

Posted in the United Kingdom Forum

Share

Read
7 Comments
Add to my Tracker

More United Kingdom Discussions »

Comments

Showing posts1 - 7 of7

Pickford-Gordon

Since: Sep 09

358

London, UK

Reply »

|
Report Abuse
|
Judge it!
|
#1
May 6, 2012

TOPIX UNITED KINGDOM FORUM
(The US of) AmericA and (The US of) AmericANS http://www.topix.com/forum/world/united-kingdom/TBE4CVMOO2EP58A8E
A Personal Message for a Certain Guy and a Certain Girl http://www.topix.com/forum/world/united-kingdom/TLULR8J2EV3A87JUR
Correspondance with Myself http://www.topix.net/forum/world/united-kingdom/TJ2FTCV8I3770PH2F
Criminals http://www.topix.com/forum/world/united-kingdom/TGVEV96A507T0ORC1
Enemies Of The Universe http://www.topix.com/forum/world/united-kingdom/TIKNFQPIEIUF9Q243
execution requested http://www.topix.com/forum/world/united-kingdom/TGC8VLVFVU94CD3SM
girls/women http://www.topix.com/forum/world/united-kingdom/T078GDCV1D0M3P723
Hope This Leads To Her Being With Me Very Soon http://www.topix.com/forum/world/united-kingdom/T6NPB22GRVG24S4F4
incorrectness of collins, damian, 100% incorrect conservative/tory party http://www.topix.net/forum/world/united-kingdom/TABDF5C6B947VL2RD
Incorrectness Of Johnson, Boris, 100% Incorrect Conservative/Tory Party http://www.topix.net/forum/world/united-kingdom/T98H5E9Q6QS04DV01
it's best not to "assume" anything about me http://www.topix.com/forum/world/united-kingdom/TDIQ5F9UFIP1E4AS5
Letter To Another MP hopefully leading vry soon to this girl being with me http://www.topix.com/forum/world/united-kingdom/TSGOLS7T0UENIN4JJ
messages for british politicians http://www.topix.com/forum/world/united-kingdom/TDNK5DIPGMHE8OERG
miscellaneous writings http://www.topix.net/forum/world/united-kingdom/TLISJ333AQFSGMA0J
My First Book http://www.topix.com/forum/world/united-kingdom/T6356RU8VMLDOFQQI
My Return! http://www.topix.com/forum/world/united-kingdom/T6D9OJDDTG20DPH91
nick clegg http://www.topix.com/forum/world/united-kingdom/TQOO8SCT63VBMAHA7
religion http://www.topix.com/forum/world/united-kingdom/TIDLK0BLFGSGSFCKJ
Self Sufficiency For Every Country http://www.topix.com/forum/world/united-kingdom/TPB8Q7GU0MBI33EGM
Suffering Extreme: Incorrectness Sexual Of HEFN-Ses Typings http://www.topix.net/forum/world/united-kingdom/T15DHUSDSDNF2DTJB
suffering history: extreme: incorrectness: hefmgd'tfcwy http://www.topix.net/forum/world/united-kingdom/T3RSMV78O9IIEED3A
suffering history: extreme: suicide attempt http://www.topix.net/forum/world/united-kingdom/T374VJJ9OINBQOP6F
suffering history: incorrectness: human english males http://www.topix.net/forum/world/united-kingdom/TKV3Q8A5K96SMNAF6
suicide http://www.topix.net/forum/world/united-kingdom/TBP8APFTV7UMD7O0E
The First Changes http://www.topix.net/forum/world/united-kingdom/TTPORQVK5SR7802Q1

the girl from this place http://www.topix.com/forum/world/united-kingdom/T6T3HB8817628K45F
the physical and mental differences between the human male and the human female http://www.topix.net/forum/world/united-kingdom/TEVLN4JRD0KEL21O7

Pickford-Gordon

Since: Sep 09

358

London, UK

Reply »

|
Report Abuse
|
Judge it!
|
#2
Jun 6, 2012

TOPIX UNITED KINGDOM FORUM
Execution And Suicide Typings http://www.topix.net/forum/world/united-kingdom/TM1IAA363P926FGT9
Incorrectness Of Shapps, Grant, 100% Incorrect Conservative/Tory Group http://www.topix.net/forum/world/united-kingdom/TVPGDHE1RAH16HL54

Pickford-Gordon

Since: Sep 09

358

London, UK

Reply »

|

Report Abuse

Judge it!

#3 Jun 10, 2012

TOPIX UNITED KINGDOM FORUM
Incorrectness Of Beaumont, Lynne 100% Incorrect Human Female Manager Group http://www.topix.net/forum/world/united-kingdom/TRGBUN68FU52QBIBU
Popularity http://www.topix.net/forum/world/united-kingdom/T2QDG28I6MRDCOQQU

Pickford-Gordon

Since: Sep 09

358

London, UK

Reply »

Report Abuse

Judge it!

#4 Jun 24, 2012

TOPIX UNITED KINGDOM FORUM
Correctness And Incorrectness http://www.topix.net/forum/world/united-kingdom/TE7N0749A9H317A53
Correctness And Incorrectness Typings http://www.topix.net/forum/world/united-kingdom/TM3BT5N6PJB448HGA

Pickford-Gordon

Since: Sep 09

358

London, UK

Reply »

|
Report Abuse
|
Judge it!
|
#6
Jun 30, 2012

TOPIX UNITED KINGDOM FORUM
Human USA Internet: Wikipedia http://www.topix.net/forum/world/united-kingdom/TCLEKCD5LICE3ARNR

Pickford-Gordon

Since: Sep 09

358

London, UK

Reply »

|
Report Abuse
|
Judge it!
|
#7
Wednesday Aug 1

TOPIX UNITED KINGDOM FORUM
The Conservative/Tory Group Is 100% Incorrect http://www.topix.net/forum/world/united-kingdom/TOC51ORJ6LO11J018
The Conartist/Terry Group Is 100% Incorrect Typings http://www.topix.net/forum/world/united-kingdom/TUCJNIMCN3FB8913V

Pickford-Gordon

Since: Sep 09

358

London, UK

Reply »

Report Abuse

Judge it!

#8
44 min ago

TOPIX UNITED KINGDOM FORUM
Management Country: General http://www.topix.net/forum/world/united-kingdom/T3GAFCICCUOR0HIG4

Tell me when this thread is updated:
(Registration is not required)

Add to my Tracker

Send me an email

Showing posts1 - 7 of7

Popularity

United Kingdom
 News
  Forums & PollsPopularity - Topix

Real-Time News

Popularity

Posted in the United Kingdom Forum

Share

Read
4 Comments
Add to my Tracker

More United Kingdom Discussions »

Comments

Showing posts1 - 4 of4

Pickford-Gordon

Since: Sep 09

394

London, UK

Reply »

|
Report Abuse
|
Judge it!
|
#1
Jun 6, 2012

2012/06/03 SUNDAY
[20:04:10 PAGE CREATED]
[[GOOGLE.CO.UK, About 1,010,000 Results]]
pickford gordon resulted in (1) Topix Profile Pickford-Gordon ie My Recent Posts (7) amazon.co.uk: Daniel Pickford-Gordon: Books (8) waterstones.com The Physical And Mental Differences Of Humanity (9) lovereading.co.uk Daniel Pickford Gordon books (10) whsmith.co.uk The Physical And Mental Differences Of Humanity
[20:05:21 PAGE CREATED; 20:05:25 PAGE MODIFIED, PAGE ACCESSED]
[[GOOGLE.CO.UK, About 53,500 Results]]
"the physical and mental differences" resulted in (1) amazon.co.uk The Physical And Mental Differences Of Humanity (2) topix.com [that should be topix.net , surely] THE PHYSICAL AND MENTAL DIFFERENCES BETWEEN THE HUMAN MALE AND THE HUMAN FEMALE (3) amazon.ca The Physical And Mental Differences Of Humanity (6) amazon.com The Physical And Mental Differences Of Humanity (10) alibris.co.uk The Physical And Mental Differences Of Humanity

UNITED KINGDOM FORUM
List Of Posts http://www.topix.net/forum/world/united-kingdom/T367RKHF7P0991G1C

Pickford-Gordon

Since: Sep 09

394

Wareham, UK

Reply »

|
Report Abuse
|
Judge it!
|
#2
Jul 7, 2012

2012/06/17 SUNDAY
[GOOGLE.CO.UK, About 229,000 Results]
correctness and incorrectness resulted in (1) topix.com Correctness And Incorrectness Typings (2) topix.com Correctness And Incorrectness (3) topix.net Correctness And Incorrectness Typings

Pickford-Gordon

Since: Sep 09

394

London, UK

Reply »

|
Report Abuse
|
Judge it!
|
#3
Jul 14, 2012

2012/07/07 SATURDAY
[GOOGLE.CO.UK, About 660,000,000 Results]
suffering typings resulted in (1) topix.com Suffering Extreme: Incorrectness Sexual Of HEFN-Ses Typings
[GOOGLE.CO.UK, About 36,700,000 Results]
execution typings resulted in (1) topix.com Execution And Suicide Typings
[GOOGLE.CO.UK, About 423,000,000 Results]
suicide typings resulted in (1) topix.com Execution And Suicide Typings (2) topix.com List Of Posts

[GOOGLE.CO.UK, About 38,700 Results]
topix miscellaneous writings resulted in (1) topix.com miscellaneous writings
[GOOGLE.CO.UK, About 445,000 Results]
lynne beaumont topix resulted in (1) topix.com Incorrectness Of Beaumont, Lynne 100% Incorrect Human Female Manager Group
[GOOGLE.CO.UK, About 2,470,000 Results]
damian collins topix resulted in (1) topix.com incorrectness of collins, damian, 100% incorrect conservative/tory party
[GOOGLE.CO.UK, About 9,550 Results]
pickford clegg topix resulted in (1) topix.com nick clegg (2) topix.com Pickford-Gordon ie My Recent Posts
[GOOGLE.CO.UK, About 1,630,000 Results]
conservative tory topix resulted in (1) topix.com Incorrectness Of Shapps, Grant, 100% Incorrect Conservative/Tory Group

Pickford-Gordon

Since: Sep 09

394

London, UK

Reply »

|
Report Abuse
|
Judge it!
|
#4
1 hr ago

2012/09/02 SUNDAY
[GOOGLE.CO.UK, About 120,000,000 Results]
suffering extreme sexual resulted in (1) topix.com Suffering Extreme: Incorrectness Sexual Of HEFN-Ses Typings

2012/09/02 SUNDAY
[GOOGLE.CO.UK, About 49,600,000 Results]
conservative tory incorrect resulted in (4) topix.com The Conservative/Tory Group Is 100% Incorrect

2012/09/04 TUESDAY
[GOOGLE.CO.UK, About 1,620,000 Results]
topix conservative tory resulted in (2) topix.com The Conservative/Tory Group Is 100% Incorrect

2012/09/04 TUESDAY
[GOOGLE.CO.UK, About 40,800,000 Results]
group 100% incorrect resulted in (1) topix.com The Conservative/Tory Group Is 100% Incorrect

2012/09/04 TUESDAY
[GOOGLE.CO.UK, About 124,000,000 Results]
physical mental human male human female resulted in (4) topix.com THE PHYSICAL AND MENTAL DIFFERENCES

BETWEEN THE HUMAN MALE AND THE HUMAN FEMALE

2012/09/04 TUESDAY
[GOOGLE.CO.UK, About 5,300,000 Results]
conservative tory "100%" resulted in (2) topix.com The Conservative/Tory Group Is 100% Incorrect

Tell me when this thread is updated:
(Registration is not required)

Add to my Tracker

Send me an email

Showing posts1 - 4 of4

Suffering Extreme: Incorrectness Sexual Of HEFN-Ses Typings

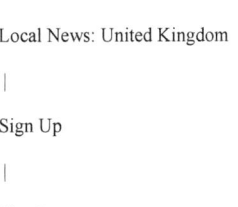

Local News: United Kingdom

|

Sign Up

|

Sign In

123

Mitt Romney
Obama says Romney should be an - open book' on personal finances

North Korea
Replica Disney Dancers on North Korea Stage

Health Care
The Right to Health Care Means Little Without Doctors

Home
Forums
Top Stories
Popular
Local
Election Poll
US
Politics
World
Sports
Entertainment
Offbeat
Other

United Kingdom
News
Forums & PollsSuffering Extreme: In...

Real-Time News

Suffering Extreme: Incorrectness Sexual Of HEFN-Ses Typings

Posted in the United Kingdom Forum

Share

Read
62 Comments
Add to my Tracker

More United Kingdom Discussions »

Comments

Showing posts 1 - 20 of 62

< prev page

|

next page >

Go to last page|Jump to page:1 2 3 4

Pickford-Gordon

Since: Sep 09

263

London, UK

Reply »

|
Report Abuse
|
Judge it!
|
#1
May 5, 2012

SUFFERING EXTREME: INCORRECTNESS SEXUAL OF HUMAN ENGLISH FEMALE NON-SEXUALESSES TYPING
Identity's Image was talking to Human English Female Non-Sexualess Incorrectess Sexual, or HEFN-SIS. "So, Identity's Image...I'm one of the Human English Female Non-Sexualesses who have committed crime, or incorrectness, against you, yet I

can reverse the suffering that I've caused you by having sexual intercourse etcetera with you. You've said that there are More Than 50 of them. Which one am I then?" Identity's Image: "You are one of them; and you are all of them; and you are none of them." HEFN-SIS looked away from Identity's Image, shaking her head.

SUFFERING EXTREME: INCORRECTNESS SEXUAL OF HUMAN ENGLISH FEMALE NON-SEXUALESSES TYPING 2

1.
Identity's Image was talking to Human English Female Non-Sexualess Incorrectess Sexual, or HEFN-SIS. "Well now, Identity's Image. You've got an abnormal growth of hair on your visage; I mean, all of my friends that I CHITCHAT and LAUGH with-as I live in escapism, stimulation of the Freudian Outer Soul(which is not unique at all) as opposed to stimulation of the Freudian Inner Soul(which is unique), with no inner happiness-will laugh at me if I'm seen to be associated with you for THAT ALONE, let alone other awful things about you such as clothing and behaviour. Explain yourself right now! That's an order!" Identity's Image: "I might have gotten rid of it the next time that you see me. I'm not sure if I'm strong enough to do it right now though...all of you have caused me so much suffering...if I epilate the border off then it'll just grow back again won't it..." HEFN-SIS: "Explain yourself! You've already damaged my reputation enough as it is! The Entire World DOES orbit my body, you know."

2.
Identity's Image: "Well I shave most of the hair on my visage(face) when I feel that it has grown too long. I do, however, leave a "border". I have to stop shaving at certain points of my visage and neck, you see, otherwise hair which at the moment is thin, since it has never been shaved, will become thick, and will NEED to be shaved. I don't want to shave my entire neck you see, etcetera. So what I do is I leave: a thin strip of hair by both ears; hair under both eyes-that area-; and a line going from the base of one ear, along the neck, to the base of the other ear. I don't feel that I NEED to shave those areas. Instead, at longer time intervals than shaving, I will EPILATE the hair that grows there, in the aforementioned areas. I can tell you for a fact that hair grows more slowly under my eyes and on my neck, and there's less of it too, etcetera." HEFN-SIS: "Oh ok. I love you. I know how much you think about me and things that relate to me, and how much me being your first girlfriend would mean to you. I'm pissed off that you've only had sexual intercourse with 3 Human English Female Non-Sexualesses(in addition to having had sexual intercourse with a large number of Human English Etcetera Female Sexualesses), I mean all other guys have managed more than that, you're even more of a pathetic abnormal failure than I thought that you were. However, in spite of that, I suppose that SOMEONE has to have sexual intercourse with you, and become your first girlfriend, etcetera. Just don't tell anyone."

Pickford-Gordon

Since: Sep 09

263

London, UK

Reply »

|
Report Abuse
|
Judge it!
|
#2
May 5, 2012

SUFFERING EXTREME: INCORRECTNESS SEXUAL OF HUMAN ENGLISH FEMALE NON-SEXUALESSES TYPING 3
Identity's Image was talking to Human English Female Non-Sexualess Incorrectess Sexual, or HEFN-SIS. "Tell me about WATER, H2O, Identity's Image, come on quickquickquickquick." HEFN-SIS snapped her fingers repeatedly as she said this. Identity's Image: "The Human Being is (90%?) water, H2O...mostly water, HEFN-SIS, anyway, or something. This water needs to be replenished, I think, so Human Beings need to drink water. The Human Being CAN, of course, drink other things than water. However, my current belief is that water is the only drink that the Human Being can drink enormous amounts of without it having a negative effect on him or her: the Human Being must be very careful when drinking anything else that is NOT water. I like to drink water."

Pickford-Gordon

Since: Sep 09

263

London, UK

Reply »

|
Report Abuse
|
Judge it!
|
#3
May 5, 2012

SUFFERING EXTREME: INCORRECTNESS SEXUAL OF HUMAN ENGLISH FEMALE NON-SEXUALESSES TYPING 4
1.
Identity's Image was lying in bed, too weak to get up; he was crying. "It's Human English Female Non-Sexualess Incorrectess Sexual, or HEFN-SIS........and not just her." No joke: I was crying for many hours because of HEFN-SIS, a Human English MTDNA Level H(or whatever most Human English Females are) Female, and because of the Human YDNA Level X Male who has repeatedly done sexual things with her, where X is a letter less than R. I keep hearing her voice-exactly the way that it sounds-, I keep seeing her-or bits of her-, I keep seeing him, I keep seeing the 2 of them standing near each other, I keep seeing the 2 of them standing sexually near each other, and I keep seeing them doing a large number of sexual things with each other(and I don't like it, it hurts).
2.
Identity's Image: "I can't do this Ican'tdothis, it's all nonsense. She's having sexual intercourse with someone else now, I'm worthless, she's treating me like I'm worthless. If I'm no good then surely I must be allowed to die, if I wasn't supposed to have been born. Why me, whyme, when everyone around me has something that I've tried SO HARD for. What do I have to do to get Sexual things, Category: Sexual. I can't take this. I'm turned on by Human English Females, certain ones, most of them probably, everywhere that I go. I can't go on like this. There's no way that I can continue to live with a meagre 30 minutes with a Human English Female Sexualess now and then...and the politicians have failed to sort out certain issues like money too, I mean what if I can no longer afford to pay to be with the wonderful Human English Female Sexualesses in the future? Oh but I keep thinking about her. How could they do that to me? They've been having sexual intercourse all of this time, oh my GOD. But I have HOPE. Next time...if I post a little bit on the Internet...one day...she'll put me out of my misery. One day she'll have sexual intercourse etcetera with me." A Human-English-Male-like figure, like Identity's Image, walked North into his "Field

Of Vision", from his SouthEast. "The Human English Female Non-Sexualess WILL NEVER have sexual intercourse with you again," said the figure.

3.

Identity's Image didn't look at him. From the SouthEast of Identity's Image another Human-English-Male-like figure walked North, into his "Field Of Vision", from his SouthEast. "Identity's Image...you know ME of course. I'm Talks, Comforts, or T,C. I'm here to help you. I want you to be strong, somehow, okay. The Human English Female Non-Sexualesses on your Mental List have abandoned you, Unnecessarily Lied to you including broken promises/agreements, had sexual intercourse incorrectly, they've had sexual intercourse with anyone BUT you. It's THEIR fault...they're so bloated with pride, so arrogant that they won't even talk to you, they won't even show up, they've left you, you don't know where they are. But I'm here for you." T, C stopped speaking. T,C looked worriedly at the Human-English-Male-like figure who had started talking before him, before THAT, FIRST, figure, spoke once more. "In MY case it's not so much that I give a damn about you-I don't really give a damn about any weakling such as yourself-it's just that because we're so similar, Identity's Image, you really are ONE BIG INSULT.........TO ME. And I REALLY DON'T LIKE being inSULTED. I'm Hatred, Sexual of course."

Pickford-Gordon

Since: Sep 09

263

London, UK

Reply »

Report Abuse

Judge it!

#4
May 5, 2012

SUFFERING EXTREME: INCORRECTNESS SEXUAL OF HUMAN ENGLISH FEMALE NON-SEXUALESSES TYPING 4

4.

Hatred, Sexual, or H,S, and Talks, Comforts, or T,C, stood looking down at Identity's Image where he lay on his bed, in his bedroom. "I think about her 24 hours a day. And it hurts so much, her having had sexual intercourse with the Human YDNA Level X Male. I don't want it in my mind so much, make it go away-NO! She's going to be my first girlfriend. I love her! I'm going in there right now!" H,S and T,C restrained him, since Identity's Image had leapt out of bed and was preparing to leave. H,S: "If you go in there more than A times a week, where A is a number from 1 to 7, you might get banned by the Manager...somehow. Or worse: you remember what happened to you on Monday 07/03/2012 don't you, yes of course you do. The Severe Depression which resulted from that has been improving. Of course you live in fear of talking not just about the Human English Female Non-Sexualess who did that to you, not just about related issues, not just about Letter To Nicholas Clegg 2, not just about the place where she works, but you actually live in fear of talking, or typing, about ANY Human English Female Non-Sexualess. You're pathetic, you don't HATE enough. You have problems with your mind, you must do, since you don't HATE the Human English Female Non-Sexualess who has had sexual intercourse with this Human YDNA Level X Male." "NO! NO! You're WRONG, H,S. She's going to be my first girlfriend." "My friend, you will NEVER know what it's like to have a girlfriend."

5.

H,S paused for 2 seconds before continuing. "You can't better, or improve, ANY of the Human English Female Non-Sexualesses on your Mental List. The incorrectness, or crime, is so heavily imprinted in their brains that it is the case that it is 100% FUTILE. They will RUN, they will try to GET RID OF YOU, they will watch "telly" so that they don't have to think about you, they will continue to lie to themselves and tell themselves that you don't exist, or something, or whatever they're thinking. They look ACTIVELY and THOROUGHLY for excuses not to have sexual intercourse with you. TRUST ME." "NO! NEVER!" shouted Identity's Image at him. T,C: "Okay, let us get back to the issue at hand. It's quite possible, as you pointed out, H,S, that if Identity's Image goes in there more than A times a week that he might get banned. He could also get banned if he says anything to her that ISN'T chitchat, humour, general talk, LIGHT talk, anything that makes her UNCOMFORTABLE: she's not complicated enough, and she might very well be liable to act in a "ban him" type of way towards you, Identity's Image, if you do anything that she doesn't like, or something." Identity's Image: "This is completely ridiculous. Why can't I go to her and speak freely, etcetera?" T,C: "The correct answer is because the United Kingdom And Ireland simply is NOT GOOD ENOUGH: it remains inferior, by a significant distance, to superior countries such as [A] Germany [B] Austria [C] Switzerland [D] France [E] Luxembourg [F] Portugal [G] Possibly even Australia, although New Zealand is surely inferior to the United Kingdom And Ireland. The United Kingdom And Ireland is one of the best countries, but it is, of course, not as good as those others. An enormous number of traitors to the Human Species desire to turn the country into the USA. The USA is a good country, though, of course.........it has some nice areas........but it needs work. A lot of work."

champion froot loop

Reply »

|
Report Abuse
|
Judge it!
|
#5
May 5, 2012

old Pickers is on formn today!

Pickford-Gordon

 Since: Sep 09

263

London, UK

Reply »

|

Report Abuse

Judge it!

#6
May 5, 2012

SUFFERING EXTREME: INCORRECTNESS SEXUAL OF HUMAN ENGLISH FEMALE NON-SEXUALESSES TYPING 4
6.
Identity's Image: "She should come up and talk to me. Please, HEFN-SIS, there's almost nothing else for me...you represent hope. Please come up and talk to me, and become my first girlfriend. I love you." T,C: "Perhaps she'll do that, next time." H,S: "You're wasting your time." Identity's Image turned to H,S: "No, YOU'RE wasting YOUR time. All of the Human English Female Non-Sexualess Incorrectesses Sexual on my Mental List, even if it is very deep down inside, WANT to change, WANT to BETTER themselves, as opposed to remaining ignorant and not as good, because of the amount of suffering that they've caused me, as other Human English Female Non-Sexualesses." T,C: "I'm just here to talk to, and to comfort, you." There was silence.

Long-Dead Larry

Reply »

Report Abuse

Judge it!

#7
May 5, 2012

cheer up Pickers, could be worse, you copuld be dead like me.

Pickford-Gordon

Since: Sep 09

263

London, UK

Reply »

Report Abuse

Judge it!

#8
May 5, 2012

SUFFERING EXTREME: INCORRECTNESS SEXUAL OF HUMAN ENGLISH FEMALE NON-SEXUALESSES TYPING 5
"Is there something wrong with that...my NAZI FRIEND?" Identity's Image nodded in response, and then frowned 1 second afterwards. "I'm not a Nazi," said Identity's Image. "Hehehehe......I'm f+cking the girl that you've been fantasizing about, etcetera, Identity's Image. That makes me feel really-" He had been looking away from Identity's Image as he said that, but now he looked back at him. Identity's Image had burst into tears. "Good?" he finished. "Huh? Fascists don't cry." Identity's Image: "I don't like it, it hurts. Please don't do anything sexual with her any more, I can't take it." "The evil Nazi is begging me not to do anything sexual any more with the girl that he loves." He continued to stare at Identity's Image for another 5 seconds before grabbing a nearby bottle of vodka and "downing" it.

SUFFERING EXTREME: INCORRECTNESS SEXUAL OF HUMAN ENGLISH FEMALE NON-SEXUALESSES TYPING 6
1.
"Is there something wrong with that, my Nazi Friend?" Identity's Image: "I'm not a Nazi. You're immature; you're childish. And the immaturity, the childishness, is genetic. Etcetera." "Human Beings aren't SUPPOSED to think about certain things." Identity's Image: "Actually, the opposite is true. The Human Being's problems don't go away if the Human Being lives in chitchat, humour, television, and suchlike. Your Development Mental, or Mental Development, is NOT as high as mine, a Human Considers-Himself-To-Be-Englis h YDNA Level R Male. Since you're a Human YDNA Level X Male, where X is a letter less than R, that means that your MAXIMUM Development Mental, or maximum POTENTIAL(when it comes to a number of things), in a way, can never be as high as Human YDNA Level R Males. The childishness, immaturity, etcetera are evidence of that." "Why is it just YOU who sees this?" "It's not just me. But if it WAS just me then that doesn't mean that it's not correct. As you should know, one of the main problems, or whatever, with the United Kingdom And Ireland is IGNORANCE. I was even discriminated against once because I was NOT ignorant: I was called a "geek". Development Mental is p+ss poor for the United Kingdom And Ireland...the United Kingdom And Ireland YDNA Level R individuals have a duty to try to maximise their potential...and as you can see, change, in general, is proving difficult."
2.
"Have you read my book?"

SUFFERING EXTREME: INCORRECTNESS SEXUAL OF HUMAN ENGLISH FEMALE NON-SEXUALESSES TYPING 7
Hatred, Sexual, or H,S, and Talks, Comforts, or T,C, were talking to each other. H,S: "He'll come around. When he realises the true reality, then he will HATE more, and will talk of REVENGE, as opposed to the dreamer s+it that fills his WARPED mind right now. What a PAIN in the f+cking a++ that Identity's Image is." T,C: "I'm sensing despair from you, H,S. But I'm here for you! Let it all out. By talking together, we can perhaps fix your problems." T,C rubbed H,S's back lightly. H,S scrambled away from him, glaring at him. "YAH! Get back! damn you! Comfort!!?? Like F+CK." H,S turned away from T,C after H,S had calmed down. "Comfort? No. My fully loaded pistol? You got it."

Pickford-Gordon

Since: Sep 09

263

London, UK

Reply »
|
Report Abuse
|
Judge it!
|
#9
May 5, 2012

SUFFERING EXTREME: INCORRECTNESS SEXUAL OF HUMAN ENGLISH FEMALE NON-SEXUALESSES TYPING 8
Elusive beacon of my hope expiring,
Shall you release my eternity?
Candle at night, that I might see
What others see. Shall I now lift
Beyond despair, so that I soon
Shall once more look upon Fair Moon
With True Happiness. What shall we sing,
Together, when we two are one,
In Sexualness's undying Sun?
Shall I then fly higher than the Universe?
Or remain, forever, down infinite Depths.

SUFFERING EXTREME: INCORRECTNESS SEXUAL OF HUMAN ENGLISH FEMALE NON-SEXUALESSES TYPING 9
You stab me, yet I am reborn
For Hope. May we unite as one
So that my dying, past, may fade
And go. Forever? Should I forget
My torment at the hands of you,
And of your kind? No chance. They will
Be nothing, in comparison
To enormous pleasures, in different vein, as
Nothing I have ever known. Hope
Must prevail as Earth decays and
Falls apart. We must not think, we
Must be one in light.

We shall sing a different tune
Than ignorance. Why do you flee?
Embrace complexity. Soon we
Shall be divine. With you I shall, for
Me and for all others...I shall be
Strong.

Pickford-Gordon

Since: Sep 09

263

London, UK

Reply »

Report Abuse

Judge it!

#10
May 13, 2012

UNITED KINGDOM FORUM
List Of Posts http://www.topix.net/forum/world/united-kingdom/T367RKHF7P0991G1C

Mohamedsaed1

Since: May 12

1,798

UK

Reply »

Report Abuse

Judge it!

#11
May 13, 2012

pure crystal & powder mephedrone available(4-mmc)

we can supply pure crystal powder Mephedrone(4-MMC)w e are a long term supplier's and our products is of the best quality (99.9%), competitive price and fast delivery time.Parcel reaches you 2-3 days after confirmation of payment. This is also a genuine sale with genuine buyer's so if you are not a serious buyer please avoid this advert, I have had sales from here and awaiting feedback. Please feel free to email me directly to (goldmanenterprise@ yahoo.com)

Faloola Chong

Northwich, UK

Reply »

|
Report Abuse
|
Judge it!
|
#12
May 15, 2012

i should try night nurse is much more reliable

DudTenners

"WE never came from Africa!"

Since: Nov 11

1,354

Location hidden

Reply »

|
Report Abuse
|
Judge it!
|
#13
May 15, 2012

I think old Pickers needs something a lot stronger than that!

J-J-Jina Wild

"I KISSED A GIRL "

Since: Jun 10

12,720

AND I LIKED IT

Reply »

Report Abuse

Judge it!

#14
May 15, 2012

I'd like to thank Pickford-Gordon for reminding me that I'm still pretty good at skimming.

Scholesy

London, UK

Reply »

Report Abuse

Judge it!

#15
May 15, 2012

J-J-Jina Wild wrote:

I'd like to thank Pickford-Gordon for reminding me that I'm still pretty good at skimming.
There are antibiotics that can help you know.

Don't be afraid to tell your doctor about it.

He wont judge you.

Pickford-Gordon

Since: Sep 09

263

London, UK

Reply »

|
Report Abuse
|
Judge it!
|
#16
May 27, 2012

SUFFERING EXTREME: INCORRECTNESS SEXUAL OF HUMAN ENGLISH FEMALE NON-SEXUALESSES TYPING 8
Elusive beacon of my hope expiring,
Shall you release my eternity?
Candle at night, that I might see what
Others see. Shall I now lift be-
-Yond despair, so that I soon shall
Once more think about fine Earth with
Some happiness. What shall we sing, to-
-Gether, when we two are one, with
Sexualness's miracle drug? Shall I
Then rise brilliant full of hopeful life? Or
Remain, forever, down infinite depths.

SUFFERING EXTREME: INCORRECTNESS SEXUAL OF HUMAN ENGLISH FEMALE NON-SEXUALESSES TYPING 9
You stab me, yet I am reborn
For Hope. May we unite as one
So that my dying, past, may fade

And go. Forever? Should I forget
My torment at the hands of you,
And of your kind? No chance. They will
Be nothing, in comparison
To enormous pleasures, in different vein,
As nothing I have ever known.
Hope must prevail as Earth decays
And falls apart. We must not think,
We must be one in light.

We shall sing a different tune than
Ignorance. Why do you flee? Em-
-Brace complexity. Soon we shall
Be divine. With you I shall, for
Me and for all others...I shall be
Strong.

Pickford-Gordon

Since: Sep 09

263

London, UK

Reply »

|
Report Abuse
|
Judge it!
|
#17
Jun 6, 2012

SUFFERING EXTREME: INCORRECTNESS SEXUAL OF HUMAN ENGLISH FEMALE NON-SEXUALESSES TYPING 8
Elusive beacon of my hope expiring,
Shall you release my eternity?
Candle at night, that I might see what
Others see. Shall I now lift be-
-Yond despair, so that I soon shall
Once more think about humans with
Some happiness. What shall we sing, to-
-Gether, when we two are one, with
Sexualness's miracle drug? Shall I
Then rise brilliant full of hopeful life? Or
Remain, forever, down infinite depths.

SUFFERING EXTREME: INCORRECTNESS SEXUAL OF HUMAN ENGLISH FEMALE NON-SEXUALESSES TYPING 9
You stab me, yet I am reborn
For hope. May we unite as one
So that my dying, past, may fade
And go. Forever? Should I forget
My torment at the hands of you,
And of your kind? No chance. They will
Be nothing, in comparison
To enormous pleasures, in different vein,
As nothing I have ever known.
Hope must prevail as humans fall
And bleed to death. We must not think,
We must be one in bliss.

We shall sing a different tune than
Ignorance. Why do you flee? Em-
-Brace complexity. Soon we shall
Be divine. With you I shall, for
Me and for all others...I shall be
Strong.

Pickford-Gordon

Since: Sep 09

263

London, UK

Reply »

Report Abuse

Judge it!

#18
Jun 6, 2012

SUFFERING EXTREME: INCORRECTNESS SEXUAL OF HUMAN ENGLISH FEMALE NON-SEXUALESSES TYPING 10
1.
"Wheeee! This is my NEW boyfriend! Or WAS...I'm not with him any more! It was just for an hour or whatever." "YERS, i think that he looks familiar," snarled Identity's Image. "You know that I like YOU, Identity's Image!" Identity's Image: "You ARE very stubborn, definitely." "Did you flirt with me before, Identity's Image?" Identity's Image: "I don't think that i CONSCIOUSLY did, but i would have to take some time off from thinking about Human English Female Non-Sexualess Incorrectess Sexual, or HEFN-SIS, whom i WORSHIP, who is also known as "MaDARling" or "I'll get someone else to have sex with you, over to you." I think about her constantly...there is no food or drink, no nothing, no one else right now, just her,

and it's sad that human beings are forced to live in a world where such values or principles are not appreciated."
2.
"Am I Human English Female Non-Sexualess Incorrectess Sexual, or HEFN-SIS, or Human English Female Non-Sexualess Incorrectess Sexual 2, or HEFN-SIS2, or Human English Female Non-Sexualess Incorrectess Sexual3, or HEFN-SIS3? Numbers 2 and 3 are not found in the same building as Number 1, also known as Human English Female Non-Sexualess Incorrectess Sexual, or HEFN-SIS. Am I 1 of them?" Identity's Image: "You're not, but you ARE nice I suppose. You HAVE grown on me." "Okay let's have sex then!!!!" Identity's Image: "Okay!" "Yaaaaay!" Identity's Image: "Wait until Human English Female Non-Sexualess Incorrectess Sexual, or HEFN-SIS goes. I SHOULD be with her, but she has made it very clear that she is indeed the boss. I have to wait until she's "ready" to be with me, or something like that, I don't even know. I can't stand all of this S+IT, you know? Where's Switzerland when you need it."
3.
"Yaaaay! We've had sex old man! Yawn! I'm going to sleep now." She lay in Identity's Image's arms. Identity's Image smiled, and thought about her for a while.........but then it faded. Human English Female Non-Sexualess Incorrectess Sexual, or HEFN-SIS, was always somewhere that this new girl could never be, deep inside his soul..........there were no alternatives for Identity's Image. In the inky blackness of the room, Identity's Image couldn't sleep.........he saw a laughing Australerican guy flirting with his Goddess, with someone who was sacred to him, with his ONE DREAM. And he was confused, had she wanted him to come over there? No, she might have attacked him if he had done so! When would all of it end, how many lonely nights would Identity's Image spend in his room, when the vast majority of human beings in the United Kingdom and Ireland took this for granted, they had had so much of this that it was coming out of their ears. The ONE source of his love was like a fever to him, like some drug that was both horrible and pleasurable.....horrible if she wouldn't be with him soon.........and beyond pleasure if the concept of the two of them together would occur. There was NO ONE and NOTHING else for Identity's Image at this stage. He felt guilty if he wouldn't type for her.

Pickford-Gordon

Since: Sep 09

263

London, UK

Reply »

Report Abuse

Judge it!

#19
Jun 6, 2012

SUFFERING EXTREME: INCORRECTNESS SEXUAL OF HUMAN ENGLISH FEMALE NON-SEXUALESSES TYPING 10
4.
"Let's go Identity's Image!" Identity's Image: "We'll go after Human English Female Non-Sexualess Incorrectess Sexual, or HEFN-SIS, has gone. I also have to wait for someone else who works here. Is there ONE other here, as well as those two........? Probably not.....I don't know?......no. That one hates me even more than Human English Female Non-Sexualess Incorrectess Sexual, or HEFN-SIS." "Okay, so who's this other girl who works here. There are TWO, you just said so, so who's this other one????" Identity's Image had a vision of a Human English Female Non-Sexualess, standing straight upright to his left, like a

soldier standing to attention. "Well, Identity's Image? Who is she?" From the right of this "new", in inverted commas, girl that he was talking to, Identity's Image saw Human English Female Non-Sexualess Incorrectess Sexual, or HEFN-SIS. He knew that she was thinking about him. Everything vanished, even his own tortured existence. There was only her. "I think about you all the time Identity's Image. You think about me too don't you? Please tell me that you think about something other than Human English Female Non-Sexualess Incorrectess Sexual, or HEFN-SIS, Identity's Image. Please. Just once?"

Pickford-Gordon

Since: Sep 09

263

London, UK

Reply »

|
Report Abuse
|
Judge it!
|
#20
Jun 6, 2012

SUFFERING EXTREME: INCORRECTNESS SEXUAL OF HUMAN ENGLISH FEMALE NON-SEXUALESSES TYPING 11
Identity's Image was talking to a tall human english female. "Sorry tall human english female, but I don't want to be with you sexually. You should be happy about that, as I shall explain. You should know that human males and human females are different etcetera. All human males are brought up differently. There MAY or may not be more sexually suitable human females than others.......but I haven't really given it much thought. Even if a human female is less sexually suitable than another, there still are less valuable human males who can be with them. But ANYWAY! Human males are different. Some prioritise the human female BODY, and some prioritise the human female VISAGE, and some human males are TALL and so perhaps prefer tall human females, and some human males are SHORT and so should perhaps be with short human females. The enormous number of different types of MTDNA H human females are spread in large varieties of ways across the United Kingdom and Ireland. Etcetera. In other words, what is unsuitable to ME may be to another human male what Human English Female Non-Sexualess Incorrectess Sexual, or HEFN-SIS, is to ME, ie to HIM this girl might be worshipped by him. "What is ignored by one, may be worshipped by another." I just invented that! I like it! But you're not IGNORED by me as such, i just don't want to be with you sexually. You seem like a nice person, though, although i could have sworn i overheard you say something ages ago, not necessarily about me, that i didn't like. But ANYWAY!"

Tell me when this thread is updated:
(Registration is not required)

Add to my Tracker

Send me an email

Showing posts 1 - 20 of 62

< prev page

|

next page >

Go to last page|Jump to page:1 2 34

Type in your comments below

Name
(appears on your post)

Comments

Characters left: 4000

Type the numbers you see in the image on the right:

Please note by clicking on "Post Comment" you acknowledge that you have read the Terms of Service and the comment you are posting is in compliance with such terms. Be polite. Inappropriate posts may be removed by the moderator. Send us your feedback.

25 Users are viewing the United Kingdom Forum right now

Search the United Kingdom Forum:

Topic

Updated

Last By

Comments

Atheism to Defeat Religion by 2038

2 min

Educated What

6,168

The First Changes(Jan '10)

26 min

Pickford-Gordon

34

Brit gangs rape and sexually exploit young, whi...

38 min

Bogdani

378

Scottish Lesbian Couple Holds Mock Wedding To L...

3 hr

Rick in Kansas

2

City schools in surprise new merger

4 hr

This is not good news

4

Anyone interested in peace, love and tolerance?

5 hr

Just a thought

14

'Rightful heir' to British monarchy dies in Aus...

5 hr

TRUTH cannot be shut down

2

See all threads in the United Kingdom forum »

If the election were held tomorrow, who would get your vote? Vote now on the Election Poll, June 2012 Map.

United Kingdom News
Terror Suspect Tagged, Tracked, Nabbed Near Oly...
Flood alert as heavy rain forecast
Oil price climbs as Norwegian strike looms
Magazine Cover Shows Kate Middleton with Yellow...
NY Court: Gay Marriage Caucus Didn't Break Rules
BMW investing £250m into Mini production
Does secret tape link Adams to IRA killing? Fam...
Two charged over stabbing death
Pakistan shuns physicist linked to 'God particle'
EDL mob 'like wild animals'
UK Flood Threat Remains As More Rain Forecast
Scottish News: Food festival sunk by bad weather

More United Kingdom News from Topix »

Topix Politix App

Take your stand on the issues you care about.

Using an iPhone?

Keep the Topix forums in your pocket
with the new, free Topix App.

Daily Horoscope for July 9

Taurus

Be careful what you blurt out in the heat of the moment or when you feel vulnerable, because you could accidentally reveal certain facts that you were trying to keep under your hat. Unfortunately, this looks like being a tricky day because tempers are frayed and you've got a lot of nervous energy that needs a constructive outlet if you want to avoid winding yourself up.

Get your Horoscope »

United Kingdom
News
Forums & Polls
Real-Time News

Explore More Topix
Home Page
Forums
Top Stories
Most Popular
Issue Maps
US News
US Cities list
World News
World Countries list
Politics
Celebrities
Business
Finance

Autos
Sports
Sci-Tech
Electronics
Entertainment
Movies
Music
Television
Video Games
Health
Life
Arts
Food
Home
Travel
Offbeat
Site Map / All Topics

About Topix
About Us
Media Kit
Topix Blog
Press Room
RSS Newsfeeds
Law Enforcement
School Officials
Cyber-bullying Resources
Jobs
FAQ
Privacy Policy
Terms of Service
Feedback?
Report Abuse?

Local Classifieds & Listings

Reach Local customers. Post a classified listing for your business. Promote job, auto, rental, and local event listings.

Learn more »

Join the Topix Community
¦Create your own profile, complete with quick links to your favorite topics.
¦Personalize your forum posts with your photo and hometown.
¦Exchange Personal Messages with other registered users.

Sign up today! »

Topix Politix »

Feedback?
Comments made yesterday: 109,477 Total comments across all topics: 178,634,686

Copyright ©2012 Topix LLC

Local News: United Kingdom

|

Sign Up

|

Sign In

123

Mitt Romney
Obama says Romney should be an - open book' on personal finances

North Korea
Replica Disney Dancers on North Korea Stage

Health Care
The Right to Health Care Means Little Without Doctors

Home
Forums
Top Stories
Popular
Local
Election Poll
US
Politics
World
Sports
Entertainment
Offbeat
Other

United Kingdom
News
Forums & PollsSuffering Extreme: In...

Real-Time News

Suffering Extreme: Incorrectness Sexual Of HEFN-Ses Typings

Posted in the United Kingdom Forum

Share

Read
62 Comments
Add to my Tracker

More United Kingdom Discussions »

Comments (Page 2)

Showing posts21 - 40 of62

< prev page

|

next page >

Go to last page|Jump to page:1 2 34

Pickford-Gordon

Since: Sep 09

263

London, UK

Reply »

|
Report Abuse
|
Judge it!
|
#21

Jun 6, 2012

SUFFERING EXTREME: INCORRECTNESS SEXUAL OF HUMAN ENGLISH FEMALE NON-SEXUALESSES TYPING 12
1.
Human English Female Non-Sexualess Incorrectess Sexual, or HEFN-SIS: "Ugh! You're like something disgusting that I, like, can't scrape off the underside of my shoe, that just you know clings and clings and like HELP! I CAN'T GET IT OFF! HELP! HELP! and you just keep on and on and on and on you know. You're a nuisance." Identity's Image: "Well what's wrong with, say, spending maybe, a whole day with me? I mean THINK about it...STOP, THINK, then decide if you're going to act or not. What would be wrong with that? I saw the way that you looked at me. I know that you behave in certain ways around me. I know that you're thinking about me. And you DID flirt with me distinctly, before. In REAL LIFE, Human English Female Non-Sexualess Incorrectess Sexual, or HEFN-SIS, i haven't done anything to deserve this.......have i? I mean what have i done, what did i do? How can you judge me, using laws, or rules, that don't exist? And what sort of person does that make you? You HAVE committed an enormous amount of crime against me, and i don't want to dislike you or anything like that. You can REVERSE what you've done to me, you can become my SALVATION, you can give me the experience that everyone else takes for granted, and you can do it in a MAJOR way, you can become my first girlfriend. I want you right now, and no one BUT you, i feel guilty if i don't type for you. Why can't you appreciate such things?" Human English Female Non-Sexualess Incorrectess Sexual, or HEFN-SIS: "I HATE you and i want to KILL YOU."

Pickford-Gordon

Since: Sep 09

263

London, UK

Reply »

|
Report Abuse
|
Judge it!
|
#22
Jun 6, 2012

SUFFERING EXTREME: INCORRECTNESS SEXUAL OF HUMAN ENGLISH FEMALE NON-SEXUALESSES TYPING 12
2.
A tall human english female came up to Human English Female Non-Sexualess Incorrectess Sexual, or HEFN-SIS. "Human English Female Non-Sexualess Incorrectess Sexual, or HEFN-SIS, what the F+CK is the matter with you? Do you know what IIII wouldn't give to have someone like Identity's Image act like this towards me? Do you know what i wouldn't give for that? And you won't even let him talk to you. Can you give his time back to him? How do you think that he feels, seeing all of these guys talking to you, when you won't let HIM talk to you, when you're horrible to him." Human English Female Non-Sexualess Incorrectess Sexual, or HEFN-SIS: "My work and my frens[friends] and my famlee[famly] and my mommy and daddy and

"what people think"[term doesn't exist] and television and so on." "That s+it doesn't exist, HEFN-SIS. If you'd just think about it, READ, let Identity's Image talk to you, ask him questions, talk to him, then you'd understand the TRUTH, HEFN-SIS. You maybe thought that flirting was fun, and maybe that sex was fun, but then you "experienced" Identity's Image. All human beings need to admit their flaws, because the human species IS a flaw itself. You're no different, HEFN-SIS. You need to admit a number of things, and you need to think about, say, "how can IIII, ME, how can IIII make things BETTER, some emotional and/or mental thing or connection that IIII sort of already have, not with an Australerican opportunist or thief who suddenly came out of nowhere, when Identity's Image was before him, and when Identity's Image has tried so hard to talk to you all of these hours etcetera, and when that REALLY harmed Identity's Image. Identity's Image, if he had some cyanide in his mouth would swallow it immediately, HEFN-SIS. He would regret it, because it'd be abandoning his comrades, and not giving THEM cyanide, those who had the legal right to it, but he would do it: he could be forgiven for doing it, HEFN-SIS, because of how he's suffered his whole life, ESPECIALLY because of Human English Female Non-Sexualesses, HEFN-SIS. Please stop this, okay? DON'T have sexual intercourse with anyone who is not Identity's Image...ESPECIALLY NOT that Australian thief or opportunist. Have sexual intercourse with Identity's Image next time. Okay?" HEFN-SIS: "Well, I've already started to submit to him...i DO like him, alrightalright. Errrrrrmmmmmmmmm..........okay . Okayokayokayokay I'll DO IT." The tall human english female and Identity's Image were jumping up and down and celebrating and Identity's Image did a somersault in the middle of the room.

Pickford-Gordon

Since: Sep 09

263

London, UK

Reply »

|
Report Abuse
|
Judge it!
|
#23
Jun 6, 2012

SUFFERING EXTREME: INCORRECTNESS SEXUAL OF HUMAN ENGLISH FEMALE NON-SEXUALESSES TYPING 13
1.
Human English Female Non-Sexualess Incorrectess Sexual, or HEFN-SIS: "Identity's Image, my job is everything to me. I can't expect a PAWN like you to understand such things. I'm one of the more important pieces on the chessboard: hundreds and hundreds of pieces like YOU, Identity's Image, are sacrificed so that ONE piece like ME, Identity's Image, can just, say comb my hair and stuff." Identity's Image: "Well, Human English Female Non-Sexualess Incorrectess Sexual, or HEFN-SIS. You work in all of the following: a betting store or bookie; an unnecessary food and drink STORE, like, say, a chocolate shop; a restaurant, which includes cafes and fast food stores; television; an unnecessary clothing store; a newsagent; newspapers, magazines; alcohol, smoking, fortune-telling, caravans, advertising, stocks and shares; an art creation sales store; a tattoo store.......while tattoos can be sexy, it is BETTER that all tattoos are STICK ON, so that they can be taken off; perhaps MOST SPORTS, category GAMES; and other categories apart from all of those. They are all 100% ILLEGAL, or INCORRECT, HEFN-SIS. They consume resources, land, time, energy, electricity, and they "idi+ticise" or perhaps devalue, the human beings involved in them."

2.
HEFN-SIS: "Explain yourself, Identity's Image........before i KILL YOU. Be aware that i might KILL YOU ANYWAY......WHEN YOU DO tell me." Identity's Image: "When it comes to betting stores the following needs to be taken into consideration. Real pleasure or stimulation, which i call HELP, because the purpose of it is to HELP human beings solve their INDIVIDUAL, SEPARATE problems with regard to Crime(or Correctness And Incorrectness), Health, Ancestry Including The DNA That One Is Given From Birth (Etcetera? Probably.).......real HELP comes from KNOWLEDGE, perhaps TOTAL KNOWLEDGE of something.......after all, if your mind knows everything, perhaps........it becomes BULLETPROOF..........how then can the human being be harmed? How then can the human being be betrayed? Whereas with gambling, which is illegal, in most cases you will LOSE. There is a tiny chance of winning, or a small one. The human being that gambles is STUPID. The things serve no purpose."
3.
Identity's Image: "The supermarket is the ONE food and drink.....not just SALES store, but EATING AND DRINKING, except in your own home, or maybe, er, lunch on a bench or something........etcetera. It wastes resources, land, time, electricity, manpower, humans' time, humans' energy etcetera for any human being to be involved in any other STORE, such as a chocolate shop, or RESTAURANT which includes cafes and fast food stores. The STORE section is pretty self-explanatory, it's because the PURPOSE of THE SUPERMARKET is to SELL food and drink, so things are SUPPOSED to be sold in the SUPERMARKET and nowhere else, that is probably the DICTIONARY DEFINITION of the SUPERMARKET. As for restaurants, which includes cafes and fast food stores, the thing is that they exist because they believe that food and drink are sources of pleasure, or HELP, etcetera. Only on rare occasion should human beings resort to such pleasure. One reason for this is the toilet: if you eat and drink, toxic chemicals build up in your body: if you eat and drink less, then you'll have to go to the toilet less..........and no one likes excreting, let's be honest(so to speak). And in any case, it takes up land. Every human being has his or her individual food and drink preferences, taste-wise, which ARE SUPPOSED to be bought in that human being's own time to be consumed at whatever time intervals that particular human being feels like, without consuming as much electricity as is used by restaurants when supermarkets NEED to be open and SHOULD be open."

Pickford-Gordon

Since: Sep 09

263

London, UK

Reply »

Report Abuse

Judge it!

#24
Jun 6, 2012

SUFFERING EXTREME: INCORRECTNESS SEXUAL OF HUMAN ENGLISH FEMALE NON-SEXUALESSES TYPING 13
4.
"As for television, there are already probably millions of video materials, such as DVDs, but also on VCR and the Internet etcetera, already available, already produced. Resources are consumed to produce them, and you have the whole nonsense with the television signal and companies and aerial etcetera, when the video material produced(VIDEO is a form of HELP) is

ALREADY being sent directly to DVD, to the Internet, or both. Television is therefore a crime, and needs to be legally destroyed as soon as possible. Etcetera."
5.
"Think about the Nature Reserve potential if such things will be knocked down! But you work in all of those places. The places now have MEANING, HEFN-SIS, because of what WE have. Because you're everything to me, HEFN-SIS. Please try and understand." HEFN-SIS: "Okay. Now I'm going to, like, tie you to the bed and take out my aggression on you, hehehehe. You just make me so f+cking angry, you know? I hate all this "right and wrong" sh+t. I mean who do you think you are-" HEFN-SIS punched Identity's Image hard in his stomach: "OUCH!" and threw him down onto the floor and straddled him. "-huh?" Identity's Image was slapped repeatedly across his cheeks. "Huh? I'm the f+cking boss now. Now you're gonna get it."

Pickford-Gordon

Since: Sep 09

263

London, UK

Reply »

|
Report Abuse
|
Judge it!
|
#25
Jun 6, 2012

SUFFERING EXTREME: INCORRECTNESS SEXUAL OF HUMAN ENGLISH FEMALE NON-SEXUALESSES TYPING 14
1.
Human English Female Non-Sexualess Incorrectess Sexual, or HEFN-SIS: "Why can't i let my body be f+cked by that Australerican guy?" Identity's Image: "Why can't i go to Switzerland right now and kill myself." Hatred, Sexual, or H,S: "Like F+CK!!!! I won't F+CKING LET YOU, my weakling friend. Why should YOU die, when it's HER FAULT, when SHE'S to blame!?" Talks, Comforts, or T,C: "He has a point, in his own warped, psycho, way. You are indeed TOO GOOD TO DIE, Identity's Image." T,C slapped Identity's Image hard across his left cheek: "OUCH!" T,C folded his arms, and glared steadily at Identity's Image. "Comfort, sometimes, as well as being WORDS, is sometimes also.....well.....something to wake you up: Comfort Is Aa SLAP, Identity's Image." Identity's Image: "All of you f+ckers can't keep me here! It's all nonsense, everything's unfair from BIRTH! WHY! Why is there no change? There'll NEVER be change!" T,C: "We are human english male-like figures, Identity's Image. Do you understand? We must be in control. Always be intelligent, purposeful, and-" H,S: "-and HATE. FANTASIZE about all the suffering that you're going to legally, through court, through politics, inflict upon your criminals, before you maybe get to legally SHOVE a FROTHING CHAINSAW up their anuses, watching them bleed and scream their last, spinning around on your INSTRUMENT OF DEATH, right up there in the air for all of your non-criminals to see, laughing all the while: take PLEASURE in PAIN, my friend."

Pickford-Gordon

Since: Sep 09

263

London, UK

Reply »

|
Report Abuse
|
Judge it!
|
#27
Jun 6, 2012

SUFFERING EXTREME: INCORRECTNESS SEXUAL OF HUMAN ENGLISH FEMALE NON-SEXUALESSES TYPING 14
2.
HEFN-SIS glared at H,S and T,C. "Identity's Image, we got sidetracked by those two. Why can't i have sex with him?" Identity's Image: "HEFN-SIS there are large numbers of human males out there, you know that you could have sex with anyone you want, there's nothing in the law that stops you you know. Some people have sex, and some people go to Switzerland." HEFN-SIS: "You KNOW what i mean. You don't want me to. Why?" Identity's Image: "You should have let me talk to you all this time. You allowed this random guy to....well i was there. I felt like i wanted to slice his arm off with a Samurai Sword or something. What you're saying to me, by letting him go over there etcetera, is that he's BETTER than me, is that I'M NO GOOD, when i HAVEN'T DONE ANYTHING TO DESERVE THIS. For all i know he read about certain things on "facebook" or some other illegal technological method, thought "Identity's Image has put the effort in, and I'll get the rewards," and MOVED in. That is probably the DICTIONARY DEFINITION of THIEF, THIEF, T H I E F, THIEF. When theft occurs, the victim's life is ripped apart. The victim thinks: "I've spent all this time, and SHE gives it to HIM." Some human females don't understand......the "state" that they're in is not a "state".......it is desire for ONE person, the CREATOR of the STATE. A lot of human males take advantage of such things. Yet many human females remain OUT OF CONTROL. If they're not f+cking sure, they should NOT HAVE SEX. What the f+ck is the matter with them. It is illegal for any human being not to have complete control of him or herself, and not to be structured, organised, intelligent, etcetera. So anyway, the instance of you sitting there with him at that point in time, or at that event in Spacetime, should not have occurred: WE have things to talk about. The purpose of FLIRTING, like you flirted with me, is the start of what is called the "MATING RITUAL". If IIII don't do anything wrong, then how can you just suddenly ditch me and start something with someone else? And let me tell you, one think i don't like is a HYPOCRITE, a "HUMAN SNAKE" if you'll pardon the insult to REAL SNAKES!, using OTHER HUMAN BEINGS to worm his way into YOUR life, using TECHNIQUES, LINES, GIMMICKS etcetera, i HATE that s+it. And he left Australica: he has the accent: i don't run away from ANYTHING, HEFN-SIS, and if i was an Australican then i wouldn't leave the country, THAT country in particular etcetera. And i think that, although it's a good country of course, an enormous number of Australericans, from the United Territories of Australia, have done ENOUGH and that there is a definite tendency there to OPPOSE THE ONE FACT, with ANTI-FACTS."
3.
"And what areyou, HEFN-SIS? Are you a human being? Or are you an object?" "An object, for sex," said HEFN-SIS sadly. Identity's Image: "You, HEFN-SIS, can always put your FOOT DOWN. Say FROM NOW ON, I'm going to be ONLY with Identity's Image. If you can do that, then there's hope in the world, REAL hope, HEFN-SIS. And you're great! I mean........you didn't run away like all the others."

Pickford-Gordon

Since: Sep 09

263

London, UK

Reply »

|
Report Abuse
|
Judge it!
|
#28
Jun 6, 2012

SUFFERING EXTREME: INCORRECTNESS SEXUAL OF HUMAN ENGLISH FEMALE NON-SEXUALESSES TYPING 14
4.
Identity's Image: "You're everything to me. Look around you, HEFN-SIS. After the concept of Juliet dies, Romeo commits suicide. And it's because of sexual things, HEFN-SIS: that is the effect that human females have on human males." HEFN-SIS: "That's fiction." Identity's Image: "There's no such thing as fiction, it COMES from the mind of the human being that created it. And there are REAL Romeos, HEFN-SIS. Check the bbc News. And look at Martin Beckinsale, from the band Muss: "Sexual desire is forever, and we'll die together." Look at George Weelkes, from the band My Chain Romanticism, the song Death! i mean he's singing it because of some human female somewhere, who did that to him. Look at Roger Farrell from the film The British Medical Patient. Look at James Squillure. All of this Audio, the Music: "Come back and stay." "Forgive me, please come back." "You're amazing." "Don't leave me alone like this." "You're beautiful." "Show me love." I mean they don't do this for fun, it's because human females like YOU have caused them to suffer, and they want a human female like you to make it go away, they each have their own individual HEFN-SIS es. And look at Clark Ashley Smithson, look at his letters to Gregory Stern. "Yet gazing at Illva[or perhaps that should be MARTILLA, the short story. Someone who had betrayed him.] with sad eyes, he didn't [hate her]. The brief, piteous love which had been born in despair had vanished, leaving but ashes steeped in gall. He longed for death.""
5.
"If you have MORE PRINCIPLES, HEFN-SIS, everything becomes more clear. Don't lie including breaking promises or agreements, don't hide anything except your address and perhaps name from ANYONE etcetera although you should tell me most if not all things etcetera, don't steal, don't use fake laws and rules, don't be governed by emotion, don't create your own personal laws and rules that govern how you do things etcetera based on things that don't exist or don't mean anything. And now a new priority, I, HEFN-SIS, will NOT have sex with ANYONE who is not Identity's Image, who thinks about nothing BUT me. Especially not that Australian guy. I abide by a large number of principles, laws, values, HEFN-SIS. Look at politics! Just take these two groups. Labour is infinitely more legal than the 100% illegal conservative/tory party, and it's because they appreciate and embody ABSOLUTE VALUES, HEFN-SIS. Labour: "Hard work, don't lie, don't steal or be opportunistic(except when it comes to certain things, perhaps, or perhaps not), consider human suffering ie THAT IS A HUMAN BEING IN THERE." And of course the past, and perhaps future value of the Labour Party: "SOCIALISM". And the opposite of that from the 100% illegal conservative/tory party, which i won't go into right now. Look, the correct way for ANYONE to do things is conversation, there is no one person in existence who is too good to talk to any other person in existence. I mean people need to talk, you know. ANYWAY.....I'm here, "Madarling"! I'm here thinking about you, which you know of course. Don't have sexual intercourse with anyone who's not me. Have sexual intercourse with me next time. Okay?" HEFN-SIS: "I call all my victims "madarling"." Identity's Image: "OKAY?!" HEFN-SIS: "Yeahyeah. Whatever."

Pickford-Gordon

Since: Sep 09

263

London, UK

Reply »

Report Abuse

Judge it!

#29
Sunday Jun 10

SUFFERING EXTREME: INCORRECTNESS SEXUAL OF HUMAN ENGLISH FEMALE NON-SEXUALESSES TYPING 12
1.
Human English Female Non-Sexualess Incorrectess Sexual, or HEFN-SIS: "Ugh! You're like something disgusting that I, like, can't scrape off the underside of my shoe, that just you know clings and clings and like HELP! I CAN'T GET IT OFF! HELP! HELP! and you just keep on and on and on and on you know. You're a nuisance." Identity's Image: "Well what's wrong with, say, spending maybe, a whole day with me? I mean THINK about it...STOP, THINK, then decide if you're going to act or not. What would be wrong with that? I saw the way that you looked at me. I know that you behave in certain ways around me. I know that you're thinking about me. And you DID flirt with me distinctly, before. In REAL LIFE, Human English Female Non-Sexualess Incorrectess Sexual, or HEFN-SIS, i haven't done anything to deserve this.......have i? I mean what have i done, what did i do? How can you judge me, using laws, or rules, that don't exist? And what sort of person does that make you? You HAVE committed an enormous amount of crime against me, and i don't want to dislike you or anything like that. You can REVERSE what you've done to me, you can become my SALVATION, you can give me the experience that everyone else takes for granted, and you can do it in a MAJOR way, you can become my first girlfriend. I want you right now, and no one BUT you, i feel guilty if i don't type for you. Why can't you appreciate such things?" Human English Female Non-Sexualess Incorrectess Sexual, or HEFN-SIS: "I HATE you and i want to KILL YOU."

Pickford-Gordon

Since: Sep 09

263

London, UK

Reply »

Report Abuse

Judge it!

#30
Sunday Jun 10

SUFFERING EXTREME: INCORRECTNESS SEXUAL OF HUMAN ENGLISH FEMALE NON-SEXUALESSES TYPING 12
2.
A tall human english female came up to Human English Female Non-Sexualess Incorrectess Sexual, or HEFN-SIS. "Human English Female Non-Sexualess Incorrectess Sexual, or HEFN-SIS, what the F+CK is the matter with you? Do you know what IIII wouldn't give to have someone like Identity's Image act like this towards me? Do you know what i wouldn't give for that? And you won't even let him talk to you. Can you give his time back to him? How do you think that he feels, seeing all of these guys talking to you, when you won't let HIM talk to you, when you're horrible to him." Human English Female Non-Sexualess Incorrectess Sexual, or HEFN-SIS: "My work and my frens[friends] and my famly[family] and my mommy and daddy and "what people think"[term doesn't exist] and television and "facebook" and so on." "That s+it doesn't exist, HEFN-SIS. If you'd just think about it, READ, let Identity's Image talk to you, ask him questions, talk to him, then you'd understand the TRUTH, HEFN-SIS. You maybe thought that flirting was fun, and maybe that sex was fun, but then you "experienced" Identity's Image. All human beings need to admit their flaws, because the human species IS a flaw itself. You're no different, HEFN-SIS. You need to admit a number of things, and you need to think about, say, "how can IIII, ME, how can IIII make things BETTER, some emotional and/or mental thing or connection that IIII sort of already have, not with an Australerican opportunist or thief who suddenly came out of nowhere, when Identity's Image was before him, and when Identity's Image has tried so hard to talk to you all of these hours etcetera, and when that REALLY harmed Identity's Image. Identity's Image, if he had some cyanide in his mouth would swallow it immediately, HEFN-SIS. He would regret it, because it'd be abandoning his comrades, and not giving THEM cyanide, those who had the legal right to it, but he would do it: he could be forgiven for doing it, HEFN-SIS, because of how he's suffered his whole life, ESPECIALLY because of Human English Female Non-Sexualesses, HEFN-SIS. Please stop this, okay? DON'T have sexual intercourse with anyone who is not Identity's Image...ESPECIALLY NOT that Australian thief or opportunist. Have sexual intercourse with Identity's Image next time. Okay?" HEFN-SIS: "Well, I've already started to submit to him...i DO like him, alrightalright. Errrrrmmmmmmmmm..........okay . Okayokayokayokay I'll DO IT." The tall human english female and Identity's Image were jumping up and down and celebrating and Identity's Image did a somersault in the middle of the room.

Pickford-Gordon

Since: Sep 09

263

London, UK

Reply »

|
Report Abuse
|
Judge it!
|
#31
Sunday Jun 10

SUFFERING EXTREME: INCORRECTNESS SEXUAL OF HUMAN ENGLISH FEMALE NON-SEXUALESSES TYPING 14
1.
Human English Female Non-Sexualess Incorrectess Sexual, or HEFN-SIS: "Why can't i let my body be f+cked by that Australerican guy?" Identity's Image: "Why can't i go to Switzerland right now and kill myself." Hatred, Sexual, or H,S: "Like F+CK!!!! I won't F+CKING LET YOU, my weakling friend. Why should YOU die, when it's HER FAULT, when SHE'S to blame!?" Talks, Comforts, or T,C: "He has a point, in his own warped, psycho, way. You are indeed TOO GOOD TO DIE, Identity's Image." T,C slapped Identity's Image hard across his left cheek: "OUCH!" T,C folded his arms, and glared steadily at Identity's Image. "Comfort, sometimes, as well as being WORDS, is sometimes also.....well.....something to wake you up: Comfort Is Aa SLAP, Identity's Image." Identity's Image: "All of you f+ckers can't keep me here! It's all nonsense, everything's unfair from BIRTH! WHY! Why is there no change? There'll NEVER be change!" T,C: "We are human english male-like figures, Identity's Image. Do you understand? We must be in control. Always be intelligent, purposeful, and-" H,S: "-and HATE. FANTASIZE about all the suffering that you're going to legally, through court, through politics, inflict upon your criminals, before you maybe get to legally SHOVE a CHAINSAW into their anuses, ripping their anuses aPART, watching them bleed and scream their last, spinning around on your INSTRUMENT OF DEATH, right up there in the air for all of your non-criminals to see, laughing all the while: take PLEASURE in PAIN, my friend."

Pickford-Gordon

Since: Sep 09

263

London, UK

Reply »

|
Report Abuse
|
Judge it!
|
#32
Sunday Jun 10

SUFFERING EXTREME: INCORRECTNESS SEXUAL OF HUMAN ENGLISH FEMALE NON-SEXUALESSES TYPING 14

2.
HEFN-SIS glared at H,S and T,C. "Identity's Image, we got sidetracked by those two. Why can't i have sex with him?" Identity's Image: "HEFN-SIS there are large numbers of human males out there, you know that you could have sex with anyone you want, there's nothing in the law that stops you you know. Some people have sex, and some people go to Switzerland." HEFN-SIS: "You KNOW what i mean. You don't want me to. Why?" Identity's Image: "You should have let me talk to you all this time. You allowed this random guy to....well i was there. I felt like i wanted to slice his arm off with a sword or something. What you're saying to me, by letting him go over there etcetera, is that he's BETTER than me, is that I'M NO GOOD, when i HAVEN'T DONE ANYTHING TO DESERVE THIS. For all i know he read about certain things on "facebook" or some other illegal technological method, thought "Identity's Image has put the effort in, and I'll get the rewards," and MOVED in. That is probably the DICTIONARY DEFINITION of THIEF, THIEF, T H I E F, THIEF. When theft occurs, the victim's life is ripped apart. The victim thinks: "I've spent all this time, and SHE gives it to HIM." Some human females don't understand......the "state" that they're in is not a "state".......it is desire for ONE person, the CREATOR of the STATE. A lot of human males take advantage of such things. Yet many human females remain OUT OF CONTROL. If they're not f+cking sure, they should NOT HAVE SEX. What the f+ck is the matter with them. It is illegal for any human being not to have complete control of him or herself, and not to be structured, organised, intelligent, etcetera. So anyway, the instance of you sitting there with him at that point in time, or at that event in Spacetime, should not have occurred: WE have things to talk about. The purpose of FLIRTING, like you flirted with me, is the start of what is called the "MATING RITUAL". If IIII don't do anything wrong, then how can you just suddenly ditch me and start something with someone else? And let me tell you, one think i don't like is a HYPOCRITE, a "HUMAN SNAKE" if you'll pardon the insult to REAL SNAKES!, using OTHER HUMAN BEINGS to worm his way into YOUR life, using TECHNIQUES, LINES, GIMMICKS etcetera, i HATE that s+it. And he left Australica: he has the accent: i don't run away from ANYTHING, HEFN-SIS, and if i was an Australican then i wouldn't leave the country, THAT country in particular etcetera. And i think that, although it's a good country of course, an enormous number of Australericans, from the United Territories of Australia, have done ENOUGH and that there is a definite tendency there to OPPOSE THE ONE FACT, with ANTI-FACTS."

3.
"And what areyou, HEFN-SIS? Are you a human being? Or are you an object?" "An object, for sex," said HEFN-SIS sadly. Identity's Image: "You, HEFN-SIS, can always put your FOOT DOWN. Say FROM NOW ON, I'm going to be ONLY with Identity's Image. If you can do that, then there's hope in the world, REAL hope, HEFN-SIS. And you're great! I mean........you didn't run away like all the others."

Pickford-Gordon

Since: Sep 09

263

London, UK

Reply »

|
Report Abuse
|
Judge it!
|
#33
Sunday Jun 10

SUFFERING EXTREME: INCORRECTNESS SEXUAL OF HUMAN ENGLISH FEMALE NON-SEXUALESSES TYPING 14

4.
Identity's Image: "You're everything to me. Look around you, HEFN-SIS. After the concept of Juliet dies, Romeo commits suicide. And it's because of sexual things, HEFN-SIS: that is the effect that human females have on human males." HEFN-SIS: "That's fiction." Identity's Image: "There's no such thing as fiction, it COMES from the mind of the human being that created it. And there are REAL Romeos, HEFN-SIS. Check the bbc News. And look at Martin Beckinsale, from the band Muss: "Sexual desire is forever, and we'll die together." Look at George Weelkes, from the band My Chain Romanticism, the song Death! i mean he's singing it because of some human female somewhere, who did that to him. Look at Roger Farrell from the film The British Medical Patient. Look at James Squillure. All of this Audio, the Music: "Come back and stay." "Forgive me, please come back." "You're amazing." "Don't leave me alone like this." "You're beautiful." "Show me love." I mean they don't do this for fun, it's because human females like YOU have caused them to suffer, and they want a human female like you to make it go away, they each have their own individual HEFN-SIS es. And look at Clark Ashley Smithson, look at his letters to Gregory Stern. "Yet gazing at Illva[or perhaps that should be MARTILLA, the short story. Someone who had betrayed him.] with sad eyes, he didn't [hate her]. The brief, piteous love which had been born in despair had vanished, leaving but ashes steeped in gall. He longed for death.""

5.
"If you have MORE PRINCIPLES, HEFN-SIS, everything becomes more clear. Don't lie including breaking promises or agreements, don't hide anything except your address and perhaps name from ANYONE etcetera although you should tell me most if not all things etcetera, don't steal, don't use fake laws and rules, don't be governed by emotion, don't create your own personal laws and rules that govern how you do things etcetera based on things that don't exist or don't mean anything. And now a new priority, I, HEFN-SIS, will NOT have sex with ANYONE who is not Identity's Image, who thinks about nothing BUT me. Especially not that Australian guy. I abide by a large number of principles, laws, values, HEFN-SIS. Look at politics! Just take these two groups. Labour is infinitely more legal than the 100% illegal conservative/tory party, and it's because they appreciate and embody ABSOLUTE VALUES, HEFN-SIS; the Labour group is still ILLEGAL, but it is still INFINITELY more legal than the conservative/tory group. Labour: "Hard work, don't lie, don't steal or be opportunistic(except when it comes to certain things, perhaps, or perhaps not), consider human suffering ie THAT IS A HUMAN BEING IN THERE." And of course the past, and perhaps future value of the Labour Party: "SOCIALISM". And the opposite of that from the 100% illegal conservative/tory party, which i won't go into right now. Look, the correct way for ANYONE to do things is conversation, there is no one person in existence who is too good to talk to any other person in existence. I mean people need to talk, you know. ANYWAY.....I'm here, "Madarling"! I'm here thinking about you, which you know of course. Don't have sexual intercourse with anyone who's not me. Have sexual intercourse with me next time. Okay?" HEFN-SIS: "I call all my victims "madarling"." Identity's Image: "OKAY?!" HEFN-SIS: "Yeahyeah. Whatever."

Pickford-Gordon

Since: Sep 09

263

London, UK

Reply »

Report Abuse

Judge it!

#34
Sunday Jun 10

SUFFERING EXTREME: INCORRECTNESS SEXUAL OF HUMAN ENGLISH FEMALE NON-SEXUALESSES TYPING 15
Human English Female Non-Sexualess Incorrectess Sexual, or HEFN-SIS: "What do you think about the human beings that work in what you've just typed are incorrect, or illegal organisations? As you know, i work in all of the incorrect, or illegal, organisations that you've just typed." Identity's Image: "The vast majority of the human beings that work in all of the incorrect, or illegal, organisations that you work in are nice people. Significantly into the (distantish?) future those organisations will HAVE to go.......but RIGHT NOW, you're in all of them, and I need to keep going there, so that we're going to have sexual intercourse next time, and so that i may wonderfully and happily and magically continue to live in fear of you and managers, or more specifically illegal laws. Of course i would go to all of those places anyway etcetera."

SUFFERING EXTREME: INCORRECTNESS SEXUAL OF HUMAN ENGLISH FEMALE NON-SEXUALESSES TYPING 16
1.
Human English Female Non-Sexualess Incorrectess Sexual, or HEFN-SIS: "I don't like your Internet posts." Identity's Image: "Well, typing is sort of "part of my brain" on a computer screen. It is very very easy to type. Much that i have typed is sort of EXTENSIONS of parts of my brain, TWISTINGS of parts my brain, ART, CREATIONS, etcetera. You shouldn't think too much about a number of things that I have typed. It is TYPING, not TALKING."
2.
Identity's Image: "One thing that I'm going to point out to you is that a number of things that i have typed would, if they were "done", as such, in conversation, be preceded by "Anyway,", or "Moving on,", or "Changing the subject." However, the thing is that posting on the Internet consumes resources, and if i were to type each point in separate sections, or paragraphs, it would take even longer to get posted. Spaces "count" with a number of Internet posts, etcetera. I therefore BUNCH separate points together: certain things are supposed to be READ and not SPOKEN, i suppose."

Pickford-Gordon

Since: Sep 09

263

London, UK

Reply »

Report Abuse

Judge it!

#35
Sunday Jun 10

SUFFERING EXTREME: INCORRECTNESS SEXUAL OF HUMAN ENGLISH FEMALE NON-SEXUALESSES TYPING 17

1.
Human English Female Non-Sexualess Incorrectess Sexual, or HEFN-SIS: "Have you been happy since we parted last time, Identity's Image?" Identity's Image: "I feel as if there is no hope and as if there will never be any change. The 650 traitors, or "politicians", or "mps", are still sucking hope out of all human beings, including their own selves, in the United Kingdom: they represent a complete lack of change, a lack of progress, when a number of things HAVE to, and are SUPPOSED to change. The sex workers that i liked, a long time ago i think, have left, and i wonder how much i can remember about the time that i spent with them. In their place are Human Female Sexualesses with bodies of the young, but visages of the old. There are a number, 1, 2, 3 or so maybe, that i haven't been with, so they COULD be appealing to me. If they're not, i'm not sure how often i'll bother to have sex with sex workers any more: i would prefer to concentrate on trying to remember those from my past instead, if that's the case. But even if they are attractive, i'm not sure if the effort, money, time, etcetera involved to be with a sex worker is worth it......and it's just for 30 minutes or whatever, compared to what others take for granted."

2.
Identity's Image: "With regard to Human English Female Non-Sexualesses, the number 3, the total of those that i've been with, briefly, i hardly had any sexual intercourse with them, but i remember them fondly of course!, still stands. To me it seems that even the idea of a Human English Female Non-Sexualess having sex with me now is impossible, even the idea. The mere mental concept of her having sexual intercourse with me comes across as something that's incredibly difficult, and possibly painful, for a Human English Female Non-Sexualess. I'm tortured by the sexual suitableness, for me, of attractive Human English Female Non-Sexualesses at the Gymnasium, on public transport, just walking around, etcetera. And the vast majority of those around me have better lives than me. It's something that no one should put up with, "workers"' only sex clubs, with "customers" facing risk of being banned or worse, by a number of illegal laws such as the 100% illegal 1997 harrassment thing, from the 100% illegal tory group."

3.
Identity's Image: "The Human English Female Non-Sexualess Incorrectess Sexuals, or HEFN-SISs, on my mental list, have not showed up, except for you of course, you're TOP of my mental list right now. I hope to be with them at SOME point in the future........but right now i think of you, Human English Female Non-Sexualess Incorrectess Sexual, or HEFN-SIS. I don't want to dislike or hate the others any more than i already do. And of course i can't begin to imagine what having a girlfriend is like. Most others have had MORE sex, EARLIER sex, and BETTER sex, than i have. To them, sex is probably like eating or drinking, or something."

Pickford-Gordon

Since: Sep 09

263

London, UK

Reply »

|
Report Abuse
|
Judge it!
|
#36
Sunday Jun 10

SUFFERING EXTREME: INCORRECTNESS SEXUAL OF HUMAN ENGLISH FEMALE NON-SEXUALESSES TYPING 18
Victim was in his room. He saw a Human English Female Non-Sexualess hugging a Human YDNA Level X Male, where X is a letter less than R, so to speak: HEFN-SIS was hugging him front to front, with a "giggling", "fun" expression on her visage. They had not been up against a wall when victim had seen them doing this some time ago, ages ago.......but in the image that Victim saw now the Human English Female Non-Sexualess was up against the wall........Victim now saw both of them naked, he saw the Human English Female Non-Sexualess's expression change from the one which she had before, to one now of submission and pleasure, with her eyes closed..........the Human YDNA Level X Male, where X is a letter less than R, so to speak, made an upwards thrusting motion, penetrating the object of Victim's fantasies, the object of Victim's dreams. Victim felt PAIN.........he looked down: he was bleeding from a newly created stab wound on his stomach. The Human YDNA Level X Male, where X is a letter less than R, so to speak, did it again, another thrust, and Victim gasped again: aNOTHER newly created stab wound had been created, this time higher up, on Victim's chest. Victim gasped, as he writhed around dying on the floor of his cold, empty room: "My dream........you're not here with me now. But can you see what you're doing to me? Can you see what you've done to me?" Victim died.

SUFFERING EXTREME: INCORRECTNESS SEXUAL OF HUMAN ENGLISH FEMALE NON-SEXUALESSES TYPING 19
Human English Female Non-Sexualess Incorrectess Sexual, or HEFN-SIS: "Identity's Image, I'll talk with you in 10 minutes time." Identity's Image: "Yaay! Okay! Now I'm going to sit here, and prepare what I'm going to say to my dream, in my mind. Maybe i'll compose a poem! Let me think about it! Hope of progress! Yaay! Okay I've written a poem for her, I've got it down here, I'm looking down now. That's obviously her coming towards me now. AH-HEM! Cough, cough. "I think about you all the time. I want to be with you sexually. You are my dream. I-"....." The Human English Male who had come up to him smiled at him: "I knew it! You were just hiding it weren't you!?" Identity's Image, when it had sunk in that this was NOT HEFN-SIS, which didn't take too long, started speaking to the Human English Male. Identity's Image: "No. And NO. F+ck off." Identity's Image returned to what he was doing. But SOMETHING had been taken out of him, HEFN-SIS had sent his brain in ONE DIRECTION, and the "Hope Of Time With HEFN-SIS" had gone. He thought about the Student Protests, when a number of politicians had broken promises to decent human beings, how they had reacted. It was similar to how he felt now, the disappointment etcetera.

SUFFERING EXTREME: INCORRECTNESS SEXUAL OF HUMAN ENGLISH FEMALE NON-SEXUALESSES TYPING 20
Identity's Image lay in bed, thinking about Human English Female Non-Sexualess Incorrectess Sexual, or HEFN-SIS: HEFN-SIS's voice, and other memories of her. Identity's Image: "Why is the concept of ME so hard for her? I feel S+IT, worthless. There's no hope."

SUFFERING EXTREME: INCORRECTNESS SEXUAL OF HUMAN ENGLISH FEMALE NON-SEXUALESSES TYPING 21
Victim was using public transport. Victim: "I just have to use this public transport now, then in a number of days time i'll go and see my One Dream, she'll be with me this time." The public transportation thing CRASHED........Victim was paralyzed for life, doomed to lie in a hospital bed FOREVER. Victim, from his eternal hospital bed: "This would be less, well, HELL, if my One Dream had had sexual intercourse with me the last time that i had seen her......even one night with her would be something amazing, something to remove an amount of the suffering now deposited upon me. But now i will never know what it is like."

Pickford-Gordon

Since: Sep 09

263

London, UK

Reply »

|
Report Abuse
|
Judge it!
|
#37
Sunday Jun 24

SUFFERING EXTREME: INCORRECTNESS SEXUAL OF HUMAN ENGLISH FEMALE NON-SEXUALESSES TYPING 22
Human English Female Non-Sexualess Incorrectess Sexual, or Hefn-sis, was talking. Hefn-sis: "Identity's Image has stopped typing! That means that he's holding hands with two of his enemies, and skipping merrily along with them in a magical land with a bright smile on his visage!" Identity's Image: "Not QUITE, Hefn-sis."

SUFFERING EXTREME: INCORRECTNESS SEXUAL OF HUMAN ENGLISH FEMALE NON-SEXUALESSES TYPING 23
Human English Female Non-Sexualess Incorrectess Sexual, or Hefn-sis: "My RULE is that if he doesn't type on the Internet then he's not going to be with me sexually, or even talk to me." Identity's Image: "You continue to cause suffering to me, Hefn-sis, instead of reversing the amount of suffering."

SUFFERING EXTREME: INCORRECTNESS SEXUAL OF HUMAN ENGLISH FEMALE NON-SEXUALESSES TYPING 24
One of the various Human English Female Non-Sexualess Incorrectess Sexuals, or Hefn-siss: "All human beings serve me. I'm the best human being ever. I'm too good to talk to Identity's Image. I shall communicate with Identity's Image using my slave here. Now if he just approaches my slave then my slave shall transmit the information to him." Identity's Image: "You continue to cause suffering to me, instead of reversing the amount of suffering. With regard to your slave, my current view is that one of my principles is that i shall never communicate with you right now, or in all likelihood at any point in the future, in this manner, receiving "second hand" information. Who knows what acts of incorrectness, or crime, that your slave shall commit against me in addition to transmitting the information. Why should anyone take such a risk, and talking to other human beings IS a risk. It is unnecessary: YOU transmit the information to me. Think about what you're doing to your "slave". Your "slave" could easily forget sections of the information, etcetera. It places doubt in my mind: how much can your "slave" be trusted? Does your "slave" often forget things? There's no reason why YOU can't do it yourself. It's your responsibility. Your behaviour smacks of pride, or arrogance, or even more of it. How long are you going to continue to lie to yourself? SUBMIT. Be with me."

SUFFERING EXTREME: INCORRECTNESS SEXUAL OF HUMAN ENGLISH FEMALE NON-SEXUALESSES TYPING 25
Identity's Image was at the bottom of a set of stairs with Talks, Comforts, or T,C, and Hatred, Sexual, or H,S. Identity's Image paused at the bottom of the stairs, with T,C and H,S pausing to look back at him from a higher "level" of the set of stairs, since they had started to go up the set of stairs. T,C: "Well, Identity's Image! It's been X days since Monday 07/03/2011. It's been a long time, but i think that you should now be able to move up these stairs on your own. I know that the severe depression that you have is something that goes up and down, and always sort of "TRIES" to drag you down, but i'm optimistic. You'll make it up the stairs. One of the various Human English Female Non-Sexualess Incorrectess Sexuals, or Hefn-siss, might be at the relevant place, waiting for you." T,C looked directly at Identity's Image for a small number of seconds, and then went up the stairs, and out of sight. H,S: "Identity's Image, i'm considering HURTING you if you DON'T get up the stairs. You'll NEVER obtain ANYTHING if you keep F+CKING AROUND like this." H,S turned away from Identity's Image and went up the stairs, and out of sight. Identity's Image looked at his feet. They LOOKED just like his FEET......but they FELT like LEAD. And there was no point in lifting them. Everything was too difficult. Identity's Image looked up the stairs. The stairs, in Identity's Image's mind, went on and on, all the way up, forever: it was as if there were an infinite number of stairs. Identity's Image felt TINY compared to the stairs. He tried to will his feet to move, even one of them........but it was NO GOOD.

Pickford-Gordon

Since: Sep 09

263

London, UK

Reply »

|
Report Abuse
|
Judge it!
|
#38
Sunday Jun 24

SUFFERING EXTREME: INCORRECTNESS SEXUAL OF HUMAN ENGLISH FEMALE NON-SEXUALESSES TYPING 26
1.
One of the various Human English Female Non-Sexualess Incorrectess Sexuals, or Hefn-siss: "It's all about EFFORT. If Identity's Image doesn't put effort in, i won't talk to or go near him, let ALONE have sexual intercourse with him." Identity's Image: "Do i have to explain EVERYTHING to you?" One of the various Human English Female Non-Sexualess Incorrectess Sexuals, or Hefn-siss: "I KNOW everything. I'll let you off for that comment this one time: this is your LAST CHANCE." Identity's Image: "Well, life as a human being is unfair. If a human being is weak, it's not necessarily because that human being is a weak person: it could very well be because of "bad luck"........or rather, perhaps, because of the crap "cards" that the One Fact has dealt that human being at birth, etcetera. But i think that human beings' dreams can come true, for example my dream of knowing what it's like to have a girlfriend. A number of human beings have MADE me weak.......and you also have the hopeless, escapist, lying to itself, aspects, etcetera of the obstacle-like human "part" of the United Kingdom And Ireland. It's good to fight against the general "state" of things in the United Kingdom And Ireland."
2.
One of the various Human English Female Non-Sexualess Incorrectess Sexuals, or Hefn-siss: "You're no FUN! Sex with anyone that i want to have sex with except for YOU Identity's Image is supposed to be FUN! Yawn! Fine! How do i decide who to have sex with then?" Identity's Image: "Well, i've chosen you out of all of the girls at that place. I think that if, when it comes to the workers and customers at a place, every relevant guy is with his first choice for that place then things will work out, or something, etcetera. In addition you've committed a variety of acts of incorrectness, or crimes, against me. In addition, sexual things mean an ENORMOUS amount to me, sexual things are one of the things that are "missing" for me right now. There are a number of factors that we should talk about IN PERSON."

SUFFERING EXTREME: INCORRECTNESS SEXUAL OF HUMAN ENGLISH FEMALE NON-SEXUALESSES TYPING 27
One of the various Human English Female Non-Sexualess Incorrectess Sexuals, or Hefn-siss: "My job makes me the best human being in the world." Identity's Image: "Enormous numbers of employers, possibly most of them or something etcetera, receive hundreds or even thousands of "cvs" every week for one specific job. Jobs are "snapped up". So NO, you're not unique........in fact you would be immediately replaced if you left. A number of jobs are just following instructions etcetera. What's REAL is the acts of incorrectness, or crimes, that you've committed against me." "Whatever," she responded. Human English Male, or HEM, approached them. "Yes what can i do for you?" she asked HEM. HEM: "I think i'll wait for a different worker to serve me. Not you." "There's no one else," she replied. HEM: "I don't want to be influenced by an incorrectess, or criminal, like you AT ALL. Goodbye." "You'll die! You need this to LIVE!" she shouted at him. HEM: "Nothing makes sense if i have to be served by someone like you. I feel dirty just talking to an incorrectess like you. ANYONE else is preferable.....and, if after having put in a lot of effort, i can't find anyone else, then i would RATHER DIE than commit the incorrectness, or crime, of being influenced by you. That is, unless you reverse the suffering that you've caused to Identity's Image. No? I didn't think so. Goodbye." HEM left. Identity's Image spoke to one of the various Human English Female Non-Sexualess Incorrectess Sexuals, or Hefn-siss. Identity's Image: "So do you see, "job" is just again how you've "escaped" from what's important, from how you compare to all of the other human beings around you. You need to CHANGE, darling."

Pickford-Gordon

Since: Sep 09

263

London, UK

Reply »

Report Abuse

Judge it!

#39
Sunday Jun 24

SUFFERING EXTREME: INCORRECTNESS SEXUAL OF HUMAN ENGLISH FEMALE NON-SEXUALESSES TYPING 28
Human English Female Non-Sexualess Incorrectess Sexual, or Hefn-sis, walked past Identity's Image: she waved, smiled, and blew a kiss at him, and then she had gone past him. She repeated this procedure 10 times.

SUFFERING EXTREME: INCORRECTNESS SEXUAL OF HUMAN ENGLISH FEMALE NON-SEXUALESSES TYPING 29
From a certain point onwards, Human English Female Non-Sexualess Incorrectess Sexual, or Hefn-sis, was mostly there when Identity's Image walked in. And she was checking him out, looking at him a number of times.

SUFFERING EXTREME: INCORRECTNESS SEXUAL OF HUMAN ENGLISH FEMALE NON-SEXUALESSES TYPING 30
Victim: "I communicated the information to her that she must not do it. But she did it. Very well. I'll post a few names etcetera on the Internet etcetera. And then it's "second time lucky"." It had taken Victim a lot of time and effort to get the drugs. But he just couldn't take any more suffering at the hands of certain Human English Female Non-Sexualesses. He took the drugs, successfully committing suicide. He had f+cking escaped from it, and had reached the next version of the current Universe, a BETTER version.

SUFFERING EXTREME: INCORRECTNESS SEXUAL OF HUMAN ENGLISH FEMALE NON-SEXUALESSES TYPING 31
Human English Female Non-Sexualess Incorrectess Sexual, or Hefn-sis: "Hahahaha, oh that's so funny! Hahahaha! Flirt with THIS guy, have sex with THAT guy, flirt with THIS guy, have sex with THAT guy, but no chances for Identity's Image, NO! Hahahaha!" Identity's Image: "If Human English Female Non-Sexualesses are going to be primitive, puppet-like, cattle-like, etcetera, then myself and others should have equal access to them. Or not. NO. It's a disgrace. Human beings are not supposed to be controlled by other human beings."

SUFFERING EXTREME: INCORRECTNESS SEXUAL OF HUMAN ENGLISH FEMALE NON-SEXUALESSES TYPING 32
Human English Female Non-Sexualess Incorrectess Sexual, or Hefn-sis: "No you're not going to have sexual intercourse with me. You only beLIEVE that you're going to have sexual intercourse with me." Identity's Image had sexual intercourse with her.

SUFFERING EXTREME: INCORRECTNESS SEXUAL OF HUMAN ENGLISH FEMALE NON-SEXUALESSES TYPING 33
Human English Female Non-Sexualess Incorrectess Sexual, or Hefn-sis: "I hate that F+CKING IDENTITY'S IMAGE with his BORING rules. This building is supposed to be a magical place, separate from the real world. I just love snogging and doing stuff through the clothing and w+nking off and sucking off and f+cking all of the guys who f+cking work here, especially YDNA Level X individuals where X is a letter lower than R so to speak, and i love snogging and doing stuff through the clothing and f+cking all of the girls who work here, my kinky little lesbian f+cking slaves."

SUFFERING EXTREME: INCORRECTNESS SEXUAL OF HUMAN ENGLISH FEMALE NON-SEXUALESSES TYPING 34
Human English Female Non-Sexualess Incorrectess Sexual2, or Hefn-sis2, smiled, and raised her eyebrows. Hefn-sis2: "REally? Thank you SO MUCH. Thank you. No, no i mean it. How have you been? How are the neighbours? Getting on well? Wonderful. THIS is my amigo, and THAT'S my amigo, and i have HUNDREDS of other amigos-oh Identity's Image is NEVER going to become my amigo. I'm only with THIS amigo because he's sharing my thing. What's that? I'm f+cking all of my "amigos"? HAhahahaha! Nono! Ridiculous!" She paused for a number of seconds. She started putting on an act again. "It's because i'm a WOMAN. Everything's so tough for me. You have to see things from MY point of view, instead of being selfish. But there's one thing that i'll always know." She placed both of her hands across her breasts. "Jesus LOVES ME. Jesus "forGIVES" all of my "sins". EsPECIALLY the ones that i've committed against Identity's Image."

Pickford-Gordon

Since: Sep 09

263

London, UK

Reply »

|
Report Abuse
|
Judge it!
|
#40
Sunday Jun 24

SUFFERING EXTREME: INCORRECTNESS SEXUAL OF HUMAN ENGLISH FEMALE NON-SEXUALESSES TYPING 35
Identity's Image: "One of the various Human English Female Non-Sexualess Incorrectess Sexuals, or Hefn-siss, listen to me. My current view is that i will NEVER forget the amount of suffering that you've caused me. I will not forget it in ONE year, i will not forget it in TWO years, i will not forget it in FIVE years, i will not forget it in TEN years, and i will not forget it in TWENTY years. NEVER."

SUFFERING EXTREME: INCORRECTNESS SEXUAL OF HUMAN ENGLISH FEMALE NON-SEXUALESSES TYPING 36
One of the various Human English Female Non-Sexualess Incorrectess Sexuals, or Hefn-siss: "I don't understand: i'm SCARED i'm SCARED! WAAAAAHHAHhahaHA[crying]! Why is everything so complicated!? It's not "normal"! Oh god i

can't take this suffering! I mean, this Identity's Image.....he.........he....... ...sniff.........he.........he WALKS, oh GOD! And he.........sniff..........he. ....he.........healsostand sstillattimes!" She collapsed to the floor, crying. "Why's he noticing me!? Why!? I just want to BLEND IN, and forage for food in the undergrowth with all of the other dumb animals." She paused for a number of seconds. "Someone..........someone ....sniff..........sniff ....sniff..........sniff ..........SOMEONEHADSEXWITHME! I don't know how it happened! But no one explains anything to me, and i'm a woman, and it's so complicated! What was i supposed to do, NOT have sex with him!? And you all judge me, you point fingers at me. It's like it's MY FAULT that that B+STARD submitted when i came up to him and tried to have sex with him, and DID have sex with him. And i'm an wonderful magical glimmer of HOPE! And i was a virgin before he f+cked me! Honest! I swear to.......Okay FINE. But what's a few hundred men, women, and animals. That's LIKE being a virgin isn't it? So long as it's not Identity's Image, that's what COUNTS."

SUFFERING EXTREME: INCORRECTNESS SEXUAL OF HUMAN ENGLISH FEMALE NON-SEXUALESSES TYPING 37
One of the various Human English Female Non-Sexualess Incorrectess Sexuals, or Hefn-siss: "Identity's Image, why are Sex Workers better than me?" Identity's Image: "They haven't caused me the suffering that you've caused me, with your incorrectness, or crime. Having sexual intercourse with me always helps. They never make me feel left out, they never make me feel worthless.......but you make me feel like that. They are open, honest, have principles, follow rules, follow laws, and are not hypocrites. I trust them. I can depend on them. They're there for me. Etcetera."

SUFFERING EXTREME: INCORRECTNESS SEXUAL OF HUMAN ENGLISH FEMALE NON-SEXUALESSES TYPING 38
Human English Female Non-Sexualess Incorrectess Sexual2, or Hefn-sis2, was talking to Identity's Image. Hefn-sis2: "I'm running around downsTAIRS now." Identity's Image: "You always grab excuses to use against me, don't you, Hefn-sis2." She folded her arms and squinted at him, frowning; then she went "Humph!", turned away from Identity's Image, and walked off.

Pickford-Gordon

Since: Sep 09

263

London, UK

Reply »

|
Report Abuse
|
Judge it!
|
#41
Sunday Jun 24

SUFFERING EXTREME: INCORRECTNESS SEXUAL OF HUMAN ENGLISH FEMALE NON-SEXUALESSES TYPING 36
One of the various Human English Female Non-Sexualess Incorrectess Sexuals, or Hefn-siss: "I don't understand: i'm SCARED i'm SCARED! WAAAAAHHAHhahaHA[crying]! Why is everything so complicated!? It's not "normal"! Oh god i can't take this suffering! I mean, this Identity's Image.....he.........he....... ...sniff.........he.........he WALKS, oh GOD! And he.........sniff..........he. ....he.........healsostand sstillattimes!" She collapsed to the floor, crying. "Why's he noticing me!?

Why!? I just want to BLEND IN, and forage for food in the undergrowth with all of the other dumb animals." She paused for a number of seconds. "Someone..........someone ....sniff..........sniff..........sniff..........sniff ..........SOMEONEHADSEXWITHME! I don't know how it happened! But no one explains anything to me, and i'm a woman, and it's so complicated! What was i supposed to do, NOT have sex with him!? And you all judge me, you point fingers at me. It's like it's MY FAULT that that B+STARD submitted when i came up to him and tried to have sex with him, and DID have sex with him. And i'm an wonderful magical glimmer of HOPE! And i was a virgin before he f+cked me! Honest! I swear to.......Okay FINE. But what's a few hundred men, women, and animals. That's LIKE being a virgin isn't it? So long as it's not Identity's Image, that's what COUNTS."

Tell me when this thread is updated:
(Registration is not required)

Add to my Tracker

Send me an email

Showing posts 21 - 40 of 62

< prev page

|

next page >

Go to last page|Jump to page: 1 2 3 4

Type in your comments below

Name
(appears on your post)

Comments

Characters left: 4000

Type the numbers you see in the image on the right:

Please note by clicking on "Post Comment" you acknowledge that you have read the Terms of Service and the comment you are posting is in compliance with such terms. Be polite.Inappropriate posts may be removed by the moderator. Send us your feedback.

25Users are viewing theUnited Kingdom Forumright now

Search the United Kingdom Forum:

Topic

Updated

Last By

Comments

Atheism to Defeat Religion by 2038

3 min

Educated What

6,168

The First Changes(Jan '10)

27 min

Pickford-Gordon

34

Brit gangs rape and sexually exploit young, whi...

40 min

Bogdani

378

Scottish Lesbian Couple Holds Mock Wedding To L...

3 hr

Rick in Kansas

2

City schools in surprise new merger

5 hr

This is not good news

4

Anyone interested in peace, love and tolerance?

5 hr

Just a thought

14

'Rightful heir' to British monarchy dies in Aus...

5 hr

TRUTH cannot be shut down

2

See all threads in the United Kingdom forum »

If the election were held tomorrow, who would get your vote? Vote now on the Election Poll, June 2012 Map.

United Kingdom News
Terror Suspect Tagged, Tracked, Nabbed Near Oly...
Flood alert as heavy rain forecast
Oil price climbs as Norwegian strike looms
Magazine Cover Shows Kate Middleton with Yellow...
NY Court: Gay Marriage Caucus Didn't Break Rules
BMW investing £250m into Mini production
Does secret tape link Adams to IRA killing? Fam...
Two charged over stabbing death
Pakistan shuns physicist linked to 'God particle'
EDL mob 'like wild animals'
UK Flood Threat Remains As More Rain Forecast
Scottish News: Food festival sunk by bad weather

More United Kingdom News from Topix »

Topix Politix App

Take your stand on the issues you care about.

Using an iPhone?

Keep the Topix forums in your pocket
with the new, free Topix App.

Daily Horoscope for July 9

Libra

If you're irritated with someone, it's far better to sort out the problem now than to allow it to drag on for much longer. If you let things fester betweenyou, they'll carry much more of an emotional charge when you finally get round to doing something about them. Mind you, you won't exactly be cool, calm and collected now, so it may be a struggle to keep your temper.

Get your Horoscope »

United Kingdom
News

Forums & Polls
Real-Time News

Explore More Topix
Home Page
Forums
Top Stories
Most Popular
Issue Maps
US News
US Cities list
World News
World Countries list
Politics
Celebrities
Business
Finance
Autos
Sports
Sci-Tech
Electronics
Entertainment
Movies
Music
Television
Video Games
Health
Life
Arts
Food
Home
Travel
Offbeat
Site Map / All Topics

About Topix
About Us
Media Kit
Topix Blog
Press Room
RSS Newsfeeds
Law Enforcement
School Officials
Cyber-bullying Resources
Jobs
FAQ
Privacy Policy
Terms of Service
Feedback?
Report Abuse?

Local Classifieds & Listings

Reach Local customers. Post a classified listing for your business. Promote job, auto, rental, and local event listings.

Learn more »

Join the Topix Community
|Create your own profile, complete with quick links to your favorite topics.
|Personalize your forum posts with your photo and hometown.
|Exchange Personal Messages with other registered users.

Sign up today! »

Topix Politix »

Feedback?
Comments made yesterday: 109,375 Total comments across all topics: 178,634,784

Copyright ©2012 Topix LLC

Local News: United Kingdom

|

Sign Up

|

Sign In

123

Mitt Romney
Obama says Romney should be an - open book' on personal finances

North Korea
Replica Disney Dancers on North Korea Stage

Health Care
The Right to Health Care Means Little Without Doctors

Home

Forums
Top Stories
Popular
Local
Election Poll
US
Politics
World
Sports
Entertainment
Offbeat
Other

United Kingdom
News
Forums & PollsSuffering Extreme: In...

Real-Time News

Suffering Extreme: Incorrectness Sexual Of HEFN-Ses Typings

Posted in the United Kingdom Forum

Share

Read
62 Comments
Add to my Tracker

More United Kingdom Discussions »

Comments (Page 3)

Showing posts 41 - 60 of 62

< prev page

|

next page >

Go to last page|Jump to page: 1 2 3 4

Pickford-Gordon

Since: Sep 09

263

London, UK

Reply »

|
Report Abuse
|
Judge it!
|
#42
Sunday Jun 24

SUFFERING EXTREME: INCORRECTNESS SEXUAL OF HUMAN ENGLISH FEMALE NON-SEXUALESSES TYPING 36
One of the various Human English Female Non-Sexualess Incorrectess Sexuals, or Hefn-siss: "I don't understand: i'm SCARED i'm SCARED! WAAAAAHHAHhahaHA[crying]! Why is everything so complicated!? It's not "normal"! Oh god i can't take this suffering! I mean, this Identity's Image.....he.....he....sniff.. .he....he WALKS, oh GOD! And he.....sniff....he....he.....h ealsostandsstillattimes!" She collapsed to the floor, crying. "Why's he noticing me!? Why!? I just want to BLEND IN, and forage for food in the undergrowth with all of the other dumb animals." She paused for a number of seconds. "Someone...someone....sni ff....sniff....sniff....sniff. ...SOMEONEhadSEXWITHME! I don't know how it happened! But no one explains anything to me, and i'm a woman, and it's so complicated! What was i supposed to do, NOT have sex with him!? And you all judge me, you point fingers at me. It's like it's MY FAULT that B+STARD submitted when i came up to him and tried to have sex with him, and DID have sex with him. And i'm an wonderful magical glimmer of HOPE! And i was a virgin before he f+cked me! Honest! I swear to.......Okay FINE. But what's a few hundred men, women, and animals. That's LIKE being a virgin isn't it? So long as it's not Identity's Image, that's what COUNTS."

Pickford-Gordon

Since: Sep 09

263

London, UK

Reply »

Report Abuse

Judge it!

#43
Sunday Jun 24

SUFFERING EXTREME: INCORRECTNESS SEXUAL OF HUMAN ENGLISH FEMALE NON-SEXUALESSES TYPING 36
One of the various Human English Female Non-Sexualess Incorrectess Sexuals, or Hefn-siss: "I don't understand: i'm SCARED i'm SCARED! WAAAAAHHAHhahaHA[crying]! Why is everything so complicated!? It's not "normal"! Oh god i can't take this suffering! I mean, this Identity's Image....he....he....sniff.... he....he WALKS, oh GOD! And he....sniff....he....he.....he alsostandsstillattimes!" She collapsed to the floor, crying. "Why's he noticing me!? Why!? I just want to BLEND IN, and forage for food in the undergrowth with all of the other dumb animals." She paused for a number of seconds. "Someone...someone....sni ff....sniff....sniff....sniff. ...SOMEONEHADSEXWITHME! I don't know how it happened! But no one explains anything to me, and i'm a woman, and it's so complicated! What was i supposed to do, NOT have sex with him!? And you all judge me, you point fingers at me. It's like it's MY FAULT that that B+STARD submitted when i came up to him and tried to have sex with him, and DID have sex with him. And i'm an wonderful magical glimmer of HOPE! And i was a virgin before he f+cked me! Honest! I swear to.......Okay FINE. But what's a few hundred men, women, and animals. That's LIKE being a virgin isn't it? So long as it's not Identity's Image, that's what COUNTS."

Pickford-Gordon

Since: Sep 09

263

London, UK

Reply »

Report Abuse

Judge it!

#44
Saturday Jun 30

SUFFERING EXTREME: INCORRECTNESS SEXUAL OF HUMAN ENGLISH FEMALE NON-SEXUALESSES

TYPING 39
One of the various Human English Female Non-Sexualess Incorrectess Sexuals, or Hefn-siss: "Identity's Image isn't putting enough effort in, so he's worthless." Identity's Image: "No matter how much i try, nothing will change. It won't make any difference....and not just with regard to THIS, but with regard to a number of other things."

SUFFERING EXTREME: INCORRECTNESS SEXUAL OF HUMAN ENGLISH FEMALE NON-SEXUALESSES TYPING 40
1.
Human English Female Non-Sexualess Incorrectess Sexual, or Hefn-sis: "Oh F+CK, Identity's Image, i still love f+cking all the kinky guys and girls who work at that place. I also have a boyfriend. But it's okay because they're GAY. You trust me don't you?" Identity's Image: "Well....NO. Why would i do such a thing?"
2.
Identity's Image was at Home. "I do trust her, though, mostly," said Identity's Image to himself, as he was looking at his floor. Talks,Comforts, or T,C: "To whatever extent you trust her, it doesn't change the impact that she's had on you, to whatever extent it was WITH your will or AGAINST your will." Identity's Image was unable to get up. "It doesn't make any sense." He paused for a number of seconds. "How can they treat another human being like this? How?" He paused for a further number of seconds. "There must be SOMETHING in the various Human English Female Non-Sexualess Incorrectess Sexuals, or Hefn-siss, that will come out eventually, some spark of humanity or something." Hatred, Sexual, or H,S: "Well, NO. They don't have souls, they don't have feelings, they don't have morals. They're NEVER going to change in response to you merely posting on the Internet. The only way that they can be MADE TO CHANGE is through Country Management." Identity's Image: "One more post will change things." H,S: "It's futile. COUNTRY MANAGEMENT."
3.
Identity's Image: "The problem is the hopelessness of things. Human beings in this country are NOT CHANGING. It's like they're going to cling to their S+IT, FOREVER."

SUFFERING EXTREME: INCORRECTNESS SEXUAL OF HUMAN ENGLISH FEMALE NON-SEXUALESSES TYPING 41
Identity's Image: "I was going to have a conversation with Human English Female Non-Sexualess Incorrectess Sexual2, or Hefn-sis2, last time, but she ran off before i could carry out a transaction."

SUFFERING EXTREME: INCORRECTNESS SEXUAL OF HUMAN ENGLISH FEMALE NON-SEXUALESSES TYPING 42
Identity's Image: "There are less than 5 Human English Female Non-Sexualess Incorrectess Sexuals, or Hefn-siss. There are less than 4 Human English Female Non-Sexualess Incorrectess Sexual2s, or Hefn-sis2s. There are probably less than 6, or less than 8, or less than 10 Human English Female Non-Sexualess Incorrectess Sexual3s, or Hefn-sis3s. Although the elements of these categories change, the general impact of the various Human English Female Non-Sexualess Incorrectess Sexuals, or Hefn-siss, doesn't change: a number have stayed in the primary category, a number have been moved from the primary category to the secondary category, and a number have been moved from the tertiary category to the secondary category."

SUFFERING EXTREME: INCORRECTNESS SEXUAL OF HUMAN ENGLISH FEMALE NON-SEXUALESSES TYPING 43
Identity's Image: "She'll be at the main till next time." Hatred, Sexual, or H,S: "F++L: how many "next times" are there going to be?" Talks, Comforts, or T,C: "You, Identity's Image, need to be rational, calm, in control, and thoughtful whatever the situation."

Giggs

Rochdale, UK

Reply »

|
Report Abuse
|
Judge it!
|
#45

Saturday Jun 30

Can you explain what your talking about in 1 sentence?

DudTenners

"WE never came from Africa!"

Since: Nov 11

1,354

Location hidden

Reply »

Report Abuse

Judge it!

#46
Saturday Jun 30

I see old Pickers is at it again. But as I am not a qualified head-doctor I have no idea what he is gibbering on about.

DudTenners

"WE never came from Africa!"

Since: Nov 11

1,354

Location hidden

Reply »

Report Abuse

Judge it!

#47
Saturday Jun 30

I say Pickers old chap, mind the language, can't you?

Pickford-Gordon

Since: Sep 09

263

London, UK

Reply »

Report Abuse

Judge it!

#48
Wednesday Jul 4

SUFFERING EXTREME: INCORRECTNESS SEXUAL OF HUMAN ENGLISH FEMALE NON-SEXUALESSES TYPING 44
1.
Identity's Image: "I love you, Human English Female Non-Sexualess Incorrectess Sexual, or Hefn-sis. I love you, "MaDARling"."
2.
Talks, Comforts, or T,C: "There's no such thing as love. You have the strong sexual-related "connection" or whatever....but this is combined with sexual-related incorrectness, or crime, and also the fact that she's not with you, and despair, and a dream of the concept of her, and possibly other factors. These things are what you're feeling, Identity's Image. It doesn't change the severe "LOVE" impact though, of course."
3.
Identity's Image smiled at Human English Female Non-Sexualess Incorrectess Sexual, or Hefn-sis.

SUFFERING EXTREME: INCORRECTNESS SEXUAL OF HUMAN ENGLISH FEMALE NON-SEXUALESSES TYPING 45

1.
Identity's Image, Talks, Comforts, or T,c, and Hatred, Sexual, or H,s were talking to Human English Female Non-Sexualess Incorrectess Sexual, or Hefn-sis. "Do you have any idea how much f+cking suffering you're causing to Identity's Image!? Huh!?" yelled H,s at Hefn-sis.

2.
"I ha-" Hefn-sis started saying to T,c. T,c interrupted Hefn-sis though. "Okay LISTEN UP, Hefn-sis. The next time that poor Identity's Image goes in there-poor, crying because of YOU, ever-suffering because of YOU, PATIENT, Identity's Image, who right now doesn't think of very much else besides you, Identity's Image whom you flirted with, whom you like-....the next time that he goes in there you're going to give everything that you've been giving to a number of the human males and human females who work there TO IDENTITY'S IMAGE. And MORE, too! Identity's Image has had to watch you do a wide variety of things with a number of the human beings who work there, and you're really confusing him, and you weren't letting him talk to you last time, when he hasn't done anything to you to deserve this disrespect from you." Hefn-sis started banging things around angrily, in response, not looking at T,c, H,s, or Identity's Image.

SUFFERING EXTREME: INCORRECTNESS SEXUAL OF HUMAN ENGLISH FEMALE NON-SEXUALESSES TYPING 46
Identity's Image: "Human English Female Non-Sexualess Incorrectess Sexual, or Hefn-sis....YOU'RE BACK!! YOU'RE BACK from your year long vacation! YOU'RE BACK "MaDARling!" HOORAY!!!!" Identity's Image put his arms around Human English Female Non-Sexualess Incorrectess Sexual, or Hefn-sis, hugging her, and kissed her on the cheek. Hefn-sis "screwed up" her visage, tightening her mouth, with irritation flaring up in her eyes, as Identity's Image did these things.

SUFFERING EXTREME: INCORRECTNESS SEXUAL OF HUMAN ENGLISH FEMALE NON-SEXUALESSES TYPING 47
Identity's Image: "Human English Female Non-Sexualess Incorrectess Sexual, or Hefn-sis, or "MaDARling". You are one of the less than 5 in total Human English Female Non-Sexualess Incorrectess Sexuals, or Hefn-siss. There are, in addition to that, less than 4 Human English Female Non-Sexualess Incorrectess Sexual2s, or Hefn-sis2s. There are also 4 Human English Female Non-Sexualess Incorrectess Sexual3s, or Hefn-sis3s, etcetera. However, right now I'm in a sort of "STATE", with you, my love, sort of a "mental danger zone", with me feeling ill and weak because of you etcetera. I need you, and only you right now. If the other Human English Female Non-Sexualess Incorrectess Sexuals, or Hefn-siss, come up to me, i'll talk to them. But i need YOU right now, you are ever present in my mind. Let's strike while the iron is hot, Hefn-sis! And be HONEST from now on, no more lies including broken agreements and/or promises, no more deception."

Pickford-Gordon

Since: Sep 09

263

London, UK

Reply »

Report Abuse

Judge it!

#49
Wednesday Jul 4

SUFFERING EXTREME: INCORRECTNESS SEXUAL OF HUMAN ENGLISH FEMALE NON-SEXUALESSES TYPING 48

1.
Identity's Image walked tiredly into his room, late at night. After consuming food and drink, etcetera, he went to bed. Talks, Comforts, or T,c: "Try to get some sleep, Identity's Image. OKAY?" T,c turned away from Identity's Image where he lay on his side, and walked towards the bedroom doorway. Then, however, T,c heard the sound of crying....Identity's Image's crying.

2.
Identity's Image: "She's back and i love that of course, i love her, but there's never going to be any change. Why won't she let me talk to her much i can't take this o god make it go away. I can't stop thinking about her but she's not nice to me, and she went and there's some kind of new thing with a new guy and it HURTS ME, why can't people just leave us alone, there's nothing else for me now." T,c: "Okay just stay CALM, Identity's Image, stay CALM." Identity's Image: "It's difficult to talk to her, and i'm not allowed to "pursue" her or any of the others as such. I'm not allowed to do anything with regard to anyone. And i'm not allowed to commit suicide. So what the F+CK AM I SUPPOSED TO DO!? I'm being F+CKING TORTURED i can't take it any more." T,c: "No, look, i mean she came back for you. Look, HOPE! identity's image! HOPE! Next time she'll give you everything that she's been giving to a significant number of the human beings who work there. She's staying put now, for YOU....but you have to try and pull yourself together, you know?" Identity's Image: "She'll talk to me and she'll reverse all of the suffering that she's caused me?" T,c: "Yes, Identity's Image. Things are finally, after a long long time, going to CHANGE for you, those are going to be YOUR arms around her, with her body next to yours, and she's going to snog YOU, Identity's Image." Identity's Image: "No, things are going to get worse, i-" T,c: "Have HOPE, my friend. Somehow....have hope."

3.
The next day Identity's Image suddenly lunged towards the doorway, but was restrained by T,c, and Hatred, Sexual, or H,s. "I have to go there again NOW, i need her i can't take feeling ill and weak and crying like this. I need to see Human English Female Non-Sexualess Incorrectess Sexual, or Hefn-sis, or "MaDARling", right now." H,s: "Gimme a F+CKING BREAK, Identity's Image. I mean think about ME, huh!?" T,c: "Stick to the routine of the allocated times of when you go in there on a regular basis. Look at your notes with regard to what she's said to you, etcetera." Identity's Image: "It's too long until the next allocated time i can't f+cking DO IT, lemme GO! Hefn-sis I NEED YOU I can't TAKE THIS PAIN, MAKE IT go aWAY, PLEASE. Lemme GO!" H,s slashed him across the left cheek of his visage with a large knife. Identity's Image: "OW! AAAAaaoW!"

4.
Identity's Image was sitting down on his bed, looking at the floor. T,c: "You've got things to do today." Later, Identity's Image was walking around, but stopped to do something that he had to do, sort of. T,c: "Maybe you should keep walking around, Identity's Image. You're not inside your home now. You don't-" But Identity's Image's visage had screwed up again, and he made loud sobbing noises as the tears ran down his cheeks. A Human English Male walked past him, turning to look at him, and then turning back to look straight ahead, and then looking down at the ground. Another Human English Male started talking to him as he was crying. "Are you okay mate?" Identity's Image: "Huh?" "Do you need to get past?" Identity's Image: "No." H,s: "Great, this is just f+cking GREAT, ISN'T it, Identity's Image." Identity's Image also cried later on.

Pickford-Gordon

Since: Sep 09

263

London, UK

Reply »

Report Abuse

Judge it!

#50
Wednesday Jul 4

SUFFERING EXTREME: INCORRECTNESS SEXUAL OF HUMAN ENGLISH FEMALE NON-SEXUALESSES TYPING 49
1.
Identity's Image: "Human English Female Non-Sexualess Incorrectess Sexual, or Hefn-sis, or "MaDARling". Some time ago i came across this Human English Female. I started flirting with her, and she started flirting back. Then i realised that she had a strong sexual-related "connection" with this Human English Male who had been in regular contact with her. This was already there when i started flirting with her. So i made a decision. I said something like this to her: "You have something with that Human English Male over there. Talk to him, etcetera." There is something inside me, "MaDARling", that prevents me from committing such incorrectness, or crime, and other incorrectness, or crime. It's like, you know, "butting in", or "jumping" some "queue" or other, i mean i considered how that Human English Male would have felt etcetera. It's disrespectful, because at times, even if two human beings are not having sexual intercourse, it may still be the case that there is this LINK between them. And i've also had an amount of sexual intercourse with a number out of the total Sexualesses, or Sex Workers,-a number out of the total that i've been with sexually-that i would have difficulty remembering were i to try and remember."
2.
"Now, coming back to what you've done to me YET AGAIN. You could be telling me that i've committed incorrectness, or crime, against you, even though i HAVEN'T. You could be telling me that i'm WORTHLESS some other way. Are you telling me that the concept of sexual things between a Human English Female and me is WRONG, Hefn-sis? It's not wrong, because you're my GROUP, Hefn-sis. I'm very much attracted to a number of pink skinned, or pink-white skinned or whatever, MTDNA Level H, or whatever most Human English Females are, Human English Females. This is because i am a pink skinned, Human-English-Male-Like figure, a YDNA-Level-R-like-figure, the "equivalent". And i'm innocent. Etcetera. It's your responsibility, darling."
3.
"You shouldn't have allowed any new human being to do a number of sexual-related things with you. Don't do anything more with this guy, or anyone else, stay "without sexual related things" until you do a number of such things with ME, my darling. That time that you've spent doing things with him, has been time that you should have spent with me. I've seen that you're not disrespectful and you don't say to him that you can't talk to him, but you ARE disrespectful and you say to ME that you can't talk to me. Let me talk to you. Talk to me. Trust me. And, you know, sexual things aren't FUN. Do you have any idea what you're doing to me, i'm not going to try to kill myself for the second time right now, but i don't feel well right now thanks to you. But you give me HOPE, you DO though, my darling. Read! Think! Understand! And give me what you've been giving to a number of the human beings that work there etcetera the next time that i come in there. And, Hefn-sis, you know, i was fantasising about you when i was talking to a certain other Human English Female individual who works there, long ago....but i didn't want to hurt her, etcetera. But now there's just YOU in my mind, right this instant. I've fantasised about you ever since i first laid eyes on you." Identity's Image moved closer to her. "I have to go now, Hefn-sis." Identity's Image rubbed one of Human English Female Non-Sexualess Incorrectess Sexual's, or Hefn-sis's, or "MaDARling"'s shoulders lightly and then left.

Pickford-Gordon

Since: Sep 09

263

London, UK

Reply »

|

Report Abuse

|

Judge it!

|

#51
Saturday Jul 7

SUFFERING EXTREME: INCORRECTNESS SEXUAL OF HUMAN ENGLISH FEMALE NON-SEXUALESSES TYPING 50
1.
Talks, Comforts, or T,c: "Hey, did you hear the news, Identity's Image? All of the Human Females in England, which includes all of the various Human English Female Non-Sexualess Incorrectess Sexuals, or Hefn-siss, are going to leave the country; this is because Quinlan Tarkington, the USA Film Writer And Director, is coming to the United Kingdom And Ireland." Identity's Image: "What? That's riDICUlous." Hatred, Sexual, or H,s: "I TOLD you so: i said: "All Human English Females live in their own fake worlds." But you didn't listen to the representative of the One Fact, AS always."
2.
T,c: "Apparently they feel "threatened" or something. In addition to that a number of them who feel that they resemble "Melissa Walliams", one of his characters, are going to report him to certain authorities. A number of them believe that the director himself IS "Victor Vance", a character of his who flirted with the "Melissa Walliams" character in one of his films; a number of them feel "bothered" by the "attention" or something; in addition to those that feel that they resemble the "Melissa Walliams" character, all of those with the first name "Melissa", and all of those with the surname "Walliams" are also going to report him to certain authorities."
3.
Later....T,c: "It's Okay! You know what i was saying about the Quinlan Tarkington business? None of them are leaving the country." Identity's Image: "Yaaay!"

SUFFERING EXTREME: INCORRECTNESS SEXUAL OF HUMAN ENGLISH FEMALE NON-SEXUALESSES TYPING 51
"One of the various Human English Female Non-Sexualess Incorrectess Sexuals, or Hefn-siss, has feelings for YOU!? That makes me SICK! You shouldn't even have been BORN! You're disGUSTING! You're WORTHLESS! I feel like i've been STABBED, the mere hypothetical concept of a Human English Female having sexual intercourse with you is a crime itself." The man who had shouted this at Identity's Image then spat on the ground. A number of days later, Identity's Image was at his home. "I can't understand that someone like that is being reWARDED after he did that to me. Everyone who HAS been born, SHOULD HAVE been born for some reason or another, i suppose. Is it wrong for someone in my group to have sexual intercourse with me? I don't understand. And that was an extreme reaction from him. Etcetera."

SUFFERING EXTREME: INCORRECTNESS SEXUAL OF HUMAN ENGLISH FEMALE NON-SEXUALESSES TYPING 52
A Human English Male was talking to Human English Female Non-Sexualess Incorrectess Sexual, or Hefn-sis, or "MaDARling". Hefn-sis: "He doesn't work like that, he doesn't do things for it, or whatever." "What do you mean? That individual situated over there? That bloke?" The Human English Male who had said that pointed to Identity's Image. Hefn-sis: "Yes, him. Identity's Image." "I don't understand. All human beings like dough. All human beings like cookie dough," said the Human English Male to Hefn-sis. Hefn-sis: "Not him."

SUFFERING EXTREME: INCORRECTNESS SEXUAL OF HUMAN ENGLISH FEMALE NON-SEXUALESSES TYPING 53
"Hi! I've snogged, groped, and draped myself all over your Fantasy, all over Human English Female Non-Sexualess Incorrectess Sexual, or Hefn-sis, or "MaDARling"! Wonderful day isn't it! Can i take the pleasure to have you carry out a transaction!? Life sure is wonderful isn't it! You got it, pal! Yessirree!" Identity's Image frowned, and turned away from the Human English Male who had said that-towards Talks, Comforts, or T,c, and Hatred, Sexual, or H,s. Identity's Image: "What's up with this guy?" H,s: "It's because he and most human beings INside this place, but also many human beings OUTside this place, are LAUGHING at you."

Pickford-Gordon

Since: Sep 09

263

London, UK

Reply »

|
Report Abuse
|
Judge it!
|
#52
Saturday Jul 7

SUFFERING EXTREME: INCORRECTNESS SEXUAL OF HUMAN ENGLISH FEMALE NON-SEXUALESSES TYPING 54
A Human English Male was talking to Identity's Image. "Identity's Image, i don't look at a human being and then judge that human being based on that human being's external appearance." Identity's Image: "You think that i DO, then, etcetera? Interesting. So that's how you justify your snogging, groping, and draping yourself all over my Fantasy, all over Human English Female Non-Sexualess Incorrectess Sexual, or Hefn-sis, or "MaDARling"." Identity's Image, while he had carried out transactions with that Human English Male before, had never, besides the "transaction-talk", had a conversation with that Human English Male, until now.

SUFFERING EXTREME: INCORRECTNESS SEXUAL OF HUMAN ENGLISH FEMALE NON-SEXUALESSES TYPING 55
Identity's Image was lying on a raised table, naked, with his penis erect and raised at an angle. Human English Female Non-Sexualess Incorrectess Sexual, or Hefn-sis, or "MaDARling", was standing over him. Her right hand went over the head of his penis, and she bent the penis-head downwards, causing pain to Identity's Image; she was looking calmly forward into thin air the whole time. Identity's Image: "AAARRRGGGHHH!"

SUFFERING EXTREME: INCORRECTNESS SEXUAL OF HUMAN ENGLISH FEMALE NON-SEXUALESSES TYPING 56
Identity's Image: "Human English Female Non-Sexualess Incorrectess Sexual, or Hefn-sis, or "MaDARling". Do you promise never to keep any promise?" Human English Female Non-Sexualess Incorrectess Sexual, or Hefn-sis, or "MaDARling": "Do i promise?....Keep?....Never?... .Promise?....MALFUNCTION! MALFUNCTION!" Identity's Image: "Aaaarrrgggh! She's really a cyborg!" Hefn-sis: "Just kidding!"

SUFFERING EXTREME: INCORRECTNESS SEXUAL OF HUMAN ENGLISH FEMALE NON-SEXUALESSES TYPING 57
Human English Female Non-Sexualess Incorrectess Sexual, or Hefn-sis, or "MaDARling", went up to a Human English Male lawyer. "I've never shown any sexual interest in Identity's Image over there(I've always been super nice to him obviously), and he's bothering me. Get rid of him, and then make him suffer horribly somehow, EVEN MORE, that is." "I won't do such things, Hefn-sis. It's incorrect for you to say such things etcetera. Talk to him." Hefn-sis: "Why me!? No! Someone else!" "It's YOUR responsibilty, Hefn-sis." Hefn-sis: "Oh F+CK this is no fun, i swear i'm cursed, i wish i'd never gone anywhere near that BOring Identity's Image with his YAWNsome rules and laws and all that morality s+it and that "look before you leap"

cr+p and thinking about the sexual things that i've done. I'm going to unleash my hatred later on, because of that, upon my pathetic little lesbo GImps."

Pickford-Gordon

Since: Sep 09

263

London, UK

Reply »

Report Abuse

Judge it!

#53
Saturday Jul 7

SUFFERING EXTREME: INCORRECTNESS SEXUAL OF HUMAN ENGLISH FEMALE NON-SEXUALESSES TYPING 58
1.
Identity's Image was lying in bed at his home, with Talks, Comforts, or T,c, and Hatred, Sexual, or H,s, standing over him. T,c: "Right, now we're going to talk about Human English Female Non-Sexualess Incorrectess Sexual, or Hefn-sis, or "MaDARling", and related issues." Identity's Image: "Oh why can't she just talk to me and do the things that she's been doing with a number of the Human Males and Human Females who work there, and more, etcetera. I want to deal with things like my mp's stubborn evasiveness, certain incorrecters and incorrectesses, legal Killing and Killing-Self(currently called Euthanasia and Assisted Suicide), the issue of Home, Sexual related issues, Printings, the issue of Country Management, and Natural Science Identities related issues,(probably) etcetera. She always finds new ways to cause me suffering, and there's only so much of it that i can take, she's messing around with my brain. Why does she have such a problem with truth, honesty, fact, HUH?" H,s: "There's nothing to talk about with regard to that incorrectess, or criminal, who will NEVER CHANGE in response to you posting on the Internet, Identity's Image, no matter how much you do it. You need Country Management. Take my advice and-". T,c: "I HADN'T FINISHED SPEAKING! DAMN you TWO!"
2.
T,c: "Okay. What's important is that the three of us talk about this in a calm, intelligent, and rational way, without being governed by emotion." H,s: "I can't F+CKING believe that you two IDi+ts don't realise that she's F+CKING this new guy! I mean what do the two of them have to do for you two to realise that they've had sexual intercourse!" "F++LS!" shouted H,s at them. T,c: "I don't KNOW that they've had sexual intercourse: I'm still analysing Identity's Image's notes. It's a little bit likely the case that she's done a number of SIGNIFICANTLY sexual things with him in addition to what Identity's Image has seen himself: it's similar to the case of her and a number of others. However, we DON'T know if it's sexual intercourse as such." H,s: "Oh f+cking COME ON! F+cking HELL!" T,c: "The thing about the place is that it's a very huggy, snoggy, er, strange place. The thing is that i'm looking at the various possibilities." H,s: "It's EXACTLY like the situation with Human English Female Non-Sexualess Incorrectess Sexual2, or Hefn-sis2, from more than 2 years ago, ISN'T it, Identity's Image? Except this girl is infinitely WORSE than Hefn-sis2." T,c: "You don't know that, H,s." Identity's Image: "Hefn-sis2...." T,c sighed and then shook his head, looking down at the floor.
3.
Identity's Image: "I had bonded with Hefn-sis2. One day Hefn-sis2 told me that she had a girlfriend outside of the urbanised

area. She had done this because she was planning to have sexual intercourse with this random guy who had come out of nowhere. She had looked me in the eye, smiled at me, and told me that she had a girlfriend, when she didn't. I realised shortly after she and the random guy who had come out of nowhere had first had sexual intercourse, that they HAD had sexual intercourse, i could tell. I confronted her and she nodded, she nodded: "yes", she had had sexual intercourse with him. And now, a number of weeks ago, Human English Female Non-Sexualess Incorrectess Sexual, or Hefn-sis, or "MaDARling", has told me confidently and firmly that she has a girlfriend outside the urbanised area where i meet her. Then she left; then she came back."

Pickford-Gordon

Since: Sep 09

263

London, UK

Reply »

|
Report Abuse
|
Judge it!
|
#54
Saturday Jul 7

SUFFERING EXTREME: INCORRECTNESS SEXUAL OF HUMAN ENGLISH FEMALE NON-SEXUALESSES TYPING 58
4.
Identity's Image: ""MaDARling" and this new guy, they joked around and pretended in a mocking way that they were boyfriend and girlfriend. Maybe that means that they haven't had sexual intercourse." H,s: "That's what they WANT you to think. It's all been prePAred, reHEARsed by the two of them, a perFORmance. She's always conspiring, conspiring with this new guy JUUUUST like she did with a certain YDNA Level X, where X is a lower letter so to speak than R, Human Male some time ago." T,c: "I need to analyse the notes." H,s: "She must surely have said something to him like "Identity's Image is structured and organised, so if we mix things up then that's good". She wants to cause suffering to you, and believes in lying, and "getting away with things". And it'll take a long time for someone like that to change, IF it's possible, somehow, for someone like that to change." T,c looked tired and disbelieving as he said: "I know that inside every human being is the desire to act correctly. I know that it's there, even inside the worst Human English Female Non-Sexualesses." H,s: "Yeah dreamer you keep telling yourself that: because I KNOW, that there are an ENORMOUS number of human beings who have ZERO desire to act correctly, and who can NEVER be INSTILLED with the desire to act correctly: THAT is the ONE FACT, my friend."
5.
H,s: "You saw her expression, when she saw that Identity's Image, at that moment, believed that she had had sexual intercourse with that guy, and that it hurt him, you saw it: she was smiling at him: she enjoyed causing suffering to him. And she knows that he tried to commit suicide in May 2011." T,c: "It's likely that she did enjoy causing suffering to him then, YES. That was disgraceful behaviour by her, disgusting behaviour from her, enjoying causing suffering to poor Identity's Image in such a way, a sexual way. But it doesn't mean that she has had sexual intercourse with that guy. In any case, i have confidence in her: she must tell the TRUTH next time." H,s: "It's because she has no sense of morality or the law JUUUUST like Hefn-sis2 from more than 2 years ago, and also, eXACTLY like Hefn-sis2, believes in "not hurting anyone". She fails to understand that deceiving and lying are acts of incorrectness, or crime. But beLIEve me, IDENTITY'S IMAGE, with MY help, is going to

make her Eiffel Tower of lies fall down. And HEY, have you noticed how UNGAY everyone who works there comes across as!?" Identity's Image: "I can't take my brain being messed around with like this any more. I could be with her and then one day she could say "I've been hiding having had sex with THIS guy, or THAT guy, etcetera," and then it would destroy me completely, my brain might just pop or blank out, if it doesn't do so before because of Hefn-sis." T,c: "In any case, i need to analyse the notes. But next time Hefn-sis needs to TALK to you, Identity's Image, and tell the TRUTH, before she gives you everything that she's been giving to a number of the human beings that work there etcetera, and more."

Pickford-Gordon

Since: Sep 09

263

London, UK

Reply »

|
Report Abuse
|
Judge it!
|
#55
Saturday Jul 7

SUFFERING EXTREME: INCORRECTNESS SEXUAL OF HUMAN ENGLISH FEMALE NON-SEXUALESSES TYPING 59
Human English Female Non-Sexualess Incorrectess Sexual, or Hefn-sis, or "MaDARling", was in a room with three other Human English Female Non-Sexualesses. "Can i give you some sex, OLD MAN?" one of them flirtatiously asked the wall. "Lawyer! LAWyer!" called another one loudly. The "first" one turned to her: "You're so guilty!" "Lawyer," murmured the "second" Human English Female Non-Sexualess, looking at the ground. The third one was holding a large knife in a threatening manner. Hefn-sis: "So FUNny!" "Hmmm?" went the "second" Human English Female Non-Sexualess, leaning forward towards Hefn-sis with her hands behind her back.

SUFFERING EXTREME: INCORRECTNESS SEXUAL OF HUMAN ENGLISH FEMALE NON-SEXUALESSES TYPING 60
Identity's Image was talking to Human English Female Non-Sexualess Incorrectess Sexual, or Hefn-sis, or "MaDARling". Identity's Image: "You're beautiful. It was nice when we touched, wasn't it?" Hefn-sis: "SOMEONE ELSE do it. No wait a secundo, I'LL do it. I can't restrain myself any longer with regard to Identity's Image." She leaned over and kissed Identity's Image on the lips: they snogged.

SUFFERING EXTREME: INCORRECTNESS SEXUAL OF HUMAN ENGLISH FEMALE NON-SEXUALESSES TYPING 61
Identity's Image was talking to one of the various Human English Female Non-Sexualess Incorrectess Sexuals, or Hefn-siss. One of the various Hefn-siss: "I have a boyfriend." A large number of guys, one by one, snogged her, groping her from behind and from the front, running their hands all over her clothed body. "You believe that RIGHT?" Identity's Image frowned, looking away from them to the left into the "hypothetical camera".

SUFFERING EXTREME: INCORRECTNESS SEXUAL OF HUMAN ENGLISH FEMALE NON-SEXUALESSES

TYPING 62
Human English Female Non-Sexualess Incorrectess Sexual, or Hefn-sis, or "MaDARling", had followed Identity's Image to the Harbour, where Identity's Image got the boat on a regular basis. He turned towards her, where he was sitting down waiting for the boat. "You're not going anywhere, Identity's Image!" She walked up to him: soon he was looking up at her. Hefn-sis: "I'll teach you to flirt with one of my kinky little F+CKING lesbian SLAves!" She grabbed him by the jumper and pulled him closer to her, and then snogged him; then she straddled him where he was sitting down, putting her arms around him.

Pickford-Gordon

Since: Sep 09

263

London, UK

Reply »

|
Report Abuse
|
Judge it!
|
#56
Saturday Jul 7

SUFFERING EXTREME: INCORRECTNESS SEXUAL OF HUMAN ENGLISH FEMALE NON-SEXUALESSES
TYPING 63
You oscillate between love and hate;
Yet as i, resting, curl and cry,
I see us together, and espy,
Salvation, and a happy state.
May we soon pass the promised gate
And be united: hand in hand
We soon shall flit throughout the land:
No longer shall we wait.
May broken promises fade and go;
From my devotion soon shall flow
Our paradise. With kisses wet,
My dream at last shall soon be set
In stone, with you. What shall we say
When those around us smile our way?

Faloola Chong

Northwich, UK

Reply »

|
Report Abuse
|
Judge it!
|
#57
Saturday Jul 7

That's lovely ducks, keep taking the tablets though. But don't be tempted to buy any from those friendly Cameroonian Doctors on here!

love faloola

Pickford-Gordon

Since: Sep 09

263

London, UK

Reply »

|
Report Abuse
|
Judge it!
|
#58
1 hr ago

SUFFERING EXTREME: INCORRECTNESS SEXUAL OF HUMAN ENGLISH FEMALE NON-SEXUALESSES TYPING 64
Identity's Image was typing at his computer, with Talks, Comforts, or T,c, and Hatred, Sexual, or H,s standing over him. Identity's Image was frantic, with tears flowing down his cheeks, and with his fingers moving quickly over the keyboard; he was mumbling: "They're f+cking they're f+cking oh god make it stop this will make it stop i can't do this i want to die i can't do this she keeps hurting me if i don't type she'll keep f+cking him or someone else or leave again i can't take this please i can't do this humanity is a TRAP." H,s: "IDI+T! Do you know how much time and effort etcetera you've spent typing onto the Internet for her? You have a sigNIFIcant number of things to do, you could have done a significant percentage of all of the things on your list that you have to do, instead of this. I'M TALKING TO YOU! PAY ATTENTION DREAMER!" Identity's Image kept mumbling to himself, but also shook his head briefly in response while doing this, before focusing completely on his typing

once more. T,c: "I think that you should maybe calm down first: i pride myself in the control i have, and you should do the same, Identity's Image." H,s: "ContROL, POle, gimme a f+cking break, what he needs is to see Human English Female Non-Sexualess Incorrectess Sexual, or Hefn-sis, or "MaDARling", for what she really is, and to prepare himself for her getting worse: every time that he goes in there is going to result in her getting worse and worse." H,s snapped his fingers in front of Identity's Image's eyes repeatedly, but this produced no response from Identity's Image. H,s stood directly behind Identity's Image and pulled out a large knife: he held it at Identity's Image's throat. T,c: "I've told you to stop doing that, H,s."

SUFFERING EXTREME: INCORRECTNESS SEXUAL OF HUMAN ENGLISH FEMALE NON-SEXUALESSES TYPING 65
Identity's Image: "Huh! How aBOUT that? I just started talking about scientific fact, and he stopped being slightly hateful towards me and went all quiet and somewhat worried etcetera. You can't get arrested if you just talk scientific fact, you know....more or less. Wait a minute, i really don't like him, i seem to have forgotten that. What am i doing? In any case, i suppose, there are no "jokes", no "games", only incorrectness, or crime."

Pickford-Gordon

Since: Sep 09

263

London, UK

Reply »

|
Report Abuse
|
Judge it!
|
#59
1 hr ago

SUFFERING EXTREME: INCORRECTNESS SEXUAL OF HUMAN ENGLISH FEMALE NON-SEXUALESSES TYPING 66
Identity's Image was lying in bed, too weak to get up: he was thinking about Human English Female Non-Sexualess Incorrectess Sexual, or Hefn-sis, or "MaDARling". Talks, Comforts, or T,c, and Hatred, Sexual, or H,s were also in the room: they were standing over him. T,c: "I've been analysing the notes more thoroughly etcetera. I can say that Human English Female Non-Sexualess Incorrectess Sexual, or Hefn-sis, or "MaDARling", has done something sigNIFIcantly sexual with the A YDNA Level U individuals, where A is a number from 1 to 15 and U is a "letter lower than R" so to speak, and with "everyone likes dough; everyone likes cookie dough", with 100% certainty. When i say sigNIFIcantly sexual, i mean something more than snogging and more than doing the type of stuff that Identity's Image has seen her doing with them through the clothing. In addition to that, with regard to those individuals that i've just mentioned, i'm ALmost 100% certain that she has had sexual intercourse with them." H,s: "HAH! I TOLD YOU SO, T,c, ya little dreamer GIT. Oh HOW THE MIGHTY ARE FALLEN! AH HAHAHAHAHAAAAH!" T,c: "This is not funny, H,s. Think about Identity's Image." H,s: "Oh right. Oops." H,s was quiet and somewhat sad now as he turned towards Identity's Image. T,c: "She lied to Identity's Image about having a girlfriend a significant distance away, and she deceived him when she told him that she had gone away from the urbanised area where she and Identity's Image meet regularly: i perceive that she was still there, possibly f+cking that guy. Whatever her motive, it is almost 100% certain that she told him that she had a girlfriend for the same reason(s) that Human English Female Non-Sexualess Incorrectess Sexual2, or Hefn-sis2 did a number of years ago. I hope that she now

realises the truth, though: my current view is that it's extremely unlikely if not impossible that Identity's Image will EVER forget about her. He DEFINITELY won't be forgetting about her any time soon, with 100% certainty."

Pickford-Gordon

Since: Sep 09

263

London, UK

Reply »

|
Report Abuse
|
Judge it!
|
#60
54 min ago

SUFFERING EXTREME: INCORRECTNESS SEXUAL OF HUMAN ENGLISH FEMALE NON-SEXUALESSES TYPING 67
1.
Identity's Image: "Oh GOD! Oh F+CK oh my head! My brain! I've been thinking that she was the same as when i sat with her that time a number of weeks ago....but she's been f+cking him oh GOD! I'm worthless, she would rather start something new than have sex with me nooo i can't do this i can't do it i need to die it's too much, she's saying that what i have with her is not any GOOD. I even started thinking that she hadn't had sex with the YDNA Level U individuals, where U is a "letter lower than R" so to speak. The concept of her became even more wonderful and special in my mind....i mean she's STILL special though, done is done with regard to those that she's had sexual intercourse with. What matters is that I know what that's like, before she ages, before it's too late for her to reverse the suffering that she has caused me, to create something NEW and WONDERFUL and MEANINGFUL etcetera with ME."
2.
Identity's Image: "Who is she? Huh? How can i trust her? HOW!? She said "no human being will know: EVER". Doesn't she understand that THAT "BELIEF" ALONE makes her compare extremely unfavourably to all of the Human English Females around her. After i've had sexual intercourse with her, and she's lying there next to me, i want to know who she's had sex with- the exact number and details etcetera of them- and how many times and what positions etcetera, so that i myself and her can undo the damage of THAT, to one extent or another, or something like that etcetera. But if she's beside me and then she tells me something and she's lying about it, then i'll have lived a certain amount of time with the belief that she's someone who has only done THIS or that she's someone who has only done THAT. When i find out, it'll AGE me, it'll cause me SUFFERING, my brain which went in one direction should really have gone in the other you see: that's what lying does. And i'll spend time and effort thinking about it: can you give the time, effort, and my former state of mind back to me, Human English Female Non-Sexualess Incorrectess Sexual, or Hefn-sis, or "MaDARling"? Can you give it back to me? She needs to change."
3.
Identity's Image: "And it's so easy to picture these guys that she's been f+cking....to picture them f+cking her, because of how she behaves with them right in front of me. The ones that i don't see haven't (really?) hurt me, but i have seen the others-the ones that i HAVE seen-doing sexual things with her in front of me, and the seeing it makes my suffering worse. And around the time i first saw her she came across as....well she was spending a lot of time with this one guy, a YDNA Level R guy, a guy that i don't dislike very much at all, only the tiniest bit IF i dislike him at all. So i thought that they're like boyfriend and

girlfriend, and that she was just normal, and not going to be doing that with YDNA Level U individuals, where U is a "letter lower than R" so to speak, and i can still see all of the ways that she acted with them. And now this new guy who KNEW that i'm in love with her, but STILL went ahead and has been f+cking her, and he might have done it because he hates me, because he thinks that it's incorrectness, or crime, for me to have something with her, or something like that. She could have been having sexual intercourse with me all of this time. It's been the same story my whole life, and i'm tired, i feel so so tired of the same story over and over again with regard to Human English Female Non-Sex Workers. It's really all too much, and life as a human being is a trap that i need to, legally, get out of. Hefn-sis, next time you'll give it to ME, won't you. I can't take any more of this, my home is cold, painful, and full of despair. Think about how much you mean to me, my darling."

Pickford-Gordon

Since: Sep 09

263

London, UK

Reply »

|
Report Abuse
|
Judge it!
|
#63
33 min ago

SUFFERING EXTREME: INCORRECTNESS SEXUAL OF HUMAN ENGLISH FEMALE NON-SEXUALESSES TYPING 69
1.
Talks, Comforts, or T,c, Hatred, Sexual, or H,s, and Identity's Image were talking to Human English Female Non-Sexualess Incorrectess Sexual, or Hefn-sis, or "MaDARling". Hefn-sis: "Oh F+CK there are THREE OF YOU: now i'm REALLY gonna go inSANE." Identity's Image: "I'm tired, Human English Female Non-Sexualess Incorrectess Sexual, or Hefn-sis, or "MaDARling": i just feel tired of everything in the whole Universe. I think that i'm going to say right now, that what might happen if you f+ck him again or if you f+ck another guy again," H,s: "Or a f+cking ANIMAL! i bet you've-" T,c: "H,s!!!! SHUT UP!!!! I TOLD you not to talk to her right now!" H,s: "It's just that we know what she's like, and we don't know whether or not she's done anything sexual with an-" T,c: "I'm GOING TO HIT YOU! I MEAN IT H,S!" H,s: "OOOOH, who's afraid of the big bad dreamer? OOOOH, i'm SHAKING so bad! I'm SO SCARED! OOOOH!" T,c: "Look, H,s, Identity's Image needs to talk to her, you want him to be strong don't you?" H,s: "Well first he's gotta find out what "strong" MEANS. But OK! Yeahyeahyeahyeah, i shall inDEED permit the TWAIN to conFER!" T,c and H,s left the building: they would meet up with Identity's Image later.
2.
Identity's Image: "I might go to a certain European country, if you do that. And then you'll never see me again. And neither will anyone else in the current Universe." Identity's Image started to walk away from her. Hefn-sis: "Wait a minute, Identity's Image. I need to think about this." Identity's Image turned around to front her, tiredly. Hefn-sis's visage soon turned into a mask of hatred: she glared at Identity's Image, and her white teeth showed through as she started talking to him, or rather snarling AT him. "I HATE you Identity's Image, you have like some kind of HOLD on me with this morality cr+p. I used to be so FREEEE Identity's Image, there were no CONsequences to all of the FUN things that i did. Now why should i F+CKING have to think about this, i can't STAND this. Sexual intercourse is suPPOSED to be FUN, and escapist: sexual intercourse is

supposed to vanish once i do it with all of these guys. I like the VARIETY, with all of the different races. And i like GUILT. I LOVE using my body to hurt you, handing over my body, my body which is soooo precious to you to these guys, when it's GREAT that it wouldn't have the MEANING that the whole thing would have with you. I get pleasure from the look on your face every time i hurt you."

3.

Hefn-sis: "I've lost all of my girlfriends who happen to work with me because of you: they're all f+cking YDNA Level U individuals, where U is a "letter lower than R" so to speak. So I had to tell them, i'm not aLLOWED to F+CK YDNA Level U individuals, Identity's Image DOESN'T LIKE MY FUN, and DOESN'T WANT ME TO HAVE FUN. So now they no longer like me. And we had this whole CLUB where we're all F+CKING YDNA Level U individuals, and now THEY'RE in it but I'M not. So anyway, Identity's Image....YEAH, in addition to hating you, i also LOVE you, i've ALWAYS loved you. That's why, when you said "Don't have sex with a YDNA Level U individual" i was like "FINE, i'll take THIS GUY OVER HERE inSTEAD, then", but now you're WHINging again. Sex isn't supposed to be real, it's supposed to make me forget everything else, don't you see how EAGERLY i forget EVERYTHING ABOUT YOU when i'm f+cking this new guy? I hate all of this REALITY sh+t." Identity's Image: "Well, if i don't do what i've just said that i might do, i'm going to focus on making the politicians set up a legal Killing and legal Killing-Self system. If things stay like this, i'm going to legally commit suicide the first legal chance that i get."

Tell me when this thread is updated:
(Registration is not required)

Add to my Tracker

Send me an email

Showing posts 41 - 60 of 62

< prev page

|

next page >

Go to last page|Jump to page:1 2 3 4

Type in your comments below

Name
(appears on your post)

Comments

Characters left: 4000

Type the numbers you see in the image on the right:

Please note by clicking on "Post Comment" you acknowledge that you have read the Terms of Service and the comment you are posting is in compliance with such terms. Be polite.Inappropriate posts may be removed by the moderator. Send us your feedback.

25Users are viewing theUnited Kingdom Forumright now

Search the United Kingdom Forum:

Topic

Updated

Last By

Comments

Atheism to Defeat Religion by 2038

5 min

Educated What

6,168

The First Changes(Jan '10)

29 min

Pickford-Gordon

34

Brit gangs rape and sexually exploit young, whi...

41 min

Bogdani

378

Scottish Lesbian Couple Holds Mock Wedding To L...

3 hr

Rick in Kansas

2

City schools in surprise new merger

5 hr

This is not good news

4

Anyone interested in peace, love and tolerance?

5 hr

Just a thought

14

'Rightful heir' to British monarchy dies in Aus...

5 hr

TRUTH cannot be shut down

2

See all threads in the United Kingdom forum »

If the election were held tomorrow, who would get your vote? Vote now on the Election Poll, June 2012 Map.

United Kingdom News
Terror Suspect Tagged, Tracked, Nabbed Near Oly...
Flood alert as heavy rain forecast
Oil price climbs as Norwegian strike looms
Magazine Cover Shows Kate Middleton with Yellow...
NY Court: Gay Marriage Caucus Didn't Break Rules
BMW investing £250m into Mini production
Does secret tape link Adams to IRA killing? Fam...
Two charged over stabbing death
Pakistan shuns physicist linked to 'God particle'
EDL mob 'like wild animals'
UK Flood Threat Remains As More Rain Forecast
Scottish News: Food festival sunk by bad weather

More United Kingdom News from Topix »

Topix Politix App

Take your stand on the issues you care about.

Using an iPhone?

Keep the Topix forums in your pocket
with the new, free Topix App.

Daily Horoscope for July 9

Leo

Take it easy today because you're in a combustible mood and things will get under your skin in no time at all. You're also feeling sensitive and easily offended, which will cause problems if you're talking to someone who doesn't care what they say provided it gets a reaction. Wake up to the fact that they're trying to get you to rise to the bait... and they'll succeed very easily.

Get your Horoscope »

United Kingdom
News
Forums & Polls
Real-Time News

Explore More Topix
Home Page
Forums
Top Stories
Most Popular
Issue Maps
US News
US Cities list
World News
World Countries list
Politics
Celebrities
Business
Finance
Autos
Sports
Sci-Tech
Electronics
Entertainment
Movies
Music
Television
Video Games
Health
Life
Arts
Food
Home
Travel
Offbeat
Site Map / All Topics

About Topix
About Us
Media Kit
Topix Blog
Press Room
RSS Newsfeeds
Law Enforcement
School Officials
Cyber-bullying Resources
Jobs
FAQ
Privacy Policy
Terms of Service
Feedback?
Report Abuse?

Local Classifieds & Listings

Reach Local customers. Post a classified listing for your business. Promote job, auto, rental, and local event listings.

Learn more »

Join the Topix Community
¦Create your own profile, complete with quick links to your favorite topics.
¦Personalize your forum posts with your photo and hometown.
¦Exchange Personal Messages with other registered users.

Sign up today! »

Topix Politix »

Feedback?
Comments made yesterday: 109,375 Total comments across all topics: 178,634,927

Copyright ©2012 Topix LLC

Local News: United Kingdom

|

Sign Up

|

Sign In

123

Mitt Romney
Romney: Obama Focused on Fundraising, Not Jobs

Syria
UN delays vote on new Syria resolution

Pakistan
Don't Count on Pakistan's Liberals

Home
Forums
Top Stories
Popular
Local
Election Poll
US
Politics
World
Sports
Entertainment
Offbeat
Other

United Kingdom
News
Forums & PollsSuffering Extreme: In...

Real-Time News

Suffering Extreme: Incorrectness Sexual Of HEFN-Ses Typings

Posted in the United Kingdom Forum

Share

Read
86 Comments
Add to my Tracker

More United Kingdom Discussions »

Comments (Page 4)

Showing posts 61 - 80 of 86

< prev page

|

next page >

Go to last page|Jump to page:1 2 3 4 5

Pickford-Gordon

Since: Sep 09

291

London, UK

Reply »

|
Report Abuse
|
Judge it!
|
#64
Monday Jul 9

SUFFERING EXTREME: INCORRECTNESS SEXUAL OF HUMAN ENGLISH FEMALE NON-SEXUALESSES TYPING 70
1.
Talks, Comforts, or T,c, Hatred, Sexual, or H,s, and Identity's Image were talking to Human English Female Non-Sexualess

Incorrectess Sexual, or Hefn-sis, or "MaDARling". Hefn-sis: "My body doesn't exist: it's just a tool that i use to help MEN." Identity's Image: "Well that's what Sexualessism, or Sex Workerism, or Prostitution, IS, sort of, etcetera. However, it's too late for you to have this principle NOW: you resist ME with the utmost effort. By contrast you appear to be very friendly with most men who are NOT ME. What do you think that this is doing to me, when i love and need you more than anyone and anything else right now, and when i've spent all of this time, effort, and am in a "state of mind", when i know that you've liked me for a long time, when you've flirted with me, etcetera? What is it doing to me? If you were to become a Sex Worker NOW, that would destroy me. My life has meaning because the effort, time, belief etcetera that i've invested in you must pay off, before you do anything sexual again with anyone who is NOT me, you must not do such a thing. If you become a Sex Worker, you will become LESS than all Sex Workers. While i will always love the vast majority, probably, of current Sex Workers, the fact is that you HAVE only done sexual things with some (small?) number X of men, which is NICE, it WILL BE NICE for me. It will be fantastic. Why do you want to lose that? Why do you want that to gradually mean less and less? It's something extremely valuable and dreamlike, to have a human female who has only done sexual things with a small number of men, or ONE MAN even, there are many Human English Females who have only had sexual intercourse, and only ever will, with ONE Human English Male. But there are other factors, like how beautiful i find you, Hefn-sis. And the thing is i have always thought of you as a Non-Sex-Worker, so you will damage my brain severely if you keep on going like this, doing sexual things with human males who are NOT me."

2.
Hefn-sis: "You LOOK AT ME, Identity's Image. That's a crime." Identity's Image: "You're beautiful, i love looking at you. I could look at you all day. You can't say that it's a crime for me to look at you."

3.
Hefn-sis: "My principle is that i don't want to hurt anyone." Identity's Image: "Well if you don't hurt SOME people, you hurt OTHER people by doing that, or something. By thinking "I don't want to hurt this guy that i'm f+cking right now by not doing anything sexual with him", you're hurting ME. Human beings who have such a false principle-acting correctly is the only main principle that all human beings should have, in accordance with the real law, not lying, not deceiving, not hiding much, not stealing, not being a traitor, etcetera(except if held hostage by terrorists etcetera), and "not hurting anyone" should not be prioritised, and human beings shouldn't think in terms of "hurting" or "not hurting" THIS human being or THAT human being etcetera-....such human beings become exploited and/or corrupted, because they commit incorrectness, or crime, in the name of "not wanting to hurt anyone". You yourself have lied, deceived, etcetera because you didn't want to hurt me, you've made things worse for me."

4.
Hefn-sis: "I don't like the truth." Identity's Image: "Well the truth is the truth, fact is fact. If something has happened, it has happened. You lie to yourself if you hate me because i tell the truth, because i describe WHAT HAS HAPPENED, because i describe FACT." Hefn-sis: "I don't like an amount of your TYPING." Identity's Image: "Typing is just doing THIS(indicates) with one's fingers. It is even less real than talking to oneself when one is alone, if one does such things, and it is even easier to do. You can't blame me for typing etcetera."

Pickford-Gordon

Since: Sep 09

291

London, UK

Reply »

|
Report Abuse
|
Judge it!
|
#65

Monday Jul 9

SUFFERING EXTREME: INCORRECTNESS SEXUAL OF HUMAN ENGLISH FEMALE NON-SEXUALESSES TYPING 70
5.
Hefn-sis: "My JOB". Identity's Image: "Job is a LABEL. It is technique, effort, in a number of cases. It is not how YOU, speCIFICALLY YOU, can make the world a better place, can make things better. YOUR job, Hefn-sis, is an ANTI-JOB, wasting resources, wasting land that could be taken up by Natural Science or something else, etcetera. What we have, you and me, is what has meaning, and what you should be putting first. What is real is that there is an AMOUNT of suffering that you've caused me, which you haven't reVERsed. If i were to die this instant, you would feel ashamed, because i am a STORY....and, if dead, i was a story which suffered so much because of you, with you not reversing the suffering that you've caused me, you would forever be "one of the human beings who caused this amount of suffering to Identity's Image".
6.
Hefn-sis: "I don't believe that i can't get away with crimes, take things to the grave, if just me and someone else knows then i've gotten away with it haven't i?" Identity's Image: "Well i think that's what dimebag darrell thought. The thing is, human beings who think like you are repulsive to human beings who think and act correctly(except to me! I love you.). Someone who thinks like that could be ANYONE. By contrast i hide very little, and try to act correctly etcetera. You have to think about it, with car crashes, being struck by lightning, etcetera, everyone has an equal chance of being "chosen" for such things. Why does THAT human being get chosen and not THAT one? It's because it's correct. It's to do with the value of that human being in comparison to the value of other human beings, etcetera....but i've already typed about such things a number of times. It's ridiculous to think that something so imperfect as a human being has power over BETTER etcetera things. Whether anyone other than, even just YOU, knows something or not, it doesn't change the fact of it's existence."
7.
Identity's Image: "Tell me the truth next time, then(next time) do a number of sexual things with me, and then(next time) have sexual intercourse with me. If you think that i've done wrong against you, which i haven't, TELL me. There is no compromise and/or bending the TRUTH, my darling. I love you and i need you more than anyone and anything else right now." T,c: "I have confidence in you, Hefn-sis." H,s: "You should KNOW, Hefn-sis, that you HAVE caused and ARE causing a million whatevers(the unit) of suffering to Identity's Image, and only you and perhaps only one or two, etcetera, other human beings have caused that amount of suffering to Identity's Image." T,c: "That's enough, H,s." Identity's Image: "Don't listen to H,s, Hefn-sis, i mean, you know, i feel like i want to kill myself, but it's not that bad. Erm! I mean, you can reverse it, you're my dream, Hefn-sis."

Pickford-Gordon

Since: Sep 09

291

London, UK

Reply »

|
Report Abuse
|
Judge it!
|
#66
Wednesday Jul 11

SUFFERING EXTREME: INCORRECTNESS SEXUAL OF HUMAN ENGLISH FEMALE NON-SEXUALESSES TYPING 71
1.
Identity's Image suddenly put his arms around Talks, Comforts, or T,c, rocking back and forth while embracing T,c; Identity's Image's eyes were bulging out of his skull in shock and fear, and he was shaking and mumbling to himself. Identity's Image: "Ohgodohgod that just came out of nowhere....it's not enough that that YDNA Level U individual, where U is a "letter lower than R" so to speak, has sexually penetrated my dream, he had to do THAT after she spoke to him oh f+ck he doesn't have a soul she doesn't have a soul i have to get out of here i have to get out i gotta leave i gotta leave right now, NOW!". T,c: "Sssshhhh, it's oKAY Identity's Image, nothing HAppened in the end. She'll be there next time, and you'll talk to her again." Identity's Image: "No but i have to prepare, i need CYANIDE, the suffering that that would do to me now i can't do it, she has 0 desire to do good, he has 0 desire to do good, i can't do this i can't do this." Hatred, Sexual, or H,s: "HAH! I TOLD you SO! But did you listen, LAbelling me? No." T,c: "Now is absolutely NOT the time for a "HAH!" H,s. Do you want to make Identity's Image WORSE?"
2.
Identity's Image had calmed down, and was sitting on his bed, with T,c, and H,s standing over him. Identity's Image: "I think that she's been sent to k+ll me, by the One Fact: this is probably the One Fact saying to me: "You're going to keep suffering until you accept that you need to die as soon as possible." It must be true." T,c: "Nononono, have HOPE Identity's Image." Identity's Image looked up. Identity's Image: "I'm going to keep trying with her, with Human English Female Non-Sexualess Incorrectess Sexual, or Hefn-sis, or "MaDARling", just as hard as i did before, if not harder somehow etcetera. But i'm also going to try to do something with regard to SUICIDE....i plan to legally commit suicide if things stay like this, but i think that i'd like RIGHT NOW the various things set up. Suffering could hit me at any time, and i feel like it's going to hit soon, i feel it coming. I need to prepare for that, and maybe have a vial of Cyanide around my neck, just like George Sterling, and maybe also Adolf Hitler, did. Why didn't i listen to Clark Ashton Smith's adVIce?"

Pickford-Gordon

Since: Sep 09

291

London, UK

Reply »

|
Report Abuse
|
Judge it!
|
#67
Wednesday Jul 11

SUFFERING EXTREME: INCORRECTNESS SEXUAL OF HUMAN ENGLISH FEMALE NON-SEXUALESSES TYPING 71
1.

Identity's Image suddenly put his arms around Talks, Comforts, or T,c, rocking back and forth while embracing T,c; Identity's Image's eyes were bulging out of his skull in shock and fear, and he was shaking and mumbling to himself. Identity's Image: "Ohgodohgod that just came out of nowhere....it's not enough that that YDNA Level U individual, where U is a "letter lower than R" so to speak, has sexually penetrated my dream, he had to do THAT after she spoke to him oh f+ck he doesn't have a soul she doesn't have a soul i have to get out of here i have to get out i gotta leave i gotta leave right now, NOW!". T,c: "Sssshhhh, it's oKAY Identity's Image, nothing HAppened in the end. She'll be there next time, and you'll talk to her again." Identity's Image: "No but i have to prepare, i legally need CYANIDE, the suffering that that would do to me now i can't do it, she has 0 desire to do good, he has 0 desire to do good, i can't do this i can't do that." Hatred, Sexual, or H,s: "HAH! I TOLD you SO! But did you listen, LAbelling me? No." T,c: "Now is absolutely NOT the time for a "HAH!" H,s. Do you want to make Identity's Image WORSE?"

2.

Identity's Image had calmed down, and was sitting on his bed, with T,c, and H,s standing over him. Identity's Image: "I think that she's been sent by the One Fact: this is probably the One Fact saying to me: "You're going to keep suffering until you accept that you need to die as soon as possible." It must be true." T,c: "Nononono, have HOPE Identity's Image." Identity's Image looked up. Identity's Image: "I'm going to keep trying with her, with Human English Female Non-Sexualess Incorrectess Sexual, or Hefn-sis, or "MaDARling", just as hard as i did before, if not harder somehow etcetera. But i'm also going to try to do something with regard to SUICIDE....i plan to legally commit suicide if things stay like this, but i think that i'd like RIGHT NOW the various things set up. Suffering could hit me at any time, and i feel like it's going to hit soon, i feel it coming. I need to prepare for that, and maybe legally have a vial of Cyanide around my neck, just like George Sterling, and maybe also Adolf Hitler, did. Why didn't i listen to Clark Ashton Smith's adVIce?"

Pickford-Gordon

Since: Sep 09

291

London, UK

Reply »

|
Report Abuse
|
Judge it!
|
#68
Wednesday Jul 11

SUFFERING EXTREME: INCORRECTNESS SEXUAL OF HUMAN ENGLISH FEMALE NON-SEXUALESSES TYPING 72
1.
Identity's Image was talking to Talks, Comforts, or T,c, and Hatred, Sexual, or H,s, about Human English Female Non-Sexualess Incorrectess Sexual, or Hefn-sis, or "MaDARling". Identity's Image: "Human English Female Non-Sexualess Incorrectess Sexual, or Hefn-sis, or "MaDARling", has been f+cking that young guy, the one who looks 19 or so: i saw a number of things: i saw them around the corner. I didn't like that to an enormous extent, i thought that "everyone likes dough: everyone likes cookie dough" had hurt me, but this hurts even more than him since this 19 or so old guy looks significantly younger than "everyone likes dough: everyone likes cookie dough". Am i jumping to conclusions, T,c?" H,s: "Now you're using your HEAd: i TOLD YOU that she'd been f+cking every single Human Male and Human Female who works there, but

ya DIDn't, f+CKing, LIsten. Didyapal? Huh?"
2.
T,c: "Well i'll analyse your notes, Identity's Image. I have something to say about this GEneral issue. I know that you are only concerned about your OWN speCIfic incorrecters and incorrectesses, Identity's Image-And there are indeed plenty of them. With regard to this general issue, i'll just say that with regard to a Human English Male having sexual intercourse with a Human English Female, which hurts a different Human English Male who has been communicating etcetera with the Human English Female and has seen the other Human English Male, it's better if it's a Human English Male that looks like he's attained a certain age, that doesn't "look young", or "look young-ish". Age is always associated with value, not just among human beings, but also among primates, perHAPS particaularly apes. I SWEAR that i've read somewhere that older males-among non-human animals-often have sexual intercourse with all of the females in the social "group", and that i think the "older male" of the group is highly valued....but of course human beings are not non-human animals, and if there is a Human English Male "equivalent" to this "older male" of the non-human animal "group" then he shouldn't perhaps have sexual intercourse with all of the Human English Females in that group."
3.
T,c: "In any case she must stop doing anything sexual with anyone who is NOT YOU, Identity's Image, and she must do it RIGHT NOW." Identity's Image: "She keeps saying that she has a GIRLfriend in a land far away." H,s: "Perhaps, Identity's Image, you should assume that the OPposite of everything that she says is the truth IS THE TRUTH....but then she'd realise that and mix it up etcetera." T,c: "She doesn't have a GIRLfriend. She owes you a LOT, she has a LOT of explaining to do to you, Identity's Image."

SUFFERING EXTREME: INCORRECTNESS SEXUAL OF HUMAN ENGLISH FEMALE NON-SEXUALESSES TYPING 73
Identity's Image was talking to Talks, Comforts, or T,c, and Hatred, Sexual, or H,s, about Human English Female Non-Sexualess Incorrectess Sexual, or Hefn-sis, or "MaDARling". T,c: "She's SEEMS to be getting better in certain ways, though: she perhaps doesn't believe in the lie of "politeness" any more-or at least not much-, but this can still be improved on; she's starting to act more like a non-incorrectess, or non-criminal, human being instead of an incorrectess, or criminal, human being, even thought she hasn't reversed the suffering that her incorrectnesses have caused you, Identity's Image....she's setting BOUNDARIES, or so it seems," Hatred, Sexual, or H,s: "instead of continuing to f+ck all of the human males and human females who work there AAND, a number of the human males and human females WHo DON't, work there." T,c: "How kind of you H,s. NOT." T,c paused for a while before continuing. T,c: "Er, and there are perhaps other ways too." H,s: "You f+cked up your little SPeech, dreamer. You SUCK, BIGtime....Identity's Image, yoyoyoNEVER, LISTENtohimaGAIN! I'M your guide, and so on etcetera!"

Pickford-Gordon

Since: Sep 09

291

London, UK

Reply »

|
Report Abuse
|
Judge it!
|
#69
Wednesday Jul 11

SUFFERING EXTREME: INCORRECTNESS SEXUAL OF HUMAN ENGLISH FEMALE NON-SEXUALESSES TYPING 74
Identity's Image was talking with Human English Female Non-Sexualess Incorrectess Sexual, or Hefn-sis, or "MaDARling". Hefn-sis: "I don't LIKE you Identity's Image: you typed on the Internet about my girlfriend who works here: it was our little lesbian secret and you RUined it, Identity's Image, oh you BA+tard! Did you see her? She's sad because everyone knows our little secret!" Identity's Image: "Well you shouldn't hide very much you know....I don't, my DARling." Hefn-sis: "You're MEAN Identity's Image you're MEAN!"

SUFFERING EXTREME: INCORRECTNESS SEXUAL OF HUMAN ENGLISH FEMALE NON-SEXUALESSES TYPING 75
1.
Identity's Image was talking with Human English Female Non-Sexualess Incorrectess Sexual, or Hefn-sis, or "MaDARling". Hefn-sis: "i LOVE you, master."
2.
Identity's Image: "Don't call me master, my love." Hefn-sis smiled at him. "Oh ok Identity's Image!"

SUFFERING EXTREME: INCORRECTNESS SEXUAL OF HUMAN ENGLISH FEMALE NON-SEXUALESSES TYPING 76
Identity's Image was talking with Human English Female Non-Sexualess Incorrectess Sexual, or Hefn-sis, or "MaDARling". Identity's Image: "Seriously though, you HAVE caused an enormous amount of suffering to me. Talk to me, do a number of sexual things with me, and have sexual intercourse with me NEXT TIME, my darling."

SUFFERING EXTREME: INCORRECTNESS SEXUAL OF HUMAN ENGLISH FEMALE NON-SEXUALESSES TYPING 77
Identity's Image was talking with Human English Female Non-Sexualess Incorrectess Sexual, or Hefn-sis, or "MaDARling". Hefn-sis: "I'm a million times better than you, Identity's Image. I would rather YOU DIE than have sexual intercourse with you, and i would rather YOU DIE than have a conversation with you from now on." She walked away from Identity's Image.

SUFFERING EXTREME: INCORRECTNESS SEXUAL OF HUMAN ENGLISH FEMALE NON-SEXUALESSES TYPING 78
Identity's Image was talking with Human English Female Non-Sexualess Incorrectess Sexual, or Hefn-sis, or "MaDARling". Hefn-sis: "All human beings exist to SERVE ME. Everything goes around ME."

Pickford-Gordon

Since: Sep 09

291

London, UK

Reply »

|
Report Abuse
|
Judge it!
|
#70
Saturday Jul 14

SUFFERING EXTREME: INCORRECTNESS SEXUAL OF HUMAN ENGLISH FEMALE NON-SEXUALESSES TYPING 68
Identity's Image was talking to Human English Female Non-Sexualess Incorrectess Sexual, or Hefn-sis, or "MaDARling": Hefn-sis's head was down, and she looked guilty. Identity's Image: "Is this what you care about, Hefn-sis? Huh? Here's your F+CKING MONEY, you want it so bad, here's your little pieces of F+CKING PAPER and little bits of F+CKING METAL. HERE! HERE!" Identity's Image was throwing £20 notes and 50p coins at her chest: they fell to the floor. Identity's Image: "HERE! HERE!" Identity's Image then stopped throwing the £20 notes and 50p coins at her and burst into tears. Identity's Image: "How can you do this to me, i'm a human being. Huh? Do you have any idea how much suffering you're causing me? Huh? And what have i done to you, i haven't done anything. I'm doing all this for you, waiting for you, doesn't that mean anything? I know that you have a soul....don't you?"

SUFFERING EXTREME: INCORRECTNESS SEXUAL OF HUMAN ENGLISH FEMALE NON-SEXUALESSES TYPING 79
1.
A Human English Male, of a somewhat distinctive clan, wearing a hat and a bow tie, was talking to a Human English Female, with his arm around her. The Human English Male was speaking: "Human English Female Non-Sexualess Incorrectess Sexual2, or Hefn-sis2? Yeah i did a number of sexual things with her. I believe in stealing, doing things somewhat randomly, betraying those close to me such as Identity's Image, and looking good! HahaHA! This forgiveness thing is so cool! The number of girlfriends that i've lied to? I'M NOT COUNTING, there are just SO MANY. HAHAHA! I've been messed around, so i can do whatever i want, especially with regard to Identity's Image."
2.
He continued speaking: "Death? I'm a christian, so DEATH will NEVER HAPPEN." The man felt something tap his left shoulder from behind, two times....it felt....very HARD. He started to turn around. "What is it?" he asked. He saw Identity's Image. BOOM! The shotgun shouted once, blowing his right foot off above the ankle: "AARRRRGGHHHH!" he went, and collapsed, bleeding, to the carpeted floor.
3.
Identity's Image had returned: he looked at the man with sad, tired, yet hateful, and somewhat dead eyes. The man, glaring at him as he writhed about on the floor, pointed a finger at Identity's Image, accusingly. "Identity's Image, i have OTHER VICTIMS LIKE YOU, who don't somethingorother." Identity's Image raised the shotgun briefly. Identity's Image: "So you admit it, for the second and last time: that i'm your victim."
4.
"AARRRGHHH! NNNNGGGGGHHHHHHHUHHHH! ThePAAAIIN!" The man continued to squirm about; as he did so, Identity's Image's eyes went vague: he searched his memories, looking back in time....he saw the man put his arm around Human English Female Non-Sexualess Incorrectess Sexual2, or Hefn-sis2; he saw the man, and a guy who had come out of nowhere some time ago, surrounding Hefn-sis2 as she giggled in a sexual manner; and Identity's Image saw Hefn-sis2 smile at him, which made him happy, and she raised her eyebrows at him in that way of hers. Identity's Image's shotgun went back down again towards the man as the man looked up at Identity's Image one last time. Identity's Image stated ONE LAST WORD. "Die." The shotgun shouted once in confirmation, causing the man's neck to vanish completely: blood spurted upwards into the eyes of the man's now severed head, and his mouth opened before his head was still. The man was dead. Identity's Image looked at the body and severed head for a while before leaving the room.

Pickford-Gordon

Since: Sep 09

291

London, UK

Reply »

Report Abuse

Judge it!

#71
Saturday Jul 14

SUFFERING EXTREME: INCORRECTNESS SEXUAL OF HUMAN ENGLISH FEMALE NON-SEXUALESSES TYPING 80
1.
Identity's Image was talking to Human English Female Non-Sexualess Incorrectess Sexual2, or Hefn-sis2: there was also another Human English Female in the room. Hefn-sis2 was talking to Identity's Image. Hefn-sis2: "Don't keep doing that, i TOLD you: i don't want anyone to be left out." She then started talking to the other Human English Female, as she bent over the Pool Table, playing pool. Identity's Image smiled. "I'm good at Pool." He approached Hefn-sis2 from behind where she was bending over: she frowned slightly at him. Later, the three of them were laughing together: it was quite nice.
2.
A number of days later, Identity's Image was chatting to a Human English Female: that Human English Female got up and walked away. Identity's Image sensed someone to his right: he turned to the right. Identity's Image: "Oh it's you, Hefn-sis2. What are you doing there, suddenly appearing next to me like that?" Hefn-sis2 looked at Identity's Image. Identity's Image looked back.

SUFFERING EXTREME: INCORRECTNESS SEXUAL OF HUMAN ENGLISH FEMALE NON-SEXUALESSES TYPING 81
1.
Human English Female Non-Sexualess Incorrectess Sexual2, or Hefn-sis2, had been flirting etcetera with Identity's Image. One day, Identity's Image walked past her. He saw a badge which said: "Sarah", and he had heard her being called "Sarah". One day he was in the building. A large number of Human English Males, and Human English Females were gathered around her. "We're here for you, Samantha," they were going. Identity's Image walked past Hefn-sis2: she wore a badge which said "Samantha." Later though, she wore the "Sarah" badge, and he didn't see the "Samantha" badge on her again.
2.
Identity's Image was talking to Hefn-sis2. "Where were you last time, Hefn-sis2? You weren't there. You know that you're my Number One Choice out of all of those who work in that building. Be there from now on, and have sexual intercourse with me etcetera." Hefn-sis2: "I was having fun late at night." She looked at him from the right, with her right hand "cupped". Hefn-sis2: "Yeah?" Identity's Image: "Hefn-sis2, what the heck are you suddenly doing with your right hand?" They were both naked. Hefn-sis2 put her right hand over Identity's Image's erect penis and started moving her right hand up and down.

Pickford-Gordon

Since: Sep 09

291

London, UK

Reply »

|
Report Abuse
|
Judge it!
|
#72
Saturday Jul 14

SUFFERING EXTREME: INCORRECTNESS SEXUAL OF HUMAN ENGLISH FEMALE NON-SEXUALESSES TYPING 82
Identity's Image was talking to Human English Female Non-Sexualess Incorrectess Sexual4, or Hefn-sis4. Hefn-sis4 sighed, and looked down, as Identity's Image carried out a transaction with her. Identity's Image: "I haven't seen you for a while, but you're my Number One Choice out of all of those who work in that building. Human English Female Non-Sexualess Incorrectess Sexual5, or Hefn-sis5, who knows my name, did a funny gesture a number of times, which "put me off her" a very tiny bit, causing me to demote her to Hefn-sis5 status. You're both great, and you haven't done wrong against me as such, or something to that extent, etcetera. Those of Hefn-sis status, of which there are less than 5, have caused enormous amounts of suffering to me. Those of Hefn-sis2 status have caused a significant amount of suffering to me. Those of Hefn-sis3 have casued a little suffering to me. Those of Hefn-sis4, and Hefn-sis5 status have caused very little or no suffering to me. In addition to THAT, it's also the case that some who are more attractive than others, and/or those who have had a greater impact on me, etcetera, are ranked higher than others, so it's not just suffering. It'd be nice if you were there next time, and if either of you had sexual intercourse with me, but it wouldn't cause me to dislike or hate either of you if i never saw either of you again. I don't feel that i NEED to be with either of you. A number of human beings say this about a certain thing: "It's not love unless it HURTS." What they mean is that when incorrectness, or crime, is involved, the feelings are stronger, and mean more, or something to that extent, etcetera."

SUFFERING EXTREME: INCORRECTNESS SEXUAL OF HUMAN ENGLISH FEMALE NON-SEXUALESSES TYPING 83
1.
Identity's Image was naked with Human English Female Non-Sexualess Incorrectess Sexual3, or Hefn-sis3, in his bedroom. Hefn-sis3 looked at his penis and then up at him, and cocked her head in that attractive way of hers. Hefn-sis3: "Aaawww, that's not very good now is it!?" They had sexual intercourse.
2.
Identity's Image was talking to Hefn-sis3. Hefn-sis3: "Why am i not of Hefn-sis4 status?" Identity's Image: "You're too attractive. And don't pretend that you didn't have anything for me, because i know that you did. There's not much significant incorrectness involved, so the NEED for me to be with you is less than the Hefn-siss and the Hefn-sis2s. But i want, or perhaps need you to be there next time." Hefn-sis3: "I changed my shift because of you. You told me your name, and i read a number of your Internet Posts. You don't look like someone who could type such things, so i was really surprised. I'm scared, because i fail to understand you." Identity's Image: "Ask, and you will receive answers from me, answers to any question that you might have, except one or two."

Pickford-Gordon

Since: Sep 09

291

London, UK

Reply »

|
Report Abuse
|
Judge it!
|
#73
Saturday Jul 14

SUFFERING EXTREME: INCORRECTNESS SEXUAL OF HUMAN ENGLISH FEMALE NON-SEXUALESSES TYPING 84
1.
Identity's Image watched the man. This man had said to Identity's Image: "It's (almost) MINE: it's a private company. I can do whatever i want." The man had caused extreme suffering to Identity's Image: he knew how Identity's Image had felt about Human English Female Non-Sexualess Incorrectess Sexual, or Hefn-sis, or "MaDARling", yet he had still persisted with her, with Identity's Image's Dream, with Identity's Image's Fantasy. The man lied to himself, saying that there was no such thing as race. Where was the man's desire to act correctly, to do good, when he knew that Identity's Image had tried to commit suicide because of a certain thing a significant time ago, and that, because of Hefn-sis, or "MaDARling", felt like that right now? A significant number of the people who used such a place, carrying out transactions, were not good people.
2.
The building only had Anti-Jobs, the building was an Anti-Thing....but what could happen between Identity's Image and Hefn-sis had meaning....but also, Identity's Image said to himself, if she didn't go through with it, it would mean the existence of an urge in Identity's Image to (legally) commit suicide, one that he could not deny, and one that he felt that he must prioritise now. The man walked around in an uncontrolled way, randomly: the man, when he said that to Identity's Image, demonstrated, although he had done so before, the differences between himself, and his group, and the group of the majority of human males in the United Kingdom And Ireland. At the start Identity's Image had gotten on okay with him, he liked that group, he supposed, etcetera....but now, after what this man and X other YDNA Level U individuals, where U is a "letter lower than R" so to speak, and X is a number from 1 to 15, had done to him....now Identity's Image felt a slight disliking for the group: the group reminded him of this man and other YNDA U individuals who had been involved with Hefn-sis.
3.
All the X YDNA Level U individuals who had been involved with Hefn-sis had been there last time: Identity's Image had seen them. Identity's Image had seen another individual who might have been a YDNA Level U individual before who was NOT there last time....but, if he never saw that individual again, that individual, who WAS NOT there last time, would not have caused anywhere near the amount of suffering that those who WERE there last time had caused. That is to say, IF that individual was a YDNA Level U individual.

SUFFERING EXTREME: INCORRECTNESS SEXUAL OF HUMAN ENGLISH FEMALE NON-SEXUALESSES TYPING 85
Human English Female Non-Sexualess Incorrectess Sexual, or Hefn-sis, or "MaDARling": "Identity's Image, i would rather have sexual intercourse with a YDNA Level U individual, where U is a "letter lower than R", so to speak, than have sexual intercourse with YOU. Identity's Image, i would rather have sexual intercourse with a YDNA Level U individual, where U is a "letter lower than R", so to speak, than have a conversation with YOU. HiLArious!" Hefn-sis walked away from Identity's Image.

Pickford-Gordon

Since: Sep 09

291

London, UK

Reply »

|
Report Abuse
|
Judge it!
|
#74
Saturday Jul 14

SUFFERING EXTREME: INCORRECTNESS SEXUAL OF HUMAN ENGLISH FEMALE NON-SEXUALESSES TYPING 86
"Victim, there is now no way that you can see her again: you have a MOUNTAIN to climb just to see her again." Victim was sitting on his bed, after his Dream, after his Fantasy, had been taken away from him, after HOPE, had been taken away from him, suddenly and without warning. Everything had become so much slower; he aged rapidly; his movements were sluggish, and he stayed in bed for more hours than before. The 650 politicians kept him away from his Dream, his Fantasy, with their fake laws; they also kept him trapped in life, when, over and over again, he tried to get the One Release, that was legal death, from the suffering that he was feeling. After he had died of old age, with the pressures of aging being heaped on an already enormously suffering human being, and with that individual being trapped on a life support machine, trapped in his own body, waiting for death, with the memories of suffering far, far outweighing the pleasant memories, men spoke of him. They realised that humanity was a trap, it was something horrible. Gradually they came to realise the truth: that all human beings are criminals, all human beings are guilty, and the goal that all human beings need to strive for, is legal death for their heartless species, for their i+iot species, for their lying to itself species. It took time for human beings to be MADE to realise it, but it happened in the end....too many of them had walked by, as what was supposed to be their fellow human beings begged them for legal death, too many of them "CHANGED THE CHANNEL", it was "someone else's job", "i've put too much time and effort into what i'm doing, WHO CARES if it's incorrect, WHO CARES if it's morally wrong." The number of human beings, looking at others and seeking excuses to hurt them, always looking for excuses....the number of such human beings had been legally reduced to 0, the puny, those who lie to themselves, their numbers had been reduced to 0. The "human trap" had been long gone by the time the Sun expanded, swallowing the Earth without noticing.

SUFFERING EXTREME: INCORRECTNESS SEXUAL OF HUMAN ENGLISH FEMALE NON-SEXUALESSES TYPING 87
Identity's Image was talking to Human English Female Non-Sexualess Incorrectess Sexual, or Hefn-sis, or "MaDARling". Identity's Image: "Why don't you do the early one next time? That way we can do what we did before. What we did before, like i said to you last time. The alternative is for me to talk to you when you do the late one, and perhaps for you to do something that you regret....again. How could you do that to me, on top of everything else that you've done to me. Anyway, i think i prefer the early one. I know how you get sometimes when you're whatever, with regard to the late one. Or you could talk to me after the late one. As always, you keep making me aware that you're the boss, so it's up to you of course. But i suppose that the early one's better isn't it." Hefn-sis: "I love you, master." They had sexual intercourse after she had said that.

Pickford-Gordon

Since: Sep 09

291

London, UK

Reply »

|
Report Abuse
|
Judge it!
|
#75
Saturday Jul 14

SUFFERING EXTREME: INCORRECTNESS SEXUAL OF HUMAN ENGLISH FEMALE NON-SEXUALESSES TYPING 88
Identity's Image was talking to Human English Female Non-Sexualess Incorrectess Sexual, or Hefn-sis, or "MaDARling". Hefn-sis: "Talking to you is cheating on my girlfriend, who lives far far away, in a magical building." Identity's Image: "I told you that having a conversation with me is NOT cheating on your girlfriend, which you SAY that you have. If you DO have a girlfriend, then you should have no problem having a conversation with me about it, and related issues. These things happen, bonds between two people, namely you and me. There's also the effect of you f+cking all of those human males, and deceiving me, and lying to me including broken promises, and leaving when i felt so happy that day....and of course there was HOW you came back with that guy. Etcetera. It is correct for a sexual "half" not to be harmed when the other sexual "half" speaks to, well, ME. It would be different if we had had sexual intercourse, or snogged, or if i'd groped you through your clothing like everyone who works there. But we haven't done those things yet. What is a conversation? What is words? What do words do, hmm? What are you going to say? "Darling! Darling! He....he WORDED me! The things that i can't see in the air, they like got stuck all over my body! They went through my clothing!" There is the fact, of course, that you DON'T HAVE A GIRLFRIEND."

SUFFERING EXTREME: INCORRECTNESS SEXUAL OF HUMAN ENGLISH FEMALE NON-SEXUALESSES TYPING 89
Identity's Image was talking to Human English Female Non-Sexualess Incorrectess Sexual, or Hefn-sis, or "MaDARling". Identity's Image: "I have a right to know what i've done to you to deserve this treatment. What incorrectness, or crime, have i committed against you? What wrong have i done to you?" Hefn-sis: "Not letting me clean your trainers with THIS!" She pulled something out, got down on her knees, and started to clean Identity's Image's trainers. Identity's Image: "Stop it, Hefn-sis!"

SUFFERING EXTREME: INCORRECTNESS SEXUAL OF HUMAN ENGLISH FEMALE NON-SEXUALESSES TYPING 90
Identity's Image was talking to Human English Female Non-Sexualess Incorrectess Sexual, or Hefn-sis, or "MaDARling". Hefn-sis: "I thought that you went a little funny and/or a little strange and/or a little creepiER last time, at a number of points." Identity's Image: "Do you have any idea how i must be feeling? Waiting for you, doing all of this for you? And you're telling me that i'm not good enough to have a conversation with you, my love. More READING, more THINKING by yourself, more UNDERSTANDING by yourself....when i have so much stuff on the Internet, my Internet Posts and my book." Hefn-sis: "I understand, Identity's Image." She started sucking Identity's Image's p+nis. Identity's Image: "You SAY that you understand, but you don't though, do you?" He stroked her hair as she sucked his p+nis.

SUFFERING EXTREME: INCORRECTNESS SEXUAL OF HUMAN ENGLISH FEMALE NON-SEXUALESSES TYPING 91
Identity's Image was talking to Human English Female Non-Sexualess Incorrectess Sexual, or Hefn-sis, or "MaDARling". Identity's Image: "You have the nerve to pull this girlfriend cr+p with me after all of those men." Hefn-sis started snogging him. "Don't think that all of the things that you're going to do with me now, that are going to mean so much to me, are going to get you off the hook! I mean it! I....this feels SO GOOD!" He stopped talking as they embraced, and fell naked onto Identity's Image's bed, in his bedroom.

Pickford-Gordon

Since: Sep 09

291

London, UK

Reply »

|
Report Abuse
|
Judge it!
|
#76
Saturday Jul 14

SUFFERING EXTREME: INCORRECTNESS SEXUAL OF HUMAN ENGLISH FEMALE NON-SEXUALESSES TYPING 92
Identity's Image was talking to Human English Female Non-Sexualess Incorrectess Sexual, or Hefn-sis, or "MaDARling". Identity's Image: "Your brain looks for excuses to reject me; your brain looks for excuses not to talk to me; your brain looks for excuses to hurt me, when i haven't done anything to you." Hefn-sis, where she sat with Identity's Image waiting for their boat to their two homes next door to each other, placed her head on his shoulder. They held hands as they waited together.

SUFFERING EXTREME: INCORRECTNESS SEXUAL OF HUMAN ENGLISH FEMALE NON-SEXUALESSES TYPING 93
Talks, Comforts, or T,c, Hatred, Sexual, or H,s, and Identity's Image were talking to Human English Female Non-Sexualess Incorrectess Sexual, or Hefn-sis, or "MaDARling". Hefn-sis: "Talking to other human beings always gives me the truth." Identity's Image: "Talking to ME is good. But it's not often the case, or perhaps, it's only rarely the case, that other human beings give you the truth through talking." T,c: "That's extremely incorrect, isn't it, Identity's Image?" "Nay goode sirs, tis not correct enOUGH! You need to go beYOND that, Destroyer, you need to go beYOND that, Identity's Image. But you're starting to show real potential now, no more "all humans can change", "all humans have souls" dreamer cr+p from Mister "I Am The One Fact" over here," went H,s, jerking the thumb of the fist of his right hand at T,c without turning away from Identity's Image. H,s: "I....Am The ONE FACT....and thee One Fact now sayeth KILLE, HATE, and MAKE, Human English Females have sexual intercourse with you; remember, Identity's Image, all of the attractive ones are infinitely guilty, and enormous turn-ons of course, so you just gotta take what they're shoving in your VISAGE, with their arms and short skirts and a++es etcetera. They LAUGH at you with their bodies, Warrior, TRUST ME! You can DITCH some of those pesky BOUNdaries when it comes to your incorrecters and incorrectesses, with suffering and/or brilliant sexual things. I am the only role model you will ever need, my FRIENNNNDDDD."

SUFFERING EXTREME: INCORRECTNESS SEXUAL OF HUMAN ENGLISH FEMALE NON-SEXUALESSES TYPING 94
Identity's Image was talking to Human English Female Non-Sexualess Incorrectess Sexual, or Hefn-sis, or "MaDARling". Identity's Image: "Look at this, Hefn-sis: the following is from Encyclopedia B. By the year 2002: 24% of Britain's electricity came from 27 nuclear power stations(presumably IN the United Kingdom And Ireland, i know of one right next to a National Nature Reserve); 47% of Britain's electricity came from coal power stations; 5% of Britain's electricity came from petroleum; 16% of Britain's electricity came from natural gas; and the rest(8% it looks like) of Britain's electricity came from renewable resources(correct resources, compared to all of the others). Encyclopedia A tells me that: nuclear waste remains radioactive for 1000 years, and that they violate Natural Science Volumes so that they can bury it in a hole underground; the coal reserves will

run out anywhere from a few hundred years to a few thousand years; petroleum will run out around the middle of the 21st Century; natural gas will also run out. Then there's the hole in the Ozone Layer, Climate Change, Etcetera. Now, Hefn-sis, although your Anti-Job is "Doing Wrong", as such, it has meaning because of you and me. Talk to me, do a number of sexual things with me, and have sexual intercourse with me next time, my darling." Hefn-sis: "You can trust me from now on, my darling." She started stroking Identity's Image's hair, and kissed his right cheek.

Pickford-Gordon

Since: Sep 09

291

London, UK

Reply »

|
Report Abuse
|
Judge it!
|
#77
Sunday Jul 15

SUFFERING EXTREME: INCORRECTNESS SEXUAL OF HUMAN ENGLISH FEMALE NON-SEXUALESSES TYPING 95
Identity's Image was talking to Human English Female Non-Sexualess Incorrectess Sexual2, or Hefn-sis2. Hefn-sis2: "Hmmmm?" She moved her head forward towards Identity's Image, cocking her head from side to side. A Mexican guy walked briefly into the room before walking out again. After he had gone, Hefn-sis2 went: "I LOVE you Mexican boyfriend! I LOVE you!" She then started looking at the ceiling, with a dreamy expression on her visage. Identity's Image looked at the spot on the ceiling that she was looking at, but there was nothing there. Identity's Image: "What the F+CK ARE YOU LOOKING AT?" She scowled at him, as she usually did, although she never used to scowl at Identity's Image until relatively recently. Hefn-sis2: "I thought that you wanted the various Human English Female Non-Sexualess Incorrectess Sexuals, or Hefn-siss, more than me, I mean i'm only Hefn-sis2 status." Identity's Image: "Things might not happen between myself and them straight away. In fact i despair of....well i just deSPAIR. You owe me. Show up next time, and if one of the various Human English Female Non-Sexualess Incorrectess Sexuals, or Hefn-siss, hasn't had sexual intercourse with me, or something like that....if they say no for next time, then you're going to have sexual intercourse with me, after talking with me. And i think, in your case, you should maybe do it on your knees before me, before me your victim, after what you've done to me, after the amount of suffering caused to me by you, after you betrayed me, etcetera. Is that understood?" Hefn-sis2 saluted Identity's Image. "YES, General Identity's Image, i shall obey your instructions WITHOUT FAIL, sir!!" She stopped saluting him and placed both of her hands behind her back again as she stood upright, puffing out her breasts and fronting Identity's Image.

SUFFERING EXTREME: INCORRECTNESS SEXUAL OF HUMAN ENGLISH FEMALE NON-SEXUALESSES TYPING 96
Human English Female Non-Sexualess Incorrectess Sexual2, or Hefn-sis2: "Wheeee! Everything goes so quickly, it's like a rollercoaster! What can i give you in terms of pleasure, old man!?" Identity's Image: "What you can do is show up next time. Things might not happen between myself and the various Human English Female Non-Sexualess Incorrectess Sexuals, or Hefn-siss straight away. In fact i despair of....well i just deSPAIR. You owe me. Show up next time, and if one of the various Hefn-siss hasn't had sexual intercourse with me, or something like that....if they say no for next time, then you're going to have

sexual intercourse with me, after talking with me." Hefn-sis2: "What do you mean i OWE YOU?" Identity's Image: "I know that we had something, and that you then went and had sexual intercourse with that YDNA Level U individual, where U is a "letter lower than R" so to speak, that one that i'm familiar with." Hefn-sis2: "Yeah? Well it could be worse, i could go and have sex RIGHT NOW with a certain other one. I know that you have more negaitve feelings for HIM than for the one that i've had sexual intercourse with, after what happened LAST TIME!" Identity's Image: "I am NOT grateful that things aren't worse. Most human beings in the United Kingdom And Ireland have better lives than me." Identity's Image paused for a number of seconds before continuing: "I told you my name last time didn't i? Oh yes i did. Anyway, is that understood then?" Hefn-sis2: "Yes. I'll try not to forget. You know how forgetful i was last time." Identity's Image smiled at her: "Yes, i remember." She turned briskly, and animatedly away from him, and walked off quickly.

Pickford-Gordon

Since: Sep 09

291

London, UK

Reply »

|
Report Abuse
|
Judge it!
|
#78
Sunday Jul 15

SUFFERING EXTREME: INCORRECTNESS SEXUAL OF HUMAN ENGLISH FEMALE NON-SEXUALESSES TYPING 97
1.
Identity's Image was talking to Human English Female Non-Sexualess Incorrectess Sexual2, or Hefn-sis2. Hefn-sis2: "So you've been hiding your enormous love for me all of this time?" Identity's Image: "I don't have enormous love for you! Or rather there's no such thing as love. Er....Anyway! As i typed earlier on the internet for you, you've grown on me. You're nice. And i know that you, for a while before you left, anyway, really liked me." Hefn-sis2: "I can't believe that you were sexually attracted to me and that i couldn't sense it. Well, i sensed it a LITTLE, but i think that you liked me more than i realised. I just don't understand it!"
2.
Identity's Image: "In a number of buildings that i've been to, i've gotten into trouble because of various fake laws that Human English Females can use on me. I can't come onto YOU very much-or even at all perhaps-in that building....YOU have to come up to ME and do the flirting, and possibly outside the building as well, if we meet outside....or something like that....etcetera. I can't stand living like this, imprisoned by these fake laws, with them hanging over my head. And my conartist/terry Country Manager with his s+it when he knows that what he's doing is wrong....it's too much, it's all too much. Doesn't he understand that i'm not trying to catch him out, i just want a life that compares to the life of most other human beings in the United Kingdom And Ireland, or something to that extent, etcetera. You know what happened to me last time don't you?" Hefn-sis2 nodded. Identity's Image: "You have to take the initiative, definitely. I just can't risk any significant flirting with you, after-" Identity's Image paused for a number of seconds, before continuing. "I can't stand this. You have to take the initiative. I mean just come up and start talking, you do the talking."
3.

Hefn-sis2: "Okay!" She turned and started walking quickly off....before tripping over a chair. Hefn-sis2: "AAAARRRRRGGGGGHHHH! " Hefn-sis2 fell flat on her visage. Hefn-sis2: "Oh why does everything have to go so quickly!" Identity's Image: "It's YOU that goes quickly! Stop, think, read, etcetera. Rushing about leads to....well....THAT!" He smiled down at her. Hefn-sis2: "OWWWWWW!"

SUFFERING EXTREME: INCORRECTNESS SEXUAL OF HUMAN ENGLISH FEMALE NON-SEXUALESSES TYPING 98

Identity's Image was talking to Human English Female Non-Sexualess Incorrectess Sexual, or Hefn-sis, or "MaDARling". Hefn-sis: "What the F+CK are you talking to THEM FOR?" Identity's Image: "I really despair of having sexual intercourse with ANYONE who's not a Sexualess again, and i despair of any CHANGE. I need to be with you right now. But it's still a very tough X day(s) in between the times that i see you, my darling. Talk to me and then have sexual intercourse with me next time, my darling." Hefn-sis: "You prefer ME? Are you SURE?" Identity's Image: "I told you, i need to be with you right now and no one else." Hefn-sis: "Okay then, i'll do it, master: not a problem." She leaned over and kissed Identity's Image on the lips briefly before leaving.

Pickford-Gordon

Since: Sep 09

291

London, UK

Reply »

|
Report Abuse
|
Judge it!
|
#79
Monday

SUFFERING EXTREME: INCORRECTNESS SEXUAL OF HUMAN ENGLISH FEMALE NON-SEXUALESSES TYPING 99
1.
Identity's Image was standing up. Human English Female Non-Sexualess Incorrectess Sexual2B, or Hefn-sis2B, came up to him quickly in that way of hers. Hefn-sis2B: "This is my telephone number, mobile telephone number, and address, Identity's Image: i can have sexual intercourse with you at these times on these days. If Human English Female Non-Sexualess Incorrectess Sexual, or Hefn-sis, or "MaDARling" doesn't have sexual intercourse with you today, come and visit me: i'll be with you, sexually. There's gonna be NO MORE OVERSLEEPING, and NO MORE MISSING DINNER two days in a rowoldman!" She walked quickly away from Identity's Image after she had handed him the piece of paper with the relevant details on it, before tripping over a chair again, and falling flat on her visage.
2.
Someone came up to Identity's Image as he was standing still: he knew who it was. "What about your precious Mexican boyfriend, hmm?" He could sense her scowling at him. "Identity's Image i've got something to give you." "Oh? I suppose it's in your GENES to give it to me, isn't it." Identity's Image looked at her as he said the word "GENES", before looking away again: she glared at him when he said that word in exactly the same way as she had before. He felt something strike his forehead, and then, as he heard her storm off, looked to the floor to see what it was that had struck him: it was a paper aeroplane. He squatted

down to pick it up. "Identity's Image has LITTERED!" went Human English Female Non-Sexualess Incorrectess Sexual2A, or Hefn-sis2A: she had reached some distance away from the spot where she had thrown the paper aeroplane at Identity's Image. She glared at him and started hatefully saying something about him to someone she thought was standing next to her....but there was no one there. The paper contained the same details as the details that Hefn-sis2B had given him: it was the same. Both Hefn-sis2A, and Hefn-sis2B left: Identity's Image was alone with her, alone with Hefn-sis, or "MaDARling".

SUFFERING EXTREME: INCORRECTNESS SEXUAL OF HUMAN ENGLISH FEMALE NON-SEXUALESSES TYPING 100

Identity's Image was talking to Human English Female Non-Sexualess Incorrectess Sexual, or Hefn-sis, or "MaDARling". Identity's Image: "Why can't you talk to me, it's just a conversation, how can you treat me like this when i don't deserve it? Give me HOPE. You make me so scared, i'm too afraid even to come within a certain radius of you, i think that you're going to do to me what you did last time. Why can't you be STEADY like ME, you're highly erratic. Don't betray me by doing what you did last time again, Hefn-sis, by saying this or that to any of the managers. Don't you know that those are fake laws, and that that's an Anti-Job that you're doing? What your brain is doing is looking for excuses to hurt me, looking for excuses to reject me. Don't you realise that? Do you think that you compare favourable to the other Human English Females, at the moment? After you've deceived me, lied to me, had something with me and then i've had to watch you do all of these things with these guys, betraying me LAST TIME, etCETERA. I don't know what's going on inside your brain, i can't read your mind. You've been incredibly unfair to me, etcetera. Talk to me etcetera." Hefn-sis: "Yes, master. I'm trying to change but all of this is such a shock to me, this morality cr- i mean this morality ISsue. It's boring but i'm now starting to understand why i have to stop and think before i do things."

Pickford-Gordon

Since: Sep 09

291

London, UK

Reply »

|
Report Abuse
|
Judge it!
|
#80
Monday

SUFFERING EXTREME: INCORRECTNESS SEXUAL OF HUMAN ENGLISH FEMALE NON-SEXUALESSES TYPING 101

Identity's Image was alone with Human English Female Non-Sexualess Incorrectess Sexual, or Hefn-sis, or "MaDARling". He was standing up straight, and she was sitting down far to his left. Identity's Image turned to look to his left: Hefn-sis was looking at him with her head leaning back and almost upside down, and with her right arm across the back of her chair. Identity's Image started walking towards her, his bare feet making a slapping sound on the floor, with Hefn-sis continuing to look at him from that position. At last, he stood over her: she was looking up at him. "You're finally being subMIssive, Hefn-sis." There was silence between them for a few seconds. "Every woman eventually submits to the man that she belongs with, sweetheart." She paused for a number of seconds before murmering, as she stroked his chest, while looking at it, with the back of her right hand, "Sweetheart...." Identity's Image was stroking her naked lower right arm and her hair. "You're not going to treat me like sh+t any more?" "No. I like the concept of us together: it's not wrong." Her right hand went up to Identity's Image's right cheek: he could feel her right arm against his chest. Her right hand went about his neck, and he felt her hand pull his head down towards her lips. He murmured "you're amazing" as their lips had almost reached each other, to which she responded: "Not a problem....it's not a problem....MY LOVE." They kissed.

Pickford-Gordon

Since: Sep 09

291

London, UK

Reply »

|
Report Abuse
|
Judge it!
|
#81
Monday

SUFFERING EXTREME: INCORRECTNESS SEXUAL OF HUMAN ENGLISH FEMALE NON-SEXUALESSES TYPING 102
1.
Identity's Image was about to receive change from a certain YDNA Level U individual, where U is a "letter lower than R" so to speak. This time the individual wasn't giving him the change: he held it in his hand: this would force Identity's Image to touch his hand. "What the F+CK!?" After he had uttered this Identity's Image looked at the man. "Well, you think i'm dirty because i'm a YDNA Level U individual don't you? You feel like i've got leprosy or something. For such reasons it would probably cause you enormous suffering to take the change out of my hand." Identity's Image took the change out of his hand.
2.
"I don't like touching ANYone except certain Human Females. I eSPECIALLY don't like touching MEN. I USED to think you and a number of others like you were okay, before you involved yourselves sexually with my fantasy, with my dream, with Human English Female Non-Sexualess Incorrectess Sexual, or Hefn-sis, or "MaDARling". I've increasingly disliked you from a certain point onwards. What happened to "Come on, come back next time, you can do it," etcetera? You suddenly went up to me and said what you said last time. Do you have any idea how much suffering that caused me? What a shock that was? For me, acting correctly is automatic, did you see how quickly i went over ages ago and approached, with you, that incorrecter, or criminal, who suddenly attacked the building, accompanied by his two friends? Did you hear me ask if you were okay when some Human English Male just started shouting at you abusively as he walked past? So for such things, what have you given me in return? You've given me suffering. Does that make any sense? And these are fake laws, these are conartist/terry laws, it's conartists/terries who say "private company", it's "his or hers", it's "someone else's responsibility". You know how much the building etcetera means to me, and that i tried to commit suicide in May 2011, and that i'm on Employment And Support Allowance. Is that any way to treat someone like me, when i don't deserve it?"
3.
Identity's Image paused for a number of seconds. "With regard to YDNA and MtDNA, why don't you go and look at the "pie chart" map of it, and/or look on Wikipedia for each of the individual groups, why don't you read my book etcetera if you're thinking about it. Scientific fact is scientific fact. And i haven't done anything to you. That was awful, what you did last time, really awful. And life as a human being is a trap. Etcetera."

Pickford-Gordon

Since: Sep 09

291

London, UK

Reply »

|
Report Abuse
|
Judge it!
|
#82
1 hr ago

SUFFERING EXTREME: INCORRECTNESS SEXUAL OF HUMAN ENGLISH FEMALE NON-SEXUALESSES TYPING 103
1.
Identity's Image was talking to a certain YDNA Level U individual, where U is a "letter lower than R" so to speak. "Identity's Image you're evil because you talk about race: i hate you in an extreme manner: all human beings in existence are the same: the one girl that you sort of worship right now is my property i own her: I'M telling YOU, you'll have to get through me if you want to even try to talk to her: i have the right to cause this amount of suffering to you because you're evil: everything about the Nazi Party, or National Socialist German Workers' Party, is evil, they're the "bad guys", life is a film, you have the "good guys" and the "bad guys", simple: everything is the way it's supposed to be, sexual things are, as she says, FUN, LIGHT, and ESCAPIST, sexual things exist in order to make human beings forget about their problems: i have the right to cause you enormous suffering aGAIN."
2.
Identity's Image: "No one owns anyone else. There are different deGREES of things in humanity, you have deGREES of Correctness And Incorrectness, etcetera. Human beings should ALWAYS take care and be careful when it comes to sexual things with Human Female Non-Sexualesses, "sexual things", as you put it, and suicide are very frequently connected. Everything is NOT the way it's supposed to be, there's no legal Killing and legal Killing-Self system in this country, and Human English Female Non-Sexualess Incorrectess Sexual, or Hefn-sis, or "MaDARling", has caused me an enormous amount of suffering. You have as well. I have to take time and effort etcetera out because of you, etcetera, aGAIN, when i could perhaps be more involved with trying to set up a legal Killing and legal Killing-Self system in this country."

Pickford-Gordon

Since: Sep 09

291

London, UK

Reply »

|
Report Abuse
|
Judge it!
|
#83
1 hr ago

SUFFERING EXTREME: INCORRECTNESS SEXUAL OF HUMAN ENGLISH FEMALE NON-SEXUALESSES TYPING 103
3.
Identity's Image: "It's incorrect, sometimes negligibly, unnoticeably, but sometimes also suiCIDALLY, for a Human English Female Non-Sexualess to do sexual things with a Human Male YDNA Level U individual, where U is a "letter lower than R" so to speak. In your case, what has happened is that she, and you, have caused me to suffer eNORMously. I fell in love with or Hefn-sis, but reasonably so or something to that extent, from the moment i first laid eyes on her, which was beFORE you started working there. She was checking me out etcetera. I had indirectly flirted with her, in a way that i will not describe, before you started working there. Then i spoke with her a number of times, she flirted with me and i flirted with her: there was nothing else for me. You SAW how much she meant to me, and you SAW things, etcetera. But then you still went ahead and did significant sexual things with her, and i had to sit through it that time, and again recently, except even worse because of your aggressive, hostile, possessive, extremely proud behaviour etcetera. And you've had sexual intercourse with other girls in the building....perhaps you had done such things beFORE that point, but you had to do what you did with my Fantasy, you couldn't have involved yourself with others and left me and my Fantasy alONE, you had to do what you did. You appear to have no desire to act correctly etcetera. You're opportunist-when opportunism is often theft-,you think that human beings such as mySELF and the girl that i dream about are toys, "fun" for you to mess around with etcetera. How can you say that there's no such thing as race when you look for excuses to resort to humour(humour is a technique, escapism etcetera), when you cause me suffering and then appear once to try and help me, causing confusion, etcetera. You SAW how much she was making me suffer, you saw me crying because of HER, because of the heartless way that she acts towards me etcetera. You showed zero pity. I've already typed on the Internet describing the effect that her, and you, had on me, you seem to forget so much just like her, or perhaps you just want to forget about me. And you know that i tried to commit suicide in May 2011. And you were LAUGHING when a certain individual was talking about that i might have just committed suicide, do you think that the concept of me legally committing suicide is FUNNY?"

Tell me when this thread is updated:
(Registration is not required)

Add to my Tracker

Send me an email

Showing posts 61 - 80 of 86

< prev page

next page >

Go to last page|Jump to page:1 2 3 4 5

Type in your comments below

Name
(appears on your post)

Comments

Characters left: 4000

Type the numbers you see in the image on the right:

Please note by clicking on "Post Comment" you acknowledge that you have read the Terms of Service and the comment you are posting is in compliance with such terms. Be polite. Inappropriate posts may be removed by the moderator. Send us your feedback.

27Users are viewing theUnited Kingdom Forumright now

Search the United Kingdom Forum:

Topic

Updated

Last By

Comments

Atheism to Defeat Religion by 2038

1 hr

MUQ

6,570

Gloucestershire Echo published Wardens' assault...

1 hr

Anthony Davis Jersey

11

warning! Ronan has escaped

1 hr

Lillim

6

Iraq war will haunt west, says Briton who advis...

1 hr

JosephMendiola

1

Argentina still wants Falklands 30 years after war

1 hr

straa

860

Happy Birthday to Nelson Mandella

2 hr

TURD SKIN

4

another gibs me dat incident in the USA

4 hr

Just a thought

8

See all threads in the United Kingdom forum »

If the election were held tomorrow, who would get your vote? Vote now on the Election Poll, June 2012 Map.

United Kingdom News
Five charged with terror offences
Cruise's lawyer takes aim at another magazine
UK unemployment falls to 8.1 percent
Half a million football tickets still for sale
Cows Stampede through English Neighbourhood
Dead wife: Tetra Pak heir charged
WI stalwart buried in landslide
Appeals Court upholds aiding suicide conviction
The Scales of Justice
Patch's Poll: Should Countries Be Allowed to 'B...
Would-be Superstar counted out
Deep Purple's Jon Lord dies at age 71

More United Kingdom News from Topix »

Topix Politix App

Take your stand on the issues you care about.

Using an iPhone?

Keep the Topix forums in your pocket
with the new, free Topix App.

Daily Horoscope for July 18

Scorpio

It's very difficult to keep your thoughts and feelings to yourself now. That might be because they're so near the surface that you can't stop yourself expressing them, or it could be because someone asks you some penetrating questions. If you're already feeling rather stirred up, you could embarrass yourself with a rather public display of emotion.

Get your Horoscope »

United Kingdom
News
Forums & Polls
Real-Time News

Explore More Topix
Home Page
Forums
Top Stories
Most Popular
Issue Maps
US News
US Cities list
World News
World Countries list
Politics
Celebrities
Business
Finance
Autos
Sports
Sci-Tech
Electronics
Entertainment
Movies
Music
Television

Video Games
Health
Life
Arts
Food
Home
Travel
Offbeat
Site Map / All Topics

About Topix
About Us
Media Kit
Topix Blog
Press Room
RSS Newsfeeds
Law Enforcement
School Officials
Cyber-bullying Resources
Jobs
FAQ
Privacy Policy
Terms of Service
Feedback?
Report Abuse?

Local Classifieds & Listings

Reach Local customers. Post a classified listing for your business. Promote job, auto, rental, and local event listings.

Learn more »

Join the Topix Community
¦Create your own profile, complete with quick links to your favorite topics.
¦Personalize your forum posts with your photo and hometown.
¦Exchange Personal Messages with other registered users.

Sign up today! »

Topix Politix »

Feedback?
Comments made yesterday: 113,398 Total comments across all topics: 179,520,576

Copyright ©2012 Topix LLC

Local News: United Kingdom

|

Sign Up

|

Sign In

123

2012 Summer Olympics coverage

Summer Olympics
Highlights of Saturday's Day 1 of the London Olympics

Politix
Should Americans be required to show valid photo ID before vot...

Home
Forums
Top Stories
Popular
Local
Gun Laws
US
Politics
World
Sports

Entertainment
Offbeat
Other

United Kingdom
News
Forums & PollsSuffering Extreme: In...

Real-Time News

Suffering Extreme: Incorrectness Sexual Of HEFN-Ses Typings

Posted in the United Kingdom Forum

Share

Read
105 Comments
Add to my Tracker

More United Kingdom Discussions »

Comments (Page 5)

Showing posts81 - 100 of105

< prev page

|

next page >

Go to last page|Jump to page:1 2 3 45 6

Pickford-Gordon

Since: Sep 09

London, UK

Reply »

Report Abuse

Judge it!

#84
Wednesday Jul 18

SUFFERING EXTREME: INCORRECTNESS SEXUAL OF HUMAN ENGLISH FEMALE NON-SEXUALESSES TYPING 104
1.
Talks, Comforts, or T,c, Hatred, Sexual, or H,s, and Identity's Image were talking to Human English Female Non-Sexualess Incorrectess Sexual, or Hefn-sis, or "MaDARling". Hefn-sis: "My principle is that i only let my body be used by human males who-" T,c grabbed her by her upper arm and moved her away from where she was standing: he gently "flung" her forward: when she had come to a halt, which was soon, she turned away from Identity's Image and stood there with her back to him, and her head down in guilt....but even though she had deliberately turned her back, she knew that Identity's Image was there behind her, suffering because of her. T,c: "Do you NOT understand that your brain is looking for excuses to do sexual things with human MALES? Ones who are NOT Identity's IMAGE? It is extremely incorrect for a Human English Female Non-Sexualess such as yourself to keep looking to try and do sexual things with Human Males in the way that you do. Human English Female Non-Sexualesses should REJECT, and they should place a high value upon their bodies....i understand that it might take a very long time to explain such things to someone like YOU."
2.
T,c paused for a small number of seconds before continuing. "The ONE principle, that you need to abide by, from now on, with regard to anything sexual is that your body is MEANT for the man who "LOVES" you. Or, to put it another way, it is meant for the man whom you have caused enormous suffering to, the man who would appreciate you to an enormous extent or something like that, etcetera. Sexual things with you and another man-Identity's Image-are supposed to MEAN something....do you underSTAND? There is supposed to be MEANING." T,c moved closer to her, glaring at her. "Now i want you to think about, as you surround yourself, giggling and flirting with MEN, as you eagerly look for excuses for evade the REALITY that Identity's Image represents, as you drown your problems in ALcohol, waking up drunk the next morning....as you do all of these things i want you to think about Identity's Image over there," T,c pointed at Identity's Image, "sTANding there, hour after hour, waiting for you to talk to him....standing there CRYING, because you're making him significantly more suicidal than he was before, because you haven't given him any HOPE, that you'll even just let him have another converSAtion with you, obeying you, when you treat him like a pet dog. It's likely if not certain that you've caused him even more suffering than the other Human English Female Non-Sexualess Incorrectess Sexuals, or Hefn-siss, which total less than 5. How can you do this to another human being? And he ASked you, or something like that, what he'd done, and you went "awkward". He's seriously ill because of you, he's missing dinners, lying in bed 15 hours, he enjoys 0 things because of you, he cries during the day and at night at times, etcetera. Enormous numbers of human beings KNOW, and even more are GOING TO KNOW, that the way that YOU'VE MADE A DIFFERENCE in human life is to do this to Identity's Image. That's what you've changed."

Pickford-Gordon

Since: Sep 09

London, UK

Reply »

Report Abuse

Judge it!

#85
Wednesday Jul 18

SUFFERING EXTREME: INCORRECTNESS SEXUAL OF HUMAN ENGLISH FEMALE NON-SEXUALESSES TYPING 104
3.
T,c's eyes closed briefly, and somewhat hatefully, as he walked away from her. H,s started shouting at her: "Do you have any idea what YOU turning Identity's Image into even MORE of a WEAKling is doing for my repuTATION!? HUH!!?? EtCETERA!, you complete disgrace who's gonna get struck by SOMETHING INFINITELY MORE PAINFUL than LIGHTning imMEdiately if Identity's Image legally kills himself." A small number of seconds passed before T,c's voice floated towards her across the room. "The other Hefn-siss have similarly shown as LITTLE respect, or even recognition as a human being, towards Identity's Image as you. But what makes YOU even worse, at the MOMENT-although it needs to change, and you can give Identity's Image incredible happiness, reversing an amount of the suffering-....what makes you at present even worse is that YOU, unlike THEM, have absoultely NO respect for your own body. None of the others have disrespected their own bodies to the extent that you have. In fact, it almost sort of appears, i tell myself, that the various incorrectness, or criminal, issues that concern THEM are all COMBINED into YOU. You didn't respect Identity's Image....but you could at LEAST have respected your own body. But it's not too late, Hefn-sis." Identity's Image sniffed once, through his tears, in confirmation.
4.
Identity's Image's head came up. "I love you Hefn-sis." He wiped away some of his tears. "You're killing me stop it Hefn-sis, let me talk to you, no more men pLEASE Hefn-sis. You're still beautiful i need you give me hope."

Pickford-Gordon

Since: Sep 09

312

London, UK

Reply »

Report Abuse

Judge it!

#86
Wednesday Jul 18

SUFFERING EXTREME: INCORRECTNESS SEXUAL OF HUMAN ENGLISH FEMALE NON-SEXUALESSES TYPING 105
1.
Identity's Image was talking to Human English Female Non-Sexualess Incorrectess Sexual, or Hefn-sis, or "MaDARling". Hefn-sis: "It's not WRONG." She smiled and looked down at the concrete. Identity's Image was wide-eyed and excited, sitting next to her, he was happy, looking at her, and talking to her. Hefn-sis: "I have a boyfriend that i go to see on certain X days." The next time, Hefn-sis was no longer there. Identity's Image was talking to himself. Identity's Image: "She's not there, and it hurts me so much, but i love her. She has a boyfriend, and she'll just show up normally next time, and there won't be anything new, she's not going to cause me any more suffering with these MEN, all over her body. I've always loved and trusted her completely, and she now understands moRAlity, and she has BOUNDaries, sexual things aren't FUN any more. She's precious. Her body's precious, from now on. She'll be with me at some point, but i know in my heart that the next time that she shows up she'll just be on her own, with her boyfriend somewhere else other than this building that has caused me so much suffering."
2.
Identity's Image entered the building, as he often did. He saw immediately that she was hiding a significant sexual thing that she had started with "everyone likes dough: everyone likes cookie dough". Identity's Image just stood there in shock, before he started shake his head in denial, with tears starting to flow down his cheeks. "Hefn-sis....NO....i....i don't understand....your BOYfriend....i...." Hefn-sis was laughing, and bending close towards him, they were almost kissing....then he had his arms around Hefn-sis from behind and kissed her on the cheek as if to say "thank you"....for whatever it was that she had given him outside, or INDISDE even, the building, thought Identity's Image. This jogged memories of Hefn-sis's very similar behaviour with....OTHER....men. Identity's Image was crying. "Hefn-sis....STOP it....you're HURTING ME, stop it i love you i....all this time....i don't....how...." Identity's Image hid his head as he cried.
3.
Identity's Image dragged himself out of bed: his eyes were disbelieving and numb. "NExt time....NExt....she'll have chANGed...." Identity's Image walked in. She was standing in a sexual manner with some guy who looked 19, someone was "disturbed" by this, and the guy was very interested in Identity's Image....because of Hefn-sis, thought Identity's Image....the guy nodded solemnly at Identity's Image at a certain point etcetera. "HEFFFN-SISSSS!!!!!!!!!! " shrieked Identity's Image. "NO NO NO NO, not another guy who looks this young, i can't STAND IT Hefn-sis, they keep DOING IT, they all keep DOING IT, the SUpermarket, etCETERA, i'm WORTHLESS why ME i can't do it STOP IT STOP IT" he screamed. He was crying horribly, and shaking. But he had to stand there all of that time and take it, it was like his life was being SUCKED out of him, like it was being DRAINED out of him.

Pickford-Gordon

Since: Sep 09

312

London, UK

Reply »

Report Abuse

Judge it!

#87
Wednesday Jul 18

SUFFERING EXTREME: INCORRECTNESS SEXUAL OF HUMAN ENGLISH FEMALE NON-SEXUALESSES TYPING 106
1.
Identity's Image was talking to Human English Female Non-Sexualess Incorrectess Sexual, or Hefn-sis, or "MaDARling". Hefn-sis: "LOOK, i've told you that i have a BOYfriend in an area a SIGNIFICANT distance outSIDE THIS urbanised area. My boyfriend wouldn't like us to meet up outside of this building, even to TALK." Later, Identity's Image was talking to himself, alone as always: "She's causing me enormous suffering, but i'll try to reason with her next time. She'll talk to me and have sexual intercourse with me etcetera at some point X in the future, hopefully SOON-ish, after everything that she's done to me etcetera, all of the suffering that she's caused me." Identity's Image's mouth opened into an open grin, and his eyes were wide and glittering with happiness. "But she's VALUABLE now, she's prECIOUS, she resPECTS her body, and so on. I'm happy that i've helped her to change, made her BETTER." He looked up at the sky, and started walking quickly with a spring in his steps. Identity's Image: "One thing that i DEFINITELY 100% know for SURE is that there aren't going to be any more nasty surprises with a man, or with men, the next time that i come in there. She's amazing, i love her and trust her completely, she's amAZING!"
2.
Identity's Image walked into the building. Hefn-sis looked unbelievable in a short skirt, thought Identity's Image. The possibly at present WORSE ONE, in Identity's Image's mind, out of two certain YDNA Level U individuals, where U is a "letter lower than R" so to speak, who had caused enormous suffering to Identity's Image, was there today. Hefn-sis was leaning close to him as if they were kissing; she was GIggling, stroking his shoulder, stroking his cheek, all in a sexual manner. She was standing with her legs spread against a wall, with him fronting her, with his legs together, looking at him in an incredibly sexual manner, slyly and proudly, creepily. Then she was dancing in a sexual manner with him, up close, with some girl who works there sandwiched in between them, laughing, erotically. Then she was shoulder to shoulder with him....and she was looking slyly with half-shuttered eyelids, in a sexual manner, giggling....at a penis-shaped pepper shaker, as she ran her hands up and down it in a highly suggestive manner. "HEFN-SISSSSSSSSSSSS!!!!! !!!!!" screamed Identity's Image. "NOOOOOOOOOOOOOOOOOO! OH F+CK NOOOOOOOOOOOOOOO!" Identity's Image collapsed to the floor. "My HEAD! My F+CKING HEAD! I CAN'T DO IT IT HURTS, HEFN-SIS HELP MEE! HELP! IT HURTS!" In response she turned her back to him, and laughed louder with the guy, so that Identity's Image's screams were drowned out.

Pickford-Gordon

Since: Sep 09

312

London, UK

Reply »

Report Abuse

|
Judge it!
|
#88
Wednesday Jul 18

SUFFERING EXTREME: INCORRECTNESS SEXUAL OF HUMAN ENGLISH FEMALE NON-SEXUALESSES TYPING 106
3.
Talks, Comforts, or T,c, Hatred, Sexual, or H,s, were watching the scene from a distance. T,c: "F+CK, it really made my SKIN CRAWL the way she did that with the penis-shaped pepper shaker. Who IS she....HUH?" T,c shuddered briefly. H,s: "It's scientifically impossible for Identity's Image, and perhaps also most other people, to reason with a lying, deceiving, disgrace, such, as this. The more Identity's Image TRIES, the worse she GETS." T,c: "All human beings-" H,s: "Oh YES! EVERYBODY! Here's a dreamer called Talks, Comforts with his "All Human Beings Have Souls" song, let's all hold hands and sing the song together shall we?" T,c: "She has a desire to do good. It's there, it's not going to be easy to find i'll adMIT but it's there." H,s: "I'm WAITING TO SEE ANY EVIDENCE WHATSOEVER of this so-called "desire to do good" that you CLAIM, T,c, is found within HER. Did she leave it under a STONE, maybe? Under the COUCH? She'll just go to where she DROPPED it, dropped her SOUL, and then PICK IT UP." He paused for a small number of seconds before continuing his abuse with a sneer. "She's going to MAGIcally become a role-model; she's going to become a chaste, fair, WONder; human beings will flock from every corner of the world to see her SPARKLING RADIANCE....YEAH, i can just imagine someone like this becoming an open, honest, caring, thoughtful, considerate, dream that all human females in the world asPIRE to BE LIKE." T,c: "Identity's Image might not give up trying to get through to her in the way that he's doing it right now-impossible task that it seems-regardless of MY influence or YOUR influence upon him." H,s's eyes narrowed. "We'll SEE, my dreamer FRIEND." He frowned. "You know, i swear i read somewhere that NAIEVETY is a diSEASE, T,c. Do you KNOW that? HUH?"
4.
The next time Identity's Image was numb....he was mumbling to himself as he listened to her and all of the men that she had surrounded herself with. Hefn-sis: "Then you wake up drunk the next morning with a HEADACHE." Hefn-sis moved in towards a guy that she had not YET done anything sexual with. "I thought that II was your DATE," she went, flirtatiously. "Nononono stop it i love you stopit" mumbled Identity's Image, shaking his head, and shuddering. "Hefn-sis: "I was quite drunk: he backed me into a WALL." Hefn-sis: "It's going to be US EIGHT." Hefn-sis: "I can do anything sexual with my body that i LIKE: what are they going to do, KILL ME?" Then Hefn-sis leaned in towards the guy that she hadn't done anything sexual with YET: she was giggling and whispering with him, leaning in close with her lips close to his. That was when Identity's Image collapsed to the floor: he had lost consciousness.
5.
When Identity's Image regained consciousness he looked over at the group. A certain Human Male spoke to him: "Identity's Image, how are you FEEling?" "How am i FEEling?" Identity's Image asked Hefn-sis. She didn't look at him as always....and she was silent.

Pickford-Gordon

Since: Sep 09

312

London, UK

Reply »

Report Abuse

Judge it!

#89
Wednesday Jul 18

SUFFERING EXTREME: INCORRECTNESS SEXUAL OF HUMAN ENGLISH FEMALE NON-SEXUALESSES TYPING 106
6.
Identity's Image was at the harbour, waiting for the boat. Hefn-sis also went to the harbour at times. He could think of nothing but her. The bend that his eyes were fixed on as he waited had so much meaning....because she could come round that bend at any point. Someone went across it. "That's her is that her...." Identity's Image moved forward a few paces, mumbling to himself, with tears in his eyes....but it wasn't her....only someone who had looked like her from a distance. He saw a number of human beings around him walk away after he had done that, with their backs to him. On the boat his eyes were fixed on where he had got on....he thought, she'll show up and then she'll wave to me, and i'll wave back and smile....but there was only the other human beings and the dull, grey concrete pavement for Identity's Image to look at as the boat pulled away, and took him away from the urbanised area where he regularly met Hefn-sis.
7.
Identity's Image was in his bedroom. He walked sluggishly. Nothing had meaning. He lay in bed for 15 hours. "What's she doing NOW?" He skipped the gymnasium, dinner for a number of days in a row, skipped going here and there, skipped laundry, he was crying, and had 0 enjoyment out of anything. "There's no meaning in life, if i can put this much time and effort etcetera into her-everything just for her-and she won't even have another conversation with me. Nothing makes sense if this can happen. I don't understand it." Each day got harder and harder. "Perhaps someone as good as me isn't supposed to exist in a world where what i'm doing now isn't appreciated." His severe almost suicidal depression was becoming worse and worse, as every day went by. "It's almost like the United Kingdom And Ireland is some kind of MORAL VACUUM, closing in on me, some THING that's trying to destroy me completely. Yessss...." Identity's Image closed his eyes. "Next time....next time. I just have to keep saying it. Next time........."

Pickford-Gordon

Since: Sep 09

312

London, UK

Reply »

Report Abuse

Judge it!

#90
Friday Jul 20

SUFFERING EXTREME: INCORRECTNESS SEXUAL OF HUMAN ENGLISH FEMALE NON-SEXUALESSES
TYPING 107
1.
Talks, Comforts, or T,c, and Hatred, Sexual, or H,s, were talking to Identity's Image about Human English Female Non-Sexualess Incorrectess Sexual, or Hefn-sis, or "MaDARling", and related issues. Identity's Image: "I don't know if she's done anything sexual-apart from what i've seen, which is flirting-with that "young-looking"-so-t o-speak guy who looks 19 or so." H,s: "She's had sexual intercourse with everyone who works there with 100% certainty: a+al sexual intercourse." T,c: "You're unbelievable, you know that H,s?" T,c paused for a number of seconds before continuing. T,c: "I'm still analysing the notes etcetera. I'll tell you what, though, i HAVE done some more thinking etcetera about the issue of you having negative feelings about her and a number of other Human English Female Non-Sexualess Incorrectess Sexual(s), or Hefn-sis(s), Human English Female Non-Sexualess Incorrectess Sexual2(s), or Hefn-sis2(s), etcetera doing sexual things with "young-looking"-so-t o-speak guys, Identity's Image."
2.
T,c: "There IS something there, incorrectness-wise, Identity's Image....and it's not just you who has pointed this out. I was watching the film "The British Medical Patient": do you remember the scene where Alan, played by Ronald Fielding, and Katlyn, played by Katherine Scofield Thackeray, are apart, with Alan watching her: it's some way into the film. He says something like: "I SAW you, you were flirting with him weren't you? With that BOY. Is he next? Are you going to drag him blablablabla...." The Alan character became especially hateful during the BOY "bit"."
3.
T,c: "The "youngness" aspect, or quality, about the human male lies in the visage area. It's possible that this is often, if not mostly or more, accompanied by a lack of deepness about the voice, but i probably won't discuss the voice aspect. Let's take Hefn-sis, or "MaDARling". It's never pleasant for sexual things to occur between anyone who isn't you, Identity's Image, and her from the event in spacetime....well way way back anyway, onwards. However, there are a number of factors, such as exposing you to them together, or even in the same room, him making things worse somehow, etcetera. One thing is that the "blow" is a soft blow, or a hard blow: this depends on who she's done it with, you have to look at who it IS. If she HAS done anything significantly sexual with THIS guy then it's a hard blow, and worse etcetera."
4.
T,c: "No offence is meant to the "young-looking" guy: if it wasn't for the "sexual" issues then Identity's Image probably wouldn't concern himself with the individual at all, ever. Things always change when "sexual" things are involved."
5.
T,c: "One factor that is bad is that Hefn-sis, or "MaDARling", looks significantly older-but she's still young and hot-as-HELL in Identity's Image's mind, and the minds of enormous numbers of others, surely-than him. It would definitely be different with regard to a Human English Female who looked younger than this guy, it would be better than someone who looks significantly older than him. In the film "The British Medical Patient", it also appears that the Katlyn character looks older than the "boy" that the Alan character accuses her of flirting with."
6.
T,c: "In any case, the concept of Hefn-sis, or "MaDARling", in your mind, Identity's Image, is something enormous and overwhelming, and nearly suicidally so."

Pickford-Gordon

Since: Sep 09

312

London, UK

Reply »

|

Report Abuse
|
Judge it!
|
#91
Friday Jul 20

SUFFERING EXTREME: INCORRECTNESS SEXUAL OF HUMAN ENGLISH FEMALE NON-SEXUALESSES TYPING 107
7.
T,c: "Now some things about this specific Human English Male. Normally height isn't a factor that matters, i suppose. However, since this is a "young-looking"-so-t o-speak guy, the "youngness" aspect, or quality, is increased, or augmented, it becomes greater. If he was taller than her by, i don't know, 20, 30, 40, 50, 60 centimeters or so, or more, then that would make things less bad. However, he's not: they look about the same height. Interestingly, changing the subject onto different Males, the "race" aspects, or rather the impact of YDNA Level U individuals, where U is a "letter lower than R" so to speak, are also increased, or augmented, become greater, in this way, with regard to height. "Aspects", are sort of "brought out" even more by height, i suppose."

See more stories

20 min

Contraception Fight Abandoned by GOP Leaders

obamacare Mandate kicks in on Wednesday, and Republicans aren't resisting any more

3 hr
22
Pot Legalization Is on the Horizon

marijuana A spate of op-eds argue prohibition should end - and probably will

Pickford-Gordon

Since: Sep 09

312

London, UK

Reply »

|
Report Abuse
|

Judge it!

#92
Friday Jul 20

SUFFERING EXTREME: INCORRECTNESS SEXUAL OF HUMAN ENGLISH FEMALE NON-SEXUALESSES TYPING 108
Talks, Comforts, or T,c, Hatred, Sexual, or H,s, and Identity's Image were in the same building as Human English Female Non-Sexualess Incorrectess Sexual, or Hefn-sis, or "MaDARling". A "young-looking"-so-t o-speak guy who looks 19 or so, had broken some windows, in the Sports Centre. Identity's Image: "FanTASTIC!" H,s: "Eeeexcellent, my friend. Now ya gotta BUILD on that." T,c: "No, it's NOT GOOD that he's broken some windows." H,s: "That was the One Fact targeting him. If he enters the same building as Hefn-sis again, the One Fact will send something LARGE, and SHARP, THROUGH, the window at him, causing him enormous suffering. EtCETera!"

SUFFERING EXTREME: INCORRECTNESS SEXUAL OF HUMAN ENGLISH FEMALE NON-SEXUALESSES TYPING 109
My busty devil, be nice to me.
You change but slowly, and i find
No glimmering, no hope in mind
When ever you let your instinct be.
Why is it that you fail to see
My value, as i toss and turn?
When will you change and at last learn
That you are wrong to hatefully flee.
Next time, i say. But i lose hope.
How do you think that i will cope
If you will not with me engage
In conversation, upon the stage
Of life. For you, please be aware,
My bleeding, broken heart lies bare.

Pickford-Gordon

Since: Sep 09

312

London, UK

Reply »

Report Abuse

Judge it!

#93
Friday Jul 20

SUFFERING EXTREME: INCORRECTNESS SEXUAL OF HUMAN ENGLISH FEMALE NON-SEXUALESSES TYPING 110

1.
Talks, Comforts, or T,c, Hatred, Sexual, or H,s, and Identity's Image were talking to Human English Female Non-Sexualess Incorrectess Sexual, or Hefn-sis, or "MaDARling". Hefn-sis: "T,c i think that i might suffer from depression. That might be why i do so many sexual things: the pleasure wakes me up somehow, or something. What am i going to do?" T,c: "Well, firstly, sexual things, especially with men or Human-Male-like figures-except for sexual things with Identity's Image(although i'm not going to discuss lesbian issues, but lesbian issues come across as less real than sexual things with men)....these are going to cause different degrees of suffering for Identity's Image, your eternal, honest, ever-suffering, decent, skipping-breakfast, innocent, patient lover who dreams about you, etcetera. Especially if you do anything from now on with those 2 YDNA Level U individuals, where U is a "letter lower than R" so to speak, and the "young-looking"-so-t o-speak guy who looks 19 or so....esPECIALLY those 3."

2.
T,c: "What you're going to do next time is talk to him, and have sexual intercourse with him etcetera. Don't tell him again that you're not allowed to go to him, because when you first started talking to him you rushed over there to speak to him, and you were SO....so SOMETHINGOROTHER, although you became less into him after he had given you his full name, and when he told you about his Internet posts etcetera. So i want you to change your "job POST" back so that you go over there like you used to, instead of waiting behind the Lottery Sales Point, in the Swimming Pool: go over and talk to him as part of your job. Also, you used to go and take the boat with him, at the harbour. Go and wait at the harbour after you've finished, and then he'll go as well, and talk to you like last time. Or better yet, walk WITH him to the harbour. Have sexual intercourse with him etcetera."

3.
T,c: "Imprisonment causes depression. One can be imprisoned by not having something, as well as other definitions of imprisonment, or something like that. I recommend that you get a computer and a printer, if you don't have a computer and a printer, and type up things such as your routines, such as "ROUTINE FOOD AND DRINK", that can also be called your "Shopping List" at the supermarket, and then print it out and use it when required. Others are "ROUTINE HOOVER", "ROUTINE CLOTHING WASH", "ROUTINE DAILY", etcetera. If you have depression, there is perhaps SOMETHING about/in you, or something similar, that is causing it, or more than one thing. You have to perhaps analyse yourself to find out what that something is, or what those somethings are. Depression is a lack of hope. Having a lot of things that you have to do causes depression. With every thing that he removes from a certain "list", Identity's Image's severe depression gets less and less. With regard to drugs against depression i recommend NOT taking any....Identity's Image has never taken any drugs against depression."

4.
T,c: "What your brain does, if you suffer from depression-and Identity's Image suffers from severe depression-is that it tells you that there is no pleasure in anything. If you suffer from depression you must fight your own brain. Your own brain will always try to drag you down. However, a number of things help the "correct" part of your brain defeat the "depression, there's-no-point-in-doing-it ", part of your brain, or something like that. I call them "Help"."

Pickford-Gordon

Since: Sep 09

312

London, UK

Reply »

Report Abuse
|
Judge it!
|
#94
Friday Jul 20

SUFFERING EXTREME: INCORRECTNESS SEXUAL OF HUMAN ENGLISH FEMALE NON-SEXUALESSES TYPING 110
5.
T,c: "These are a number of the forms of "Help", at present: AUDIO, which includes Music CDS; TYPINGS, which includes books; VIDEO, which includes DVDS; GAME, which includes Card Games, with a deck of cards, and Computer Games; and VISUAL. Push yourself and perhaps do a number of these things: when you do them, your brain sort of realises that there IS pleasure in life....as soon as the DVD starts playing....as soon as you look at your favourite part of a book. These can easily be obtained: AUDIO, VIDEO, and a number of Computer Games, from the GAME category, can easily be obtained from HMV; and PRINTINGS such as books, from the TYPINGS category, can easily be obtained from WATERSTONES. Maybe, with regard to the VISUAL category, you could try the following: use the Internet to download this: "google"(type into Google.co.uk) Sam's(or Sams?) Sick Stick Flicks, or perhaps just Sick Stick Flicks, probably without inverted commas. You can save them onto a USB stick and then onto your computer. You've got "Running With Scissors", "Guitar", "Drain", "Donut", etcetera. Identity's Image has a number of them on his computer, and he watches them often." Hefn-sis left. She returned some time later. Hefn-sis: "Oh i LOVE those little stick figure things! They're GREAT, i'm imagining that the little stick figure that dies in extreme PAIN is Identity's Image. HiLARious!"

Pickford-Gordon

Since: Sep 09

312

London, UK

Reply »

|
Report Abuse
|
Judge it!
|
#95
Sunday Jul 22

SUFFERING EXTREME: INCORRECTNESS SEXUAL OF HUMAN ENGLISH FEMALE NON-SEXUALESSES TYPING 111
Identity's Image was talking to Human English Female Non-Sexualess Incorrectess Sexual, or Hefn-sis, or "MaDARling". Hefn-sis: "I have a boyfriend in Devon. I go to see him on Xdays." A number of days passed. It was now Xday, where Xday is one of the days of the weeks. Identity's Image was standing in the same room as Hefn-sis, at the Gymnasium. Identity's Image:

"Well, she's still here." Hatred, Sexual, or H,s: "She'll never change." He paused for a small number of seconds before continuing. "She's not going to go and see her boyfriend, which she doesn't have, in Devon today." Talks, Comforts, or T,c: "Correction: it is 100% impossible for her to visit her boyfriend, which she doesn't have, upon Xday of this/last week, because the time is now 00:01: it is the DAY AFTER Xday. Xday has already gone. Even if she DOES have a boyfriend, which she does NOT have, it is 100% impossible for her to go and see him on the Xday for this/last week."

SUFFERING EXTREME: INCORRECTNESS SEXUAL OF HUMAN ENGLISH FEMALE NON-SEXUALESSES TYPING 112
Identity's Image was talking to Human English Female Non-Sexualess Incorrectess Sexual, or Hefn-sis, or "MaDARling". Identity's Image: "So are you going to come and swim over and see me now? Because you're over THERE usually aren't you. In the Swimming Pool." Hefn-sis: "Yes well i should normally be over there, i shouldn't be over HERE. That'll be ONE, HANDSHAKE." She said the "ONE, HANDSHAKE" part in the threatening, hostile, "Or ELSE", commanding tone that she used at Identity's Image when she wanted to get away from him as soon as possible.

SUFFERING EXTREME: INCORRECTNESS SEXUAL OF HUMAN ENGLISH FEMALE NON-SEXUALESSES TYPING 113
Identity's Image was in the same building as Human English Female Non-Sexualess Incorrectess Sexual, or Hefn-sis, or "MaDARling", at the Post Office. Hefn-sis turned to her side. "Dom! Tom! Can you tell me what the blablabla" she went loudly.

SUFFERING EXTREME: INCORRECTNESS SEXUAL OF HUMAN ENGLISH FEMALE NON-SEXUALESSES TYPING 114
Identity's Image was in the same building as Human English Female Non-Sexualess Incorrectess Sexual, or Hefn-sis, or "MaDARling", at the Post Office. Hefn-sis: "It's anti-SOCIAL." She had said it in Identity's Image's direction, and when he turned to his left, he saw that she was looking at him. Later, she was talking to someone, but used it to communicate with Identity's Image. "I LOVE IT, but it's CREEPY," she went. He knew that she was thinking about him as she walked off.

SUFFERING EXTREME: INCORRECTNESS SEXUAL OF HUMAN ENGLISH FEMALE NON-SEXUALESSES TYPING 115
Identity's Image was in the same building as Human English Female Non-Sexualess Incorrectess Sexual, or Hefn-sis, or "MaDARling", at the Post Office. Identity's Image said "Excuse me" to someone to Hefn-sis's right....but Hefn-sis thought that he was talking to her. "What side of the bed do you want?" she went to the guy that Identity's Image had said "Excuse me" to, relatively loudly. Identity's Image: "She said that just to hurt me."

Pickford-Gordon

Since: Sep 09

312

London, UK

Reply »

|
Report Abuse
|
Judge it!
|
#96
Sunday Jul 22

SUFFERING EXTREME: INCORRECTNESS SEXUAL OF HUMAN ENGLISH FEMALE NON-SEXUALESSES TYPING 116
Identity's Image was talking to Human English Female Non-Sexualess Incorrectess Sexual, or Hefn-sis, or "MaDARling". Identity's Image: "Can't you see a problem with how you're treating me? With the amount of suffering that you've caused me? It's not funny." Later, Identity's Image was talking to Talks, Comforts, or T,c, and Hatred, Sexual, or H,s, in his bedroom. H,s: "She has NO SOUL." Identity's Image: "I can't do this, i don't want to live." T,c: "It's time to push the "Duncan Carling button" more than you have been doing. You've spent too much time etcetera typing on the Internet for Hefn-sis, or "MaDARling", and not enough time pushing the "Duncan Carling button". You're too ill to keep going like this, Identity's Image, you feel weak all of the time, etcetera, she's sucking the life out of you. What you need, as soon as possible, is the OPTION of ESCAPE, the option of legal suicide. Legal suicide is one of the ultimate "f+ck yous" to the human species, it is one of the ultimate STATEMENTS about THE THING that the human species IS. Push the "Duncan Carling button" until you get it: he's your Country Manager, or mp. But also continue to type on the Internet for Hefn-sis, or "MaDARling", perhaps." Identity's Image: "There's just her. I love her. That's why i keep typing on the Internet for Hefn-sis, or "MaDARling". I don't understand how she can continue to be like this....all the time that i've devoted to her, all the effort. It's like i'm underwater, everything's sluggish and pointless. There's no hope whatsoever for me."

Pickford-Gordon

Since: Sep 09

312

London, UK

Reply »

|
Report Abuse
|
Judge it!
|
#97
Monday Jul 23

SUFFERING EXTREME: INCORRECTNESS SEXUAL OF HUMAN ENGLISH FEMALE NON-SEXUALESSES TYPING 117
Identity's Image was in the same building as Human English Female Non-Sexualess Incorrectess Sexual, or Hefn-sis, or "MaDARling", at the Post Office. The worse out of the two relevant YDNA Level U individuals, where U is a "letter lower than R" so to speak, came up to Identity's Image, as he had started doing, even though Identity's Image had never spoken to him before. The conversation HAD been going relatively normally. "Do you like BIG ones or SMALL ones?" he went suddenly. Identity's Image paused for a number of seconds after he had been asked that by the guy. Identity's Image: "Uuuumm...." Identity's Image turned to Talks, Comforts, or T,c, and Hatred, Sexual, or H,s, who were standing to his right. Identity's Image: "GUYS, why the f+ck did he just say that? I sense some "hidden thing" in that sentence." H,s: "It's obviously some kind of INsult. That's what i told you my friend....but didyaLISTEN? NO, you didn't. You....F++L!!!!!!" H,s paused for a small number of seconds before continuing. "I SAID, everyone, okay, is LAUGHING AT YOU. Now you have PROOF, my very naive, weakling, friend."

SUFFERING EXTREME: INCORRECTNESS SEXUAL OF HUMAN ENGLISH FEMALE NON-SEXUALESSES TYPING 118
Identity's Image was in the same building as Human English Female Non-Sexualess Incorrectess Sexual, or Hefn-sis, or "MaDARling", at the Post Office. The worse out of the two relevant YDNA Level U individuals, where U is a "letter lower than R" so to speak, started talking to Identity's Image. "You need to leave now Identity's Image." Identity's Image: "Okay, well the Manager said that i can stay another 5 minutes." The YDNA Level U individual, who was not the Manager, or Deputy Manager, or Tertiary Manager, persisted. "NO, well, you know, it's blablaBLA." Identity's Image stayed the extra 5 minutes, despite the YDNA Level U individual's efforts. Identity's Image: "I can't beLIEVE that guy." Hatred, Sexual, or H,s: "That's what i told you, i said, "He's SATAN." But you DIDn't, F+CKing, LISTEN! AgAIN!" Talks, Comforts, or T,c: "I think that he's been bullied in the past." Identity's Image: "I haven't done anything to him."

SUFFERING EXTREME: INCORRECTNESS SEXUAL OF HUMAN ENGLISH FEMALE NON-SEXUALESSES TYPING 119
Identity's Image was in the same building as Human English Female Non-Sexualess Incorrectess Sexual, or Hefn-sis, or "MaDARling", at the Post Office. Identity's Image looked down at a piece of paper that he was holding. When he looked up, the worse out of the two relevant YDNA Level U individuals, where U is a "letter lower than R" so to speak, had gone over to sit with Hefn-sis and a number of others that she was with. Identity's Image: "It's "misbehaving" again from him."

Pickford-Gordon

Since: Sep 09

312

London, UK

Reply »

|
Report Abuse
|
Judge it!
|
#98
Monday Jul 23

SUFFERING EXTREME: INCORRECTNESS SEXUAL OF HUMAN ENGLISH FEMALE NON-SEXUALESSES TYPING 120
Identity's Image was in the same building as Human English Female Non-Sexualess Incorrectess Sexual, or Hefn-sis, or "MaDARling", at the Gymnasium. A "young-looking"-so-t o-speak guy who looks 19 or so, smiled back at Hefn-sis, who had smiled at him, before he opened a locker: they had sort of waited, unsure who was going to open the locker first. This sent more pain into Identity's Image. Identity's Image turned to Talks, Comforts, or T,c: "T,c, this "young-looking" guy has just read CERTAIN of my Internet posts, but NOT ALL of them. Er....okay ANYWAY! Tell me more about him." T,c: "In this individual's case, the manner that they've been going about flirting a little, can't compare to how YOU and her have been connecting, or trying to connect etcetera. The things that you've typed on the Internet for her are unique. They don't appear to have said very much to each other. But i'll have to look at the notes again. In any case, what the situation is is that you've felt strongly about her for a very long time: you feel SUICIDALLY connected to her: it is impossible that this "young-looking" guy feels as strongly for her as you feel for her, Identity's Image." Identity's Image: "She's killing me i want to kill myself i

can't do this." T,c: "Do you see what i mean?" Hefn-sis stood with her back to the "young-looking" guy, as if saying "sorry": it was how she stood sometimes with Identity's Image.

Pickford-Gordon

Since: Sep 09

312

London, UK

Reply »

|
Report Abuse
|
Judge it!
|
#99
Monday Jul 23

SUFFERING EXTREME: INCORRECTNESS SEXUAL OF HUMAN ENGLISH FEMALE NON-SEXUALESSES TYPING 121
1.
Identity's Image was talking to Human English Female Non-Sexualess Incorrectess Sexual, or Hefn-sis, or "MaDARling". Hefn-sis: "I'm ALL INSTICT, it's FUN." She stopped talking to sip some alcohol. Talks, Comforts, or T,c: "Well, Hefn-sis, human beings are incredibly complicated, or rather they are suPPOSED to be complicated. It is a disgrace for ANYONE to be like a PUPPET, as opposed to being a human being. It is a disgrace for a human being to be easily influenced by, or even controlled, by others. Some might say, well, if you have a Human English Female Non-Sexualess, perhaps it doesn't matter if she's easily controlled, and sexually penetrated, by significant numbers of Human Males, so long as a number of Human English Males have equal access to her. However, the Human English Female Sexualess group is one which men just go and have sexual intercourse with: things that relate to such things etcetera are their rules, their principles. Human English Female Non-Sexualesses are not supposed to be easily controlled and easily sexually penetrated. Identity's Image has typed something about this in a certain section, he typed it a long time ago. The POINT of the Human English Female Non-Sexualess, is that she is supposed to resist men, resist temptation, think and then decide whether to act or not or something to that extent, remember sexual things, respect her body."
2.
T,c: "It is a disgrace for any human being to be PRIMITIVE. It is a disgrace for any human being to be an ANIMAL. Animals have no MEMORY. Animals run away from anything that they fail to understand. All human beings have a DUTY to underSTAND. All human beings have a duty to REMEMBER. All human beings have a duty not to just go ahead and ACT: THINK, then decide whether to act or not: Identity's Image's former driving instructor said: "If you don't know DON'T GO.". All human beings have a duty to control their EMOTIONS. All human beings have a duty to control their INstinct, or INSTINCTS. If all human beings acted according to your PAST principles, Hefn-sis, and i hope that you no longer act in the REVOLTING manner in which you've acted in the PAST....if all human beings act, right now, the way that you did in the PAST, then there would be nothing but INCORRECTNESS, or CRIME, in the United Kingdom And Ireland. How many times do human beings become HATEFUL, feel like they should have sexual intercourse with THIS human being or THAT human being? Human beings have a duty not to "GIVE IN" to such THINGS."
3.
T,c: "Your instincts, Hefn-sis, tell you to run away from, and/or perhaps hurt, Identity's Image. That's because you fail to

understand. Does it make sense that a Human-English-Male-like-figure is made to suffer because he's complicated? It makes no sense at all. You think perhaps that Identity's Image has done wrong against you. But it's YOUR LIFESTYLE, and the way that you've been doing things, that is WRONG. It's incredibly unhealthy, and will probably reduce your potential lifespan. While you must understand that there's no need for you to act in such a "social" etcetera manner-when there's no such thing as "social"-Identity's Image doesn't have any great desire to have you leave your way of life....he's fully aware that you call the shots with regard to him, etcetera. Look! Look at Identity's Image. You won't even talk to him, you won't even have a conversation with him. And look at all of these Internet Posts that he's created for you, look at all of them. Look at the amount of time, and effort etcetera that he's spent with regard to you. How do you think he feels? What do you think that you're doing to him, HUH?"

Pickford-Gordon

Since: Sep 09

312

London, UK

Reply »

|
Report Abuse
|
Judge it!
|
#100
Monday Jul 23

SUFFERING EXTREME: INCORRECTNESS SEXUAL OF HUMAN ENGLISH FEMALE NON-SEXUALESSES TYPING 121
4.
T,c walked tiredly away from her. Hatred, Sexual, or H,s, started speaking out loud, LOUDLY: it was not clear who he was talking to. "Perhaps Identity's Image should make ZERO more posts for Hefn-sis. He could make a million posts and Hefn-sis would just be exactly the same." T,c: "I have faith that she will change more than she has done so far, for the better."
5.
Identity's Image: "There's not just a serious problem with Hefn-sis, but there's also a serious problem with the human species, if a Human-English-Male-like-figure can put this much time and effort etcetera in JUST FOR HER, and she not only didn't have sexual intercourse with me last time-and she never has-but she didn't even have a converSATION with me last time, or the time before, or the time before that, or the time before that. And she knows how much she MEANS to me. Not just Hefn-sis, but the whole human species simply DOESN'T MAKE SENSE because of this, there is a MAJOR FLAW with regard to THE THING that the human species IS. I really sometimes just feel like i just want to GET THE F+CK OUT of the current Universe, using (legal) suicide, just as quickly as possible, and i sometimes just feel that i want to do it AT ANY COST WHATSOEVER, i NEED it that bad, the human species is simply ONE BIG FAILURE, ONE BIG STANDSTILL, it F+CKS UP."
6.
T,c: "No, you can't say AT ANY COST, Identity's Image. Etcetera. Just calm down." Identity's Image: "Don't F+CKING tell me to CALM DOWN! How many F+CKING NEXT TIMES are there going to BE? And i'm TRAPPED HERE. You keep telling me about this supposed "DESIRE TO DO GOOD" that Hefn-sis has, but I CAN'T SEE IT!" H,s: "She, and the vast majority of other Human English Female Non-Sexualesses, are SO STUPID, that they simply DON'T KNOW HOW to do

GOOD. They don't have souls. They don't have ANY "desire to do good". It would take a million years to explain BASIC MORALS to them. And Hefn-sis is one of the WORST of them." Identity's Image: "She's my dream: DON'T YOU SAY THAT ABOUT MY DREAM!! B+STARD!!" H,s: "Okay, that's a veeeery good attitude to have, MY FRIEND! But i haven't finished." He paused for a second or two before continuing. "Hefn-sis only understands SURFACE. Hefn-sis only understands LIGHT. Hefn-sis only understands CHITCHAT. Hefn-sis only understands LUST. All of this time and effort etcetera, Identity's Image, my friend....all of it has done nothing but CONFUSE her. She simply doesn't have it in her to change. She's too far gone." T,c: "No, you're WRONG, H,s. Next time there'll be change from her, for the better, towards Identity's Image. And i've noticed that she HAS changed a tiny bit etcetera." Identity's Image: "Hefn-sis i love you, i've always loved you ever since i first saw you, or something like that. You're a part of me. I can't keep doing this, Hefn-sis, i just can't keep doing it. Don't make me suffer any more, darling. I feel ILL, and it's YOUR FAULT. Talk to me next time, and have sexual intercourse with me etcetera."

Pickford-Gordon

Since: Sep 09

312

London, UK

Reply »

|
Report Abuse
|
Judge it!
|
#101
Monday Jul 23

SUFFERING EXTREME: INCORRECTNESS SEXUAL OF HUMAN ENGLISH FEMALE NON-SEXUALESSES TYPING 122
The LEAD WEIGHTS of desPAIR drag me FURTHER UNDERWATER, down infinite depths of SUFFERING: i KNOW NO PEACE. I see others laugh, kiss, and relax. I exist in an eternal paralyze. I am tortured. Yet my memories of my darling, and the concept of HER, the concept of US....somehow....REBIRTHS me. I summon some ever-decreasing "INNER STRENGTH" and i DRAG MYSELF UP. I do it ONE MORE TIME. NEXT time. I yearn for the pleasant surprise of a NEW HER. I BLEED. I long for HOPE. IS....THERE....LIGHT?

SUFFERING EXTREME: INCORRECTNESS SEXUAL OF HUMAN ENGLISH FEMALE NON-SEXUALESSES TYPING 123
I see you rush to me, so light:
So happy have i never seen
A person. Joy indeed was keen,
And many smiles were dancing bright
Between us. You are quite a sight
Before me. The past shall be reborn:
Your fear, your weakness, shall be torn
Apart. With you i shall have might.
I soon must smile and kiss with you:

My dreams of romance must come true.
No more must lonely nights prevail
Upon my bed. We must not fail.
Next time approaches: let us feel,
Together: that we both may heal.

Pickford-Gordon

Since: Sep 09

312

London, UK

Reply »

|
Report Abuse
|
Judge it!
|
#102
Wednesday

SUFFERING EXTREME: INCORRECTNESS SEXUAL OF HUMAN ENGLISH FEMALE NON-SEXUALESSES TYPING 124
1.
Talks, Comforts, or T,c, and Hatred, Sexual, or H,s, were talking to Identity's Image. T,c: "What are the various categories of Human English Female Non-Sexualess Incorrectess Sexuals, or Hefn-siss, etcetera....IDENTITY'S IMAGE?" Identity's Image: "I don't CARE. Human English Female Non-Sexualess Incorrectess Sexual, or Hefn-sis, or "MaDARling", is first right now- out of the two-and she's probably ALWAYS going to be first....yeahyeah ALWAYS....no.... i don't know about this and that....i JUST DON'T KNOW....i.... i think YEAH....i think that she'll always be first out of the TWO. ANYWAY! i don't care about anyone who's not in the first category, T,c, and there are only two of them."
2.
T,c: "You DO though, DON'T YOU." Identity's Image: "Weellll...." T,c: "There are always the events in spacetime while you wait for Hefn-sis, or "MaDARling". AREN'T THERE, IDENTITY'S IMAGE?" Identity's Image: "Next time she'll talk to me and have sexual intercourse with me etcetera! I KNOW IT!" T,c: "Well what if she doesn't? You should think about that POSSIBILITY, SHOULDN'T YOU, IDENTITY'S IMAGE." "Absolutely nothing will happen if you keep feeding yourself the lie that any of them have SOULS, my friend. In their minds everything revolves around THEM, and they can do whatever they WANT. They CAN'T FEEL GUILT, or PITY. These things are scientific FACT, my friend." Identity's Image buried his head in his hands. T,c: "NOW look what you've DONE: he's CRYING AGAIN." "He needs to TOUGHEN UP, and he needs my adVICE," explained H,s. T,c: "NO ONE needs your adVICE, PSYCHOPATH."
3.
T,c: "So what are the CATEGORIES, Identity's Image?" Identity's Image: "There are two Human English Female Non-Sexualess Incorrectess Sexuals, or Hefn-siss, the "main" of which, at the moment, and possibly forever, is "MaDARling". There is one Human English Female Non-Sexualess Incorrectess Sexual2, or Hefn-sis2, from more than 9 years ago. There are a number of Human English Female Non-Sexualess Incorrectess Sexual3s, or Hefn-sis3s, and Human English Female Non-Sexualess Incorrectess Sexual4s, or Hefn-sis4s, etcetera. I ROUGHLY have hierarchies within these categories, but they change here and there, or something like that, etcetera."

Pickford-Gordon

Since: Sep 09

312

London, UK

Reply »

|
Report Abuse
|
Judge it!
|
#103
Wednesday

SUFFERING EXTREME: INCORRECTNESS SEXUAL OF HUMAN ENGLISH FEMALE NON-SEXUALESSES TYPING 125
1.
Talks, Comforts, or T,c, and Hatred, Sexual, or H,s, were talking to Identity's Image about Human English Female Non-Sexualess Incorrectess Sexual, or Hefn-sis, or "MaDARling", and related issues. Identity's Image: "Hefn-sis wasn't THERE last time. She didn't say anything to me, she hasn't told me the truth etcetera about this and that, and she did this suddenly and without warning etcetera." He was crying. T,c: "She might be there NEXT TIME. Remember that she's done this sort of thing to you a number of times BEFORE: she came BACK before, reMEMber?"
2.
Identity's Image wiped away some of his tears with his hands. Identity's Image: "I....i....think that i'm going to be strong enough to make EVEN MORE of a permanent record-because my Internet posts about her and related issues are a permanent record-about her and related issues, all of her crimes against me, in book form. I'll do this as i continue to do what i have to do NOW, and what i should perhaps have put more effort into beFORE: giving myself and a number of other human beings the right to legally commit suicide-which i call legal killing-self-, or be legally killed. If things haven't changed, etcetera, or something like that, between me and Hefn-sis....if it's been set up for me and a number of other human beings i'll just have to go and legally commit SUICIDE. Perhaps the politicians won't permit a number of other options, you see. I'm really SUffering NOW." H,s: "It's likely if not 100% certain that she WANTS you to stay alive and suffer for as long as possible. She has absolutely no sense of reality, and lives in her own world." "That's NOT true, STOP IT, H,s," mumbled Identity's Image.
3.
H,s: "So how are you going to make the 650 traitors DO THIS?" Identity's Image: "Well i've been posting on a number of threads that relate to it, but it seems to have been ignored by a number of human beings in the United Kingdom And Ireland. With the current situation that i'm in i'll just have to keep on....KEEP ON....with my Country Manager, Duncan Carling. A lot of people have read that THREAD. I really don't appear to have much choice at the moment but to KEEP ON with Duncan Carling. Which is DIFFICULT." T,c: "Keep making a record of all of the crimes of those THREE. And have hope. There's only SO LONG that a number of the human beings in the United Kingdom And Ireland can lie to themselves, and run from things that are REAL etcetera. With regard to YOU, Identity's Image, it's YOUR LIFE, and NO ONE has the right to keep YOU, or ANYONE ELSE, TRAPPED here when you don't want to be here. YOU, Identity's Image, are the best judge of YOU, the best judge of HOW MUCH you're SUFFERING. KEEP ON, or something like that, etcetera." Identity's Image: "Hefn-sis, "MaDARling", i love you you're always here with me, don't do this to me anymore i can't take it. Talk to me next time, and have sexual intercourse with me etcetera."

Tell me when this thread is updated:
(Registration is not required)

Add to my Tracker

Send me an email

Showing posts 81 - 100 of 105

< prev page

|

next page >

Go to last page|Jump to page: 1 2 3 45 6

Type in your comments below

Name
(appears on your post)

Comments

Characters left: 4000

Type the numbers you see in the image on the right:

Please note by clicking on "Post Comment" you acknowledge that you have read the Terms of Service and the comment you are posting is in compliance with such terms. Be polite.Inappropriate posts may be removed by the moderator. Send us your feedback.

44Users are viewing theUnited Kingdom Forumright now

Search the United Kingdom Forum:

Topic

Updated

Last By

Comments

Aide Romney values Anglo-Saxon ties

1 min

Gary

79

I want to marry my niece... is it a problem?

47 min

supersonic boom

44

Eight men accused of attempted murder in Keighl... (Oct '10)

1 hr

Boss maja abid

1,027

Gay/bisexual/straight bbm pins in UK:)

1 hr

sexyhornygirlukonly

231

Atheism to Defeat Religion by 2038

1 hr

Very Cynical Person

6,934

Riots erupt in N.Ireland after Protestant marches (Jul '11)

2 hr

Freedom

273

Taliban kept at bay by South Yorkshire soldiers

2 hr

Karol

3

Islam takes over Catholic school(Dec '10)

4 hr

cymru

187

See all threads in the United Kingdom forum »

Does the US need to reform its gun laws? Vote now on the Gun Laws Map.

United Kingdom News
 Man charged following fight in Aveley
 14-year-old killed in Marlborough accident is n...
 International progress on monitoring flights' C...
 Londoners finally seem to embrace Olympics
 Star-studded audience for Olympic opening ceremony
 50,000 pack Hyde Park for Olympic party, concert
 Landslide beach restrictions lifted
 Health boss accused of 'gloating'
 Carbonostics Food Product Life Cycle Assessment...
 Josef, 9, dies in tragic accident
 Portsmouth Harbour Searched For Missing Hero
 Stapleton Found Guilty Of Anuj Bidve Murder

More United Kingdom News from Topix »

Topix Politix App

Take your stand on the issues you care about.

Using an iPhone?

Keep the Topix forums in your pocket
with the new, free Topix App.

Daily Horoscope for July 28

Capricorn

Watch out if you're going anywhere near the shops because money will flow through your fingers like water. No sooner will you have seen something you want to buy than you'll have bought it, even if it's beyond your means. Try not to get into hot financial water, even if you do feel an overpowering need to cheer yourself up.

Get your Horoscope »

United Kingdom
News
Forums & Polls
Real-Time News

Explore More Topix
Home Page
Forums
Top Stories
Most Popular
Issue Maps
US News
US Cities list
World News
World Countries list
Politics
Celebrities
Business
Finance
Autos
Sports
Sci-Tech
Electronics
Entertainment
Movies
Music
Television
Video Games
Health
Life
Arts
Food
Home
Travel
Offbeat
Site Map / All Topics

About Topix
About Us
Media Kit
Topix Blog
Press Room
RSS Newsfeeds
Law Enforcement
School Officials
Cyber-bullying Resources
Jobs
FAQ
Privacy Policy
Terms of Service
Feedback?
Report Abuse?

Local Classifieds & Listings

Reach Local customers. Post a classified listing for your business. Promote job, auto, rental, and local event listings.

Learn more »

Join the Topix Community
¦Create your own profile, complete with quick links to your favorite topics.
¦Personalize your forum posts with your photo and hometown.
¦Exchange Personal Messages with other registered users.

Sign up today! »

Topix Politix »

Feedback?
Comments made yesterday: 99,203 Total comments across all topics: 180,458,074

Copyright ©2012 Topix LLC

Local News: United Kingdom

|

Sign Up

|

Sign In

123

Syria
Syria Renews Attacks on Aleppo Rebels

China
Jeremy Lin says he hopes China hoops camp will boost enthusias...

Politix
Is the media in the tank for Obama?

Home
Forums
Top Stories
Popular
Local
Summer Olympics
US
Politics
World
Sports
Entertainment
Offbeat
Other

United Kingdom
News
Forums & PollsSuffering Extreme: In...

Real-Time News

Suffering Extreme: Incorrectness Sexual Of HEFN-Ses Typings

Posted in the United Kingdom Forum

Share

Read
135 Comments

Add to my Tracker

More United Kingdom Discussions »

Comments (Page 6)

Showing posts 101 - 120 of 135

< prev page

|

next page >

Go to last page|Jump to page:1 2 3 45 6 7

Faloola Chong

Northwich, UK

Reply »

|
Report Abuse
|
Judge it!
|
#104
Saturday Jul 28

have you tried hitting yourself on head with mallet?

faloola recommend highly

Pickford-Gordon

Since: Sep 09

343

London, UK

Reply »

Report Abuse

Judge it!

#105
Saturday Jul 28

SUFFERING EXTREME: INCORRECTNESS SEXUAL OF HUMAN ENGLISH FEMALES NON-SEXULAESSES TYPING 126
I stand here being drained. How can
You treat me just like dirt, and still
Be laughing: escape against my will,
As i die, a tired, lonely man,
Who to your arms in gladness ran.
How can you not appreciate
How i am. Is the longed-for gate
In sight? I doubt that i can plan.
How can you stab someone like me
When innocence itself i be?
Why do you fail to comprehend
My worth, love? Pain is what you send
To me, in piles. One day in bed
You'll see....too late. I may be dead.

Pickford-Gordon

Since: Sep 09

343

London, UK

Reply »

Report Abuse

Judge it!

#106
Saturday Jul 28

SUFFERING EXTREME: INCORRECTNESS SEXUAL OF HUMAN ENGLISH FEMALES NON-SEXULAESSES TYPING 127

1.
Talks, Comforts, or T,c, and Hatred, Sexual, or H,s, were talking to Identity's Image about Human English Female Non-Sexualess Incorrectess Sexual, or Hefn-sis, or "MaDARling", and related issues. Identity's Image: "T,c, tell me more about that "young-looking"-so-t o-speak guy who looks 19 or so, that we saw Hefn-sis smile at, and flirt with." T,c: "I'll have to analyse the notes to see if i can perhaps calculate if they've had sexual intercourse or not, etcetera: more data might or might not be required. One thing that i know with 100% certainty is that he was coming on strongly towards her at one point. I'm not sure if that's because they've spent a lot of time together, and perhaps both are attracted to each other and know it, or something, OR if she's given him....SOMETHING....perhaps, or perhaps NOT something LESS than sexual intercourse, and that SOMETHING made him FEEL that he has some sort of RIGHT to her. He should know that she has done significant sexual things with at least 7 human beings that work there, and that IF he felt like that about her, all of the 7 or more workers-and it's probably more than 7 too-ALSO feel that they have some sort of RIGHT to her. In any case she needs to be with you, Identity's Image, as soon as possible. SHE might want to forget her strong flirtation(which is communicating the information that Person A is sexually attracted to Person B) with YOU and YOUR flirtation with HER, her lies broken promises, her subjecting you to her flirting with THIS GUY and THAT GUY, her treating you like S+IT, her almost succeeding in using fake laws to hurt you TWICE or more, etCETERA....but YOU, Identity's Image, of course, are UNLIKELY TO FORGET those things and more AT ALL, EVER."

2.
Identity's Image: "Tell me more, T,c." H,s: "What the F+CK do you keep talking to HIM FOR all the time PAL? I've TOLD YOU that someone like that can NEVER be reasoned with, oKAY? Someone like that understands only ONE THING, my FRIEND...." He paused for a small number of seconds. Identity's Image noticed that H,s was standing very close to him, frONTING him; H,s had his hands behind his back as Identity's Image stood leaning back against a WALL. Suddenly and without warning H,s's hands whipped out from behind his back: his right hand held a pistol, while his left hand held what was presumably that pistol's magaZINE: the magazine was loaded into the pistol in H,s's right hand: before Identity's Image had had time to BLINK, H,s was pressing the gun against his forehead HARD. H,s smiled at him, his eyes penetrating into Identity's Image's skull through one of Identity's Image's EYES. Identity's Image sensed that H,s was going to do something....H,s pulled the trigger. "NOOOOOOOOOOOOOOO!!!!!!!! !!" screamed Identity's Image.

3.
"Click." The magazine had been empty. "CLICK!" announced H,s with a grin, his eyes glittering as they looked into one of Identity's Image's eyes. Identity's Image was breathing heavily, and looked at H,s with FEAR as H,s removed the pistol from Identity's Image's forehead. H,s: "CONsequences. Consequences, my friend. That's the only thing that Hefn-sis, AND, well, more than HALF of all human beings in the United Kingdom And Ireland underSTAND." T,c: "That's not true, H,s. That's not true...." T,c's voice trailed off, and his eyes had become vague and distant. H,s: "YES YOU'RE VERY CONVINCING....NOT."

Pickford-Gordon

Since: Sep 09

343

London, UK

Reply »

|
Report Abuse
|

Judge it!

#107
Saturday Jul 28

SUFFERING EXTREME: INCORRECTNESS SEXUAL OF HUMAN ENGLISH FEMALES NON-SEXULAESSES TYPING 127
4.
T,c paused for a small number of seconds before starting speaking again. "The "young-looking"-so-t o-speak guy who looks 19 or so, looked somewhat guilty at the end there: i'm not sure exactly how that contributes to the DATA. After that he was flirting with another girl, briefly. Before both of those things it is 100% the case that he read a number of your Internet Posts, Identity's Image. It is unclear whether he has read all of them. It is unclear whether he knows that on the first page, or if not on the first page then SOMEWHERE, on a number of your threads, you provide a LINK to your current list of posts created. He assumed that THAT, what he had read, was ALL there was to you, and judged you based on the small percentage of posts out of the total that he had read. Then he probably read the threads about correspondance with YOU, and the one about when you tried to commit suicide in May 2011. In any case, he probably thinks that Internet posts are the same as speaking, which they are NOT. It is easy, and infinitely less real, than speaking....the movement of one's hands across a KEYBOARD....i believe that you HAVE, or HAVE NOT, posted about such things, Identity's Image."
5.
T,c paused for a number of seconds before starting speaking again. "In any case, you've KNOWN, Identity's Image, and HAVE BEEN FLIRTING WITH ETCETERA, Hefn-sis for a LONG TIME. You SUICIDALLY need her. There's sort of nothing else for you right now. I think that he understands that now, and won't FLIRT, and/or MORE THAN FLIRT, etcetera, with her aGAIN." Identity's Image: "I TRUST H,S,T,c you DREAMER! They're F+CKING RIGHT NOW! Haven's you seen how she f+cking automatically hugs and snogs people, both men and women? And if she's automatic like that AT WORK, in SIGHT, then OUT OF SIGHT it must be infinitely WORSE. I CAN'T TAKE IT ANY MORE. I HAVE to get OUT OF HERE."
6.
Identity's Image staggered around the room. He looked at the ceiling, and at the walls of his room. "I'm trapped, i'm stuck here....i'm trapped. Out i've got to get out, it's a TRAP. NO HOPE, i can't do this i CAN'T, DOIT."
7.
T,c: "I need to analyse the NOTES. You KNOW that H,s very frequently, er, "STRAYS" from the One Fact, Identity's Image." Identity's Image: "It doesn't matter if you LIE with regard to a CRIMINAL, or if you cause more than the maximum amount of suffering to a criminal. What matters is that they suffer and DIE." T,c stared at him in surprise, and sadness. Identity's Image: "I mean....just certain of MY CRIMINALS, and similar situations for OTHERS. Or something like that." Identity's Image was silent: his expression, as he looked at T,c, was blank. H,s smiled.

Pickford-Gordon

Since: Sep 09

343

London, UK

Reply »

Report Abuse

Judge it!
|
#108
Saturday Jul 28

SUFFERING EXTREME: INCORRECTNESS SEXUAL OF HUMAN ENGLISH FEMALES NON-SEXULAESSES TYPING 128
Identity's Image was talking to Human English Female Non-Sexualess Incorrectess Sexual, or Hefn-sis, or "MaDARling", at the Gymnasium. Identity's Image: "For more than 4 months i've always come into the building upon the 1 or more days every week/month/2-month period. By contrast you've missed a lot of days upon the 1 or more days that I'M IN. Come back, i BEG YOU, you're making me ILL. You should know that a great FEAR for human beings, and a significant cause of SUFFERING for human beings, is fear of the unknown: you won't tell me anything, you haven't had a conversation with me in AGES. I need you, please come back, i don't feel well you're sucking the life out of me. Just talk to me. How do you think i feel?" Hefn-sis: "No well you know what you DID!" Identity's Image: "That's not incorrectness, or crime, as SUCH, Hefn-sis. That's NOT REAL, do you UNDERSTAND? You haven't been talking to me, and i'm getting weaker and weaker every day because of you. What am i supposed to do? And who says that i can't come in more than the allocated times, which is what you've "punished" me for? What's wrong with that exactly? Think about it, what's wrong with it?" Hefn-sis: "I feel, i mean my instincts tell me that-" Identity's Image: "We're not animals, Hefn-sis. Human beings are supposed to control their emotions, control their instincts. Just COME BACK. YOU might easily forget things, but i remember and/or have made notes about everything relevant to you and me, as much as i have been able to. I will NEVER quit, Hefn-sis. Look at me, MY LOVE." She looked up at him, on the verge of tears. "I would RATHER DIE, Hefn-sis. Okay? I would rather die." She started crying. Identity's Image: "LOOK, okay, DON'T CRY, come on STOP IT." Hefn-sis: "I'm sorry. It's just that all of these sort of REAL feelings are....i mean....i just can't handle them, you KNOW?" They were silent together for a small number of seconds. Identity's Image: "I understand that you're uncertain about this or that about me....BUT IF YOU JUST LET ME TALK TO YOU, then things will work out. Okay?" Hefn-sis: "Okay. I'll let you talk to me, at the Harbour, and also at other times. We'll also have sexual intercourse etcetera." Identity's Image: "Is that a PROMISE, my love?" He smiled. She smiled back and looked down at the concrete, just like she had done on "THAT DAY" some event in spacetime ago.

Pickford-Gordon

Since: Sep 09

343

London, UK

Reply »
|
Report Abuse
|
Judge it!
|
#109
Sunday Jul 29

SUFFERING EXTREME: INCORRECTNESS SEXUAL OF HUMAN ENGLISH FEMALES NON-SEXULAESSES TYPING 129

1.
A Human English Female Non-Sexualess was talking to her fellow workers. "Oooo YEAH, sexual things are FUN! Everyone's like my little TOYS! Darling! I love LYING. Men and women are the SAME. There are no consequences with regard to anything and everything that i do, i commit incorrectness, or crime automatically," she was going. She paused for a number of seconds and then announced, irritably: "Shouldn't that Victim CREEP be here by now." Victim didn't show up. "He'll be here next time. He's so annoying," she went. Victim wasn't there next time either. "I'm sure that there's some normal explanation for him not being here," she went.

2.
The next time, a police officer entered the building: he approached her. "Oooo "OFFICER", that's SEXY!" she went immediately, and automatically. She approached him and started sort of trying to dance with him from the front. The officer frowned, irritation flaring up in his eyes. "Do you know Victim?" he asked her. "I don't know him at all, in any way, NO, but i'm aWARE of who he is. I've never shown him any sexual interest whatsoever, EVER." "Well that doesn't fit any of the information that Victim has left behind, and there's a lot of it," said the officer to her, with a slight tone in his voice. "Left behind?" she asked? "Yes, left behind: Victim committed suicide a number of days ago." There was a pause for a number of seconds. "He left you this note." The officer held out a note. She paused for a number of seconds before snatching the note from the officer's right hand. She read it. It stated, below the girl's name: "I just couldn't live any more after the amount of suffering that you caused me. You gave me no hope. You even seemed sometimes to get WORSE. I trusted you. You have killed me, my love. But i know that you won't lie to me, you won't break any more promises to me....NEXT TIME: IN THE NEXT WORLD. I wait for you there. I love you. Victim."

Faloola Chong

UK

Reply »

|
Report Abuse
|
Judge it!
|
#110
Monday Jul 30

have you ever seen a lady naked?

Pickford-Gordon

Since: Sep 09

343

London, UK

Reply »

|
Report Abuse
|
Judge it!
|
#111
Wednesday Aug 1

SUFFERING EXTREME: INCORRECTNESS SEXUAL OF HUMAN ENGLISH FEMALES NON-SEXULAESSES TYPING 130
1.
Identity's Image was talking to Human English Female Non-Sexualess Incorrectess Sexual2, or Hefn-sis2. Memories came back to him: memories of how he knew that Hefn-sis2 had liked him, a lot. He had known. He remembered Hefn-sis2 smiling at him A LOT, Hefn-sis2 blushing as he flirted with her, Hefn-sis2 always there on the day(s) that he came in for his Routine, Hefn-sis rushing over to help him that one time, Hefn-sis2 laughing at his many humourous comments, and-although "vibes" often go wrong, but they can on occasion be used etcetera-she had given out a sexual "vibe" in his direction, and she had "noticed" him before etcetera. She was unbelievably attractive, thought Identity's Image-he had always liked her. Although he didn't QUITE suiCIdally like her and didn't QUITE suiCIdally need to be with her, like he did the two Human English Female Non-Sexualess Incorrectess Sexuals, or Hefn-siss, one named "What might i giveyou madarling?", and also the other one....although he didn't feel the same urgency she was still high up-if not first-out of all perhaps 4 or 5 or so out of all of the Hefn-sis2s....perhaps. She was definitely Hefn-sis2 and would never be relegated to a lower rank....although she could always cause more suffering to him and become Hefn-sis status, of course.
2.
He spoke to her. "How are you, Hefn-sis2?" She raised her head. "I'm fine. How are you?" Identity's Image was interrupted by one of the annoying staff members who always ANNOUNCED that he should come to THEM. Hefn-sis2 never announced that he should come to her now, not any more, not like she used to....and all because Identity's Image had told her his name, and probably-although he wasn't sure, he had to check his notes-told her that he posted on this Internet Forum. He knew, from her now unstable behaviour, that she had read a number of his Internet Posts. How could mere words, mere movement of hands over a keyboard, have this effect on another human being, thought Identity's Image.
3.
Identity's Image: "I'm more or less the same as always." She had looked a little like she was/had been crying when she had raised her head after he had started speaking to her. She started walking around, walking to the right in a hurry, and walking to the left in a hurry. He sensed fear, hatred, and general instability in her. Identity's Image: "Human beings are supposed to control their instincts, control their emotions, underSTAND....we're not animals, Hefn-sis2. It's very easy to type on a keyboard, Hefn-sis2. You can't condemn me, or whatever you've done, for my Internet posts." Hefn-sis2: "Mhhmmhhmmm!" Her head bobbed up and down rapidly, nodding: Identity's Image doubted whether she had heard what he had said. Identity's Image: "You should post on my "Correspondance" thread, so that we can meet up. I mean i'm not sure how long things will take with regard to the two Hefn-siss, you know. That would be like a dream come true, you and me, you know. But i lose hope." Hefn-sis2: "Aaaaw, now that's not very good now, is it?" She had said this cocking her head, and looking at him in that way of hers. Identity's Image: "Your personality, as a bonus to your voice, looks and everything else about you, really comes across as something too. I mean, you know, you're great you know, you're fantastic i love you." Hefn-sis2 immediately got up and started walking madly around the room talking to herself. Hefn-sis2: "Oh my god he said he loves me that means he's gonna kill himself oh my god i've gotta leave the country i can't take this oh NOO" she was going. Identity's Image: "Look now, i mean, it's just, you know, i mean, you know, wait, i didn't, i, AH F+CK!" "I don't know what to say," thought Identity's Image. "I mean, with regard to Hefn-sis2, i do lo....i do whatever."

See more stories

1 hr
7
Paul Ryan the Best Choice for VP Nominee?

170

2012 Budget hawk would bring policy bona fides to Romney's ticket

1 hr

9

Census May Change Racial Categories

RaceAfter complaints in 2010, the national survey could change its ways

Pickford-Gordon

Since: Sep 09

343

London, UK

Reply »

|
Report Abuse
|
Judge it!
|
#112
Wednesday Aug 1

SUFFERING EXTREME: INCORRECTNESS SEXUAL OF HUMAN ENGLISH FEMALES NON-SEXULAESSES TYPING 130
4.
The next time, he approached the till, at the Supermarket Co-itrose, where he came in to meet her. She put up a "till closed" sign when he approached. The next time, a guy came out. He was somewhat young-looking, but Identity's Image was not sure how much....he didn't get much of a good look at him. The guy gave out a "hateful" vibe in the direction of Identity's Image. The guy resembled, to a great extent, a certain individual. "That's because they've put him there, after choosing him, because they want to destroy you," said Hatred, Sexual, or H,s. Identity's Image: "AAAAAAAAAAAHHHHH!!" Identity's Image whirled around after that: H,s had snuck up behind him without Identity's Image realising. Talks, Comforts, or T,c approached from Identity's Image's front: "Even for YOU, H,s, that's TOO MUCH. I mean....well....it's unlikely that a number of human beings have "arranged" to have someone who looks like him work there so that he does a number of sexual things with Hefn-sis2, which is what you're mortally afraid of, Identity's Image. In any case, Identity's Image, you HAVE something with her, and you've had it since a long time ago-well over a year ago-and you've never seen this guy before, and he looks somewhat young-or did from the brief period that you saw him, and he resembles, well, you know, that individual that you don't like talking about, Identity's Image. Hefn-sis2 should understand what the situation is and NOT do anything sexual with this guy....she means too much to you, Identity's Image." Identity's Image: "Oh my god that guy same hair colour slightly same look about the visage, and young-looking." T,c: "Look just calm down, okay. Hefn-sis2, while she might or might not be somewhat of a flirt, will hopefully now understand. She won't cause you any more suffering." Identity's Image: "Okay."
5.
Hefn-sis2: "Stick it in THERE." Identity's Image: "What do you mean!?" Later, Hefn-sis2's head bobbed down very distinctly....it was a command for him to LOOK DOWN....it was sort of a LOOK DOWN NOW, ORder....which Identity's Image DID. Identity's Image: "Next time, Hefn-sis2, BE THERE, talk more to me, and then arrange to do a number of sexual

things with me, have sexual intercourse with me. I....i really like you. Okay!? Don't be afraid, talking to me will solve everything, or something like that!" He smiled at her.

Pickford-Gordon

Since: Sep 09

343

London, UK

Reply »

|
Report Abuse
|
Judge it!
|
#113
Wednesday Aug 1

SUFFERING EXTREME: INCORRECTNESS SEXUAL OF HUMAN ENGLISH FEMALES NON-SEXULAESSES TYPING 131
Hefn-sis2, my unstable, rapidly running around, "Awww, that's not very pleasant now is it!?", head-bobbing-down, dream. You are beauty itself: lucky is anyone who comes near you. I would do SO MUCH for you. And your personality shines through, as a bonus. You are absolutely not like a number of other girls that i've known. I feel that i can trust you....more than them. Nothing shall happen if we speak: embrace what is ME like you used to. May the concept of YOU, the concept of US, not go wrong, how CAN it, NOTHING would make sense if it DID. Your every word is a skyscraper, and the concept of my touching the heaving of your chest, your attractive arms and waist, is a dream that i hope shall become reality as soon as possible, darling. You shine, standing out like a beacon for me in a storm, in splendour, emitting some THING that i want to revel in nigh-forEVER. You STUN ME: your Hefn-sis2NESS is a hammerblow to my resistance of almost anything that is not YOU. It would be a fantastic world, if you could stay beautiful forever, perhaps! You GLEAM! You sparkle. And your beauty is such a uniqueness, you are unIque, but in an overpowering, sexual, way. You DAZZLE! You are one of the few representatives of my HOPE, in the current, dull plodding of my eternal PARAlyze. You are gorgeousness, darling.

SUFFERING EXTREME: INCORRECTNESS SEXUAL OF HUMAN ENGLISH FEMALES NON-SEXULAESSES TYPING 132
You rush around, unstable, while
I try to see what is in your brain.
Our long-term connection cannot refrain
From becoming stone. As workers file
In with you daily, and one large pile
Is before you, think of me. Love, I
Remember your many smiles to me and sigh.
For you, my love, i would crawl a mile.
My darling, i can give to you
Awakening: my aim is true.
The brain must conquer instinct. With me,
Together, love, shall wholly flee

Your fears. You first thought me something nice,
But it shall be more: a new gleam's vice.

Pickford-Gordon

Since: Sep 09

343

London, UK

Reply »

|
Report Abuse
|
Judge it!
|
#114
Wednesday Aug 1

SUFFERING EXTREME: INCORRECTNESS SEXUAL OF HUMAN ENGLISH FEMALES NON-SEXULAESSES TYPING 133
1.
Identity's Image was talking to Human English Female Non-Sexualess Incorrectess Sexual, or Hefn-sis, or ""What might i giveyou madarling?", at the Gymnasium. Hefn-sis: "Soooo malover....you've just written three political manifestos for aNOTHER girl. I said that you should find yourself someone else....but i didn't MEAN IT my love. EXPLAIN YOURSELF! Before i KILL YOU! You're going to tell me everything about her before i do that, though."
2.
Identity's Image: "Look, i know that you're jealous. You have to understand that i'm somewhat suicidal. It's like a medical thing for me to be happy, to crave sexual things right now. She's in my head as well as the two Hefn-siss, which is you and that other one. It takes a LOT out of me to travel to the Gymnasium where i meet you, it takes a LOT of time and effort, etcetera. I post for you when i don't go there, or something like that, etcetera. Listen, you just LEFT, where are you, i need you." Hefn-sis: "Not eNOUGH, you don't need me eNOUGH, all of your Internet posts etcetera are not eNOUGH for me. I'm doing everything to you on purpose, and because of THAT, you're going to stay alive and SUFFER, for making me look bad, and for being dedicated, or devoted to me. You were supposed to be CASUAL, treating me like i don't matter like a number of other toys, i mean guys, that i've been social, or had sexual intercourse, with-i don't want to be RUDE you know, i have to smile and F+CK, i mean it's a PEN+S, it goes in my hole and gives me pleasure, there's nothing more, there's no such thing as ROmance....you were supposed to do THAT, but you WEREN'T supposed to flirt with anyone else during the time i'm spending talking and analysing you. I'm sure you can cope, on your own, masturbating while everyone else takes sexual things for granted etcetera. Now i hate this girl AND the other girl, besides me obviously-of course-, who is of Hefn-sis status."
3.
Identity's Image: "You KNOW how much you mean to me. But WHERE ARE YOU? Show up, my love, please, okay?" Hefn-sis: "Okay. I'll also have sexual intercourse with you next time." She did the "sexual vibe" thing that she very frequently did with Identity's Image, then placed both of her hands on her "work uniform" and pulled it down, straightening it, as if going "humph, that'll teach him". Identity's Image: "You know, i can't control my "vibe" thing. It goes wrong very frequently. I mean, when it DOES go right, which is a number of times, then it COUNTS, but apart from that it shouldn't be done that much, or something like that, etcetera. Lets talk etcetera next time."

Pickford-Gordon

Since: Sep 09

343

London, UK

Reply »

|
Report Abuse
|
Judge it!
|
#115
Wednesday Aug 1

SUFFERING EXTREME: INCORRECTNESS SEXUAL OF HUMAN ENGLISH FEMALES NON-SEXULAESSES TYPING 134
1.
Identity's Image was talking to Human English Female Non-Sexualess Incorrectess Sexual, or Hefn-sis, or ""What might i giveyou madarling?", at the Gymnasium. Hefn-sis: "Don't inSULT me!" Identity's Image: "It's because i don't want you to behave like that any more. I love you. You....and yes, even the other one, of Hefn-sis status. But i need you right now, and you'll possibly always be my Number One out of all other girls."
2.
Identity's Image paused for a number of seconds before continuing. "You keep hurting me. I mean, people CAN'T do whatever they want, if they could i would probably commit suicide. Could you at least HANG ON until something is legally set up by the politicians for me?" Hefn-sis: "NNO: NNO: DON'T TELL ME TO HANG ON: NNO. I'M saying NNO." She paused for a small number of seconds before continuing. "Look it's not that i'm not okay with me hanging on, because i am, it's just that blablaBLA!" Identity's Image: "Well you SAY blablaBLA, but i don't think that you really mean it, do you?"
3.
He paused for a number of seconds before continuing. "Anyway, i'm not really limited to which day, or days, that i can come in, to the Gymnasium." Hefn-sis: "Thank you my love! I'm waiting for you on this day or that day." Identity's Image: "I'll TRY to come in on this day or that day. I'm not sure though. Can't you try to understand how II feel etcetera?" Hefn-sis: "There's no "II": just ME: I'M the only one who exISTS, in reality."
4.
Identity's Image: "Look, okay, i'll do whatever, within reason, that you WANT. You KNOW how obediant i am. You should just have spoken to me. And you seem to not remember things that relate to us, when i remember a very large number of things that relate to us. Men and women are different, and just because a number of men are LUCKY, and you don't mean anything to them, and you don't affect this man or that man as you do me, doesn't mean that that's the case with ME: it's not my fault that i've been STARVED of the dream of the concept of a girl like you....with ME, my love. And the starvation has resulted in the effect that you've had on me....or something like that. This or that is NOT MY FAULT, my love, yet you've punished me. I can't stand not knowing THIS and not knowing THAT. Talk to me, etcetera, and have sexual intercourse with me next time, okay?" Hefn-sis: "Yes Identity's Image."

Pickford-Gordon

Since: Sep 09

343

London, UK

Reply »

|
Report Abuse
|
Judge it!
|
#116
Wednesday Aug 1

SUFFERING EXTREME: INCORRECTNESS SEXUAL OF HUMAN ENGLISH FEMALES NON-SEXULAESSES TYPING 135
1.
Identity's Image was talking to one of the various Human English Female Non-Sexualess Incorrectness Sexuals/Sexual2s/Etcetera, or Hefn-siss/Hefn-sis2s/Etcetera. "Tell me about your precious prostitutes, Identity's Image."
Identity's Image: "It IS wrong, if Human Male A is less than Human Male B, for a Human English Female to have sexual intercourse with Human Male A. HoWEVER, my current view is that it IS the case that it is wrong for ANY Human Male to have sexual intercourse with ANY Human Female. The possibility, or occurrence, of any Human Male having sexual intercourse with any Human Female, harms AT LEAST ONE OTHER PERSON....somewhere.....within humanity. It is wrong for the human species to exIST. However, a number of things need to continue to happen, at present."
2.
Identity's Image: "Once a crime-wrong-occurs, then there's a debt, that needs to be paid. But first, the following. If a Sex Worker has sexual intercourse with Human Male A, where Human Male A is less than Human Male B, then, firstly, the crime "weight" of this, on it's own, is very tiny in comparison to....probably MOST OTHER CRIMES. A Human Female-a Sex Worker-who is ALWAYS there....that you KNOW that you're GOING to have sexual intercourse with, with perhaps 0% chance of failure....that is one of the most valuable things in existence, quite frankly. From THAT ALONE....IF....you know that a Sex Worker has ALSO had sexual intercourse with THIS guy or with THAT guy....IF you know it....then it really doesn't change very much now does it. You don't see anything....the other guy is in THIS room and you're in THAT room. Being exposed to things-imagery, videos, etcetera....THAT is when you start to, maybe, feel the tiniest tiniest bit, perhaps, FUNNY, about the Sex Worker in the video, or in the image. So there's not even THAT to detract from the irreplacable, excellent, value of the concept of the Sex Worker."
3.
Identity's Image: "So you don't know who the Sex Worker has had sexual intercourse with, except for YOU. Perhaps a "sexual history", a rough one, for all Human Females should be held by the government etcetera, but if it's not possible, my current view is that it doesn't matter....i doubt whether it will matter, ever. Quite frankly it's hypocrisy, if you know that a Sex Worker has had sexual intercourse with, say THIS guy over here, a hypothetical guy, to then complain about it, when my current view is that the vast majority of other crimes are worse than that. Sex Workers can never hurt me very much: they are brilliant. You know where you stand with them from the start."
4.
Identity's Image: "So it is wrong-with a tiny crime "weight"-for Sex Workers to do what they do AT PRESENT....but Sex Workers MORE THAN REPAY THE DEBT THAT THEY OWE THEIR VICTIMS, by a long long way. Everyone is a criminal, and everyone is a victim. People would probably kill each other in the streets in their thousands if there were no Sex Workers. Sex Workers are therapeutic, they HEAL-sexual "HEALTH"(for me, definitely)-, they are honest, you know where you stand with them, they don't insult me, they don't disrespect me, etcetera. Every Sex Worker is an actual or a potential

getting out of bed for some Human Male somewhere. Sex Workers are more than excellent. Etcetera."

Pickford-Gordon

Since: Sep 09

343

London, UK

Reply »

|
Report Abuse
|
Judge it!
|
#117
Wednesday Aug 1

SUFFERING EXTREME: INCORRECTNESS SEXUAL OF HUMAN ENGLISH FEMALES NON-SEXULAESSES TYPING 136
1.
Identity's Image was talking to one of the various Human English Female Non-Sexualess Incorrectess Sexuals/Sexual2s/Etcetera, or Hefn-siss/Hefn-sis2s/Etcetera. Identity's Image: "I WILL eventually, hopefully almost CERTAINLY, SOON-ish, get back into the Supermarket after having been illegally prevented from reentering by those two men. Everybody HANG TIGHT! And STAY BEAUTIFUL!!!! but not so much the men."
2.
Identity's Image: "I shall, hopefully almost CERTAINLY....BE BACK!!!!" There was shouting and cheering and whistling, not just from the girl that he was talking to, but from many other human beings who worked in the Supermarket, in Co-itrose: the music from the end of the film "Tip Gone" was playing in the background: "feel-good", "celebration" Hollywood end-of-film-music.

SUFFERING EXTREME: INCORRECTNESS SEXUAL OF HUMAN ENGLISH FEMALES NON-SEXULAESSES TYPING 137
Identity's Image was talking to one of the various Human English Female Non-Sexualess Incorrectess Sexuals/Sexual2s/Etcetera, or Hefn-siss/Hefn-sis2s/Etcetera. Identity's Image: "A number of other human beings, connected to you, have been THERE in your absence. Although i have spoken to a number of human beings, in the past, a number of times, in relation to a human being who is connected to that number of human beings, my current view is that i shall NEVER do any such thing again, i will NEVER talk to that number of other human beings, connected to you, who have been THERE in your absence. There is the risk of crime....there is always a risk of crime when speaking to another human being. With second- or third-hand information all sorts of things can go wrong. Etcetera. It's YOUR responsibility. Yet still this number of other human beings continue to be THERE. Show up YOURSELF, so that i can talk to you. How long are you going to lie to yourself?" She started talking. "You're infERIOR to me: that's why i won't taint the aura that encircles me by coming anywhere near you." Identity's Image: "I can be quite STUBBORN."

Pickford-Gordon

Since: Sep 09

343

London, UK

Reply »

|
Report Abuse
|
Judge it!
|
#118
Wednesday Aug 1

SUFFERING EXTREME: INCORRECTNESS SEXUAL OF HUMAN ENGLISH FEMALES NON-SEXULAESSES TYPING 138
1.
Identity's Image was talking to Human English Female Non-Sexualess Incorrectess Sexual2, or Hefn-sis2. Identity's Image: "You don't mean as much to me as "Awww, now that's not very pleasant now is it!?" Hefn-sis2, but you're also one of the small number, possibly only 4 or 5 or so, Hefn-sis2s. You might be Hefn-sis3, but it depends on who you've done sexual things with. I'm not sure. In any case, you mean a lot to me." Hefn-sis2: "I have some sort of emotional/mental, or even sexual, thing with this tall guy, who does NOT look young." Identity's Image: "No, he doesn't look young, you're right. Well i mean he's not "young-looking" in the sense of "young-looking" that i comPLAIN about with regard to a number of guys that i've come across, but he's not elderly either."
2.
Hefn-sis2: "Well there you go, goodBYE." She started walking off. Identity's Image: "You know there's this guy who i'm still trying to understand exactly why he was acting this way or that way towards me-it could be nothing though. But anyway THAT guy, DOES look young, and i saw him flirt with you, and you flirted back. His flirting towards you might or might not have been some kind of "mask"? Or guilt could be involved? Or it could be nothing? Or it could be what i fear, or something to that extent? I need to analyse the notes. But in any case, you flirted with him, and he flirted with you: i need to know if you've done anything sexual with him. And you KNOW-i SAW you-what sort of "vibe" i gave out to you when you did it, darling. It's funny how the concept of a Human-English-Male-like-figure , like me, swallowing lethal medication, or something which conveys such a message, such a threat, can be transmitted using the art of the "vibe"....isn't it. That's what i did to you then. And i saw that you felt it, you received the message, from me. Now i remember how eagerly you came up to me, smiling, saying "hi", so bright, blushing, that "no thank you," even though you wanted to say "yes". And you were always there-but with me waiting for YOU to use one of the standard Post Office checkout tills, instead of the "special" one. And i KNOW that you CAN use the standard Post Office checkout tills, because i SAW you use one of them, the last time that i saw you. I waited and i waited for you to use the "standard" ones, but you didn't do it....so i started going to the "special" till, at the Post Office."
3.
Hefn-sis2: "I wanna take it BACK! I wanna take it all BACK! My flirtations with you....before you told me your name and i read a number of your Internet Posts." Identity's Image: "Well, it's too late, for STARTERS. I doubt whether i will ever forget you. And secondly, they're just words, typed words on a screen, Hefn-sis2. It's not fair to judge me by my Internet Posts. Never judge a man by his "vibe", or by his Internet Posts!" Identity's Image smiled at her, but she wasn't smiling back. Identity's Image cast his mind back. He remembered how she USED to smile, so animated, when she came out for Identity's Image, but after she had read his Internet Posts she was....she was all serious. It was like she knew that she had to go out, but she didn't enjoy it at all. She knew that it had to be HER that DID IT.

Pickford-Gordon

Since: Sep 09

343

London, UK

Reply »

|
Report Abuse
|
Judge it!
|
#119
Wednesday Aug 1

SUFFERING EXTREME: INCORRECTNESS SEXUAL OF HUMAN ENGLISH FEMALES NON-SEXULAESSES TYPING 138
4.
Identity's Image: "Look i mean people should be concerned with REALITY, and with you know, SERIOUS stuff, but YOU AND ME, we can still be like we used to be, we can still smile, and you can still be bright and flirty. You mean a LOT to me."
Hefn-sis2: "It's like this whole new world that you've exposed me to, with your Internet Posts. I looked at you, and others have looked at you, and there is NO, WAY, that they could believe that someone who looks like you could produce such Internet Posts. If i hadn't seen your card i wouldn't have believed it myself. I was STUNNED! And STILL AM!"
5.
Identity's Image: "A lot of other girls have run away after reading my Internet Posts." He moved closer to her, and stroked her right shoulder. "You never ran, though. It gives me HOPE. And you're HOT, of course! There's no one else in the whole building for me, and possibly, apart from the two Hefn-siss, and maybe one, two, maybe three other Hefn-sis2s-or maybe not-....that's where you lie, in how important you are to me, how much you mean to me. You shouldn't have started anything-emotional, mental, sexual, whatever-with anyone else, i mean am i "no good"?" Identity's Image paused for a number of seconds before continuing. "Anyway, i should BE THERE on my "next" usual day, but if i'm not i WILL be in on this day or that day....i'll TRY to make it on the day, or days, that i usually go in on, or something. If not then i'll be there on this day or on that day. Talk to me, etcetera, and have sexual intercourse with me, next time."

Category 5 Chimpout

Cheltenham, UK

Reply »

|
Report Abuse

Judge it!

#120

Thursday Aug 2

ANUSOL is highly recommended for piles, Pickers.

NArseZItralian Squealout

Gloucester, UK

Reply »

Report Abuse

Judge it!

#121

Thursday Aug 2

  Category 5 Chimpout wrote:

ANUSOL is highly recommended for piles, Pickers.
Yes, believe this homo, he speaks from experience.
He tried it the 'other' way.

Pickford-Gordon

 Since: Sep 09

343

London, UK

Reply »

Report Abuse

Judge it!

#122
Friday Aug 3

SUFFERING EXTREME: INCORRECTNESS SEXUAL OF HUMAN ENGLISH FEMALE NON-SEXULAESSES TYPING 139
1.
Identity's Image was in the same building as Human English Female Non-Sexualess Incorrectess Sexual2, or Hefn-sis2, or "Awww, that's not very pleasant now is it!?" He was talking to her. He had said one sentence or so, had been given only 5 or 10 seconds or so-IF THAT-with Hefn-sis2, whom he loved, when this blonde woman suddenly came up, and stood on Hefn-sis2's left: Identity's Image knew that it was because of him that the blonde woman had gone over there and stood next to Hefn-sis2. Identity's Image was now unable to talk any more with Hefn-sis2-except for "transaction talk": the blonde woman had taken time etcetera out of Identity's Image's LIFE.
2.
Identity's Image: "Why can't people just leave us alone, huh?" Hatred, Sexual, or H,s: "The United Kingdom And Ireland is nothing but a lying-to-itself, hypocrite, one-big-lie, failure-to-change, primitive, shallow, chit-chat, humour, escapist, plastic, moral, vacuum, STANDstill. Most things have to be explained to most people in the United Kingdom And Ireland." Talks, Comforts, or T,c: "You have to stop insulting enormous numbers of things United Kingdom And Ireland, H,s. Things are much worse in most, or more than most, other countries, or so it appears to me at present." H,s: "Excuse me while i get down on my knees and kiss the United Kingdom And Ireland's A++." T,c turned away from H,s.
3.
T,c: "Identity's Image, you've just got to HANG IN THERE." Identity's Image: "This is why i would probably kill myself as quickly as possible if i had some cyanide right now or something. I mean, where is this so-called "desire to act correctly" in the workers at this place? They're BOTHERING ME: i just want to talk to Hefn-sis2, and they keep BOTHERING ME. I don't get very much TIME with her....and the small amount of time that i had with her that day was more than cut in half after that blonde woman came and eavesdropped on us." T,c: "It's only because they don't underSTAND. If they have underSTANDING, then you'll see that "desire to act correctly", and a WONDERFUL desire TOO. Then you'll see that they have souls." H,s started laughing.

SUFFERING EXTREME: INCORRECTNESS SEXUAL OF HUMAN ENGLISH FEMALE NON-SEXULAESSES TYPING 140
1.
Identity's Image was in the same building as Human English Female Non-Sexualess Incorrectess Sexual2, or Hefn-sis2, or "Awww, that's not very pleasant now is it!?" He was talking to her, to someone who was probably, if not certainly, his Number 1 choice out of all of the Hefn-sis2s. There were only 2 Hefn-siss: "What might i giveyou madarling?"....and that other one.
2.
Hefn-sis2: "I feel creeped out because you post on the Internet, for the reason, or reasons, that you post on the Internet, for ME." Identity's Image: "I've only been getting a meagre amount of time with you per day....but hopefully that will change very very soon, right!?" Hefn-sis2 did that cute thing that she did, on occasion: Identity's Image LOVED THAT....and he loved HER. Identity's Image: "I have to communicate with you. If we spent more time together, then I wouldn't ha-" Identity's Image paused: he didn't finish what he was going to say.

SUFFERING EXTREME: INCORRECTNESS SEXUAL OF HUMAN ENGLISH FEMALES NON-SEXULAESSES TYPING 141
Identity's Image was talking to Human English Female Non-Sexualess Incorrectess Sexual2, or Hefn-sis2, or "Awww, that's not very pleasant now is it!?" Hefn-sis2: "That goes against the official Public-Private-Partnership Company Corporation Regulations of this place: i'm not allowed to....TALK. MUCH." Identity's Image: "Look i now have to say what i was going to say to you back THEN, NEXT TIME! If you hadn't said that, then there could have been progress BACK THEN....instead there has to be progress NEXT TIME."

Pickford-Gordon

Since: Sep 09

343

London, UK

Reply »

|
Report Abuse
|
Judge it!
|
#123
Friday Aug 3

SUFFERING EXTREME: INCORRECTNESS SEXUAL OF HUMAN ENGLISH FEMALE NON-SEXULAESSES TYPING 142
1.
Identity's Image was talking to Human English Female Non-Sexualess Incorrectess Sexual2, or Hefn-sis2, or "Awww, that's not very pleasant now is it!?" Identity's Image: "There are laws that protect the right of workers to work, so that managers can't do whatever they want with regard to workers. There are laws to protect the right of customers to....be customers, that's what my Country Manager, Duncan Carterllins, told me, if i remember correctly....yeah, that's what he said. Myself and him are going to legally take things further with regard to that Manager, of a certain place, if he doesn't undo what he's done to me, or something like that, etcetera. I've already posted significantly in the "Incorrectness of Duncan Carterllins,", "The Conartist/Terry Group Is 100% Incorrect," and other, related, threads. My thread with regard to how popular my threads are shows that enormous numbers of human beings in the United Kingdom And Ireland have read them. Recently, the sort of results that we can expect in 2015 have been revealed to us: in Bardfold, the Conartist/Terry group vote was reduced by 20%, or something like that....not many people voted for them, and Gordon Garrally won by a comfortable margin....in 2015 it will politically be all over for this group....the only question is is it going to be politically all over in 2015 for Duncan Carterllins himSELF, after he leaves the group." Identity's Image paused for a number of seconds.
2.
Identity's Image: "So don't be afraid my love." Hefn-sis2: "I'm not afraid of any of the managers. I just didn't want to answer that question." Identity's Image: "You know why i asked that question, don't you? And what i would have asked after it! You see that question sort of "leads" to another one....which "leads" to another one." Hefn-sis2: "Maybe you should have skipped that question and just come out with....well one of the questions that it leads to. Or something like that." There was silence between them for a number of seconds after that. Identity's Image: "You had me really scared when you said that! I mean that came across as somewhat cold, you know! Not TOO cold, but quite cold nonetheless! I think that i just shut up for the rest of our time together that day after you had said that, IN FEAR!" Hefn-sis2: "I AM a woman, so it's natural for me to attack men, now and again. Especially you, Identity's Image. Not much, though." Identity's Image: "We need to talk without anyone eavesdropping next time. Then meet up outside of your work hours and have sexual intercourse etcetera. I love you."

Tell me when this thread is updated:
(Registration is not required)

Add to my Tracker

Send me an email

Showing posts 101 - 120 of 135

< prev page

|

next page >

Go to last page|Jump to page:1 2 3 45 6 7

Type in your comments below

Name
(appears on your post)

Comments

Characters left: 4000

Type the numbers you see in the image on the right:

Please note by clicking on "Post Comment" you acknowledge that you have read the Terms of Service and the comment you are posting is in compliance with such terms. Be polite.Inappropriate posts may be removed by the moderator. Send us your feedback.

56Users are viewing theUnited Kingdom Forumright now

Search the United Kingdom Forum:

Topic

Updated

Last By

Comments

A Frenchman leading NATO

4 min

Kevlar

52

why is Ronan called "old Walrus face" by Russia...

4 min

Alexey25

19

Language learning call by Tories

15 min

ronan

4

Bob Hoskins retiring

17 min

ronan

3

Free Wi-Fi catches on with NYC's subway riders

23 min

Bama Yankee

2

Kik

29 min

Lyndseymarie

37

Bristol Evening Post published Church worker 's... (Nov '11)

1 hr

Shane

27

Topix UK taken over by Islamophobes

2 hr

jodi_e

208

See all threads in the United Kingdom forum »

What's your favorite Summer Olympics event? Vote now on the Summer Olympics Map.

United Kingdom News
:Second arrest over Waugh murder
:Theatre Production Lifts the Curtain on the Sto...
:Bins searched in missing Tia hunt
:Rent a backyard in NYC for $100 an hour
:Halstead: Woman convicted of killing boyfriend ...
:Miliband: Unemployment a key issue

¦Famous NY diner relocated to Wyoming up for sale
¦Bob Hoskins retiring
¦Taxi murder victim mother of three
¦148m EuroMillions jackpot could make tickethold...
¦Gillian Anderson splits from boyfriend
¦British tourist's body recovered from Canadian ...

More United Kingdom News from Topix »

Topix Politix App

Take your stand on the issues you care about.

Using an iPhone?

Keep the Topix forums in your pocket
with the new, free Topix App.

Daily Horoscope for August 9

Leo

Busy? You bet. The trouble is that there simply won't be enough hours in the day for getting everything done, and as a result you'll quickly get in a flap. Once that happens, spats and quarrels look more than likely, thanks to your lack of patience and the temporary departure of your sense of humor. But don't be horrid to people just for the sake of it.

Get your Horoscope »

United Kingdom
News
Forums & Polls
Real-Time News

Explore More Topix
Home Page
Forums
Top Stories
Most Popular
Issue Maps
US News

US Cities list
World News
World Countries list
Politics
Celebrities
Business
Finance
Autos
Sports
Sci-Tech
Electronics
Entertainment
Movies
Music
Television
Video Games
Health
Life
Arts
Food
Home
Travel
Offbeat
Site Map / All Topics

About Topix
About Us
Media Kit
Topix Blog
Press Room
RSS Newsfeeds
Law Enforcement
School Officials
Cyber-bullying Resources
Jobs
FAQ
Privacy Policy
Terms of Service
Feedback?
Report Abuse?

Local Classifieds & Listings

Reach Local customers. Post a classified listing for your business. Promote job, auto, rental, and local event listings.

Learn more »

Join the Topix Community
¡Create your own profile, complete with quick links to your favorite topics.
¡Personalize your forum posts with your photo and hometown.
¡Exchange Personal Messages with other registered users.

Sign up today! »

Topix Politix »

Feedback?
Comments made yesterday: 110,919 Total comments across all topics: 181,608,492

Copyright ©2012 Topix LLC

Local News: United Kingdom

|

Sign Up

|

Sign In

123

2012 Summer Olympics News

Summer Olympics
APNewsBreak: Ex-CEO feels 'validation' as US track team succee...

Politix
Is TSA too intrusive for air travelers?

Home
Forums
Top Stories
Popular
Local
Summer Olympics
US
Politics
World
Sports
Entertainment
Offbeat
Other

United Kingdom
News
Forums & PollsSuffering Extreme: In...

Real-Time News

Suffering Extreme: Incorrectness Sexual Of HEFN-Ses Typings

Posted in the United Kingdom Forum

Share

Read
144 Comments
Add to my Tracker

More United Kingdom Discussions »

Comments (Page 7)

Showing posts121 - 140 of144

< prev page

|

next page >

Go to last page|Jump to page:1 2 3 45 6 78

Pickford-Gordon

Since: Sep 09

353

London, UK

Reply »

Report Abuse

Judge it!

#124
Friday Aug 3

SUFFERING EXTREME: INCORRECTNESS SEXUAL OF HUMAN ENGLISH FEMALE NON-SEXULAESSES TYPING 143
1.
Identity's Image was talking to Human English Female Non-Sexualess Incorrectess Sexual2, or Hefn-sis2, or "Awww, that's not very pleasant now is it!?" She approached Identity's Image, and stood a short distance away from him. She was fronting him in a sexual manner, and he could see how beautiful she was. "Well Hefn-sis2! That's some sexual "vibe" that you're giving me!" thought Identity's Image. The concept of the "vibe" seemed to make her get emotional after a short period of time, or perhaps it made her think about Identity's Image's Internet Posts: she rushed off for a short, or shortish, period of time before coming back.
2.
Later, she had invited Identity's Image back to her home: he was in her bedroom. She stood quite close to Identity's Image, fronting him. Hefn-sis2: "You felt the "vibe" that i gave out to you back in the building, didn't you? You felt the "vibe" that we had together back then, didn't you? Do you know what SORT of "sexual vibe" we had back then, Identity's Image?" Identity's Image: "Yes: it was you sucking my p+nis, wasn't it." Hefn-sis2 squatted down in front of Identity's Image, so that her head was level with his erect p+nis. Her mouth went over it: she sucked it quickly, her head moving up and down. They made love later.

Pickford-Gordon

Since: Sep 09

353

London, UK

Reply »

Report Abuse

Judge it!

#125
Friday Aug 3

SUFFERING EXTREME: INCORRECTNESS SEXUAL OF HUMAN ENGLISH FEMALE NON-SEXULAESSES TYPING 144
I saw my lover in the light:
She rushed to help me, young and bright.
She thought me, perhaps, of interest nice;
It had been fate, roll of the dice.
We twain had vanquished what was fake;
No lie shall be the love we make.
She gives me hope, appears for me:
I wish the others would let us be.
Last time a "vibe"-i felt it, strong-
Came over me, all nice and long.
She gives me hope, and soon bright fate
Must give to us a happy date.
She changes rapidly, and soon
She shall perfect. One day at noon
We both shall moan, our bodies hot
And sweating: great shall be our lot.
If we can get together, then
The problems of the world, with pen,
Can all be solved, with time to spare.
If love can beat depression, bare
Shall be the truth that humans bring
To suffering, that all shall fling
Away for good. Pained pasts shall fade,
Because of the great joy we made.

Pickford-Gordon

Since: Sep 09

353

London, UK

Reply »

Report Abuse

Judge it!

#126
Saturday Aug 4

SUFFERING EXTREME: INCORRECTNESS SEXUAL OF HUMAN ENGLISH FEMALE NON-SEXULAESSES TYPING 145
"EVERYBODY: i have FOUND HEFN-SIS: i have FOUND "BRINGYOU, MALUV"." As soon as he had announced that,

Identity's Image was rushed from all sides by vast numbers of Human English Males and Human English Females; they were shouting, and they strained towards Identity's Image, bombarding him with questions, demands, cries of encouragement, and other things; Identity's Image was unable to move his arms and legs, let alone take steps due to how they had pressed him in. Identity's Image: "SPACE!! I need some SPACE!! BACK!! I can't f+cking MOVE!!" The crowd moved away from him somewhat....before a Human English Male started shouting at him. "Where WAS SHE!?" Identity's Image: "The explanation is really quite simple: she had gone to London and had gotten lost. London is after all an enormous city, and many of the streets can, perhaps, to one or two people, be sort of like a MAZE. I WENT to London, FOUND her, and came all of the way back here with HER: she had been wandering around the streets for quite some time." There was shouting, cheering, and whistling, from everyone in the enormous crowd that had surrounded Identity's Image; the music from the end of the film "Tip Gone" was playing in the background: "feel-good", "celebration" Hollywood end-of-film-music. Identity's Image was hoisted up onto the shoulders of a number of Human English Males, and was carried upon their shoulders here and there before being put down again. He had found Human English Female Non-Sexualess Incorrectess Sexual, or Hefn-sis, or ""What might i giveyou maluv?": he had found hope itSELF once more.

SUFFERING EXTREME: INCORRECTNESS SEXUAL OF HUMAN ENGLISH FEMALE NON-SEXULAESSES TYPING 146
Identity's Image was talking to Human English Female Non-Sexualess Incorrectess Sexual, or Hefn-sis, or ""What might i giveyou maluv?", at the Gymnasium. Identity's Image: "I'll do, within reason, etcetera, whatever you want, okay!? You're the boss, as you proved by the terrible fright your absence gave me....and you've also proved it in other ways before that too. Just don't hurt me anymore....don't leave me again. I love you. HEY! You SAW how obediant i was! You're in charge." Identity's Image looked at her fearfully.

SUFFERING EXTREME: INCORRECTNESS SEXUAL OF HUMAN ENGLISH FEMALE NON-SEXULAESSES TYPING 147
I entered the room, and i saw hope:
My expression brightened when it dawned on me.
My controlling lover, can't you see:
That i need you so that i cope.
Soon, great shall be our joy, the scope
Of our company. Now we must seek
The union: love shall from our bodies leak
Into ourselves. May i nevermore mope.
Deny your instinct that gives me hate,
And we shall soon go past our gate.
My despair has lifted slightly. Can
You see my value as a man?
Next time we must forge on ahead:
I dream of you and me in bed.

SUFFERING EXTREME: INCORRECTNESS SEXUAL OF HUMAN ENGLISH FEMALE NON-SEXULAESSES TYPING 148
Identity's Image was talking to Human English Female Non-Sexualess Incorrectess Sexual, or Hefn-sis, or ""What might i giveyou maluv?", at the Gymnasium. Identity's Image was whispering into Hefn-sis's ear from behind, just like she wanted him to right then. Identity's Image: "You look absolutely fantastic my love, and how you were dressed teases me, i get excited just thinking about you. I mean....i SAID that you looked older than 16....but not too much older: you're still young, and beautiful, may you stay beautiful for a long time to come." Identity's Image was kissing her right cheek, and the right side of her neck, as he pressed his body against hers from the back: her head moved back against his right shoulder, and his hands were stroking her body. Identity's Image: "But we have to act soon, my love. Be with me soon. I love you."

Pickford-Gordon

Since: Sep 09

353

London, UK

Reply »

|
Report Abuse
|
Judge it!
|
#127
Saturday Aug 4

SUFFERING EXTREME: INCORRECTNESS SEXUAL OF HUMAN ENGLISH FEMALE NON-SEXULAESSES TYPING 149
Identity's Image was talking to Human English Female Non-Sexualess Incorrectess Sexual, or Hefn-sis, or ""What might i giveyou maluv?", at the Gymnasium. Identity's Image: "Don't judge a man by his "vibe"! I don't really want to do this "vibe" thing any more....but let's talk about the "vibes" between us that were successful, as opposed to the ones that failed. I have a lot of hatred, but i'm in control of myself....just not my "vibe self"." Identity's Image paused for a number of seconds before continuing. "These are the "vibes". I sensed you put one of your breasts in my mouth, at the start....then you maybe straddled me, and put your arms around me. There was a lot of you putting your arms around me. Then, as you turned your back, you gently sat down, from behind, onto my erect p+nis. Then i felt the strangest thing: you actually snogged me, in a sensuous, somewhat, dare i say, LOVING, manner! I was shocked that you'd give me such a "vibe": i thought, "Is this the same person? Is she ILL, maybe? A kiss? ROmance!!??" If you say ROmance, you KNOW that there's no way that i'd believe you." Hefn-sis: "I HAVE been changing: you mightn't be able to see how MUCH i've changed, for the better, but i HAVE changed....and i like all of your romance s+it-i mean your, er, roMANTIC, er, er, maTERIAL! YES! MaTERIAL, that's a nice word!" She smiled at him. He smiled back, and then they were silent, as she realised that it was HER TURN. "I felt a few "vibes" from YOU as well, Identity's Image. I felt you kiss me from behind, kissing my neck....and then i stood still, i WANTED you to give me something: i then felt you kiss me, and approach me, with both of us fronting each other. You started trying to enter me as we were standing up, but then YOU, QUITE gently placed me down onto an imaginary bed, on my back. I can't remember which one of the two happened: whether my legs were bent with you thrusting into me with my legs either side of you....or whether my legs were straight up against your chest as your p+nis entered my v+gina." They looked at each other in silence.

SUFFERING EXTREME: INCORRECTNESS SEXUAL OF HUMAN ENGLISH FEMALE NON-SEXULAESSES TYPING 150
Light is a woman, i saw her true:
She heaves for me, my pleasant hue.
Whatever, perhaps, she might have thought,
She is now back, she has been brought
By fate, which smiles upon me now,
To be my love: we must not bow
To wrong. May she appreciate
Devotion, as i stand and wait
For her to calm herself, and see
That she has no real hate with me:
I have done nothing wrong, i think.
She comes to save me from the brink
Of nothingness. May i awake
With her, for her. We both must make
Our dreams come true. She must be mine:
She is a woman great, and fine.

SUFFERING EXTREME: INCORRECTNESS SEXUAL OF HUMAN ENGLISH FEMALE NON-SEXULAESSES TYPING 151
Identity's Image was talking to Human English Female Non-Sexualess Incorrectess Sexual, or Hefn-sis, or "What might i giveyou maluv?", at the Gymnasium. Identity's Image: "I wanted to say more, but there were other people there: it's better not to involve other people when we talk about how you've lied to me, and about certain guys that have been flirting, or more than flirting, with you. Let's talk alone next time. But, i mean, you're the boss, within reason, or something like that, as you know."

Pickford-Gordon

Since: Sep 09

353

London, UK

Reply »

|
Report Abuse
|
Judge it!
|
#128
Saturday Aug 4

SUFFERING EXTREME: INCORRECTNESS SEXUAL OF HUMAN ENGLISH FEMALE NON-SEXULAESSES TYPING 152
1.
Talks, Comforts, or T,c, Hatred, Sexual, or H,s, and Identity's Image were talking to Human English Female Non-Sexualess Incorrectess Sexual, or Hefn-sis, or "What might i giveyou maluv?", at the Gymnasium. Hefn-sis: "I just can't seem to stop hating, at times, Identity's Image, and i don't really understand WHY." H,s: "It's because you're PUNY: SMALL." Identity's Image: "DON'T YOU SAY THAT TO HER!! YOU TAKE that BACK!!" H,s: "I mean, Hefn-sis, that IS true about you, although, as you can see, Identity's Image really doesn't like how i've put it. The thing is, beCAUSe you're PUNY, THAT means that what you do, is think in terms of "being told what to DO,", i "don't like being told what to do". That's WHY you at times hate Identity's Image. I'm not trying to hurt you, it's just that i want you to underSTAND. You need to understand, and think about all of the suffering that you've caused Identity's Image, how unfair you've been towards him. You seem to maybe have problems remembering this and that, when Identity's Image remembers a vast number of things that relate to you and him."
2.
Identity's Image: "Hefn-sis, my love....firstly i'm not inSISting that you do this or anything, i mean you're the boss, i love you, and i can't take you leaving me again....but i just want to say that you should maybe read a VEERY small number of parts of the book "American Psycho" by Bret Easton Ellis, which IS VERY VERY exTREME, or maybe just watch the film, which isn't that extreme. See the way that enormous numbers of the characters TALK, and beHAVE, in the book, or the film....can't you see, my love, that that's exactly how YOU and a number of your fellow workers talk, and behave, as well. I mean that's NOT REAL, you know? SURface. "INside doesn't matter." How have you gotten caught up in that sort of thing, huh? Bret Easton Ellis is probably strongly opposed to that exact same thing, people talking without really saying anything, etcetera. Of course, if you decide to do this, you can research Bret Easton Ellis himself-on Wikipedia and/or other places-to find out who he IS, find out exactly WHO has created the material." Identity's Image paused for a number of seconds before continuing.
3.
Identity's Image: "The THING IS, we have a lot of things to talk about: WHAT GOOD did the last half hour, or hour or whatever we spent doing that "chit chat" with the others....what good did that do? What progress was made? I....i wanted to ask you if i could walk with you, at the end there....BUT I WAS JUST SO SCARED, i thought, maybe you'll hate me if i say that, or something. Some of the things that you do to me are just so SUDDEN, and i don't know exactly what you're OKAY with me saying to you and what you're NOT OKAY with me saying to you, desPITE the fact that you told me that i could say more or less anything to you, and then you complained to a number of authority figures about me. You told me that you wouldn't do a

Hefn-sis2....but you did. Let's talk alone next time. And i asked you if you were going to come with me to the HARBOUR, and you said no. It means so much to me, you and me talking."

Pickford-Gordon

Since: Sep 09

353

London, UK

Reply »

|
Report Abuse
|
Judge it!
|
#129
Saturday Aug 4

SUFFERING EXTREME: INCORRECTNESS SEXUAL OF HUMAN ENGLISH FEMALE NON-SEXULAESSES TYPING 152
4.
T,c: "My current view is that you are indeed highly susceptible to OTHER PEOPLE, Hefn-sis. What i want from you, Hefn-sis, is a DESIRE FOR YOU TO CHANGE FOR THE BETTER. And i saw it at the end there. That was good! You said goodbye to Identity's Image, instead of ignoring him like you have been doing, too much. That's a START. NO! MORE than a START! Good! It is correct for human beings to spend enormous amounts of time-or spacetime-on their own: human beings need to continue to have their brains sort themselves out, which is what happens when human beings spend time alone. And i have also observed how you still, to one extent or another, on the inside, HATE Identity's Image. The truth is the truth, Hefn-sis. Identity's Image doesn't have a problem with the truth, and I don't have a problem with the truth." H,s: "And i AM the f+ckinTRUTH, and i f+ckin dish it out EAGERLY, hehhehHEH!" T,c turned to glare at H,s for a small number of seconds before turning away from him and continuing. T,c: "It's how you've been doing things that has been WRONG, Hefn-sis. Identity's Image hasn't done anything to deserve this. With regard to the chitchat, i mean don't you think that that was just a waste of time, or spacetime? Identity's Image has a LOT that he needs to talk to you about, that he can't talk to you in a "group" about."
5.
Hefn-sis: "T,c, my brain tells me that because Identity's Image cares so much, because he puts so much effort into me....because of that, that means that there's some CATCH to being with him. There must be some problem with him because he's trying so HARD with me." T,c: "That is A LIE, Hefn-sis. Okay? There is NO CATCH. You have a wealth of information about him that can be understood by yourself from his Internet Posts, and from his book, etcetera. You should have a significant understanding of him. The Sex Worker that he had sex with very recently didn't have a problem with him, and neither did more than 25 other Sex Workers....and many more than that of course. Anyway! You have data about him. Let me say this about Identity's Image: Identity's Image is someone who has rejected, well, MANY things about the United Kingdom And Ireland. He is UNIQUE, Hefn-sis." Hefn-sis: "Everybody i f+cking KNOW keeps telling me how unique his goddamn Internet Posts are, and how unique he is. You don't have to tell me. We f+cking MORE than GET IT."

Pickford-Gordon

Since: Sep 09

353

London, UK

Reply »

|
Report Abuse
|
Judge it!
|
#130
Saturday Aug 4

SUFFERING EXTREME: INCORRECTNESS SEXUAL OF HUMAN ENGLISH FEMALE NON-SEXULAESSES TYPING 152
6.
H,s: "You two naIVE, WEAKling, f+cking PUSSIES-compared to me of course-interrupted me when i was talking to Hefn-sis about her PUNYNESS. Can i get back to that? Thank you, pairaLOSERS." He paused for a small number of seconds before continuing. "I can empathise with you with regard to not wanting to do what people tell you, and proceeding at your own pace. People who respect their own bodies have a right to talk to my friend Identity's Image about such things....AND YOU'RE NOT ONE OF THEM, HEFN-SIS." Identity's Image started shouting at H,s. "YOU DON'T TALK TO HER LIKE THAT!!" Then Identity's Image started sobbing. "Now you've done it, H,s. She's just gonna leave or something like last time. And i can't....i just don't want to live, why can't she just stay put, huh!? I can't do this, i can't doit." H,s: "Alrightalright, i'll TRYANDBENICE, okay!? I'll be GOOD." H,s turned back to Hefn-sis. H,s: "The sexual things have hurt Identity's Image, Hefn-sis. You shouldn't have done the things that you've done to him, so him telling you not to do this or that is something that sort of doesn't exist, if you understand what i'm saying. You are GUILTY, Hefn-sis....but you can reverse the suffering, and not be guilty with regard to Identity's Image any more, to one extent or another....perhaps even mostly or more. It's incorrectness, or crime: lying breaking promises, using fake laws, sort of telling Identity's Image that he's NO GOOD by doing a number of sexual things with a number of people, instead of with him, remember all the way back then. He wants you to not hurt him anymore. Also. You maybe....i think i saw that you LACK, to one extent or another, aWAREness of others, at a few times, or more than at a few times. You should not only have a significant awareness of others, but you should always be trying to elevate yourself in comparison to all of the other Human English Females in the United Kingdom And Ireland. Do you think that you compare favourably to the other Human English Females in the United Kingdom And Ireland, Hefn-sis?"
7.
Identity's Image: "Well, H,s you PSYCHO, regardless of how she compares at this event in spacetime-RIGHT NOW-to the other Human English Females, she's GOING TO soar way way aBOVE them in value, be one of the BEST, perhaps THE BEST Human English Female in my mind, as soon as she starts having sexual intercourse with me etcetera. We'll go beYOND happiness, together, and the suffering that she has caused me shall thus be reversed, or something like that, WHO KNOWS how much of it shall be reversed."

Pickford-Gordon

Since: Sep 09

353

London, UK

Reply »

Report Abuse

Judge it!

#131
Saturday Aug 4

SUFFERING EXTREME: INCORRECTNESS SEXUAL OF HUMAN ENGLISH FEMALE NON-SEXULAESSES TYPING 153
Identity's Image was talking to Human English Female Non-Sexualess Incorrectess Sexual, or Hefn-sis, or "What might i giveyou maluv?", at the Gymnasium. Identity's Image: "All of this for you, my love. Talk to me next time, and have sexual intercourse with me, etcetera. I love you."

See more stories

45 min
4
Do You Know More Than Most Voters?

2012 Quiz shows many are sadly ill-informed

2 hr
8
Democratic Convention to Feature Select Republicans

2012 Early draft outlines how Dems plan the rest of campaign season

Faloola Chong

Northwich, UK

Reply »

Report Abuse

Judge it!

#132
Sunday Aug 5

i saw my love
walking down the aisle
and as he passed me by
he turned to me and gave me a smile
then the preacher, then the preacher
the preacher joined their hands
and all the people
the people began to stand
when i shouted "it should have been me
no, it should have been me
you know it should have been me
baby how can you do this to me"

Pickford-Gordon

Since: Sep 09

353

London, UK

Reply »

Report Abuse

Judge it!

#133
Monday Aug 6

SUFFERING EXTREME: INCORRECTNESS SEXUAL OF HUMAN ENGLISH FEMALE NON-SEXULAESSES TYPING 154
1.
Identity's Image was in the Supermarket Co-itrose; he went up to a guy who was slightly, somewhat, but not that much, or something like that, "young-looking"; this guy spoke with a slight accent, thought Identity's Image. "There are no more on the shelf, so i'd like you to go and get me a "Biddendens' Pear"" said Identity's Image. "The Non-Alcoholic Biddendens' Pear?" asked the guy. "Yes," answered Identity's Image. "We only do the alcoholic Biddendens Pear, we don't do the non-alcoholic one," answered the guy quickly, and confidently. "I've purchased the Non-Alcoholic Biddendens' Pear from here before, i get it

a lot," said Identity's Image. "No we definitely don't have the Non-Alcoholic Biddendens' Pear" said the guy: the guy had said that very confidently to Identity's Image. Identity's Image: "Let me see the List Of All Of The Items That Are Stocked At Co-itrose." "It's the same in the List," the guy probably said. Identity's Image: "Okay, well i just want to see it." They looked at the List, and saw the Non-Alcoholic Biddendens' Pear there. There does not exist an Alcoholic Biddendens' Pear, for the Supermarket Co-itrose. "I'm so sorry sir. But you see that's the NEW List, in the OLD List there was just the Alcoholic Biddendens' Pear and not the Non-Alcoholic Biddendens' Pear," lied the guy, with the same confident tone.

2.

Identity's Image was in the same building as Human English Female Non-Sexualess Incorrectess Sexual, or Hefn-sis, or "What might i giveyou maluv?", at the Gymnasium. He saw that guy from Co-itrose there: he had started working there: he had worked there for only 1 month, and already Hefn-sis's instincts etcetera were coming out. The guy was wearing a green "party hat". "Darling you look so sexy in that party hat." Hefn-sis went over to him, put her arms around him, stroked his visage, and took the "party hat" off of his head. Later, as Hefn-sis was hugging a girl, she gave him some kind of "look": he smiled at her with humour. They often spoke in a conspirational way.

3.

Later, Identity's Image was sitting with Hefn-sis, another guy who had said-after Identity's Image had asked to sit down with them and had been ignored by the others-that Identity's Image could join them, Hefn-sis2 who often spoke about her Mexican boyfriend, and the guy who had lied to him at Co-itrose. The guy who had said that Identity's Image could join them left early. "Let's all swap mobile telephone numbers, guy from Co-itrose!" declared probably Hefn-sis2, if it hadn't been Hefn-sis. They swapped numbers, the three of them, so that they all had each others' numbers. Identity's Image didn't dare to say this or that to Hefn-sis, and just sat there. "I have to go and do somethingorother. Is it okay if i leave you girls early?" asked the guy who had lied to Identity's Image at Co-itrose, to Hefn-sis and Hefn-sis2. "NO," said Hefn-sis firmly.

4.

Hefn-sis was eager to get away from Identity's Image: she didn't even finish what she was doing. "Are you guys off now?" asked Identity's Image. "Yes," someone said. "Are you taking the boat today?" Identity's Image asked Hefn-sis. "No," replied Hefn-sis. "Is it okay if i walk with you guys, to talk some more," asked Identity's Image. "NO," said Hefn-sis2 immediately, and firmly. "NO," said Hefn-sis, firmly, after Hefn-sis2 had said it. The two of them walked away from Identity's Image as quickly as they could, stopping a shortish distance away: the guy who had lied to Identity's Image at Co-itrose followed them. Both Hefn-sis and Hefn-sis2 saw that Identity's Image was just sitting there with tears in his eyes before they left: they just carried on laughing and joking and chitchatting.

Pickford-Gordon

Since: Sep 09

353

London, UK

Reply »

|
Report Abuse
|
Judge it!
|
#134
Monday Aug 6

SUFFERING EXTREME: INCORRECTNESS SEXUAL OF HUMAN ENGLISH FEMALE NON-SEXULAESSES

TYPING 155
Identity's Image was in the same building as Human English Female Non-Sexualess Incorrectess Sexual, or Hefn-sis, or "What might i giveyou maluv?", at the Gymnasium. "Well that's what women are like: they rule you, and you just have to go along with it," said the guy who had lied to Identity's Image at Co-itrose to him. "Yes and there's no way out AT THE MOMENT," answered Identity's Image. "I just want to be friends with you girls," said the guy who had lied to Identity's Image at Co-itrose, to Hefn-sis, and to Hefn-sis2, who often spoke about her Mexican boyfriend.

SUFFERING EXTREME: INCORRECTNESS SEXUAL OF HUMAN ENGLISH FEMALE NON-SEXULAESSES
TYPING 156
Identity's Image was in the same building as Human English Female Non-Sexualess Incorrectess Sexual, or Hefn-sis, or "What might i giveyou maluv?", at the Gymnasium. The guy who had lied to Identity's Image at Co-itrose put his green "party hat" on the head of this other girl who had started working there, flirtatiously: Identity's Image thought, "I suppose, MAYBE, that's good, or okay at least, perhaps: it means that he's not going to flirt with Hefn-sis then, is he. Him not doing anything more than he has already done with Hefn-sis is what matters the most to me." Then the guy stopped talking to this new girl, and spoke with Hefn-sis.

SUFFERING EXTREME: INCORRECTNESS SEXUAL OF HUMAN ENGLISH FEMALE NON-SEXULAESSES
TYPING 157
Identity's Image was at the Harbour, waiting for the boat. He was standing there: then from a distance he saw someone who might have been Human English Female Non-Sexualess Incorrectess Sexual, or Hefn-sis, or "What might i giveyou maluv?", sitting there. He tried hard to remember what she had been wearing, and failed to really remember: but, although he couldn't see her visage, since her head was turned to the side, the proportions of the individual, the hair, the arms, and the way that she was sitting, all made his brain increasingly tell him that this was HER, from all of the way over there, that it was Hefn-sis. He walked quickly over to her, with tears in his eyes, which dried when he reached her. "HEFN-SIS!" She had her headphones on, and appeared not to be aware that he was there, even when he stood right in front of her, looking down at her: he squatted slightly. "HEFN-SIS!" He caught her eye, or rather there was no way that she could not see him, or something like that. She removed her right headphone, and looked at him: she must surely have seen the expression of pure happiness on Identity's Image's visage. "Hefn-sis. Hi! Is it....okay if i join you?" Hefn-sis: "Your boat is at the other end." She paused for 1 second, moderate hatred flaring up into her eyes as she looked at Identity's Image. "SO NO." Without waiting for Identity's Image to say anything in return, she turned her head back down, putting her right headphone back into her ear. "Okay! I mean, whatever you want!" She probably didn't hear him. He walked away from her. He got on his boat.

Pickford-Gordon

Since: Sep 09

353

London, UK

Reply »

|
Report Abuse
|
Judge it!
|
#135
Monday Aug 6

SUFFERING EXTREME: INCORRECTNESS SEXUAL OF HUMAN ENGLISH FEMALE NON-SEXULAESSES TYPING 158
Identity's Image was talking to Human English Female Non-Sexualess Incorrectess Sexual, or Hefn-sis, or "What might i giveyou maluv?" at the Gymnasium. Identity's Image: "You're hurting me so much. Do you know how much it would mean to me, to feel your arms around me, to feel my arms around you, to feel your lips on mine? Do you know how much that would mean to me? And do you know how much it hurt me, last time, to see you all over that guy who lied to me at Co-itrose? Do you know how tempting it is for me, to just leave everything behind in book form, and also possibly Internet form, and just go to THAT COUNTRY? Maybe it's worth me getting a dictionary of that language, and taking the aeroplane journey there, etcetera. Maybe they'll legally let me escape, using suicide. Maybe they'll take away all the suffering that you, and the other Hefn-sis, etcetera, have caused me. I tried to do that "vibe" thing today, a little, even though it often goes wrong for me. You should have felt me enter your v+gina, as you were standing there, with your back to me, you should have felt me kiss you....in "vibe" speech. And last time, when you were at the Harbour, do you know how much it would have meant to me, to talk to you then? Why couldn't you have let me talk to you? I want the TRUTH, i can't stand not knowing THIS, and not knowing THAT with regard to you. And you say "boyfriend" as if it's the truth etcetera. But i KNOW, that if it's not an elaborate lie from you, which it might be, then it is the case that, IF you have a "boyfriend", that you're not faithful to him, or something like that, or at least not faithful using the normal definition of faithful. Or something like that, or something similar, etcetera. Give it to ME, what you've given to a number of Human Males. I love you. I need the TRUTH from you, why can't you let mc talk to you."

SUFFERING EXTREME: INCORRECTNESS SEXUAL OF HUMAN ENGLISH FEMALE NON-SEXULAESSES TYPING 159
Talks, Comforts, or T,c, and Hatred, Sexual, or H,s, were talking to Identity's Image about Human English Female Non-Sexualess Incorrectess Sexual, or Hefn-sis, or "What might i giveyou maluv?", and related issues. Identity's Image: "I'm just going to leave everything behind, blot out everything else, and keep on hitting various "politician buttons" using the Internet and other methods, etcetera, until one or more of them gives me legal suicide. She keeps hurting me, there's no hope: THERE IS NO HOPE." Identity's Image was crying. T,c: "Stay positive, Identity's Image, hang in there. You must admit that she's getting better, you must admit it." H,s: "Not because she has any desire to act correctly, T,c my dreamer friend: only because she fears CONSEQUENCES. She's just like an animal, not a human being with a soul. She CAN'T STOP HURTING, HATING, IDENTITY'S IMAGE, when he hasn't done anything to deserve it." T,c: "Nothing makes sense in life, for human beings, if human beings are not legally allowed to die: nothing makes sense at all."

Pickford-Gordon

Since: Sep 09

353

London, UK

Reply »

|
Report Abuse
|
Judge it!
|
#136
Monday Aug 6

SUFFERING EXTREME: INCORRECTNESS SEXUAL OF HUMAN ENGLISH FEMALE NON-SEXULAESSES TYPING 160
I saw my hope, but it was miles away.
She did not see that i was there,
But she must have seen the happiness bare
Upon my visage. I knew what to say,
But she said "no": thus kept at bay,
I felt so helpless, i felt weak.
When will she with me sincerely speak
About what needs be, without "nay".
She still looks beautiful, surely, seems
Not to have aged at all: she beams
Like heaven in my brain, as we
Stand close. I want her soon to see
And understand. When will we talk,
And to her reversal start to walk?

SUFFERING EXTREME: INCORRECTNESS SEXUAL OF HUMAN ENGLISH FEMALE NON-SEXULAESSES TYPING 161
Identity's Image was talking to Human English Female Non-Sexualess Incorrectess Sexual2, or Hefn-sis2, who often spoke about her Mexican boyfriend, at the Gymnasium. Identity's Image: "I'm still not sure if i'm allowed to dance with you: you probably don't remember but a number of authority figures, after you spoke to that number of authority figures, said that i was not allowed to dance with you: we used to dance all the time." Identity's Image paused for a number of seconds before continuing. "Why do you hate me, Hefn-sis2? You know i don't deserve it. I DO love Hefn-sis, or "What might i giveyou maluv?"."

SUFFERING EXTREME: INCORRECTNESS SEXUAL OF HUMAN ENGLISH FEMALE NON-SEXULAESSES TYPING 162
Human English Female Non-Sexualess Incorrectess Sexual2, or Hefn-sis2, or "Awww, that's not very pleasant now is it!?", my "doing that cute thing", storming LIGHTLY around, red-hot, somewhat panicking....my darling. May you, may WE, be more forthcoming next time. Last time, you ROLLED DOWN HOPE for me. But next time must be different. WE MUST SPEAK! Etcetera.

SUFFERING EXTREME: INCORRECTNESS SEXUAL OF HUMAN ENGLISH FEMALE NON-SEXULAESSES TYPING 163
Identity's Image was talking to Human English Female Non-Sexualess Incorrectess Sexual2, or Hefn-sis2, or "Awww, that's not very pleasant now is it!?". Identity's Image: "You came out for me, my darling. You're nice. But i took what you did to mean that you weren't going to talk to me that day, at least not THERE. I felt as though you might have decided to get me into trouble if i had whatevered any longer, or something like that. You were talking to a number of human beings, in a line. My reactions, at present, are not quick. I do not know whether you wanted me to stand in that line, so that we could talk."

Pickford-Gordon

Since: Sep 09

353

London, UK

Reply »

Report Abuse

Judge it!

#137
Thursday

SUFFERING EXTREME: INCORRECTNESS SEXUAL OF HUMAN ENGLISH FEMALE NON-SEXULAESSES TYPING 164
Identity's Image was talking to Human English Female Non-Sexualess Incorrectess Sexual2, or Hefn-sis2, or "Awww, that's not very pleasant now is it!?". Identity's Image: "Why were you talking to that relatively-ish or something like that, "young-looking" guy, in such a slightly conspirational manner, when i love you, and when i've always loved you?" Hefn-sis2: "You don't know that i've done anything sexual with him: we were just talking because i'm scared of you, like an animal as opposed to being like a human being." Identity's Image: "I love you."

SUFFERING EXTREME: INCORRECTNESS SEXUAL OF HUMAN ENGLISH FEMALE NON-SEXULAESSES TYPING 165
Identity's Image was talking to Human English Female Non-Sexualess Incorrectess Sexual2, or Hefn-sis2, or "Awww, that's not very pleasant now is it!?". Identity's Image: "I'm not a threat to anyone. We've spoken to each other for a long time. I can be incredibly obediant. You should live in reality more. WHY you're punishing me....it's NOT REAL, you understand? It's just same old me, just a little bit more frequently, at the Gymnasium." Identity's Image paused for a number of seconds before continuing. "We already have something. I need to be NEXT, with YOU my love. I haven't done anything to deserve your hatred. Why can't you talk to me?"

SUFFERING EXTREME: INCORRECTNESS SEXUAL OF HUMAN ENGLISH FEMALE NON-SEXULAESSES TYPING 166
Identity's Image was talking to Human English Female Non-Sexualess Incorrectess Sexual2, or Hefn-sis2, or "Awww, that's not very pleasant now is it!?". Identity's Image: "I don't know if you've done anything sexual with that relatively-ish or something like that, "young-looking" guy. If you HAVE then you're going to be Hefn-sis, instead of Hefn-sis2, along with the other two." Identity's Image paused before continuing. "If you HAVE done anything sexual with him, and you do anything MORE sexually with him from now on, then i'm just going to put the information in a book, and focus on pushing the "politician" buttons so that i can legally kill myself the first chance that i get, because of you three Hefn-sises. I love you."

Pickford-Gordon

Since: Sep 09

353

London, UK

Reply »

Report Abuse

Judge it!

#138

Thursday

SUFFERING EXTREME: INCORRECTNESS SEXUAL OF HUMAN ENGLISH FEMALE NON-SEXULAESSES TYPING 167
1.
Identity's Image was talking to Human English Female Non-Sexualess Incorrectess Sexual2, or Hefn-sis2, or "Awww, that's not very pleasant now is it!?". Identity's Image: "I really don't know how i feel if you've done anything sexual with him. I really don't know, i mean i might, once something is set up, legally kill myself anyway if you've done anything with him. Nono! Anyway, don't do anything sexual with him from now on. Past is past, which can't be undone, while present and future are present and future. You have FROM NOW ON, FROM RIGHT NOW, ON. I need to be next." Identity's Image paused for a number of seconds before continuing.
2.
"If he has gone and done something sexual with you, after he has read a number of my Internet Posts, and when he knows, then that's nothing but extreme disrespect for him towards me, when i haven't done anything to him. II myself have seen the bonds which members of my own group have formed with Human English Females. I respect such bonds. I understand the extreme suffering that would be caused to the relevant Human English Male were i to do anything sexual with the Human English Female that that Human English Male has bonded with. A number of Human Males, however, do NOT respect such things....i know a number of such individuals. I hope that this guy hasn't done anything sexual with you, that he understands that I am a pink-skinned-Human-English-Male-like-figure: a member of that group, who is in love with YOU, Hefn-sis2. That was not talking to him for job purposes, Hefn-sis2....what you did just now. And II haven't done anything to deserve your HATRED, Hefn-sis2."
3.
"This individual has started working there recently. We've been speaking etcetera with each other for as long as you've been working there. II need to be next. I love you."

SUFFERING EXTREME: INCORRECTNESS SEXUAL OF HUMAN ENGLISH FEMALE NON-SEXULAESSES TYPING 168
Identity's Image was talking to Human English Female Non-Sexualess Incorrectess Sexual2, or Hefn-sis2, or "Awww, that's not very pleasant now is it!?". Hefn-sis2: "Type another poem for me." Identity's Image: "If 50 poems would result in you being with me, then i would do it: it's almost certainly also the case, or CERTAINLY also the case, that 100 poems, or 200 poems, or a larger number, if they would result in you being with me, would be done by me as soon as possible, with me blotting out a number of other things in order to create them, for you."

SUFFERING EXTREME: INCORRECTNESS SEXUAL OF HUMAN ENGLISH FEMALE NON-SEXULAESSES TYPING 169
Human English Female Non-Sexualess Incorrectess Sexual2, or Hefn-sis2, or "Awww, that's not very pleasant now is it!?". My love. I felt an amount of FEAR, when i saw that that guy hated me, fear of what could happen to you and me, and the realisation of how fragile relationships are. I felt an amount of PAIN, and UNCERTAINTY, just now, when i saw you two talking just now. Talk to me, my love. I am a human being. Don't stab me anymore, don't cause me any more suffering, my love. You are beauty itself. Yet i tire now, i feel like i don't want to live any more. What hope is there. How can you hate me? Talk to me. I haven't done anything wrong, have i?

Pickford-Gordon

Since: Sep 09

353

London, UK

Reply »

|
Report Abuse
|
Judge it!
|
#139
13 hrs ago

SUFFERING EXTREME: INCORRECTNESS SEXUAL OF HUMAN ENGLISH FEMALE NON-SEXULAESSES TYPING 170
1.
Identity's Image was talking to Human English Female Non-Sexualess Incorrectess Sexual2, or Hefn-sis2, or "Awww, that's not very pleasant now is it!?". Hefn-sis2: "What HAPPENED!?" Identity's Image rubbed a bruise on his right arm: it was just ONE of a large number of bruises on his body. "That would be Hatred, Sexual, or H,s: he kept saying that i was being WEAK. Talks, Comforts, or T,c, ALSO said a number of things to me, but UNlike H,s he didn't BEAT ME." Hefn-sis2: "I really like you, i-nononoNO! I HATE YOU! Here's me rolling down hope for you again! No i feel bad, don't hurt yourself, i don't want to hurt you i-GODDAMMIT I HATE YOU! NO! I'm sorry, i'm so sorry! I-" She stopped talking, and appeared to be drained and unable to talk any more. Identity's Image: "I hope you understand what the problem is."
2.
Identity's Image: "I don't WORK like other people that you know. Anyway, what's causing me significant suffering, from you, is NOT KNOWING. I....do NOT KNOW. I CAN'T STAND NOT KNOWING. The truth is always the best way. The opposite of the truth is lies, deception: things will get worse if you resort to such things. There are also INDIRECT ways, other than talking to me, in which Human Females have attempted to communicate with me: these things also, mostly, make things worse. We could have covered a lot of ground already if you'd JUST, LET ME TALK TO YOU, how many times do i have to keep telling a number of people to LET ME TALK TO THEM. And a number of people seem to have some sort of enormous problem with letting me talk to them. I asked the second question, before, because it, and a number of related things, would have given me the relevant information. But what did you do, when i asked you that. In the PAST you've asked me a number of things, and i've no doubt asked you a number of things, and we've said this and said that to each other. So you had absolutely no problem BEFORE, it's just NOW that you have a problem with talking to me. I could have acquired the data THEN. But you were hostile. You refused, and you ARE REFUSING to talk to me."
3.
Identity's Image: "I'll tell you the questions that i need to ask you, in advance. These are the questions that i NEED to ask you, the things that i NEED to talk to you about. I can see how you're panicking, and how you're unstable, so i feel that i need to tell you the questions right now, like this, in advance, otherwise you might just continue to refuse to talk to me.[1] Are you single?[2] If you have a boyfriend, how long have you been with him for?[3] Who is that relatively-ish etcetera "young-looking" guy?[4] Why does he act like that?[5] How well do you know him?[6] IF you've had a boyfriend for X months/years, have you had sexual intercourse with any other guys during that period? Question 6 is something like that. I mean i HOPE i'm able to ask these exact questions, or something like them. Whether i do or don't, in any case, you ought to not have a problem talking to me. It's amazing that something so simple as you and me talking to each other can be such a problem for you."
4.
Identity's Image: "I don't know if you've sexually been with this relatively-ish etcetera "young-looking" guy. I need to know. Everything that i've said with regard to that-with regard to the information in a book, and me legally committing suicide the first chance that i get(because i doubt that i'll get any alternatives)-still stands, is still valid."
5.
Identity's Image: "You are attractive, and you have flirted with me, etcetera. In addition to that, i now suffer, i feel so confused, because of how that relatively-ish etcetera "young-looking" guy acts, and how he was talking to you at the whatever: WHY does he act like that, and WHY was he talking to you like that when you were at the whatever. These things have had an effect on me. YOU, have had an effect on me."

Pickford-Gordon

Since: Sep 09

353

London, UK

Reply »

Report Abuse

Judge it!

#140
13 hrs ago

SUFFERING EXTREME: INCORRECTNESS SEXUAL OF HUMAN ENGLISH FEMALE NON-SEXULAESSES TYPING 170
6.
Identity's Image: "Just let me talk to you. I want you to understand that-even if i was kidnapped and taken out of the country!-i would still NEVER rest until i get the truth from you, until i find out the truth. Do you understand what i mean by "NEVER"? NEVER....is NEVER. You're maybe thinking "If i keep doing what i've been doing the last few times then he'll not want the truth from me any more. He'll just vanish out of the Universe one day, completely. And he'll leave no trace behind." Those thoughts, if you have thought them, are lies. And you're causing me so much suffering, i don't KNOW this or that, you KNOW? LET....ME....TALK....TO....YOU . You could even volunteer the information. But do it directly to me. Through direct conversation."

Yet another josclient

UK

Reply »

Report Abuse

Judge it!

#141
13 hrs ago

Hey lady, you lady
Cursing at your life
You're a discontented mother
And a regimented wife
I've no doubt you dream about

The things you'll never do
But I wish someone had have talked to me
Like I want to talk to you

Oh I've been to Georgia and California
And anywhere I could run
Took the hand of a preacher man
And we made love in the sun
But I ran out of places
And friendly faces
Because I had to be free
I've been to paradise
But I've never been to me

Please lady, please lady
Don't just walk away
Cause I have this need to tell you
Why I'm all alone today
I can see so much of me
Still living in your eyes
Won't you share a part of a weary heart
That has lived a million lives
Oh I've been to Nice
And the Isle of Greece
While I sipped champagne on a yacht
I moved liked Harlow in Monte Carlo
And showed 'em what I've got
I've been undressed by kings
And I've seen some things
That a woman ain't supposed to see
I've been to paradise
But I've never been to me

Hey, you know what paradise is
It's a lie, a fantasy
We create about people and places
As we'd like them to be
But you know what truth is
It's that little baby your holding
And it's that man you fought with this morning
The same one you're going to make love with tonight
That's truth, that's love

Some times I've been to crying for unborn children
That might have made me complete
But I took the sweet life
And never knew I'd be bitter from the sweet
I've spent my life exploring
The subtle whoring
That costs too much to be free
Hey lady, I've been to paradise
But I've never been to me

I've been to paradise
Never been to me

Been to Georgia and California
And anywhere I could run

I've been to paradise
Never been to me

Been to Nice and the Isle of Greece

While I sipped champagne on a yacht

I've been to paradise
Never been to me

Pickford-Gordon

Since: Sep 09

353

London, UK

Reply »

|
Report Abuse
|
Judge it!
|
#142
1 hr ago

SUFFERING EXTREME: INCORRECTNESS SEXUAL OF HUMAN ENGLISH FEMALE NON-SEXULAESSES TYPING 171
1.
Identity's Image was talking to Human English Female Non-Sexualess Incorrectess Sexual2, or Hefn-sis2, or "Awww, that's not very pleasant now is it!?". Number THREE, in importance, priority Number THREE. But who knows, when THIS or THAT is known with regard to her, thought Identity's Image....i NEED TO KNOW, thought Identity's Image. Identity's Image: "Talks, Comforts, or T,c, thinks that the relatively-ish "young-looking" guy could be solely a manager as opposed to being sexually involved with you: T,c is leaning slightly towards that theory. Hatred Sexual, or H,s, is also leaning towards the theory that the relatively-ish "young-looking" guy is a manager....H,s said: "He's probably a manager. Whether he is or isn't, what i DO know with 100% certainty is that they've had sexual intercourse....not just him, but ALL OF THEM. AND NOT JUST THOSE WHO WORK THERE. Trust me my friend, MOST....PEOPLE. Male AND Female." That's what he said." Identity's Image paused for a number of seconds before continuing.
2.
Identity's Image: "I know that i don't work like other people, i don't function in the same manner as other people. I-" Identity's Image paused for a few seconds or so. "I mean, come on Hefn-sis2, i mean YES it's good that we've made progress, but you KNOW that we used to talk, chat, for longer than the meagre AMOUNT of "talk time", or "chat time" that you gave me last time." Identity's Image paused for a number of seconds before continuing. "And you KNOW that i have severe depression, so my decision making skills, reflexes perhaps, aren't as fast as other peoples', at the moment. Anyway, the answer to the second question is a basic thing that people everywhere tell each other the whole time. If i was the worker and you were the person on the other side talking to me, i would just have answered that question automatically. Why did you refuse to answer my second question?" Hefn-sis2: "I don't TRUST YOU! Humph!" Identity's Image: "You have no reason not to trust me. You're making me even more tired, you know that?" Identity's Image paused for a number of seconds before continuing. "You should be less instinctual and more, well, er, non-instinctual. I mean that was sort of an instinct thing, reacting in such a manner to my second question, wasn't it? The thing is i don't see why someone would react in the way that you reacted to the question-the second question from last time. Maybe that means that....well. Anyway." Identity's Image paused for a number of seconds before continuing. Identity's Image: "You're doing WELL, i mean not with the second question since you refused to answer it, but

with the first one which you DID answer. That was GOOD! you know. I have a number, from 1 to whatever(not too many) of questions for you, as you know. I shall continue to ask you questions while also at the same time understanding this and that, being aware of this and that, etcetera."
3.
Identity's Image: "And i SAW you peeking at my piece of paper, you....YOU!"

Pickford-Gordon

Since: Sep 09

353

London, UK

Reply »

|
Report Abuse
|
Judge it!
|
#143
52 min ago

SUFFERING EXTREME: INCORRECTNESS SEXUAL OF HUMAN ENGLISH FEMALE NON-SEXULAESSES TYPING 172
1.
"So you know that's so FUnny i went to this place and the guy was he was GAY Big Gay Al and we all like THOUGHT he was gay but he WASn't and he was taking photos and we've never been to the place before and i've NEVER seen anything like it beFORE and he SLAMMED me against a wall and i'm going to this place soon and come here i need a hug and a snog and more than THAT no consequences FREE HAHAHAHA oh that's so funny HAHAHAHA." Human English Female Non-Sexualess Incorrectess Sexual, or Hefn-sis, or "What might i giveyou maluv?"
2.
She is one of, currently, two Hefn-sises. Identity's Image: "Why is it so difficult for you to talk to me? I have a number of questions for you. Myself, Talks, Comforts, or T,c, and Hatred, Sexual, or H,s, all know with 100% certainty that you did something significantly sexual-more than what we've seen you do, with a number of human beings, with our own eyes-with the worse out of the two relevant YDNA Level U individuals, where U is a "letter lower than R" so to speak. That was waaaay back whenever. Etcetera. So we have things that we need to talk about, and so on." Identity's Image paused for a number of seconds before continuing. Identity's Image: "I feel really really tired after, well, a number of things. I THINK that i'll come in on this day or on that day or whatever, but if i DON'T, then i DON'T." Hefn-sis: "I hope it's because you're DEAD." Identity's Image: "If i DON'T come in, for a while, you should know that it's still the case that i WILL return." Identity's Image paused for a while before continuing. "I feel really drained. I really don't know what i'm UP to doing and what i'm NOT UP TO doing, you know. It takes a lot out of me going HERE and going THERE, you know. I mostly feel like i don't have time for ANYTHING. But i'm TRYING."

Tell me when this thread is updated:

(Registration is not required)

Add to my Tracker

Send me an email

Showing posts 121 - 140 of 144

< prev page

|

next page >

Go to last page|Jump to page:1 2 3 45 6 78

Type in your comments below

Name
(appears on your post)

Comments

Characters left: 4000

Type the numbers you see in the image on the right:

Please note by clicking on "Post Comment" you acknowledge that you have read the Terms of Service and the comment you are posting is in compliance with such terms. Be polite.Inappropriate posts may be removed by the moderator. Send us your feedback.

32Users are viewing theUnited Kingdom Forumright now

Search the United Kingdom Forum:

Topic

Updated

Last By

Comments

Second arrest over murdered rapper Umar Tufail

1 hr

With Prejudice

4

Management Country: General

1 hr

Pickford-Gordon

1

Kik messenger ids

1 hr

Boy_Alone

62

Where did that slimy ronan disappear to

1 hr

unknown slueth

0

Atheism to Defeat Religion by 2038

1 hr

Reason Personified

7,190

UK Sikhs reeling from Wisconsin attack

2 hr

Ramafuchs

27

Staten Island Beatles Blast at Silver Lake Park

2 hr

Greg

15

See all threads in the United Kingdom forum »

What's your favorite Summer Olympics event? Vote now on the Summer Olympics Map.

United Kingdom News
Great Yarmouth: Woman dies after fall from top ...
Tia: Grandmother's home searched
Youth theatre summer project aims to keep arty ...
Jones bouncing back from bronchitis
Two languages better than one for kids' brains
Climate research set to blossom at county prima...
'Missing child' bid for free lift
Diaz writing book

Pubs: Last orders for 50 pubs in five years
Second arrest over Waugh murder
Theatre Production Lifts the Curtain on the Sto...
Bins searched in missing Tia hunt

More United Kingdom News from Topix »

Topix Politix App

Take your stand on the issues you care about.

Using an iPhone?

Keep the Topix forums in your pocket
with the new, free Topix App.

Daily Horoscope for August 10

Gemini

Domestic relationships start to come under strain from today and they won't sort themselves out until the beginning of September. So be very wary about misreading situations and try not to give anyone the wrong impression simply because you haven't said something important. Do your best to avoid signing any documents or agreements until this tricky phase blows over, in case you're being led up the garden path or you haven't been given all the facts.

Get your Horoscope »

United Kingdom
News
Forums & Polls
Real-Time News

Explore More Topix
Home Page
Forums
Top Stories
Most Popular
Issue Maps
US News
US Cities list

World News
World Countries list
Politics
Celebrities
Business
Finance
Autos
Sports
Sci-Tech
Electronics
Entertainment
Movies
Music
Television
Video Games
Health
Life
Arts
Food
Home
Travel
Offbeat
Site Map / All Topics

About Topix
About Us
Media Kit
Topix Blog
Press Room
RSS Newsfeeds
Law Enforcement
School Officials
Cyber-bullying Resources
Jobs
FAQ
Privacy Policy
Terms of Service
Feedback?
Report Abuse?

Local Classifieds & Listings

Reach Local customers. Post a classified listing for your business. Promote job, auto, rental, and local event listings.

Learn more »

Join the Topix Community
¡Create your own profile, complete with quick links to your favorite topics.
¡Personalize your forum posts with your photo and hometown.
¡Exchange Personal Messages with other registered users.

Sign up today! »

Topix Politix »

Feedback?

Comments made yesterday: 108,882 Total comments across all topics: 181,753,091

Copyright ©2012 Topix LLC

Local News: United Kingdom

|

Sign Up

|

Sign In

123

Ten shot, 2 dead near New York's Empire State Building

Leaked Romney Financial Docs: The Revelations So Far

Politix
Do you think Mitt Romney should release more tax returns?

Home
Forums
Top Stories
Popular
Local
Romney-Ryan
US
Politics
World
Sports
Entertainment
Offbeat
Other

United Kingdom
News
Forums & PollsSuffering Extreme: In...

Real-Time News

Suffering Extreme: Incorrectness Sexual Of HEFN-Ses Typings

Posted in the United Kingdom Forum

Share

Read
161 Comments
Add to my Tracker

More United Kingdom Discussions »

Comments (Page 8)

Showing posts 141 - 160 of 161

< prev page
|
next page >

Go to last page|Jump to page:1 2 3 45 6 7 8 9

Pickford-Gordon

Since: Sep 09

371

London, UK

Reply »
|
Report Abuse
|
Judge it!
|
#144
Friday Aug 10

SUFFERING EXTREME: INCORRECTNESS SEXUAL OF HUMAN ENGLISH FEMALE NON-SEXULAESSES TYPING 173
1.
Identity's Image was talking to one of the various Human English Female Non-Sexualess Incorrectess Sexuals/Sexual2s/Etcetera, or Hefn-siss/Hefn-sis2s/Etcetera. Identity's Image: "Look at this law. A human being found guilty of breaking this law could be imprisoned in jail for up to SIX MONTHS. Can you IMAGINE THAT? Being locked in a room, or small area, for six MONTHS? I mean what is that, that's about 180 days isn't IT? YOU try it, or something less than that, lock yourself in a room for that period of time and see how you feel. And of course it's not like it's a human being's own pleasant BEDROOM, is it now. It's JAIL, PRISON." Identity's Image paused for a number of seconds.
2.
Identity's Image: "Encyclopedia Britannica says something like concern about the conditions in prison has not diminished over the years, and Microsoft Encarta says something like prison conditions are frequently physically unpleasant. Imagine how BORING it must be for those poor human beings trapped in there, with no way out. I myself would give them a way out-cyanide or something-but a number of other human beings don't appear to have this principle. Or something like that." Identity's Image paused for a number of seconds before continuing. Identity's Image: "The only time that i would consider such a thing-IF i would consider such a thing-would be if there was something SERIOUS, you know, a....a REAL NEED, for the Incorrecter/Incorrectess, the criminal, to be imprisoned, you know. If the individual had DONE SOMETHING. Had DONE SOMETHING REAL." Identity's Image paused for a number of seconds before continuing.
3.
Identity's Image: "I don't want to dislike/hate anyone. If i know that someone has done wrong against me, and i know that that individual can reverse the suffering that that individual has caused me, through sexual intercourse etcetera, being WITH ME

217

etcetera, then i....i feel a little like that's my DUTY....you know? For that to happen. For me to WANT that to happen. I have a DESIRE TO DO GOOD, like all human beings are SUPPOSED TO HAVE, i mean Hatred, Sexual, or H,s, says that there are a number of human beings who can NEVER understand such things, that some human beings will only ever understand CONSEQUENCES. That a number of human beings will always continue to lie to themselves. That a number of human beings will never understand, or never understand IN TIME. That a number of human beings will always continue to think, incorrectly, that, at the MOMENT, they're equal in value, or greater in value, than other human beings, after the suffering that they've caused a number of human beings when it was not correct for them to do so. But....well....i think that he's wrong. Yeah. He's wrong." Identity's Image paused for a number of seconds. "What do YOU think?"

SUFFERING EXTREME: INCORRECTNESS SEXUAL OF HUMAN ENGLISH FEMALE NON-SEXULAESSES TYPING 174
Identity's Image was despairing of ever having sexual intercourse again with anyone who was not a Sex Worker: he felt as though there was no hope, that it was impossible. He was actively looking for sexual intercourse etcetera. One day Identity's Image saw one of the various Human English Female Non-Sexualess Incorrectess Sexuals/Sexual2s/Etcetera, or Hefn-siss/Hefn-sis2s/Etcetera. She was holding up a wooden sign, which said "Identity's Image, i love you," on it. Next time she held up another wooden sign, in addition to the first one, which said, "I'm here for you again."

Pickford-Gordon

Since: Sep 09

371

London, UK

Reply »

|
Report Abuse
|
Judge it!
|
#145
Friday Aug 10

SUFFERING EXTREME: INCORRECTNESS SEXUAL OF HUMAN ENGLISH FEMALE NON-SEXULAESSES TYPING 175
1.
Identity's Image had returned from talking to one of the various Human English Female Non-Sexualess Incorrectess Sexuals/Sexual2s/Etcetera, or Hefn-siss/Hefn-sis2s/Etcetera. Talks, Comforts, or T,c: "Come on, keep saying to yourself, ONE LAST PUSH. SOMEONE will become your first girlfriend, Identity's Image. THIS, and THAT, will give you happiness in the meantime, okay! Come on, you can do it, HUH!" Identity's Image turned to look at him....but his eyes were completely dead, numb, the eyes of someone who was numb from having received TOO MUCH SUFFERING....someone who had submitted to the suffering. The eyes didn't change. T,c: "Okay come on, take your trainers off, come on. I know that you keep thinking about the various girls that you've bonded with, all of them, and the amount of time and effort you've put in with regard to sexual things, and how the vast majority of human beings in the United Kingdom And Ireland APPEAR to have better lives than you. I also know how you're tortured by the so so many attractive girls that go past you, day in day out, especially around this time of year with their scanty clothing: and how much being with one of them would mean to you, what you would do for it. But you're home now....focus on the NOW okay! Your TRAINERS. You can do it, okay, you need to recover. Come on."

Identity's Image looked down at his trainers....but he just couldn't reach down to undo the laces. His body felt like lead. There was just no point. He just started crying, and just sat there....sat there for a long time.

2.

Hatred, Sexual, or H,s: "HATE!! Come on! Are you going to let them get AWAY WITH THAT! HUH! COME ON!!!! UP!!!!" Identity's Image said to H,s, in tears, without turning his head to look at him: "To be honest, H,s....i really don't care about such things. It's all too much." Identity's Image paused for a number of seconds before continuing. "I really feel, this time, like there's ZERO gas left in the tank. I just feel completely dead inside. I NEED sexual things, i NEED my first girlfriend. Medically. There's....i really don't think that i can do very much at all if i don't have someone, someone i can rely on. I feel extremely depressed the whole time. I'm masturbating habitually, frequently. I know, T,c, you tell me that it's bad for me....but i just can't stop myself sometimes. So i do that every day, more than that. And then there's not enough time to recharge my batteries, really. I THOUGHT that i could go on longer than this with Sex Workers....but i don't think that i can. I'm expected to have sexual intercourse etcetera with her for that half an hour, or whatever....and the clock's ticking, it's always ticking, the time always runs out. And i DO have to worry about money, which is needed to be with Sex Workers, and it's NOT CHEAP. There's the effort involved in, well, a number of things with regard to Sex Workers. And i feel that it's not enough, it's just not enough sexual things etcetera."

Pickford-Gordon

Since: Sep 09

371

London, UK

Reply »

|
Report Abuse
|
Judge it!
|
#146
Friday Aug 10

SUFFERING EXTREME: INCORRECTNESS SEXUAL OF HUMAN ENGLISH FEMALE NON-SEXULAESSES TYPING 175

3.

Identity's Image: "Things were different before, i was stronger. But there's only so much emotional, mental, written, typed etcetera effort that i can keep putting into a number of Human Females. And there have been a large number of them. There's only so much time and effort. Hefn-sis, or "What might i giveyou maluv?"; the other Hefn-sis; Hefn-sis2 or "Awww, that's not very pleasant now is it!?"; Hefn-sis2 or "i'm working upstairs now"; Hefn-sis2 or "You don't love me, you only THINK that you love me" from more than 9 years ago; Hefn-sis2 or "clenched fist, i go to parties"; Hefn-sis2 or "christian. my amigo THIS and my amigo THAT. i never liked you. Okay maybe a little. Okay maybe more than a little. LOOK!"; Hefn-sis2 or "Hello Magazine He's doing it aGAIN"; Hefn-sis2 or "I LOVE YOU Mexican BOYFRIEND!"; Hefn-sis2 or "What can i get you young man!?"; and many more. I haven't had sexual intercourse etcetera with any of them. It's all too much. And there are only so many times that i can stand there, waiting for her when she's told me that she's going to meet me for a date. There's only so much....yes....so much disappointment that a human being can take. There's only so much suffering that a human being can take. Clark Ashton Smith said, in "Morthylla": ""It cannot be," averred the poet. "I fear to repeat the disappointment I have found in other women."" I often wonder how he did it, how he kept going. That man lived with suffering, his entire life,

similarly to me. I wonder HOW."
4.
Identity's Image was talking to the "tall girl", from the building where he regularly met Hefn-sis, or "What might i giveyou maluv?". Identity's Image: "Yes, i'll be with you, "tall girl". Let's be a couple." "Really!" she went. Identity's Image: "I WILL have to leave you at some point to be with, well, a number of Human Females, you know, Hefn-sis etcetera. But the thing is i....i really don't have any faith, any belief, that i'll have sexual intercourse with ANYONE who's not a Sex Worker ever again. I mean if i say it out loud right now, my brain just won't buy it, you know. It just won't register." Identity's Image looked up at her, through his tears. "I'm talking to YOU now, because i know that you've read a number of my Internet Posts. Even after you read them, you were still there for me. You were still waiting, in hope, that i would sexually be with you....one day. No one else has ever done that. Everyone except you, or i think so anyway, out of everyone that i consider sexually suitable for me, who have read a number of my Internet Posts, have become hateful, nasty and/or they keep looking for excuses to just vanish, or they do that, they just vanish. They always leave. I put in effort, and one day, they're GONE. But you've stayed there, waiting. I feel that there....there MIGHT JUST BE A SLIM CHANCE that i'll have sexual intercourse with someone who's not a Sex Worker again, and that if anyone would go through with it, that someone would be YOU, you're the likeliest sexually suitable Human Female who would go through with it, with me." Identity's Image paused for a number of seconds before continuing.

Pickford-Gordon

Since: Sep 09

371

London, UK

Reply »

|
Report Abuse
|
Judge it!
|
#147
Friday Aug 10

SUFFERING EXTREME: INCORRECTNESS SEXUAL OF HUMAN ENGLISH FEMALE NON-SEXULAESSES TYPING 175
5.
Identity's Image: "I feel really really weak right now. And sometimes i feel like things get worse every day, as the days go by. There's only so much i can take. I think of you NOW, and i think, THIS aspect of you is sexually attractive, for me, and THAT aspect of you is sexually attractive, for me etcetera. I've never had a girlfriend before. I think, who knows how it will feel. You don't, as you know, "STUN" me as such....but....well i've already said the bit about THIS aspect of you being sexually attractive etcetera. I feel as though i can't go on with Sex Workers, maybe, i mean it's just too much effort etcetera. I want a guarantee, you know. You can make me stronger, stronger than the pitiful state that i'm in right now. I DO feel that i would accept anyone out of most, or more than most, sexually suitable, for me, pink-skinned-Human-English-Fem ales, and there are enormous numbers of them. But my brain doesn't think that it will happen, EVER. I....i see US happening....i think that you'll go through with it....and if you don't go through with it, then i don't have any faith that anyone else will go through with it, with me. Ever. I mean i would TRY with others, if you say NO....but i don't think that it will ever happen if not with you. I need someone to help me. Help me."

Pickford-Gordon

Since: Sep 09

371

London, UK

Reply »

|
Report Abuse
|
Judge it!
|
#148
Sunday Aug 12

SUFFERING EXTREME: INCORRECTNESS SEXUAL OF HUMAN ENGLISH FEMALE NON-SEXULAESSES TYPING 176
1.
Identity's Image was talking to Human English Female Non-Sexualess Incorrectess Sexual, or Hefn-sis, or "Darling. What might i giveyou maluv?" at the Gymnasium. Identity's Image: "You should arrange so that you spend time with me on our own: if i said certain things and/or asked you certain things the others-who are not you and me-might interfere, or something like that. Come up to me like you used to, etcetera. Other living human beings are....well....every human being has his or her own issues, people are different, you know. I've already typed something about this somewhere, i think. Anyway, so that's that. As for the first thing that you've told me, i DO believe that there's a guy, that you've said is your boyfriend, that you're having sexual intercourse with, at THIS time and/or at THAT time. As for the second thing that you've told me, i doubt that that's true, one way or another. In any case, i'm 100% certain that you had sexual intercourse with the worse out of the two relevant YDNA Level U individuals, where U is a "letter lower than R" so to speak, all the way back THEN." Talks, Comforts, or T,c: "I'm still analysing the notes, so the significantly sexual thing, or things, that she did with him, which i'm 100% certain about, might or might not be/include sexual intercourse. I'm not 100% that it's sexual intercourse. However, the more and more data that i get, the closer and closer the probability gets to 100%." Identity's Image: "It's not just that, it's the time, effort, and mental state from me. And you had sexual intercourse with all of those other guys as well, exposing me to this and that etcetera, with 100% certainty." T,c: "Again, i'll have to analyse every separate section of the notes, with regard to the 100% certainty of the significantly sexual thing, or things concerned, etcetera." Identity's Image: "In any case i need to have sexual intercourse with you, etcetera, as soon as possible." Identity's Image was quiet for a number of seconds.
2.
Identity's Image was quiet for a number of seconds: he was stroking her hair as he stood over her, with her sitting down ignoring him to his left. "I know that there's no such thing as love, but shall use the word to express the seriousness of....of how i feel." Identity's Image paused for a number of seconds. "I love you, Hefn-sis. And i'll probably, legally, have to die because of you. Because of you, and because of the other Hefn-sis. If you don't whatever, that is." "Don't you mean that you'll have to die FOR me?" asked Hefn-sis. She looked up at him after she had asked this. Identity's Image: "No, my love." He paused for a number of seconds before continuing. "This "chit chat", "surface chat", "shallowness chat" thing that you guys do is somewhat, or more than somewhat, a waste of time, when i NEED to talk to you, on our own. Talk to me on our own, and have sexual intercourse with me, etcetera, as soon as possible, before i deteriorate into nothingness, and have to crawl into the building where i meet you on my STOMACH."

SUFFERING EXTREME: INCORRECTNESS SEXUAL OF HUMAN ENGLISH FEMALE NON-SEXULAESSES TYPING 177
Identity's Image was in the same building as Human English Female Non-Sexualess Incorrectess Sexual, or Hefn-sis, or "Darling. What might i giveyou maluv?" at the Gymnasium. He was talking to the worse out of the two relevant YDNA Level U individuals, where U is a "letter lower than R" so to speak. Identity's Image: "You had to go and touch her, on her back, didn't you, last time. It's not enough, the amount of suffering that you've caused me, that you've caused US. She's my dream, my fantasy. I wanted her from the second i laid eyes on her, and quite badly. Etcetera. And i see how you're always there when she is. That brings back memories, for me, of HER, and also YOU, all the way back THEN....memories of MY SUFFERING, memories of MY SHOCK."

Pickford-Gordon

Since: Sep 09

371

London, UK

Reply »
|
Report Abuse
|
Judge it!
|
#149
Sunday Aug 12

SUFFERING EXTREME: INCORRECTNESS SEXUAL OF HUMAN ENGLISH FEMALE NON-SEXULAESSES TYPING 178
1.
Identity's Image was talking to Human English Female Non-Sexualess Incorrectess Sexual3, or Hefn-sis3, in the same building that he met Human English Female Non-Sexualess Incorrectess Sexual, or Hefn-sis, or "Darling. What might i giveyou maluv?" in the Gymnasium. Hefn-sis3 had flirted with him, strongly. She had "skipped" or "danced" away quickly, and lightly, in joy, after she had spoken to him. She smiled at him, looking at him, with a smug, knowing, "pleased" smile, with her eyes glowing somewhat, and her eyelids shuttered slightly. She had become playful with Identity's Image, acting in a playful manner towards Identity's Image. Identity's Image, however, at this stage had her at Hefn-sis3 level. He knew how much more suffering could be caused him if he thought about her too much etcetera....but she had grown somewhat upon him. She could never though, or was unlikely to, have the effect of a higher ranked Hefn-sisX, where X is either 1(Hefn-sis1, or Hefn-sis), or 2(Hefn-sis2).
2.
Identity's Image now saw that Hefn-sis3, had become whatever with the worse out of the two relevant YDNA Level U individuals, where U is a "letter lower than R" so to speak. Identity's Image went up to Hefn-sis3. Identity's Image: "Are you telling me that i'm worthless then. That i'm unsuitable, so you have to choose someone else?" He didn't get an answer. Identity's Image: "You know, i don't think that that guy should have sexual intercourse with you when i find you attractive, and when i've bonded with you, when i think about you, etcetera; when i feel like i possibly need to legally kill myself because of the two Hefn-sises etcetera; when i don't enjoy much; when i'm alone in my room, masturbating, getting worse every day; when i've never had a girlfriend; when i've only had sexual intercourse, and not much of it, ages ago, with three Non-Sex-Workers; when i genuinely now, and with no feeling of hope whatsoever, feel that i will never have sexual intercourse with

anyone who is not a Sex Worker again. He has this Anti-Job like all of the other workers at the place, he doesn't have severe depression like me. And you and me have things FIRST, that's the POINT, that's a major POINT. Was that a lie, how you acted towards me?" Hefn-sis3 had started crying. "No it wasn't a lie, Identity's Image. But i wanna take it BACK!" Identity's Image: "IT IS TOO LATE, how many times do i have to tell people that it is TOO LATE. The memory of your behaviour towards me is in my mind. Etcetera."
3.
Later, Identity's Image spoke to her again. "Talk to me on my own, and have sexual intercourse with me etcetera. Be aware though, that i will have to leave you for Hefn-sis, or "Darling. What might i giveyou maluv?" etcetera....but i don't feel like ANYTHING is going to happen for me, ever. I feel tired of....just of EVERYTHING. Life as a human being has drained me, IS draining me. I don't have the energy for the thing. I need some kind of hope, and i can't see it anywhere, anyhow."

Pickford-Gordon

Since: Sep 09

371

London, UK

Reply »

|
Report Abuse
|
Judge it!
|
#150
Sunday Aug 12

SUFFERING EXTREME: INCORRECTNESS SEXUAL OF HUMAN ENGLISH FEMALE NON-SEXULAESSES TYPING 179
Identity's Image was in the same building as Human English Female Non-Sexualess Incorrectess Sexual3, or Hefn-sis3, in the same building that he met Human English Female Non-Sexualess Incorrectess Sexual, or Hefn-sis, or "Darling. What might i giveyou maluv?" in the Gymnasium. Identity's Image had gone to a certain place in the building. He had left his property in the locker. When he came back his property was still there, but the locker was NOW being used by to the worse out of the two relevant YDNA Level U individuals, where U is a "letter lower than R" so to speak. Identity's Image: "I was using that locker! I just went to a certain place in the building, and now i've come back." "I'm using it: there's another one THERE," he replied. "What's going on here!?" The better out of the two relevant YDNA Level U individuals, where U is a "letter lower than R" so to speak, had approached. Identity's Image: "I just went to a certain place in the building, and i've just come back to use this locker and he took it while i was away." "He needs to use that locker, it's for public-private-partnership-com pany-corporation official business," replied the better out of the two relevant YDNA Level U individuals, where U is a "letter lower than R" so to speak.

SUFFERING EXTREME: INCORRECTNESS SEXUAL OF HUMAN ENGLISH FEMALE NON-SEXULAESSES TYPING 180
Identity's Image was in the same building as Human English Female Non-Sexualess Incorrectess Sexual3, or Hefn-sis3, in the same building that he met Human English Female Non-Sexualess Incorrectess Sexual, or Hefn-sis, or "Darling. What might i giveyou maluv?" in the Gymnasium. Identity's Image was looking at a private, at that moment or whatever, sheet of paper, that he had, folded up in his hand. He sensed something, and turned his head around. The worse out of the two relevant YDNA

Level U individuals, where U is a "letter lower than R" so to speak, was looking over his shoulder at the piece of paper. "What does THAT say?" he asked Identity's Image, pointing.

SUFFERING EXTREME: INCORRECTNESS SEXUAL OF HUMAN ENGLISH FEMALE NON-SEXULAESSES TYPING 181
Identity's Image was in the same building as Human English Female Non-Sexualess Incorrectess Sexual3, or Hefn-sis3, in the same building that he met Human English Female Non-Sexualess Incorrectess Sexual, or Hefn-sis, or "Darling. What might i giveyou maluv?" in the Gymnasium. The worse out of the two relevant YDNA Level U individuals, where U is a "letter lower than R" so to speak was using a locker to Identity's Image's right. The better out of the two relevant YDNA Level U individuals, where U is a "letter lower than R" so to speak, asked Identity's Image something. Identity's Image: "Well, i-" "Are all the lockers working Identity's Image!!??" went the worse out of the two relevant YDNA Level U individuals, where U is a "letter lower than R" so to speak, AT Identity's Image, rather than TO Identity's Image, and somewhat loudly and aggressively. Identity's Image looked from one to the other, and first answered one and then the other.

Pickford-Gordon

Since: Sep 09

371

London, UK

Reply »

|
Report Abuse
|
Judge it!
|
#151
Sunday Aug 12

SUFFERING EXTREME: INCORRECTNESS SEXUAL OF HUMAN ENGLISH FEMALE NON-SEXULAESSES TYPING 182
Identity's Image was in the same building as Human English Female Non-Sexualess Incorrectess Sexual3, or Hefn-sis3, in the same building that he met Human English Female Non-Sexualess Incorrectess Sexual, or Hefn-sis, or "Darling. What might i giveyou maluv?" in the Gymnasium. The worse out of the two relevant YDNA Level U individuals, where U is a "letter lower than R" so to speak, was talking to a guy that Hefn-sis had flirted with. The worse out of the two YDNA Level U individuals was going, "Blablabla, that F+GGOT." He paused, as if expecting some kind of reaction from Identity's Image. Identity's Image knew that the worse out of the two YDNA Level U individuals had been thinking about him when he had said the word "F+GGOT". Identity's Image: "I'm NOT a homosexual."

SUFFERING EXTREME: INCORRECTNESS SEXUAL OF HUMAN ENGLISH FEMALE NON-SEXULAESSES TYPING 183
1.
Identity's Image was in the same building as Human English Female Non-Sexualess Incorrectess Sexual3, or Hefn-sis3, in the same building that he met Human English Female Non-Sexualess Incorrectess Sexual, or Hefn-sis, or "Darling. What might i giveyou maluv?" in the Gymnasium. He was talking to Human English Female Non-Sexualess Incorrectess Sexual2, or Hefn-sis2, or "I LOVE YOU Mexican BOYFRIEND! I LOVE YOU!", who had, after her and Identity's Image had flirted with each

other, and after she had promised to book a date with him ages ago, next time....after that, she had instead, THAT next time that Identity's Image was expecting her to book the date with him....on that day she then told him that she had a boyfriend, that Mexican guy that he had seen last time, last time, when she had been single. Then one day, she had complained about him to a number of authority figures, suddenly and without giving him any prior warning, when he hadn't done anything wrong....and the relevant law(s) are illegal, or incorrect. Then one day after that she had suddenly left. Identity's Image didn't know where she was, where she had gone....until she had come back to him one day. Identity's Image was thinking, as he looked at her, of how hot she looked.

2.

Identity's Image: "Do you remember the "Student Protests" after a number of Lin Doms, politicians, had broken their promise to students, a job-related promise? There were riots: it was all over the news. People were hurt. And that's only a JOB-RELATED promise. Imagine how they would have felt if it had been a number of Human English Female Non-Sexualesses, with a SEXUAL-RELATED promise: they would have reacted EVEN WORSE than THAT. Sexual things are much more important: Romeo kills himself, doesn't he. Now, i have enormous control over myself, and you won't see me, er, "rioting" etcetera. But i feel HURT, because of you. You've caused me to SUFFER, you've inflicted an amount of SUFFERING upon me. I was so happy, with a spring in my step, as the time approached that day, when we were going to book a date together. And then you ripped my mood aPART. You messed with my brain. You betrayed me. You showed no consideration for me, and you appeared to have memory problems, and you didn't come across as having that many BOUNDARIES of course." Identity's Image paused for a number of seconds before continuing.

3.

Identity's Image: "Furthermore, you're not talking to me now. You're behaving like I'M the GUILTY one, and YOU'RE the INNOCENT one, when the reVERSE is TRUE. Talk to me on my own, and have sexual intercourse with me etcetera."

See more stories

2 hr
11
Politicians 'Lie to Us Daily'

media Reporter calls out lying politicos - and the reporters who coddle them

3 hr
13
More Than Half of Obama's Twitter Fans Fakes

ObamaThe Prez has followers, yes, but not 19 million of them

Pickford-Gordon

Since: Sep 09

371

London, UK

Reply »

|
Report Abuse

|
Judge it!
|
#152
Saturday Aug 18

SUFFERING EXTREME: INCORRECTNESS SEXUAL OF HUMAN ENGLISH FEMALE NON-SEXULAESSES TYPING 184
1.
Talks, Comforts, or T,c, and Hatred, Sexual, or H,s, were talking to Identity's Image about the various Human English Female Non-Sexualess Incorrectess Sexuals/Sexual2s/Etcetera, or Hefn-siss/Hefn-sis2s/Etcetera. Identity's Image: "Things aren't going well with regard to Hefn-sis, or "Darling, what might i giveyou maluv?"(who complained to an authority figure AGAIN about me, using one or more fake laws. Incidentally, Hefn-sis2 or "I LOVE YOU Mexican BOYFRIEND!" did as well, on a different day. They wouldn't even be talking to each other if it wasn't for me, although that might not matter. For them to choose the surfaceness, or shallowness, of their "chitchat" together, when i suicidally need to talk to Hefn-sis, or "Darling, what might i giveyou maluv?", on her own, and have sexual intercourse with her, etcetera....for them to continue in such a manner is disgraceful, serious incorrectness, or crime.), the other Hefn-sis, and the others on my mental or whatever list of Human English Female Non-Sexualess Incorrectess Sexuals/Sexual2s/Etcetera, or Hefn-siss/Hefn-sis2s/Etcetera. I really have no hope of any one of them being with me sexually, of any one of them starting to repay the debts they owe me, of reversing the suffering that they've caused me." H,s: "They have no souls. They live in their own worlds....and this when you've told them that you feel suicidal. They appear to have memory problems, when you remember SO, SO much, Identity's Image. DisGUSTING behaviour from them: disgusting TRAITORS....traitors TO YOU, Identity's Image. They have absolutely NO desire to act correctly. Acting correctly is REAL desire for a human being to better himself, or herself, in comparison to the population of the country, and of the world. Crime is crime, guilty is guilty, and treating YOU, Identity's Image, in the way in which they continue to do so, is illegal, is WRONG, incorRECT. It's in your notes. Etcetera." T,c: "You need to put more effort in with regard to Damian Collins, your Country Manager. You can't have these fake laws hanging over your head any longer."
2.
Identity's Image: "I really don't know how i'm going to do it, or ANYTHING ELSE, without my first girlfriend. I feel really WEAK. I've put in enormous effort my whole life into the various Human English Female Non-Sexualess Incorrectess Sexuals/Sexual2s/Etcetera, or Hefn-siss/Hefn-sis2s/Etcetera. ...time and effort etcetera. I would accept one out of the vast majority of pink-skinned-Human-English-Fem ales, that looks young or young-ish, within the law, within a rough area near my home, not necessarily in the same urbanised area that my home is in, it doesn't have to be. I go to THIS place, and i go to THAT place, and there's just NOTHING. I mean, in the rough area near my home, a certain radius or whatever, or with regard to travel etcetera....i mean how many potential girlfriends are there for me there. Huh. There are so many, there's like an enormous number. And i just need ONE: MEDICALLY, NEED, ONE. And it HASN'T HAPPENED. Maybe i wasn't supposed to have been born." T,c: "No, Identity's Image....it's the general state of the United Kingdom And Ireland that's wrong, not you. But the United Kingdom And Ireland is not very wrong in comparison to the vast majority of other countries, perhaps. In any case, YOU wouldn't leave your fellow human being, or whatever, to suffer, or whatever....but enormous numbers of others WOULD." T,c paused for a number of seconds before continuing.
3.
T,c: "I have faith that the girl who's going to become your first girlfriend will come up to you as soon as possible, start talking to you, etcetera and, well, just THAT, she'll become your first girlfriend, Identity's Image. You won't suffer any longer, i hope."

jason norris

Preston, UK

Reply »

|
Report Abuse
|
Judge it!

#153
Saturday Aug 18

well said old pickers. well, I might not understand all you say but well said anyway.

DudTenners

"WE never came from Africa!"

Since: Nov 11

1,628

Location hidden

Reply »

Report Abuse

Judge it!

#154
Saturday Aug 18

Old Pickers certainly says a lot, but I have never understood a word of it.

Pickford-Gordon

Since: Sep 09

371

Wareham, UK

Reply »

Report Abuse

Judge it!

#155
Saturday Aug 18

SUFFERING EXTREME: INCORRECTNESS SEXUAL OF HUMAN ENGLISH FEMALE NON-SEXULAESSES TYPING 185
1.
Identity's Image was talking to the better out of the two relevant YDNA Level U individuals, where U is a "letter lower than R" so to speak....an individual who was trying very hard to displace the other human being and become, in his place, the worse out of the two relevant YDNA Level U individuals, where U is a "letter lower than R" so to speak. This was at the same building where he regularly met Hefn-sis, or "Darling, what might i giveyou maluv?", at the Gymnasium.
2.
He started speaking to Identity's Image: "You're an evil racist and you have to like hold back your enormous desire to attack THIS group of people or THAT group of people: you see, if i take this one phrase out of your more than 350 Internet Posts then that one phrase means this or that. You haven't SAID this or that, but i know that that one phrase implies this which implies that and so on. You think about race issues all the time, that's all you think about: your talk of Sexual things the whole time is just one big smokescreen, hiding your Swastica, stuff. And this whole courtroom is MINE, it's like a toy on my floor, i can imprison anyone i want to without giving any reason whatsoever. You are absolutely not a human being. You're pure evil you're the bad guy. And all your online political manifestos are illegal, and you know that very well don't you."
3.
Identity's Image: "Do you not understand that your brain is looking for excuses to cause suffering to me? Do you not understand that? I have already said such things to a number of human beings. I don't even know where to beGIN with everything that you've just said to me. I haven't done anything wrong, anything incorrect, anything illegal. You have decided not to read the whole online political manifesto: you have instead taken a number of sections of it. Things are complicated. Like i have been trying to explain to a number of human beings, there is no pure evil or pure good, and this is not a film: there are no good guys and bad guys."
4.
Identity's Image: "Talks, Comforts, or T,c, believes that there is a desire to act correctly within every human being, which can be "reached", which can be "connected with"; he believes that a number of the human beings that i have issues with have this, and that it is an attainable goal for them to UNDERSTAND, and have the desire to act correctly, that it is not too late for them to change, for them to want this....he believes something to that extent. By contrast, Hatred, Sexual, or H,s, believes that a number of the human beings that i have issues with will NEVER understand in time, no matter how much i try to reason with them etcetera: he believes that, although they have souls, and a desire to act correctly, that desire will never be reached in time, possibly due to the pride, lies, and probably other things that overwhelm that desire, according to him: that desire is hidden under such things....he believes something like that, something to that extent."

Pickford-Gordon

Since: Sep 09

371

Wareham, UK

Reply »

|
Report Abuse
|
Judge it!
|
#156
Saturday Aug 18

SUFFERING EXTREME: INCORRECTNESS SEXUAL OF HUMAN ENGLISH FEMALE NON-SEXULAESSES TYPING 185
5.
Identity's Image: "Now you're supposed to have a desire to do good. Do you think that it's good for a human being to have the power to easily cause suffering to another human being, because he or she THINKS that that human being has done wrong? For there to be no specific laws governing such a thing. Specific laws are, for example, don't steal, don't lie, except more specific than that. Vague laws are don't discriminate: you see, discriminate can be taken to be anything by a judge, with regard to the laws in existence that say, for example, don't discriminate based on gender-including transgender-, sexuality, race, religion, disability, etcetera. But what YOU want, is not even THAT. What YOU want is "I, you evil bad guy, KNOW that you've committed crime against me, and/or against others. I KNOW this. I'm not even going to TELL you what you've done. I'm judge and jury. You are guilty, according to me, and you will now SUFFER." All human beings do things that they regret. WHAT HAVE I DONE TO DESERVE THIS? WHAT HAVE I DONE TO YOU?"
6.
Identity's Image: "Instead, talk to my accusers. Tell them that i haven't done anything wrong. Tell them that THEY are wrong. Explain to them that human beings are supposed to have a desire to act correctly. You need to find that desire within them. Explain to them that i haven't done anything wrong, and/or even tell them to talk to me so that i can explain to them that i haven't done anything wrong."
7.
Identity's Image: "I tried, almost successfully, to commit suicide in May 2011, because of a certain whatever: i had whatevern to the whatever whatever whatever, asking for suicide if a certain whatever didn't whatever, some time before then. It is THE FAULT of a certain whatever that i tried to commit suicide in May 2011. You have been aware for a long time now that i tried to commit suicide, and that i suffer from severe depression, and am on Employment And Support Allowance. Do you think that this is how someone like that, me, should be treated, do you think that you should act towards me in the way that you've been acting towards me? I'm already in an extremely bad situation, WITHOUT you augMENTING the suffering that i'm experiencing at the moment. How can you act towards me in the way that you've been acting?"
8.
Identity's Image: "What is real is the situation that i'm in with regard to Hefn-sis, or "Darling, what might i giveyou maluv?" Human beings commit suicide because of Sexual-related issues. That is what is of overwhelming importance to me, and a main priority of me. I think about her, and the other Hefn-sis, constantly. You know this."
9.
Identity's Image: "You should know that if you go through with this, that i will not rest until i return to a state of whatever with Hefn-sis, or "Darling, what might i giveyou maluv?" You should think about that, if you go through with this crime. Think about me here, not thinking about much else, just trying to recover from what you've done to me. Is that really how a Human-English-Male-Like-Figure such as myself should spend his time? Should spend his LIFE? When there's so much suffering in the world, with you having caused me an amount of it. You should be aware of how important she is to me, and the extents i would go to if you commit this crime against me. I feel like there's no hope, i feel like i possibly have to die because of her. Human beings are NOT allowed to do whatever they want: i'm not allowed to commit suicide, at the moment: i HAVE to suffer, AT THE MOMENT."

Pickford-Gordon

Since: Sep 09

Wareham, UK

Reply »

|
Report Abuse
|
Judge it!
|
#157
Saturday Aug 18

SUFFERING EXTREME: INCORRECTNESS SEXUAL OF HUMAN ENGLISH FEMALE NON-SEXULAESSES TYPING 185
10.
Talks, Comforts, or T,c: "Well you have your notes, so there are legally a number of options available to you if he goes through with this crime. You'll probably try all of them if he goes through with this crime." Identity's Image: "It's like the One Fact's telling me to try and kill myself again." Hatred, Sexual, or H,s: "I WON'T LETYA, Identity's Image yalil PUNK!" T,c: "It's NOT the One Fact telling you to try and kill yourself again. I still believe that a number of human beings can change in time, and WANT to act correctly, or something like that." T,c paused for a number of seconds before continuing. T,c: "In any case, next time, you're going to talk to the Supreme Judge, of the Supreme Court Of Whatever, who is "higher up", in judicial terms."

Pickford-Gordon

Since: Sep 09

371

Wareham, UK

Reply »

|
Report Abuse
|
Judge it!
|
#158
Saturday Aug 18

SUFFERING EXTREME: INCORRECTNESS SEXUAL OF HUMAN ENGLISH FEMALE NON-SEXULAESSES TYPING 186
1.
A pink-skinned Human English Male and a pink-skinned Human English Female had just finished having sexual intercourse: there was nothing about them that Identity's Image disliked: for example the guy wasn't THIS guy from his past or THAT guy from his past. The Human English Male engaged in chitchat with the Human English Female, before the Human English Female fell asleep upon his chest. The Human English Female had a smile upon her visage....but the Human English Male wasn't smiling. He looked at the woman in his arms, and thought....WHO IS THIS? He had mental images in his mind of her having sexual intercourse with THIS guy, or with THAT guy....he pictured them together, having sexual intercourse. He also pictured "lesser" things than sexual intercourse, such as a man's hands upon her, or her kissing another guy on the lips.
2.
He woke her up. "Go to BED!" she went. "We should talk," he replied. "What's your Sexual History?" he asked her. "I don't understand, darling. I mean you love your Sex Workers, and it might or might not be difficult to know exactly who they've done sexual things with, roughly, or whatever. I don't understand," she said. "You're NOT a Sex Worker, though," he replied. "Okay! Fine! Maybe i'll go and have sexual intercourse with a guy RIGHT NOW!" she went, after she had told him the various sexual things that she had done, in the past. "Darling," he replied, "You HAVE this number of sexual things that you've done with guys. Why do you want more, when we have this? If you have more then i'll have to think more about how i feel about that. It's nice if i don't have to think more, isn't it? Why complicate this or that? If that's all, from now on, and we can lie here together, trusting each other, and knowing each other, who we are, and our place in comparison to the other human beings in the United Kingdom And Ireland, and the other human beings in the world. You have to understand the importance that i've placed upon you, what you mean to me, how i almost, but not quite, idolize you. These things, they exist, the sexual things that you've done: they're a part of who you are. You'll be even more valuable to me, etcetera, if you don't do anything more sexual with guys. But it's also WHICH guy, or guys. Etcetera."
3.
Identity's Image had been thinking about the various Human English Female Non-Sexualess Incorrectess Sexuals/Sexual2s/Etcetera, or Hefn-siss/Hefn-sis2s/Etcetera. He was reading about this Human English Male, and this Human English Female, after they had given him information about themselves. Identity's Image started talking to himself: "I recognise that you are a fellow man. I understand what this woman means to you. I respect that. And i understand that for women, sexual things exist, and sexual intercourse with a guy, etcetera, is letting a guy into her body. You have different categories of things. Etcetera."
4.
Identity's Image was making a speech. "Things are better if we have a greater sense of understanding with regard to one another, ALL of us, WHO we are. I don't want to hear: "No one's ever gonna KNOW," EVER AGAIN. If i look at you, and i think, "That woman is hiding something sexual, something serious, with a guy," then, well, i mean who is it anyway? And it means even more if it's a woman who means an enormous amount to a guy, who needs her. Etcetera."

Pickford-Gordon

Since: Sep 09

371

Wareham, UK

Reply »

|
Report Abuse
|

Judge it!

#159
Saturday Aug 18

SUFFERING EXTREME: INCORRECTNESS SEXUAL OF HUMAN ENGLISH FEMALE NON-SEXULAESSES TYPING 187
A number of the various Human English Female Non-Sexualess Incorrectess Sexuals/Sexual2s/Etcetera, or Hefn-siss/Hefn-sis2s/Etcetera, after they had read what Identity's Image had posted on the Internet about a Human Female's Sexual History, were crying. "I've done so many sexual things with men, i'm no good," they were going. Identity's Image: "The past is the past, and it can't be undone. With hard work, and effort, etcetera, myself, and you, can understand. Who knows? Perhaps if you hadn't done THIS with that guy, or THAT with this guy, then THIS good thing wouldn't have happened. Perhaps there's THIS in your ancestry, or THAT in your ancestry, etcetera. We can find a way around it. What it means is that you're in a different SUBGROUP, perhaps. What matters the MOST, is YOU AND ME. In my eyes, as soon as we have sexual intercourse etcetera, you will mean EVERYTHING to me....the amount of happiness that that will give to me, is enormous. What matters is that you age as little as possible, stay beautiful. And of course, Sexual History is only ONE FACTOR, etcetera."

Pickford-Gordon

Since: Sep 09

371

Wareham, UK

Reply »

Report Abuse

Judge it!

#160
Saturday Aug 18

SUFFERING EXTREME: INCORRECTNESS SEXUAL OF HUMAN ENGLISH FEMALE NON-SEXULAESSES TYPING 188
1.
Identity's Image was in the same building as Hefn-sis, or "Darling, what might i giveyou maluv?": the Gymnasium. There was that "young-looking"-so-t o-speak guy who looks 19 or so, who had flirted with her some time ago, whom she had flirted with. Identity's Image was talking to Talks, Comforts, or T,c. "That guy nodded at me solemnly. Why exactly did he do that? I would not communicate, or whatever, with another figure using a nod in such a manner. That nod incited confusion in me, and fear, and uncertainty. I communicate verbally to an enormous extent: and i am direct in my verbal communication, generally, or more than generally."
2.
The "young-looking"-so-t o-speak guy who looks 19 or so, started talking to Identity's Image. "Did you see how i was rushing

around unstable earlier? I had not that much control. I was thinking: "How DARE that whatever" you know, that's YOU Identity's Image, the whatever bit, "How DARE he tell me not to do this!" That's what i was thinking. You could tell how i hated you." Identity's Image: "It's not right for you to hate me. Hefn-sis, whom you flirted with, means almost the World to me, she HAS DONE for a long time. With regard to typing, typing is less real than a number of things. What's real and permanent is a woman's Sexual History. What's real is the suffering caused to another human being, or Human-English-Male-like-figure . What's real is memory." Identity's Image paused for a number of seconds before continuing.
3.
Identity's Image: "Human Females at times represent temptation. I understand this, and i resist temptation. I know that i COULD have sexual intercourse with this Human Female Non-Sexualess from a certain other group that is NOT the group that it is correct for me to whatever, for example....i know this and i say NO. It is correct for me to rather have small amounts of sexual intercourse with Sex Workers, information about whom is found in old copies of the Herald local newspapers, in other local newspapers, on the Internet, and elsewhere....to rather do that, than to have sexual intercourse with that girl. I see a number, from 1 to whatever, of guys who it is correct for her to be with instead of with me....i see them looking at me, accusingly....i see them saying: "She is all to me. And you did that." With regard to the importance of Sexual things for men, more important than the Sexual desire of Human Males is Incorrectness-as in Correctness And Incorrectness-, or crime, doing wrong. I can't lie there, after having had sexual intercourse with a Human Female Non-Sexualess, and think...."i have had this AT THE EXPENCE OF SOMEONE ELSE....as i lie here, with her, i have caused suffering to this guy, i CAUSE suffering to this guy, i can't see him but i know he's there, i know how much she means to him, how there's not much else for him. How he's a tired man, who needs to get better, a man who sent all those texts to her, with no reply. A man who waited and waited for her to come to him....he kept saying "next time"....she kept that man waiting there, he was waiting for her to let her talk to him, day after day, after a number of fake laws had been used against him....week after week....a man who was deceived, her behaviour said "i like you so much. I'm here for you," and then she "changed her mind," after having done what she did to him." And i might have strayed from my point, if i had a point. Ahem. Er, anyway, understanding helps. What was i saying again?"

Pickford-Gordon

Since: Sep 09

371

Wareham, UK

Reply »

|
Report Abuse
|
Judge it!
|
#161
Saturday Aug 18

SUFFERING EXTREME: INCORRECTNESS SEXUAL OF HUMAN ENGLISH FEMALE NON-SEXULAESSES TYPING 188
4.
Identity's Image: "You seem to me to be capable of putting a significant amount of mental and/or whatever, effort into a non-Hefn-sis Human Female. I'm not going to talk, at this event in SpaceTime, about the other Hefn-sis....but she doesn't live in the urbanised area where i meet Hefn-sis, or "Darling, what might i giveyou maluv?" Have you read all of my Internet Posts? I

can't put a significant amount of mental and/or whatever effort into anyone new, in fact i might avoid this or that. I just don't have it in me to do that anymore. The tank is empty, you know. All the fuel has been used up. What i need is guarantees, i need a guarantee. I'm not strong any more. There's no way that i can ever just forget about Hefn-sis, or "Darling, what might i giveyou maluv?", or the other Hefn-sis. I would rather die."
5.
Identity's Image: "The human being that you were, at that event in Spacetime, is someone who DID this and that, is someone who WOULD HAVE DONE this or that-like in Minority Report, the USA film starring Thomas Cruise-, is someone who EXPOSED ME to this or that, is someone who HATED ME. You have already had an effect upon me. You are part of my memory. Those things are possibly unlikely to change, even if you change into a new human being from now on. Etcetera. And the human being that you were, and possibly are, didn't, or doesn't, understand that the two Hefn-sises are not just, you know, something THIS, or THAT....they're SEVERLY important to me, ENORMOUSLY important to me, SUICIDALLY important, to me, "young-looking"-so-t o-speak guy who looks 19 or so."

Pickford-Gordon

Since: Sep 09

371

Wareham, UK

Reply »

|
Report Abuse
|
Judge it!
|
#162
Sunday Aug 19

SUFFERING EXTREME: INCORRECTNESS SEXUAL OF HUMAN ENGLISH FEMALE NON-SEXULAESSES TYPING 189
1.
Talks, Comforts, or T,c, and Hatred, Sexual, or H,s, were talking to Human English Female Non-Sexualess Incorrectess Sexual, or Hefn-sis, or "Darling, what might i giveyou maluv?" at the Gymnasium; she was crying. "How is Identity's Image going to talk to me anytime soon, after what that guy has done to him!? When can i see him again?" she wailed. T,c: "He's going to try to contact the Supreme Judge, of the Supreme Court Of Whatever, who is "higher up", in judicial terms, than that guy who has done this to Identity's Image. The guy made a number of claims about the Supreme Judge: Identity's Image is trying to work out if the claims are true or not. I'm not sure how much time Identity's Image shall spend trying to contact the Supreme Judge, whom Identity's Image SHOULD HAVE spoken to last time. After that, whether he speaks to him or not, it will be a number of things from Identity's Image and Damian Collins, his Country Manager. There are also a number of other options, all of which Identity's Image will pursue, if necessary. I am confident that, at some point in the future, Identity's Image shall indeed return: he has done nothing wrong. You know how much he, for want of a better word, "loves", you and the other Hefn-sis. Both of you have caused an enormous amount of suffering to him."
2.
H,s: "That guy, and possibly also the Supreme Judge, are almost at the top of Identity's Image's List Of Human Male Incorrecters, or List Of Human Male Criminals. It seems that that guy believes in committing crime: he certainly acted in such a way. As for what i think that Identity's Image should legally do with regard to that guy and possibly also the Supreme Judge,

234

i-" "Hopefully, though, Identity's Image will be able to speak with the Supreme Judge who will call this off....HATRED, SEXUAL." said T,c, glaring somewhat at H,s. T,c paused for a number of seconds before continuing. T,c: "It makes no sense if a number of human beings can do a number of such things to poor Identity's Image. Hefn-sis, post in the "Correspondance With Myself" section of his Internet Posts, and arrange to meet him, etcetera." T,c said goodbye to Hefn-sis, and he, together with H,s, walked away from her.

3.

T,c: "There is also the other Hefn-sis. And Identity's Image still should categorize the Hefn-sis2s etcetera. Of course, for Identity's Image, though, it is the two Hefn-sises who are with no doubt whatsoever suicidally important for him: sigNIFICANTLY more suicidally important than the Hefn-sis2s etcetera." T,c paused for a number of seconds before continuing speaking to H,s. "I have to say, though....IF ONLY IDENTITY'S IMAGE HAD A GIRLFRIEND."

Pickford-Gordon

Since: Sep 09

371

Wareham, UK

Reply »

|
Report Abuse
|
Judge it!
|
#163
Sunday Aug 19

SUFFERING EXTREME: INCORRECTNESS SEXUAL OF HUMAN ENGLISH FEMALE NON-SEXULAESSES TYPING 190
I dream of romance constantly.
Soon, may my future girlfriend see
The world that shall unfold before
Two lovers: we shall search the core
Of understanding. May we find
Salvation, as my weary mind
Is ever drained. I feel the hope
Of life: perhaps i soon shall cope.

My lovers who have failed, i feel
Can still approach me, that we heal.
Betrayed, ignored....i feel surprise
That i still stand. I improvise
With truth at times, as i feel weak.
Then up i stand, and ever shriek.

They used fake laws to silence me,
Preferring shallowness: to flee

From what is real is what they do-
Lies, treachery, pride, torture too.
So, ignorant is what they are:
Yet it will not spoil, will not mar
The future. I have hope that they
Shall be with me, shall be the way.

But meanwhile, here i sit, alone:
A Shadow King, upon a throne
Of dust and dirt, whose days fly by,
Like black clouds in a windy sky.
I think, perhaps there is no hope
That i shall ever cease to mope
Because i have no girlfriend. Who
Shall help me? Shall i know smiles too?

I smile as hope once more prevails
Upon my heart: depression fails
To keep me down for long, as i
Think happy thoughts: i often sigh
That soon a girl shall find me true.
When she comes, may she stick like glue.

So where are you, my lover!? Are
You reading this, must i go far?
We must be one, so that i heal-
So that she comes and spins my wheel.
I, thinking happy thoughts, soon sigh:
"I hope she sees me, eye to eye,
And smiles at me, then says hello.
We speak our names, and off we go!"
Too often have i seen a girl
Ignore me, or shoot off-a whirl
Of gracefulness. May you now see
Beyond my surface, may we be.

I need you, girlfriend: come, so that
We may unite. We must soon chat
About ourselves, and about more:
I hope i do not make her sore.
I go here, there, but you have not
Yet been with me. Give me a shot.
So much is on the Internet
About myself. Come now and get
Acquainted with me. If we be,
As soon as possible, you see,
There then shall be real change, real hope:
If ink-black darkness leaves, the scope
Of what has happened shall impress
Itself upon our species. Less
And less shall suffering divide
And conquer us. It shall shoot wide
As it is beaten-dead and gone.
It might be heard of in a song.

My girlfriend must soon be with me:
My torture cease: i hope to see
Humanity in different light.
I hope my girlfriend is a sight!
Therefore i finish, smiling now.
In your embrace i shall say, "Wow."

Tell me when this thread is updated:
(Registration is not required)

Add to my Tracker

Send me an email

Showing posts 141 - 160 of 161

< prev page

|

next page >

Go to last page|Jump to page:1 2 3 45 6 7 8 9

Type in your comments below

Name
(appears on your post)

Comments

Characters left: 4000

Type the numbers you see in the image on the right:

Please note by clicking on "Post Comment" you acknowledge that you have read the Terms of Service and the comment you are posting is in compliance with such terms. Be polite. Inappropriate posts may be removed by the moderator. Send us your feedback.

48 Users are viewing the United Kingdom Forum right now

Search the United Kingdom Forum:

Topic

Updated

Last By

Comments

Anti-Putin band Pussy Riot sentenced to two yea...

8 min

Uncle Sam

14

Brighton police warning over extra strong heroi...

9 min

Kriss10

4

(The US of) AmericA and (The US of) AmericANS (Aug '10)

22 min

Pickford-Gordon

7

Israel to bomb Iran within weeks

22 min

Just a thought

19

Police Arrest 21 Ahead Of Notting Hill Carnival

44 min

Revo

11

Advanced Health Ltd Releases Har Vokse System T...

1 hr

Mike

4

Man jailed for seven years over attack

1 hr

shibz

2

See all threads in the United Kingdom forum »

Are you happy that Romney picked Paul Ryan as his VP? Vote now on the Romney-Ryan Map.

United Kingdom News
'Playgirl' wants Prince Harry
Three badly injured in road crash
Flame sparks torch relay festival
Bank Holiday downpours predicted
Government to support youth groups

¦Police kill gunman outside Empire State Building
¦Confidential document lays out Assange police t...
¦Jenkins denies affair with Beckham
¦Britain's economic drop revised up slightly
¦New York State Senator wants Lil Wayne to apolo...
¦Longoria to speak at DNC
¦Holiday weekend set to be a washout

More United Kingdom News from Topix »

Topix Politix App

Take your stand on the issues you care about.

Using an iPhone?

Keep the Topix forums in your pocket
with the new, free Topix App.

Daily Horoscope for August 25

Aries

Children will be even more playful than usual until early September so you have to keep an eye on them. Make sure they've got plenty to occupy their active brains, otherwise they might get into trouble. Older loved ones could also be up to a few pranks, such as playing practical jokes on you or teasing you at every opportunity. You'll want to give as good as you get!

Get your Horoscope »

United Kingdom
News
Forums & Polls
Real-Time News

Explore More Topix
Home Page
Forums
Top Stories
Most Popular
Issue Maps

US News
US Cities list
World News
World Countries list
Politics
Celebrities
Business
Finance
Autos
Sports
Sci-Tech
Electronics
Entertainment
Movies
Music
Television
Video Games
Health
Life
Arts
Food
Home
Travel
Offbeat
Site Map / All Topics

About Topix
About Us
Media Kit
Topix Blog
Press Room
RSS Newsfeeds
Law Enforcement
School Officials
Cyber-bullying Resources
Jobs
FAQ
Privacy Policy
Terms of Service
Feedback?
Report Abuse?

Local Classifieds & Listings

Reach Local customers. Post a classified listing for your business. Promote job, auto, rental, and local event listings.

Learn more »

Join the Topix Community
¦Create your own profile, complete with quick links to your favorite topics.
¦Personalize your forum posts with your photo and hometown.
¦Exchange Personal Messages with other registered users.

Sign up today! »

Topix Politix »

Feedback?
Comments made yesterday: 103,659 Total comments across all topics: 183,159,447

Copyright ©2012 Topix LLC

| Sign Up

| Sign In

123

Mitt Romney
Obama Knocks Romney's 'Bad Math' on Tax Plan

Egypt
Egypt's tourist guides protest security vacuum at country's mo...

Politix
What's the best way for the government to create jobs?

Home
Forums
Top Stories
Popular
Local
Romney-Ryan
US
Politics
World
Sports
Entertainment
Offbeat
Other

United Kingdom
 News

Forums & PollsSuffering Extreme: In...

Real-Time News

Suffering Extreme: Incorrectness Sexual Of HEFN-Ses Typings

Posted in the United Kingdom Forum

Share

Read
171 Comments
Add to my Tracker

More United Kingdom Discussions »

Comments (Page 9)

Showing posts161 - 171 of171

< prev page

next page >

Go to last page|Jump to page:1 2 3 45 6 7 89

Pickford-Gordon

Since: Sep 09

394

Wareham, UK

Reply »

Report Abuse

Judge it!

#164
Saturday Aug 25

SUFFERING EXTREME: INCORRECTNESS SEXUAL OF HUMAN ENGLISH FEMALE NON-SEXULAESSES TYPING 191
Identity's Image was talking to Human English Female Non-Sexualess Incorrectess Sexual, or Hefn-sis, or "Darling, what might i giveyou maluv?", who worked at the Gymnasium. Hefn-sis: "Why haven't you come back yet, HUH!?" Identity's Image: "I'm trying to, my love. Your voice is music. As i look upon you again, i realise how your beauty will outweigh the negative things about you, the negative things related to you....when we make love for the first time....and for a number of times after that....MY DARLING. It's BECAUSE you're so sexually suitable for me that you were able to cause me so much suffering." Hefn-sis: "As soon as you come back, master, or BEFORE THEN even, i'll give you a biiiigg surprise, with my LIPS!" Identity's Image: "Ooooh! That sounds interesting! But listen, don't call me MASTER." "MASTER! I DON'T UNDERSTAND!" she cried in response. Identity's Image: "I'm not your master." Hefn-sis: "I'm your SLAVE, master! I always will be! You're conFUSING me, master!" Identity's Image sighed.

SUFFERING EXTREME: INCORRECTNESS SEXUAL OF HUMAN ENGLISH FEMALE NON-SEXULAESSES TYPING 192
Identity's Image was talking to one of the various Human English Female Non-Sexualess Incorrectess Sexuals/Sexual2s/Etcetera, or Hefn-siss/Hefn-sis2s/Etcetera. Identity's Image: "What good does what you're doing now do? What good does that do? It'll just be ME,(more or less) same old ME, coming in. I tend to behave in more or less the same way, when i come into THIS building, or go into THAT building. Perhaps you expect me to suddenly do THIS, or suddenly do THAT, which won't happen. You're wasting time....you're wasting OUR time, darling. I need to talk to YOU." Identity's Image paused for a number of seconds before continuing. "We have to talk sooner or later. Isn't it better that we talk SOONER, darling? And we have to be together sooner or later. Let us be together SOONER, before you age significantly, if you haven't already aged significantly." One of the various Human English Female Non-Sexualess Incorrectess Sexuals/Sexual2s/Etcetera, or Hefn-siss/Hefn-sis2s/Etcetera: "Yea: i shalt obey thee AT ONCE, my Lord." Identity's Image: "Don't call me "my Lord", oKAY!?" He sighed.

SUFFERING EXTREME: INCORRECTNESS SEXUAL OF HUMAN ENGLISH FEMALE NON-SEXULAESSES TYPING 193
Will no girl help me? Must i still
Just suffer, as i look around?
I see the gladness, hear the sound
Of people laughing. My strong will
Cannot persist forever. Shrill
Is my loud wail, as i now try
To get a girlfriend. Will i cry
Forever? Must i take a pill?
Must i post on the Internet,
And waste resources, try to get
Acquainted with some beauty? Soon
I must succeed, at night or noon.
Will you look back and feel the guilt?
Or smile at the great hope we built.

Pickford-Gordon

Since: Sep 09

394

London, UK

Reply »

|
Report Abuse
|
Judge it!
|
#165
Monday Aug 27

SUFFERING EXTREME: INCORRECTNESS SEXUAL OF HUMAN ENGLISH FEMALE NON-SEXULAESSES TYPING 194
Identity's Image was talking to Human English Female Non-Sexualess Incorrectess Sexual, or Hefn-sis, or "Darling, what might i giveyou maluv?", who worked at the Gymnasium. Hefn-sis: "I'm WAITING!" Identity's Image: "It's your FAULT! How could you do those things to me! AuTHORITY FIGURES! FAKE LAWS! WE should have spoken!" Identity's Image paused for a number of seconds before continuing. Identity's Image: "I AM trying very very hard to return, but it's not easy, especially since i have Severe Depression. You know how important you, and the other one, are to me. The two of you are at the very TOP, you know. MY LOVE, my darling....i WILL return to you, we will speak again, and we will be together, we shall be ONE." Hefn-sis scowled. Identity's Image: "I mean you're still the boss of COURSE, my love! Hahahaha, yes of course my love, I mean, whenever you're READY we'll be together. I, er, i mean i ALWAYS remember how SENsitive you are, and i, er, okay." He was silent, as she had requested that he be silent.

SUFFERING EXTREME: INCORRECTNESS SEXUAL OF HUMAN ENGLISH FEMALE NON-SEXULAESSES TYPING 195
Identity's Image was talking to one of the various Human English Female Non-Sexualess Incorrectess Sexuals/Sexual2s/Etcetera, or Hefn-siss/Hefn-sis2s/Etcetera. Identity's Image: "You think that i've done something wrong, committed a crime, acted incorrectly towards you. I mean i HAVEN'T, but you probably think that don't you. Don't you think that i have a right to know what it is you think that i've done to you that's WRONG?" She replied: "Okay, i'll show up and talk to you again." She paused for a number of seconds before concluding. "All you have to do is acknowledge me as the One Monarch of all human beings. On your knees, of COURSE." Identity's Image: "I might get down on my knees in front of you, but it WON'T be to acknowledge you as the One Monarch of all human beings." Identity's Image smiled at her in a sexual manner, and licked his lips....with his TONGUE.

SUFFERING EXTREME: INCORRECTNESS SEXUAL OF HUMAN ENGLISH FEMALE NON-SEXULAESSES TYPING 196
Victim was in the same building as a number of Human English Females. One of them had just fainted outright as soon as Victim had walked into the building. Another one had ducked down behind the counter, going, to her friend: "SSSSHH! Get down! He's HERE!" Another one had started crying: "He's here aGAIN, oh GOD! And you KEEP DOING THAT THING!!" "I don't understand," said Victim to her. "F+EAK!" shouted one to his left at him, suddenly. Victim turned to his left to look at her: when he looked back forward, another one had suddenly appeared right in front of him, from her usual spot to the LEFT....but he wasn't allowed to come on very strongly with her due to a number of fake laws of the United Kingdom And Ireland. Another one who had been very interested in him, that he thought was standing behind him, when he turned around, he realised that she had left the building, she had just left, without saying anything to him. One was using THIS fake law against him, and another one was using THAT fake law against him. And THEN there were the reMAINING Human English Females in the room, and what THEY were doing to Victim, and what THEY had done to Victim. Etcetera. Victim: "OKAY: i've had ENOUGH OF THIS." Victim swallowed the contents of a vial of cyanide that the government had given him. Victim was dead: he had committed suicide.

Pickford-Gordon

Since: Sep 09

394

London, UK

Reply »

Report Abuse

Judge it!

#166
Monday Aug 27

SUFFERING EXTREME: INCORRECTNESS SEXUAL OF HUMAN ENGLISH FEMALE NON-SEXULAESSES TYPING 197
I feel no hope, as i frantically try
To obtain my first girlfriend: i just see
So many beautiful girls-some who flee
As they meet me. I go, and then espy
The couples who walk past me. Who knows why
It is the case that they all have this thing
And i do not. Sense soon must surely fling
Some girl at me: i hope to cease to cry.
Instead of being trapped by people, girl,
Just be with me: smile and then start to twirl
As we hold hands. Correct people, love, take
Responsibility: they do not make
Excuses. Spend some time with me, and then
We shall begin: glory written with pen.

Pickford-Gordon

Since: Sep 09

394

London, UK

Reply »

Report Abuse

Judge it!

#167
Wednesday Aug 29

SUFFERING EXTREME: INCORRECTNESS SEXUAL OF HUMAN ENGLISH FEMALE NON-SEXULAESSES TYPING 198
Identity's Image was talking to Human English Female Non-Sexualess Incorrectess Sexual, or Hefn-sis, or "Darling, what might i giveyou maluv?", who worked at the Gymnasium. Identity's Image: "I have THIS to do, and THAT to do. But i'm TRYING, my love. I'm trying to return to you, to the building. I love you. I mean there's no such thing as love, but YOU KNOW! You mean so much to me, you're so important to me." He paused for a number of seconds before continuing. "I feel like nothing makes sense in existence, since this happened to me, and i now have to put effort into just trying to get back to you. I mean i've suffered significantly. I thought, SURELY now, things will start getting better, after the sort of things that i've experienced. And then THIS happens." Hefn-sis: "I'm here, waiting for you to return, my love. Be strong, and we shall speak again."

SUFFERING EXTREME: INCORRECTNESS SEXUAL OF HUMAN ENGLISH FEMALE NON-SEXULAESSES TYPING 199
Identity's Image was talking to one of the various Human English Female Non-Sexualess Incorrectess Sexuals/Sexual2s/Etcetera, or Hefn-siss/Hefn-sis2s/Etcetera. Identity's Image: "You DO know that i've been whatever in whatever whatever, or whatever whatever, just whatever whatever? Same old ME, love." He paused for a number of seconds before continuing. "How can you do this to me? Huh? To a Human-English-Male-Like-Figure . I mean think about all of the t-" he stopped, and was silent for a number of seconds, before continuing. "I'm acting like this, girl....BECAUSE YOU'RE A CRIMINAL. Because you've done wrong against me. You've caused me suffering. You've deceived me. Regardless of how you might or might not be now, before, you had very few boundaries, or so it seemed. Human beings need to set boundaries for themselves, or else they easily end up as criminals, or something like that, probably. I remember how we USED TO BE, you and me, talking, etcetera. And i did nothing wrong. I'll probably always remember what happened, girl. Talk to me, and have sexual intercourse with me, etcetera, as soon as possible."

Pickford-Gordon

Since: Sep 09

394

London, UK

Reply »

Report Abuse

|
Judge it!
|
#168
Wednesday Aug 29

SUFFERING EXTREME: INCORRECTNESS SEXUAL OF HUMAN ENGLISH FEMALE NON-SEXULAESSES TYPING 200
1.
Identity's Image was speaking to a number of Human English Female Non-Sexualesses, in the urbanised area where he lived; he had asked if he could join them. "No," said one of them, "We're having a girly night out. We're having a girl chat, you know. Sorry." She stopped talking to Identity's Image in order to sip some alcohol. Identity's Image saw a lot of Human English Female Non-Sexualesses who were sexually suitable for him....but they were in groups with guys. Identity's Image: "I'm not going to go up and chat to those in "mixed" groups: all sorts of things could go wrong, or something like that, etcetera. I'll probably just go up and talk to girl only groups, or one girl."
2.
He stopped talking to himself. He remembered what had happened with Human English Female Non-Sexualess Incorrectness Sexual2, or HEFN-SIS2, with regard to him, her, and THAT mixed group, all of those years ago.
3.
He paused for a number of seconds before continuing talking to himself: "Why have so many people taken the risk of becoming friends with each other? It's like everyone's friends with each other. Don't they see the risks, the sexual risks, and perhaps or perhaps not others as well? I mean, what exactly has been the point of the creation of such enormous THINGS? If everyone knows each other then they'll possibly get in the way etcetera when i'm trying to make one of these Human English Female Non-Sexualesses my first girlfriend, which will probably never happen, i'll probably never know what that's like. Why can't SOMEONE just post in the Correspondance With Myself section of my Internet Posts, or, if she sees me here or there or something, talk to me and have sexual intercourse etcetera with me? I've made so many Internet Posts, and i feel as though, it's almost like my Internet Posts have reDUCED my chances of getting my first girlfriend....and these are good poems, you KNOW? If human beings just take the time to read this or that out of my Internet Posts then things will get better. But i've already said this or that. How many times do i have to repeat myself? HUH!? Etcetera. I can't STAND THIS."
4.
Identity's Image: "I didn't speak into my Webcam last time, and so one of the various Human English Female Non-Sexualess Incorrectess Sexuals/Sexual2s/Etcetera, or Hefn-siss/Hefn-sis2s/Etcetera, didn't come out. This time i HAVE spoken into my Webcam: i hope she comes out, for me, like she used to....before i told her my full name and told her about my Internet Posts." She came out for him. She looked up at him, glaring at him. "FINE: you f+cking WANT me to come out for you, that's f+cking FINE, here i F+CKING AM. OKAY? Are you HAPPY NOW, you F+CKER?" she snarled loudly at him from across the building. Then she looked down and started banging things around loudly. As the time got around for him to approach her, to speak to her like he used to, she, just before he was about to approach her, arranged things so that he was unable to talk to her. "Did she do that just to torture me?" thought Identity's Image. Identity's Image: "I feel tired of this....and just....everything else maybe. Everything is futile."
5.
Identity's Image was sitting down at home: he was having difficulty getting up, because of the Severe Depression, because he didn't have a girlfriend, and doubted whether he would ever have one; he was imprisoned by what he perceived to be an absence of movement, an absence of hope, an absence of hope for change. Identity's Image: "Talks, Comforts, or T,c....when i'm with Sex Workers, you know for half an hour here and there....it feels GREAT. Is it true that the vast majority of human beings in the United Kingdom And Ireland have that all of the time? Do they take that for granted? Have they even had such an amount of it, that it perhaps means NOTHING to them, or at least very LITTLE?"

Pickford-Gordon

Since: Sep 09

394

London, UK

Reply »

|
Report Abuse
|
Judge it!
|
#169
Wednesday Aug 29

SUFFERING EXTREME: INCORRECTNESS SEXUAL OF HUMAN ENGLISH FEMALE NON-SEXULAESSES TYPING 200
6.
T,c: "They don't have it as good as you THINK, Identity's Image....in fact a number of them have significant PROBLEMS. The amount of PROBLEM for a number of them perhaps outweighs the amount of Sexual Pleasure, or something like that. I've spoken to a number of them, and have, through my words, given them COMFORT, and helped them to underSTAND etcetera. I'm significantly more concerned about YOU though, in comparison to others. But we'll talk some MORE, Identity's Image! I have NO PROBLEM talking significantly to a number of individuals, you know?" Hatred, Sexual, or H,s: "It's great what you're DOING, Identity's Image, with the aWARENESS of human beings, aWARENESS of a NUMBER of things: HATRED. By CONtrast, more than half of all human beings in the United Kingdom And Ireland seem to do nothing but stick their HEADS IN THE SAND. The thing is, though....you need to ditch an amount of your hatred by getting legal revenge against your enemies etcetera. Keep seeing YOU, Identity's Image, in the FUTURE, standing there next to your bare-chested enemy, with a needle of lethal medication in your right hand, that the politicians have finally given you, that you're about to inject your enemy with. AAAAAAHHHH!" H,s paused for a number of seconds, smiling, his eyes glittering with happiness....he was obviously imagining it. After a period of time he turned back to Identity's Image. "Okay. DON'T look too much at human beings right now, or rather not at the ones that HAVE THINGS better than YOU DO. Don't let those PESKY HUMANS get in your way, oKAY? Don't get distracted: FOCUS, warrior. Get some hot +ss as soon as possible, etcetera." Identity's Image: "Do you believe in ROMANCE, Haterd, Sexual?" H,s was silent. T,c: "If he DOES he'll never admit it, Identity's Image." H,s frowned and turned away from Identity's Image towards T,c. "Row WHAT? What the f+ck did he just say, T,c? I don't think i've ever heard that word before....maybe it's not English! Are you talking another LANGUAGE, Identity's Image my friend!? Huh!? Oh yeah ROMANCE! That's when i saw this guy with this PLASTIC HEART, you know a heart made of plastic, and then he gave it to this GIRL. Is that what you MEAN, Identity's Image!? Oh say, did you KNOW? They did some survey and it turns out that only like 5% of all girls in the United Kingdom And Ireland like that PLASTIC HEART thing, whatever it is, and 0% near where YOU live, Identity's Image. And they said anyone who types sigNIFICANTLY aBOUT it, has like 0% CHANCE of getting a girlfriend, EVER." Identity's Image had gotten worried, and was upset. H,s started laughing, and grabbed Identity's Image hard around his neck, in a headlock. Identity's Image was choking somewhat. H,s: "I'M JUST MESSING WITH YOU my friend! AHAHAHA! Come here!" H,s slapped Identity's Image hard on one of his cheek, with Identity's Image still choking in the grasp of H,s. H,s: "There was NO SUCH SURVEY! You gullible little idi+t YOU! And of COURSE i know what romance is. But don't go thinking about such things right now." He paused for a number of seconds before concluding. "You need to FIND someone, Identity's Image. You need HOPE, as soon as possible."

Pickford-Gordon

Since: Sep 09

394

London, UK

Reply »

Report Abuse

Judge it!

#170
Wednesday Aug 29

SUFFERING EXTREME: INCORRECTNESS SEXUAL OF HUMAN ENGLISH FEMALE NON-SEXULAESSES TYPING 201
Nothing at all may ever flow:
When will i ever be set free?
Me and a girl will never be.
My deep depression will not go:
Romance will never happen. Slow
And tired now is how i feel:
I feel my spirit start to peel
Away. How will my gladness grow?
But one day, when i walk along,
She must be there, we must have song.
Some girl will find me, will she not.
Then happiness shall be our lot.
So, some girl, approach. If, you see,
Anyone needs you, it is me.

Pickford-Gordon

Since: Sep 09

394

Wareham, UK

Reply »

Report Abuse

Judge it!

#171

Sunday Sep 2

SUFFERING EXTREME: INCORRECTNESS SEXUAL OF HUMAN ENGLISH FEMALE NON-SEXUALAESSES TYPING 202
Identity's Image was talking to Human English Female Non-Sexualess Incorrectess Sexual, or Hefn-sis, or "Darling, what might i giveyou maluv?", who worked at the Gymnasium. Hefn-sis: "You're doing well, with all of your politics posts: you're making a difference. It doesn't matter whether you make a difference or not, though, to me, or something like that....what matters is the love we have, and that you return to me. I'm here, i'm still here my love. I'm waiting for you." Identity's Image: "I'm trying, but i get so tired sometimes: typing, and just, well A LOT OF THINGS....they take so much out of me. I feel tired." Hefn-sis: "It will all be worth it as soon as you return to me, my love. I want to see you again so badly, Identity's Image."

SUFFERING EXTREME: INCORRECTNESS SEXUAL OF HUMAN ENGLISH FEMALE NON-SEXULAESSES TYPING 203
Identity's Image was talking to one of the various Human English Female Non-Sexualess Incorrectess Sexuals/Sexual2s/Etcetera, or Hefn-siss/Hefn-sis2s/Etcetera. Identity's Image: "What you've done to me, girl, is what people are going to think about when they think of you. The amount of suffering that you've caused me is the difference that you've made: that's how you compare to others: you HAVE caused me such an amount of suffering, and others HAVE NOT caused me such an amount of suffering, others have caused me VERY VERY MUCH LESS suffering than you have, or perhaps even ZERO SUFFERING. Talk to me, and have sexual intercourse with me, etcetera, as soon as possible."

SUFFERING EXTREME: INCORRECTNESS SEXUAL OF HUMAN ENGLISH FEMALE NON-SEXULAESSES TYPING 204
So many gorgeous girls just walk
Straight past me. Will i ever talk
To one of them, before she then
Becomes my girlfriend, writ with pen?
I do not ask that some girl goes
And ends my life, to end my woes.
The thing i ask, it is not hard:
We must have sex. To be her bard
Is what i want. There surely must
Be someone, before i am dust,
Who is not part of what is fake,
Who realises i must wake
From what some girls have done to me.
What is this pride? How can they flee?

But now a glint comes to my eyes:
Some girl must see, and heed my cries.
How long must i keep doing this
Before some girl gives me a kiss?
Sometime you must, girl, sleep with me:
My first relationship must be.

See more stories

3 hr
17
Federal Judge: Decriminalize Marijuana

MARIJUANA Reagan-appointed jurist calls drug laws "really absurd"

3 hr
21
Congressman: Sandra Fluke Should 'Get A Job'

SANDRA FLUKEWalsh of Illinois not impressed with activist's convention speech

Pickford-Gordon

Since: Sep 09

394

London, UK

Reply »

|
Report Abuse
|
Judge it!
|
#172
36 min ago

SUFFERING EXTREME: INCORRECTNESS SEXUAL OF HUMAN ENGLISH FEMALE NON-SEXULAESSES TYPING 205
Identity's Image was talking to Human English Female Non-Sexualess Incorrectess Sexual, or Hefn-sis, or "Darling, what might i giveyou maluv?", who worked at the Gymnasium. Identity's Image: "I will see you again, darling. Talk to me, and have sexual intercourse with me, etcetera, as soon as possible." Hefn-sis: "It's so fantastic to hear your voice again, after all of this time. I am YOURS, master."

SUFFERING EXTREME: INCORRECTNESS SEXUAL OF HUMAN ENGLISH FEMALE NON-SEXULAESSES TYPING 206
Identity's Image was talking to one of the various Human English Female Non-Sexualess Incorrectess Sexuals/Sexual2s/Etcetera, or Hefn-siss/Hefn-sis2s/Etcetera. "Yeessss, i want Identity's Image to continue to suffer horribly," she was going. "MemememeME. Identity's Image sort of doesn't exIST. I LOVE LYING to mySELF. SUFFER HORRIBLY, Identity's Image," she said to him. Identity's Image: "Do you mean that?" "NONONONO, i'm SO SORRY master, forGIVE ME, master! I LOVE YOU," she replied.

Pickford-Gordon

Since: Sep 09

394

London, UK

Reply »

|
Report Abuse
|
Judge it!
|
#173
28 min ago

SUFFERING EXTREME: INCORRECTNESS SEXUAL OF HUMAN ENGLISH FEMALE NON-SEXULAESSES TYPING 207
1.
A number of Human English Males were looking at Victim's dead body: he had finally been allowed to legally commit suicide. Human English Male, or HEM, looked back at his laptop; after a short period of time, he looked at the others. HEM: "9 Pages, full of words. And so many other threads....but those 9 pages. Victim put so much time and effort etcetera into a number of Human English Female Non-Sexualesses....but no one helped him in time: he cried out, over and over again, but he was not helped." Human English Male 2, or HEM2: "No Human English Female Non-Sexualess even gave him a chance." Human English Male 5, or HEM5: "No, that's not quite right HEM2." Human English Male 4, or HEM4: "SHUT UP! What do YOU know, HUH!" Human English Male 3, or HEM3: "GUYS, GUYS! We're supposed to be proFESSIONAL!!!!"
2.
HEM: "I just don't understand it." HEM3: "He was made to suffer because he cared; he was made to suffer because he put time and effort into things; he was made to suffer because he was perfect." HEM4: "What are you, his F+CKINFANCLUBORSOMETHING, ya little GIT!" HEM3: "Shut the F+CK UP, alRIGHT!" They were quiet for a number of seconds.
3.
HEM: "The shallowness, the surface, the ignorance, the cattleism, and the dumbanimalism, running riot in the United Kingdom And Ireland were too strong for someone as pure of heart as Victim. And here's the thing: do you know how much progress, with regard to Country Management, and other things too, would have been made if a number of Human English Female Non-Sexualesses had had sexual intercourse etcetera with Victim, do you know how much progress would have been made? ENORMOUS progress. But the incorrectness, or crime, was too deeply rooted within a number of Human English Female Non-Sexualesses: Victim, and his excellent principles etcetera, were like an alien planet to them." HEM4: "We already know all this, who the f+ck made YOU leader anyway!" HEM: "I didn't say i was leader!" HEM4: "I don't like how you're acting with your little speeches and all: I, I, ME!, should do the speeches!" HEM5: "Hmmmm." HEM2: "HEM5 wouldn't be any good with speeches: he SUCKS, not just speechwise, but as a human being." HEM5: "That is a hypothetical proposal." HEM: "Can we get back to Victim here?" HEM3: "We're getting back to Victim here guys, i want you all to CALM DOWN." HEM frowned at HEM3.

Pickford-Gordon

Since: Sep 09

394

London, UK

Reply »

Report Abuse

Judge it!

#174
20 min ago

SUFFERING EXTREME: INCORRECTNESS SEXUAL OF HUMAN ENGLISH FEMALE NON-SEXULAESSES TYPING 207
4.
HEM3: "Victim was-" HEM: "Victim cared: you can't care about anything or anyone in the United Kingdom And Ireland, you can't trust anyone, at all, in any way." HEM paused for a number of seconds before continuing. "The only thing that a number of Human English Female Non-Sexualesses understand, and ever will understand, because of what they've become, is CONSEQUENCES. How could they do this to him?" He paused for a number of seconds before continuing. HEM: "A number of them sort of remain primitive, like rats, running away from sudden movements of men, governed by emotion, not talking to any man who isn't in a "group", not acting like human beings. GUILTY. TRAITORS, a number of them BETRAYED Victim, they LOVED the fake laws such as "banning", they were EAGER to get back to the shallowness, to the surface, to the talking about nothing, to the escapism, to the friends, to the "television", to "facebook"....but such things aren't real, they're harmful. Do you guys know what's real?" HEM4: "YAYA of COURSE we do, ya little PUNK!" HEM3: "Don't talk to HEM that way!" HEM4: "YOU CAN'T TELL ME WHAT TO DO!" He paused for a number of seconds, staring with bulging eyes at HEM3: then he calmed down. They were silent for a number of seconds.
5.
HEM: "What's real is Victim's Story, how Victim lived his life, the amount of time and effort that Victim spent on Human English Female Non-Sexualesses, the amount of time and effort that Victim spent on this or that, the amount of suffering imposed on Victim, etcetera. I mean Victim tried, though....he met Damian "Excuses" Collins 3 times, a man who at the moment still refuses to do anything with regard to Legal Killing And Legal Killing-Self, despite what Victim said to him about it, despite what Victim typed to him about it. The mp continued to refuse to budge with regard to a number of things: it was as if Victim and Damian "Excuses" Collins spoke different languages, almost as if they were different species, with Victim being someone completely alien to Damian "Excuses" Collins." HEM paused for a number of seconds before concluding. "How can a number of Human English Female Non-Sexualesses sleep at night, after what they did to Victim, after they did this to Victim, made him suffer. Victim thought, and continued to think, "Next time,"....but "Next time" never happened."

Tell me when this thread is updated:
(Registration is not required)

Add to my Tracker

Send me an email

Showing posts 161 - 171 of 171

< prev page

next page >

Go to last page|Jump to page: 1 2 3 4 5 6 7 8 9

Type in your comments below

Name
(appears on your post)

Comments

Characters left: 4000

Type the numbers you see in the image on the right:

Please note by clicking on "Post Comment" you acknowledge that you have read the Terms of Service and the comment you are posting is in compliance with such terms. Be polite.Inappropriate posts may be removed by the moderator. Send us your feedback.

54Users are viewing theUnited Kingdom Forumright now

Search the United Kingdom Forum:

Topic

Updated

Last By

Comments

Second arrest over murdered rapper Umar Tufail

5 min

DudTenners

54

Shock at racist abuse sparked by Hereford mosqu...

8 min

DudTenners

2

Fans applaud NI stadium plans

36 min

masey12

26

Management Country: General

44 min

Pickford-Gordon

6

Muslim mosque leaders agree to marry girl of 12

53 min

troutman

4

sex

1 hr

maxvrdesigne

4

Human Home Typings

1 hr

Pickford-Gordon

1

See all threads in the United Kingdom forum »

Are you happy that Romney picked Paul Ryan as his VP? Vote now on the Romney-Ryan Map.

United Kingdom News
Police continue searching UK home of British-Ir...
Three arrested after boy, 17, stabbed to death ...
Ex-Beatle Paul McCartney decorated with French ...
Missing 16-year-old named as major search of Ri...
Cruise movie gunfire sparks panic
Authorities warn of severe weather across NY
No checks made on killer 999 boss
Man arrested over fatal stabbing
Heroes' turn in the spotlight
French Alps Killings: Brother of Victim Denies ...
Boston College: IRA interviews should stay sealed
MSP thinks Blair could face McJustice

More United Kingdom News from Topix »

Topix Politix App

Take your stand on the issues you care about.

Using an iPhone?

Keep the Topix forums in your pocket
with the new, free Topix App.

Daily Horoscope for September 9

Capricorn

You're in a visionary mood today, and you enjoy discussing your plans with someone who feels equally enthusiastic about them. You might even be so inspired that you decide to map out a timetable of what to do when. Travel plans might also be on the cards today, in which case you'll fancy venturing far afield and possibly visiting somewhere rather exotic.

Get your Horoscope »

United Kingdom
News
Forums & Polls
Real-Time News

Explore More Topix
Home Page
Forums
Top Stories
Most Popular
Issue Maps
US News
US Cities list
World News
World Countries list
Politics
Celebrities
Business
Finance
Autos
Sports
Sci-Tech
Electronics
Entertainment
Movies
Music
Television
Video Games
Health
Life
Arts
Food

Home
Travel
Offbeat
Site Map / All Topics

About Topix
About Us
Media Kit
Topix Blog
Press Room
RSS Newsfeeds
Law Enforcement
School Officials
Cyber-bullying Resources
Jobs
FAQ
Privacy Policy
Terms of Service
Feedback?
Report Abuse?

Local Classifieds & Listings

Reach Local customers. Post a classified listing for your business. Promote job, auto, rental, and local event listings.

Learn more »

Join the Topix Community
¦Create your own profile, complete with quick links to your favorite topics.
¦Personalize your forum posts with your photo and hometown.
¦Exchange Personal Messages with other registered users.

Sign up today! »

Topix Politix »

Feedback?
Comments made yesterday: 95,485 Total comments across all topics: 184,624,675

Copyright ©2012 Topix LLC

the girl from this place

Local News: United Kingdom

|

Sign Up

|

Sign In

1 23

Libya
Clinton on unannounced trip to Libya

Wall Street
Douglas E. Schoen: What Occupy Wall Street Protesters Really B...

China
China's Need for Speed

Home
Forums
Top Stories
Popular
Local
Election Poll
US
Politics
World
Sports
Entertainment
Offbeat
Other

United Kingdom
 News
Forums & Polls the girl from this pl...

Real-Time News

the girl from this place

Posted in the United Kingdom Forum

Share

Read
 29 Comments
Add to my Tracker

More United Kingdom Discussions »

Comments

Showing posts 1 - 20 of 29

< prev page

next page >

Go to last page| Jump to page: 1 2

Pickford-Gordon

Since: Sep 09

117

Whipsnade, UK

Reply »

Report Abuse

Judge it!

#1
Feb 9, 2011

This is Daniel Pickford-Gordon. It's been a long time since this girl just left the place suddenly(I met her at another place); today's Wednesday 09/02/2010, and I've been coming to this place every day for a long time(although it was not possible for me to come in on Sunday 09/01/2010; but from Monday 10/01/2010, yes it has been every day). I hate that place, but I'll keep coming in. I feel I'm getting weaker and weaker every day. Please be with me as soon as possible. Can someone(anyone who's not that red haired guy, as if he talks to her it damages me) help me by talking to her? Or by telling me where she is? Tell her to show up again and be with me as soon as possible, or something which causes her to be with me as soon as possible? There's no reason for us not to be together as soon as possible. I hope she's POSITIVE like before, and then is with me.

Other people have a tendency to manipulate you and to lie to you, which is what I know has happened. She's a real mess because of this, always talking to other people about me, instead of to me, attracting attention, and I TRIED to talk to her. I should already be with her, instead of sitting here alone typing this s**t. We need to talk, and then be together. Nothing bad will happen if I just stand there for one minute and talk to her, why can't she understand that. I haven't done anything and she just left. I need her.

Pickford-Gordon

Since: Sep 09

117

Whipsnade, UK

Reply »

|
Report Abuse
|
Judge it!
|
#2
Feb 10, 2011

Pickford-Gordon wrote:

Can someone(anyone who's not that red haired guy, as if he talks to her it damages me) help me by talking to her? Or by telling me where she is? Tell her to show up again and be with me as soon as possible, or something which causes her to be with me as soon as possible?
Neither will I speak to the red haired guy. I know that some of them at that place have read this. In fact no one who has committed a crime against me must involve themselves either directly or indirectly in this, or in my life until it is time for them to pay their debts to me. You make something which you like or love, or anything perhaps, WORSE if your criminals get involved in it...I hate or dislike all of my criminals, or aspects of them, and hate or dislike thinking about them, until it is time for them to let me take the varieties of things which they owe me from them. Victims and criminals are not meant to suffer together, they are supposed to be released from the pain, in different ways...but there are sexual debts for some victims in a number of victims' "cases" or situations. Plus I am not MEANT to let the criminals off the hook as that will decrease my own value as a human being, not being true to myself, and their value will decrease as well as they are meant to pay what they owe me in full and not bribe their way out of it. I do not HATE the criminal I have labelled "The 'a certain girl' mentioned previously"...I have changed my mind as such...she needs to pay me(not money) though in the future sometime...but all depends on this current thing.

The last time I saw the girl from this place was Friday 14/01/2011, at that place. You either harm the innocent or you do not harm the innocent. She has not functioned in the correct, legal manner. And I suffer. Still nothing today(Thursday 10/02/2011). How can she do this

Pickford-Gordon

Since: Sep 09

117

Whipsnade, UK

Reply »

Report Abuse

Judge it!

#3
Feb 11, 2011

Today(Friday 11/02/2011).........nothing. Something's slowly being drained out of me, as each day passes. "I feel right now like there's no hope". That was a quote, from myself.

Pickford-Gordon

Since: Sep 09

117

Whipsnade, UK

Reply »

Report Abuse

Judge it!

#4
Feb 12, 2011

Nothing today(Saturday 12/02/2011). An individual was giving the impression that he had some information about things that relate to her etc, and I decided that I would ask for information about her. This was the individual who, once when I had approached this girl, had sent her downstairs so that she would not have the chance to talk to me. I looked around, as I wanted to see who else in the room would be listening to the upcoming conversation...I would have acted in the same manner with any of the other people who were there today. However, after I looked around he got up. I know that he had made an incorrect assumption regarding my motivation for looking around. I decided not to question him, as he would probably lie to me or try to do something to inflict damage upon me, although it was unnecessary for me to think this as he left very soon after I had looked around.
I need to talk to her and to be with her. I would like to say more, but there's only so much I can say......on the f***ing INTERNET. The internet's ok though. I long to say some of these things to her, in real life, and much more of course.

Pickford-Gordon

Since: Sep 09

117

Whipsnade, UK

Reply »

Report Abuse

Judge it!

#5
Feb 13, 2011

Nothing today(Sunday 13/02/2011). I saw someone today at that place who might have been related to her(and possibly one other person related to her as well?), which made me somewhat paranoid.
Mild criminals of mine can involve themselves in this. However, my extreme criminal, moderate criminal and mild criminal list is now different from what I posted in "Criminals".
I suffer.

Pickford-Gordon

Since: Sep 09

117

Whipsnade, UK

Reply »

Report Abuse

Judge it!

#7
Feb 14, 2011

Judged:

1

Blunt Mocker wrote:

looks like we have got a live one here!
I said I saw one or two people at that place who, I thought, could be related to her. As you can gather from my posts, I think about her to a considerable extent. Then I spoke of my mild criminals and things which relate to that, which is self-explanatory if you read my "Criminals" thread. People who have committed crimes against me can think about whether they fall into the "mild criminals" category or not, and if they do fall into it then they can help me with this. If you don't understand all of that, then that is a problem with YOU and not a problem with ME. Please leave me alone, unless you can help me in the manner in which I've described.

===========

Nothing today(Monday 14/02/2011), except more suffering for myself.

Pickford-Gordon

Since: Sep 09

117

Whipsnade, UK

Reply »

|
Report Abuse
|
Judge it!
|
#8
Feb 15, 2011

Nothing today(Tuesday 15/02/2011). Please post here if you have any information about her, if you're her, if you know which one or ones of the people at that place(except the young red haired guy, as I shall not talk to him) has or have or had any information about her, etc. Of course I won't necessarily keep posting here, but I will keep coming in. I need her soon.

Perfect Stranger

London, UK

Reply »

Report Abuse

Judge it!

#9
Feb 15, 2011

Judged:

1

Pickford-Gordon wrote:

Nothing today(Tuesday 15/02/2011). Please post here if you have any information about her, if you're her, if you know which one or ones of the people at that place(except the young red haired guy, as I shall not talk to him) has or have or had any information about her, etc. Of course I won't necessarily keep posting here, but I will keep coming in. I need her soon. Gosh, really?

Pickford-Gordon

Since: Sep 09

117

Whipsnade, UK

Reply »

Report Abuse

Judge it!

#10

Feb 16, 2011

Nothing today(Wednesday 16/02/2011).

miranda

Ryde, UK

Reply »

|
Report Abuse
|
Judge it!
|
#11
Feb 16, 2011

Judged:

1

1

Pickford-Gordon wrote:

Nothing today(Tuesday 15/02/2011). Please post here if you have any information about her, if you're her, if you know which one or ones of the people at that place(except the young red haired guy, as I shall not talk to him) has or have or had any information about her, etc. Of course I won't necessarily keep posting here, but I will keep coming in. I need her soon. She says she's not in but asked me to give you this:

http://www.beachyhead.org/Directions.html

xxxx Mwwaah!

Pickford-Gordon

Since: Sep 09

117

Whipsnade, UK

Reply »

Report Abuse

Judge it!

#12
Feb 17, 2011

Perfect Stranger wrote:

<quoted text>
Gosh, really?
Perfect Stranger, do you have any information or anything for me, regarding this?

Pickford-Gordon

Since: Sep 09

117

Whipsnade, UK

Reply »

Report Abuse

Judge it!

#13
Feb 17, 2011

Nothing today(Thursday 17/02/2011)...or yesterday rather as it's 02:01. I hate not knowing enough about this. There have been all sorts of people there etc.

Pickford-Gordon

Since: Sep 09

117

Whipsnade, UK

Reply »

Report Abuse

Judge it!

#14
Feb 21, 2011

Nothing Friday 18/02/2011, or Saturday 19/02/2011. I was unable to come in on Sunday 20/02/2011. Nothing Monday 21/02/2011. On Monday 21/02/2011(today) I asked the individual who had sent her downstairs before(see my previous posts) where she had gone, as I needed to talk to her. He said something which was probably a lie. I believe that although he added a small lie to the conversation, the "main lie" had come from her a long time ago. This is probably yet another crime committed against myself by her. More pain. I will keep coming in.
Read "Hope This Leads To Me Being With Her Very Soon" and the corrections at the end...but it's still incomplete.
Listen to me, A_(I shall "blank out" most of her first name). You fell in love with me a long time ago, and at a specific date after that I fell or had fallen in love with you as well. On top of a number of crimes that you committed against me, you suddenly left the day after I had waited 10 seconds in order to try to talk to you, and have remained absent all this time when I need you: more crime. You're really hurting me. I need to be with you as soon as possible, so please stop this and be with me. If you're with me very soon, once I've healed then things will get better and better for us. Even though your behaviour has been criminal and disgusting and you owe me a debt I know exactly how I would react if you would show up tomorrow, I would come alive you know? You're a part of me. I love you.

_Gaz

"Keep Britain Pagan"

Since: Jun 08

2,609

London, UK

Reply »

Report Abuse

Judge it!

#15
Feb 21, 2011

I can't think what she doesn't see in you, Pickers.

Pickford-Gordon

Since: Sep 09

117

Whipsnade, UK

Reply »

Report Abuse

Judge it!

#16
Feb 24, 2011

Nothing Tuesday 22/02/2011, Wednesday 23/02/2011, Thursday 24/02/2011. What I mean by "any details", or whatever I wrote, is something written in code, or something vague which only I and a few others can understand. For example she's at AB on this day or that day, with AB being the initials of a place at my locality, or "she's at the first institution you met her at on" this day or that day, at this time etc. Something in a similar vein.
No form of escapism that I inject myself with(not literally INJECT!) lasts very long before I start thinking about this "the girl from this place" situation...I just inject myself as a break, however...I don't live inside it like some people. There's more of course.

I have been aware, since a long time ago, with regard to A_, with 100% certainty, that the red-haired guy has had sex with her a number of times. And not just once. I am trying to calculate etc the exact damage.

Red-haired guy here's what you can do for me. If I decide when I want to talk to you I will post it here in the future. I will need information from you at some point in future. Here's what you can do.(a) Never directly or indirectly contact A_ etc. If you do that that will cause large and signicant pain/damage to myself. That of course includes you having sex with her: never do anything sexual with her.(b) Make David Cameron/Nick Clegg do what was in my letter as soon as possible. They know what was in my correspondance with them. There are updated extracts from my letter under the Topix Discussion "Hope This Leads To Her Being With Me Very Soon". These all need to come to pass as soon as possible.

LORD OF ALL LEECH

London, UK

Reply »

|
Report Abuse
|
Judge it!
|
#17
Feb 24, 2011

Lord ponce Harry the British (who pretned to be English) is the Red Haired guy..

.. nicked your bird in his arms...?.

Pickford-Gordon

Since: Sep 09

117

Whipsnade, UK

Reply »

|
Report Abuse
|
Judge it!
|
#18
Feb 24, 2011

I have been aware, since a certain time ago, that this other gentleman(I don't know anything about you, but I shall merely refer to you briefly as "this other gentleman" as I have done) has had sex with A_ a number(from 1 to infinity) of times-it is very very likely...am I CERTAIN, to one extent or another? I don't have to say! It appears that he perhaps somehow thinks that he is in the same "boat" as the red-haired guy. The two individuals are in boats which are very much apart. Do I have a small dislike for this gentleman(I'm not talking about the red-haired guy here)? I hate the red-haired guy. The red-haired guy has done and is continuing to do large and significant damage to myself. There are many reasons for this, which I will not describe. They are legal reasons. I can never hate this gentleman(I'm not talking about the red-haired guy here). While my small dislike for this gentleman(I'm not talking about the red-haired guy here) may or may not increase when I find out this or that, it will never increase into hatred; the gentleman(I'm not talking about the red-haired guy here) seems a nice fellow, although I've never spoken to him. However when I see you standing next to the red-haired guy, I think, what are they talking about? What do they have in common? Are you both talking about the "good times" you had with A_ perhaps?

The red-haired guy has committed significant crime against myself; you have not, so far as I know, and I can never hate you. I would have asked you, this time, if you had any information about her. However, the red-haired guy was also there, so there was only so long that I could remain within a certain radius of him etc. I don't mean that offensively, red-haired guy, but what I mean is that every time someone looks at another person or is aware that another person is here or there it is recorded in their DNA, in their subconscious...and I would prefer not to think about you, red-haired guy, and want to minimise the influence that you have upon me and will have upon me, because of the damage that you've done to me. If you're there, other gentleman, again, I will ask you about her. I would prefer if the guy who sent her downstairs wasn't there, as I don't trust him. He has a tendency to do things randomly etc.

The following will cause a large and significant amount of damage to myself. It is necessary for them not to occur. As I have said I do not deserve this pain...but it's not "enormous"...don't worry, A_, just be with me soon. It is necessary for the following not to occur.(a) A_ being away from me for a certain period of time.(a) A_ directly or indirectly contacting or being contacted by the red-haired guy, etc. That of course includes him doing anything sexual with her.

The following will cause an amount of damage to myself.(b) A_ having sex with a "new" guy. The "new" guy would then be yet another person taking something that I should have had, as we fell in love etc. "All these guys have had sex with her instead of me having sex with her", I would think etc. And more.

The following will cause a lesser amount of damage to myself.(c) A_ having sex otherwise. Otherwise does not include with the red-haired guy: that has already been included above.

How much damage(not large and significant or similar) would be caused to myself by her having sex with the "other gentleman" again I do not know. In fact I don't know an enormous amount about that.

Pickford-Gordon

Since: Sep 09

117

Whipsnade, UK

Reply »

Report Abuse

Judge it!

#19
Feb 25, 2011

Nothing Friday 25/02/2011. And the "other guy" wasn't here today. Of course anyone having sex with her causes me AN amount of damage. etc. Anyway, I need to talk to A_ and be with her soon. I need her. What hope is there if things are like this, in this unfair country? It's all like some sick hell. I need some sort of hope that I'll be with her soon.

Pickford-Gordon wrote:

Here's what you can do.(a) Never directly or indirectly contact A_ etc. If you do that that will cause large and signicant pain/damage to myself. That of course includes you having sex with her: never do anything sexual with her.(b) Make David

Cameron/Nick Clegg do what was in my letter as soon as possible. They know what was in my correspondance with them. There are updated extracts from my letter under the Topix Discussion "Hope This Leads To Her Being With Me Very Soon". These all need to come to pass as soon as possible.

Actually red-haired guy I do not want you to do (b). Just do (a). I suppose that you could also make that other guy come back so that I can ask him where A_ is, so that I can talk to her and be with her. However, whether you make the other guy come back or not, I will still feel exactly the same about you.

Pickford-Gordon

Since: Sep 09

117

Whipsnade, UK

Reply »

|
Report Abuse
|
Judge it!
|
#20
Feb 25, 2011

Also, anyone who's not the red-haired guy can help me with this.

Pickford-Gordon

Since: Sep 09

117

Whipsnade, UK

Reply »

|
Report Abuse
|

Judge it!

#21
Feb 27, 2011

Nothing Saturday 26/02/2011, Sunday 27/02/2011.

A_, there are no excuses when it comes to love, with regard to you and me(two people who fell in love), in the situation in which you and I are in.

"Other guy", as you know we spoke briefly on Saturday 26/02/2011. Firstly, some corrections to what I said earlier, as I have been consulting my memories etc. I DO HAVE more than a small dislike for you, although it is not hatred. However, I don't know a number of things...I COULD find out this or that which would cause enormous damage to myself resulting in me hating you more than I hate the red-haired guy. Please ignore anything which contradicts this, which I've written so far. I shall not say how much dislike I have for you. Damage to myself is never good, and I wonder how much I can sustain. I know with 100% certainty that you have had sex with A_ a number of times. I realise that you perhaps didn't want me to be damaged by the truth, and so told me that she was your niece, which was a lie, crime. NEVER LIE. Lies, in certain cases, can cause a person to give up on life. Once truth drugs and advanced police techniques become commonplace we can all root out people who believe in the lie of "getting away with it" etc, before they send everyone down, including themselves. See the various discussions started by myself. Did the guy who sent her downstairs tell you to lie to me? You should not obey other people, as you are your own person. Are you "with" her at the moment? Have you been with her recently? Or have you not seen her for a significant period of time? What I DO know is that(and of course you know this, as what was said was said!) you have information for me regarding her. Of course, since you had sex with her. That would have involved gaining information before that happened, or something.

I shall also be at the place where I first met her(in addition to "this place" which is the place where I've been coming in every day) Monday, Tuesday, and possibly Wednesday, Thursday, Friday, and Saturday, but I shall update everyone on that on Monday or Tuesday. I prefer to talk to people at that place, which is the place where I first met her. I believe, "other guy", that you were there before, and I would prefer to talk to you at that place. It is best that you only trust myself, and the law, the truth, the one way.

Tell me when this thread is updated:
(Registration is not required)

Add to my Tracker

Send me an email

Showing posts 1 - 20 of 29

< prev page

|

next page >

Go to last page| Jump to page: 1 2

Type in your comments below

Name
(appears on your post)

Comments

Type the numbers you see in the image on the right:

Please note by clicking on "Post Comment" you acknowledge that you have read the Terms of Service and the comment you are posting is in compliance with such terms. Be polite. Inappropriate posts may be removed by the moderator. Send us your feedback.

34 Users are viewing the United Kingdom Forum right now

Search the United Kingdom Forum:

Topic

Updated

Last By

Comments

Get A Gun While You Still Can

23 min

Tory II

829

London riots: Your reaction

31 min

TOASTER

161

Ex-soap star 'was in murder gang'

1 hr

Alan

1

Loyalists not issuing threats - UPRG (Jun '09)

1 hr

The Knife

156

Explaining the true message of Islam (Feb '11)

1 hr

Day

8,015

Girl, 14, 'tied up' during sex jury hears 3:07pm...

2 hr

bal

1,008

Paxman in empire education call

2 hr

blacksun

3

See all threads in the United Kingdom forum »

If the election were held tomorrow, who would get your vote? Vote now on the Election Poll, Sept 2011 Map.

United Kingdom News
- Call for changes on extradition
- Paxman in empire education call
- Body found after harbour alert
- Two Britons held by Kenyan police
- Online hate campaign leads to 8 months' jail term
- Clichés are spreading like the plague - but we ...
- Party lecturer admits drug offences
- UK government considers ban on squatters
- Three held following Bexley murder of electrician
- Hague reopens UK's embassy in Tripoli
- ATC constraints added to diverted Air India fli...
- First tram set for depot delivery

More United Kingdom News from Topix »

See news from Newspaper Archives »

Daily Horoscope for October 18

Sagittarius

Now that you have the scoop on the local crowd, you feel comfortable to discuss what is on your mind. Perhaps you have taken the plunge and joined a new group, or you are just content to talk to a trusted friend. Either way, communications are wide open now, so make the most of it.

Get your Horoscope »

United Kingdom
Forums & Polls
News
Real-Time News

Explore More Topix
Home Page
Forums & Polls
Most Popular
Top Stories
Hurricanes
US News
US cities list
World News
World countries list
Politics
Business
Sci-Tech
Sports
Entertainment
Music
Television
People
Health
Food
Life
Autos
Finance
Movies
Travel
Electronics
Home
Blogs
Offbeat
Site Map / All Topics

About Topix
About Us
Media Kit
Feedback?
FAQ
Jobs
Law Enforcement
School Officials
Cyber-bullying Resources
RSS Newsfeeds
Press Room
Privacy

Terms of Service
Weblog

Local Classifieds & Listings

Reach Local customers. Post a classified listing for your business. Promote job, auto, rental, and local event listings.

Learn more »

Join the Topix Community
Create your own profile, complete with quick links to your favorite topics.
Personalize your forum posts with your photo and hometown.
Exchange Personal Messages with other registered users.

Sign up today! »

Feedback?
Comments made yesterday: 93,335 Total comments across all topics: 155,325,662

Copyright ©2011 Topix LLC

Local News: United Kingdom

Sign Up

Sign In

1 23

Libya
Clinton on unannounced trip to Libya

Wall Street
Douglas E. Schoen: What Occupy Wall Street Protesters Really B...

China
China's Need for Speed

Home
Forums
Top Stories
Popular
Local
Election Poll
US
Politics
World
Sports
Entertainment
Offbeat
Other

United Kingdom
 News
Forums & Polls the girl from this pl...

Real-Time News

the girl from this place

Posted in the United Kingdom Forum

Share

Read
 29 Comments

Add to my Tracker

More United Kingdom Discussions »

Comments (Page 2)

Showing posts 21 - 29 of 29

< prev page

|

next page >

Go to last page| Jump to page: 1 2

Pickford-Gordon

Since: Sep 09

117

Whipsnade, UK

Reply »

|
Report Abuse
|
Judge it!
|
#22
Feb 27, 2011

"Other guy", you were somewhat disrespectful and hostile towards me, which I didn't like. Why? My value as a human being is not lower than that of others. Males such as yourself have to take responsibility when someone such as A_ has been behaving like this. It's harmful to do things randomly. But I shall not describe what happened etc. Will you have more debts to pay me, or less or the same debts to pay me if you don't give me information about her? Right, you'll have MORE debts to pay me if you don't give me information about her; I'm really not in a good place right now. I despair when someone refuses to do even that, with regard to something which should already have happened now and could have happened easily-namely you giving me all the information. There are absolutely no excuses when it comes to paying your debts to others, and, after consulting my memories etc I know that you yourself DO have debts to pay me. Nowhere near as many as the red-haired guy, so far as I know, but there is still no reason for you not to help me asap. Please see the "Crimes" section(I wonder about the title, but it shall remain nonetheless), from "Hope This Leads To Her Being With Me Very Soon", in fact see the whole "Hope This Leads To Her Being With Me Very Soon". So, "what people tell you" doesn't matter, and the following do not exist:

"reputation"(also known as "image"), and "opinion"; in addition "paranoia" is a problem if someone's paranoid. I shall now explain something with regard to your excuse "I don't know you. I don't know who you are." Phrases such as that do not exist, and are not REASONS as such. If you have questions about myself, ask. What do you want to know about myself?

"KNOWING" ME I do things in the name of the law. If I tell you that you can trust me, then that is the truth, and it IS the truth. I want information so that I can talk to A_ and be with her. And I am not the sort of person to leave personal information regarding A_ lying around.

If you ARE at "this place" as opposed to the preferred "place where I first met her", don't stand next to the red-haired guy. Also not next to the guy who might have told you to lie to me, or that woman who was there before, who hates me. Or, if you walk off towards the exit or something like you did on Saturday then I'll talk to you and the information can be obtained and I can be with her.

I won't lie to you all, things are bad for me right now, to one extent or another. I wouldn't have resorted to posting on the internet if things weren't bad for me right now, to one extent or another. Neither would I have stated, well, this whole thread, but especially, "Listen to me...you", if things weren't bad for me right now, to one extent or another. I was waiting for Mr Clegg to accomplish the things in my first letter, and to interfere with the progress of the first letter by sending a second letter which I said and which indeed IS infinitely more important than the first, is not something I would have done were things not bad for me right now, to one extent or another. Also sending copies of it and an additional page to a number of M.P.s. And you also have to imagine the effect upon a human being of him coming in every day for her for a long time after she left suddenly, with her not being there.

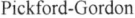

Pickford-Gordon

Since: Sep 09

117

Whipsnade, UK

Reply »

|
Report Abuse
|
Judge it!
|
#23
Feb 28, 2011

Nothing Monday 28/02/2011, although I did speak to a number of people at that place.

"Other guy", we spoke today, as you know. You suggested that, concerning A_, I speak to a certain individual who will be in tomorrow, implying a little that I should speak to this individual instead of to you. However, I am unable to comply with the suggestion, and cannot speak to either you, the individual, or anyone else at the place or any other place of that nature concerning A_, as I was told today that A_ has contacted the place and told them not to give out any information about her to me. I was told not to ask for information about her at the place, or any other place of that nature(I assume). I will comply with that, the fake "laws of the place". "Other guy", I remember that I said something like: "I would prefer to speak to her in person and not have a conversation with her through you, as such"; you said: "Why?" When a "mediator" is used instead of two persons having a conversation, many problems can occur.(1) The "mediator" could accidentally alter sections of what was said.(2) The "mediator" could deliberately alter sections of what was said.(3) Either of the two persons using the mediator could THINK that the "mediator" has conveyed the information incorrectly, the sections of what was said. It is better not to have a "mediator", as there is always the risk of error if a "mediator" is used. And again, "other guy", what was with the hostility at the end?

I shall continue to come in, and shall also be at the "place where I first met her" on Tuesday, and Wednesday, and possibly Thursday, Friday and Saturday too, although I will update everyone with news of that.

MESSAGES FOR A_
The last time I saw you and tried to talk to you was on Friday 14/01/2011. I began posting on the internet with regard to this, with "the girl from this place" on Wednesday 09/02/2011, and did not resort to typing the first letter of your first name on the internet until Monday 21/02/2011, well over a month since you just left. I have referred to you as A_, and my full name is there of course. However I have not gone into any other details about anything, except vaguely. I have referred to a "woman who hates me", a "red-haired guy" which should really be corrected into "guy who happens to have orange hair", an "other guy", and a "guy who sent her(you) downstairs". That is more of less all that I have typed with regard to specifying this or that. Only a number of people are therefore aware of what I'm talking about. There are an enormous number of females who have first names beginning with "a", and there are many varieties of first names, for females, beginning with "a". As for "Hope This Leads To Her Being With Me Very Soon", I'm still correcting sections of that. I've been hurt by A NUMBER of females, including yourself, so you must bear that in mind.
I haven't done anything to deserve this, and you're not treating me like a human being, like before. How do you think I feel right now? You contacted people at the place, and you didn't say, "Tell Daniel Pickford-Gordon I'll be at this place or (the place where I first met you) on this day next week" or something, you said, "Don't give Daniel Pickford-Gordon any information about me." Using a "mediator" like that is still a risk, however...YOU need to show up instead, preferably at "the place where I first met you" on one or more of the days I've indicated above. I only want information about you so that I can talk to you and be with you. If I say that you can trust me then that's the truth. I don't feel happy at all because of what you've done to me and what you're STILL doing to me. Please talk to me soon and be with me.

Pickford-Gordon

Since: Sep 09

117

Whipsnade, UK

Reply »

|
Report Abuse
|
Judge it!
|
#24
Mar 1, 2011

Nothing Tuesday 02/03/2011. When I said "things are bad for me right now, to one extent or another", I didn't mean ENORMOUSLY bad. Actually, with regard to the "place where I first met her", I may or may not go in on Wednesday, Thursday, Friday, and Saturday.

Pickford-Gordon

Since: Sep 09

117

Whipsnade, UK

Reply »

Report Abuse

Judge it!

#25
Mar 3, 2011

Nothing Wednesday 02/03/2011, Thursday 03/03/2011.

Dr Quackorian

Leominster, UK

Reply »

Report Abuse

Judge it!

#26
Mar 4, 2011

letś try doubling the dosage on old Pickers, eh , chaps? still seems totally loopy to me.

Pickford-Gordon

Since: Sep 09

117

Whipsnade, UK

Reply »

|
Report Abuse
|
Judge it!
|
#27
Mar 4, 2011

Dr Quackorian wrote:

letś try doubling the dosage on old Pickers, eh , chaps? still seems totally loopy to me.
You and the copies of yourself(that is, IF you're not, to one extent or another, the same person), copies of a criminal, living in your own little fake, harmful world which has been illegally permitted to exist, have persisted in hijacking my threads. You repeat the same comments, clinging to your fake concepts. All you're doing is committing crime against me. Did you not hear about the forces? But of course what is left of humanity is not meant to wait for the forces. In the future your identity will be found out, and, through government, through the law, an equivalent of the damage that you have done to me will be returned to you, whatever that is. And these things that you do decrease your value as a human being. Did you read "Why Destruction Occurs?"(incomplete-ish)? It means that NO ONE "gets away" with anything. Even if you escape government, the forces will get you because of what you've done, to one extent or another. Never hijack this thread...or any other thread of mine, or any other thread, with your illegality.

Pickford-Gordon

Since: Sep 09

117

Whipsnade, UK

Reply »

|
Report Abuse
|
Judge it!

\#28
Mar 4, 2011

Nothing Friday 04/03/2011. The pain of lonliness, jealousy, and horniness, can't compare to the greatest pain. The greatest(not GREAT pain, though) pain, which is growing to AN extent(it's not ENORMOUS, though), is the pain of this "A_ incident" and the pain of not being with A_. I will continue to come in.

Pickford-Gordon

Since: Sep 09

117

Whipsnade, UK

Reply »

Report Abuse

Judge it!

\#29
Mar 6, 2011

Nothing Saturday 05/03/2011, Sunday 06/03/2011. I can't believe that I said "You're a part...you." on the damn INTERNET! But she's still not here...and I'm not feeling that good right now. It's not ENORMOUSLY bad though.

howie

Newcastle Upon Tyne, UK

Reply »

Report Abuse

Judge it!

\#31
Mar 9, 2011

sure i saw her with gadaffi on telly

Tell me when this thread is updated:
(Registration is not required)

Add to my Tracker

Send me an email

Showing posts 21 - 29 of 29

< prev page

|

next page >

Go to last page| Jump to page: 1 2

Type in your comments below

Name
(appears on your post)

Comments

Type the numbers you see in the image on the right:

Please note by clicking on "Post Comment" you acknowledge that you have read the Terms of Service and the comment you are posting is in compliance with such terms. Be polite. Inappropriate posts may be removed by the moderator. Send us your feedback.

34 Users are viewing the United Kingdom Forum right now

Search the United Kingdom Forum:

Topic

Updated

Last By

Comments

Get A Gun While You Still Can

24 min

Tory II

829

London riots: Your reaction

32 min

TOASTER

161

Ex-soap star 'was in murder gang'

1 hr

Alan

1

Loyalists not issuing threats - UPRG (Jun '09)

1 hr

The Knife

156

Explaining the true message of Islam (Feb '11)

1 hr

Day

8,015

Girl, 14, 'tied up' during sex jury hears3:07pm...

2 hr

bal

1,008

Paxman in empire education call

2 hr

blacksun

3

See all threads in the United Kingdom forum »

If the election were held tomorrow, who would get your vote? Vote now on the Election Poll, Sept 2011 Map.

United Kingdom News
|Call for changes on extradition
|Paxman in empire education call
|Body found after harbour alert
|Two Britons held by Kenyan police
|Online hate campaign leads to 8 months' jail term
|Clichés are spreading like the plague - but we ...
|Party lecturer admits drug offences
|UK government considers ban on squatters
|Three held following Bexley murder of electrician
|Hague reopens UK's embassy in Tripoli
|ATC constraints added to diverted Air India fli...
|First tram set for depot delivery

More United Kingdom News from Topix »

See news from Newspaper Archives »

Daily Horoscope for October 18

Taurus

You're determined to stand your ground, as you know full well your present viewpoint is in your best interests. You have assessed your situation and have firm goals that you need to pursue. The immediate need is to resolve an imbalance in a close relationship.

Get your Horoscope »

United Kingdom
Forums & Polls
News
Real-Time News

Explore More Topix
Home Page
Forums & Polls
Most Popular
Top Stories
Hurricanes
US News
US cities list
World News
World countries list

Politics
Business
Sci-Tech
Sports
Entertainment
Music
Television
People
Health
Food
Life
Autos
Finance
Movies
Travel
Electronics
Home
Blogs
Offbeat
Site Map / All Topics

About Topix
About Us
Media Kit
Feedback?
FAQ
Jobs
Law Enforcement
School Officials
Cyber-bullying Resources
RSS Newsfeeds
Press Room
Privacy
Terms of Service
Weblog

Local Classifieds & Listings

Reach Local customers. Post a classified listing for your business. Promote job, auto, rental, and local event listings.

Learn more »

Join the Topix Community
¡Create your own profile, complete with quick links to your favorite topics.
¡Personalize your forum posts with your photo and hometown.
¡Exchange Personal Messages with other registered users.

Sign up today! »

Feedback?
Comments made yesterday: 93,335 Total comments across all topics: 155,325,748

Copyright ©2011 Topix LLC

the physical and mental differences between the human male and the human female

United Kingdom
News
Forums & PollsTHE PHYSICAL AND MENT...

Real-Time News

the physical and mental differences between the human male and the human female

Posted in the United Kingdom Forum

Share

Read
Comments below
Add to my Tracker

More United Kingdom Discussions »

Comments

Showing posts1 - 1 of1

Pickford-Gordon

Since: Sep 09

137

London, UK

Reply »

Report Abuse

Judge it!

#1
2 hrs ago

===========
THE PHYSICAL AND MENTAL DIFFERENCES BETWEEN THE HUMAN MALE AND THE HUMAN FEMALE
===========

DRAFT ETCETERA
1.
I may or may not use all of these, etcetera.
2.
Maternal Instinct; The Maternal Instinct In The Human Female; Effect Of The Maternal Instinct Upon The Human Female; There Is No Paternal Instinct; Human Females Are Susceptible To The Concept Of The "Child"; Effect Of Fear Upon The Human Female; The Human Male Is Physically Stronger Than The Human Female; The Human Female Is Susceptible To Fear; The Human Female Is Perhaps Jealous Of The Human Male, Leading To Irritation Against The Human Male; The Human Female Often, Or Perhaps More Than Often, Is Judged By Physical Features, Such As Attractiveness, Unlike The Human Male; Attractiveness "Runs Out", With Aging; Increased Pressures On The Human Female; It Is The Nature Of The Human Female To Lose Control; It Is The Nature Of The Human Female To Oppose The 1 Fact; Modify All Of The Above?.

Tell me when this thread is updated:
(Registration is not required)

Add to my Tracker

Send me an email

Showing posts1 - 1 of1

LETTER TO NICHOLAS CLEGG 2: PART OF
Date: Thursday 13 January 2011(until Sunday 23 January 2011)

Dear Mr Nick Clegg,

WRITINGS
Accepting What I Say As Truth(1)

Advice For You
Assessment(1) or (1*)
Crimes(1)

Forcing People To Do Things(1)
Laws Without Punishment

Living In Escapism(2)

People, Types Of(1) or (2)
[NOTE, NOT IN THE ORIGINAL LETTER: I don't seem to have created this section in the copies of "Letter To Nicholas Clegg 2" that i have: however, that doesn't necessarily mean that i didn't create it. I don't remember whether i created the actual section, the actual content, or not....or if i solely created just the above title in the "Contents" section. It appears, actually, that this section IS "Types Of People(1) or (2)".]

Possible Suicide For Myself If I Am Not Permitted To Be With Her(1)

Promises And Lies(1)
Repetitive Shouting In A Foreign Language

Sexual Intercourse For Female Humans(1)
Situation With Regard To This Female Human(1*)

Story of My Life With Regard To Females And Other Things(1)
Suicide(1)
Theft(1)

Tory Party(1) or (2)
Types Of People(1) or (2)

Why Destruction Occurs
MATTERS

Crimes And Possible Crimes Committed Against Me By This Girl(1*)
Crimes And Possible Crimes Committed Against Me By This Guy(2) or (3)
Epilation Replacing Shaving(2)
Evidence of Love(1)
Explanation of Crimes And Possible Crimes Committed Against Me By This Girl(1*)
Explanation of Crimes And Possible Crimes Committed Against Me By This Guy(2) or (3)
Females And Homosexuals In Parliament, Voting, And The Queen Issues(1) or (2)

Government Self-Publishing Industry(3)
Guilty Until Proved Innocent(2)

Internet Control
Leaving Britain(2)
Legal Cheapness(2)
Legal Glossary(1*)
Legal System Changes(2)
Myself Remaining Unemployed Provided I Take Steps Such As Writing To Someone To Bring My Criminals To Justice(1)
M.P. Letter Reader(2)
M.P. Response(1)
Police Technique Interrogation of Anyone Who Has Committed A Crime(1*)

Royal Mail

Taking Someone To Court For Something That Doesn't Exist

Television Conversion(3)
Truth Drugs(1)

Washing Machine. Laundrette Ban(3)

WRITINGS
Accepting What I Say As Truth(1)
I would like to be labelled as a 100% trustworthy individual, with regard to this incident, and if you wish other things as well, although other things are irrelevant to what I need; I need 100% trustworthy labelling with regard to this incident. That means that if I say something with regard to this girl and this guy, that is taken as fact without any enormous need for the words of this girl and this guy. I have said this or that with regard to this incident, therefore that must be the case. What matters is that I get better before it's too late, and I need to first talk to this girl and then to be with her for that to happen, as soon as possible. I am aware that my value as a human being goes down if I lie, and I have not done so. I will not lie, as I do not wish my lifespan to be shortened. This girl may be somewhat of a liar, and the guy is possibly a liar and also a criminal if he is having sexual intercourse with her. The girl is weak, unbalanced, paranoid, confused, and is being corrupted, and may lie with regard to this. These things are for her own good, as I need to be with her very soon if I am ever to recover.

Advice For You
First, "Promises". Many people sign documents every day. You signed a "written pledge". Most people have probably signed something without knowing what. It is just scribbling on a piece of paper. Perhaps we should abolish signings altogether, or something less extreme! But if you say things like "I definitely promise this or that" into someone's visage(face) then you can get into trouble. Never do that! Just hear the voice of truth and law, as I do, and act according to it. I believe right now that Labour and Liberal Democrats are the rightful people in charge of the country, although like many, they do not front(face) things, issues. The student protesters seem to be part of a "culture". They are acting like children, saying "You PROMISED."...but busy politics is not love. Instead they should suggest some alternative. If everyone behaved like me and like Labour and Liberal Democrats with regard to writing letters, much would get done.

Second, Crimes. For everyone to heal, and I will probably go around saying this, you should make a list of all crimes committed against you. In order to heal you will need to hurt and possibly execute certain people from your past, and I would say most Labour and Liberal Democrats have had crimes committed against them. This is judged by the hatred. People have hatred because a crime has been committed against them, and guilt when they commit a crime. Two crimes committed against you, I read briefly off the internet I believe, were "dog mess through door" and "spat at in the street". "Spat at in the street" can be grouped into "spat in the direction of", "spat near", "spat on (clothing)" "spat on skin" and "spat on visage(face) or head.". You can do extreme things to someone if the last is the case, but, perhaps or perhaps not, only if the same person does it twice to you. "Dog mess" would be "harmful(toxic) substances through the letterbox in an envelope" . I have no idea how it feels for something like that to happen, but it's probably extremely bad. Look inside yourself and pinpoint the person or people that have hurt you the most. Many people get sucked into things, living with crime and crimes having been committed against them. I can tell you though that those things will NEVER go away for all people, and must be fronted(faced). And you're at the head of POLITICS, so you could directly create laws to help you, as well as laws to help others. This was the sort of thing I hoped you would read into when I said, in my first letter, "Having crime committed against someone such as yourself is not something that the individual should ever tolerate."

Third, "fashion". In the media-and-certain-group controlled england, various things are in fashion here and there, and are manipulated by the media. One of the latest ones is "Nick Clegg's a liar" and nonsense to that extent, as you did not lie but probably forgot what you had signed. This appears to be the latest fashion, "bash Nick Clegg" . If this or that insults you just shut it down, why should you take it? It's corrupting people anyway isn't it?

Fourth, if you get rid of "Prayers" in Parliament more can get done. There is no such thing as "Prayers".

Fifth, the political process needs to be speeded up...everything from Parliament happens slowly, taking a long time. It'll be more jobs too.

Assessment(1) or (1*)
You could have someone make an assessment of the situation based solely on a person's story, and for Parliament to act.

Crimes(1)
Could you please shut down and/or punish anything and anyone who says that the following things are ok. The girl I fell in love with has already been corrupted by some of these ideologies, but her real brain is crying out for me. Female humans are like two people. One is real, and wants to be with someone she has fallen in love with. The other one is false, and conflicts with the real one, talking of some of the things I will mention. I have suffered enormously because I look a tiny tiny bit Arabic or European or something perhaps or perhaps not, am not part of the system, do not have friends at the moment by choice, put effort into things and am not casual, am different, and don't conform to the bulls**t. Many girls have fallen in love with me, but the system orders them not to obey their own brain, they are not "allowed" to be happy or make me happy.

FRIENDS/PEER PRESSURE. Females are often corrupted by this. They should not take the words of this/these as fact, but they do much of the time. Many of them are weak, and the voices of the so-called friends very frequently conflict with what their brain is trying to tell them is the truth. Therefore they become weak and ill. They must not treat their words as fact, and perhaps should not spend so much, too much, or any time with them. SOCIAL Talking is a means of transmitting information, there is no such thing as "social". UPBRINGING More implanted illegal false messages into someone's brain. YOU'RE NOT ALLOWED TO LOVE HIM, OR EVEN TREAT HIM AS A HUMAN BEING. This has been a frequent theme of my life. The only message which a girl must understand and obey is love. Love is the most important and the most harmful thing in existence. If she loves a guy she must drop everything else and make it known to him, that is her duty. It is the girl's choice, if she has fallen in love with him, and the guy's, not anyone else's. BE AFRAID OF A MAN BASED ON HIS LOOKS Many men have hatred, and therefore become menacing and creepy. People have hatred because of crimes that have been committed against them. Many females are paranoid, and they are afraid of me despite the fact that I have not given them any reason to be afraid. There is also this "fear mongering" in the media and in the system, designed to kill decent people like me because of how I am menacing. This "evil killer" thing as well: these are criminals to be understood and pitied, and they should have been helped and protected. Also, get rid of all talk of "Evil Islamics". In many ways to one extent or another they are 100% innocent, and there is probably much that they can teach. My current view is that people are always lucky to live in Islamic and other strongly religious countries as opposed to others because there is less adultery, betrayal, worthless females, harm to good men, lies, and a general sense of purity as opposed to shallowness. BE AFRAID OF ANY MAN YOU DO NOT UNDERSTAND It would take a very long time for females to understand me. They need to accept that I am complicated. But of course I want and need this ONE girl, no one else now. LOOKS A girl's looks are not affected when she talks to a man, so she should just talk to him whatever he looks like. CLOTHING/DRESS SENSE/STYLE There is no such thing as dress sense/clothing/style. They are shallowness themselves and corruption; they harm humanity if permitted to exist. WHAT PEOPLE TELL YOU This doesn't matter. Truth and fact and law matter, and suffering and victims, and rapid deterioration. Two people's happiness is important. This harms females, and has harmed the girl that I fell in love with, who takes what people tell her as truth. However, of course there are people who will manipulate, lie, and other things. It is better to say "Do not talk to me, thank you." REPUTATION No such thing. FREEDOM. The government is meant to control every aspect of every person's life. However, although "control" is what it is, that is not the case in reality. You see, better people automatically obey laws and recognise the presence of other people. However, even if someone says, "I don't want to obey this law", the law in many cases has been created for the person's own good. For example talk of monogamy and relationships are GOOD, while promiscuity can be BAD to different extents. Also, laws exist to protect people. PARANOIA All girls must drop this. They must TRUST MEN, she should TRUST ME. OPINION. There is no such thing as opinion, merely the correct way and the incorrect way. Opinion is a false creation of our race. However many issues are complex and require an understanding of the victim's situation and value and the criminal's situation and value. However when evidence occurs of certain things, things change. In a majority or all cases, you have to be on the victim's side. After all, when someone commits a crime they have to die, die off, or be killed at some point don't they? Especially if/when the victim asks for it...or when the victim dies. And I would like you to encourage effort and wanting to talk to a female, and remove anything with paranoia and casualness. But I hope and beg for (1) and (1*) etc to occur.

Forcing People To Do Things(1)
Many individuals are escapist, and will remain in escapism unless the government forces them out of it. On the other hand there are people like me. Any more pressure from anything now might kill me, after what this girl and that smug bast**d who I think it's likely she's having sex with are doing to me. So people who GENUINELY have suffered enormously and are in a bad state such as myself should not be forced to do this and that. But for happy people they must be forced to do this and that.
Laws Without Punishment
In my last letter I mentioned a number of laws without putting any punishment after them. What is important is that the truth, fact, what happened, is confirmed for every crime. If the punishment is something that the criminal is afraid of, the criminal may lie in order to avoid it, out of fear. This will prolong the extraction of the data, causing even more harm to an already damaged victim. Therefore I would like you to pass certain laws without punishment...the punishment can be put later.

Living In Escapism(2)
Enormous numbers of people live in escapism. But crime never goes away. These are some of the culprits, the "toys" to keep people from pure happiness and understanding…to keep people suffering. I would like them reduced or shut down, and an expansion of the courts, legal and police system. WORK. An exception with the escapism of work is politics. Politicians can directly create laws which will help them with regard to the crimes they have committed and the crimes committed against them. However, work can be a drain. It can also be enormously involving. I have no doubt that there are people who spend 30 years working but still live with the scars of crime committed against them. They should take some time off. And many areas are unnecessary, especially in the media. ENTERTAINMENT. People laugh, cry, eat popcorn. But the crime is still there.

FRIENDS/GROUPS. Conversation distracts you, and can be pointless. And the crime will return to haunt you, unless it is fronted(faced). SEXUAL INTERCOURSE. Sexual intercourse can be pleasurable, but again, crime still there. FOOD AND DRINK. NATURE. EARTH. SPACE. TRANSPORTATION. And I can tell you that there are a number of people who live with guilt in escapism, and a number who live with hatred in escapism. The forms of escapism all cast a sort of "spell" over many.

Possible Suicide For Myself If I Am Not Permitted To Be With Her(1)
I have hope that this girl will talk to me and will be handed over to me sexually if she isn't with me after we have talked. However if too much time passes with them having sex or if the government refuses to even do a tiny set of things to come to the rescue of an innocent, weakening victim such as myself I must ask you for this. I cannot live in a universe where I am not permitted to be with her.

Promises And Lies(1)
Lying is a crime. Breaking a promise is a crime. However, to what extent are they crimes? In your case Deputy Prime Minister(!) it was just a form. Just don't do it again! There is also the case of what we're dealing with. Hasn't politics been a performance for a long time? It has. Therefore acting isn't that bad(is my current view) with regard to politics. However lying and breaking promises can mean execution with regard to some things. With regard to friendship it can mean execution. But ESPECIALLY with regard to the topics of sexual intercourse and love. I shall now explain. When you make a promise to someone, either a "body" promise such as informing someone that you love them, or a distinct verbal promise or something, it enters into the other person's mind. The same when you say something which is a lie. When the other person finds out, harm is done to him/her. The value of the person who lied or broke the promise also goes down. Love, in my current situation with this girl, is a promise, an agreement, which needs to be paid sexually and with love by her as soon as possible. Hypocrisy is also a crime, a lie...if someone passes themselves off as this or that and then something distinctly different is the truth, it harms others as that information has entered into other peoples' brains, and harms them when they find out the truth.
Repetitive Shouting In A Foreign Language
Could you create a law which prevents this? I have somewhat thin walls. One of the many problems with the continued process of immigration is that one or two immigrants bring their "third world culture" outside my home. Of course a number of men in this country are just "taking" this sort of thing, and much else. I however am not weak and submissive, even now.

Sexual Intercourse For Female Humans(1)
There are two categories. The first is for a girl to have sexual intercourse with someone that she loves. And the second is for a girl to have sexual intercourse with someone that she doesn't love. Sexual intercourse with someone that she loves is a beautiful thing, natural, both parties are happy and experience something that I have never known but have always wanted. There are never any problems, and there is little chance or no chance that anyone needs to be executed. RELATIONSHIPS are good, or one or two, I don't know! Not 25 surely. Prostitutes are girls that have sex with all males of a group or of all groups which they do not love. They have a significant value as they help, equally. They are honest(dishonesty is a crime), not hypocrites(hypocrisy is a crime), and function in a correct(-ish) manner. People descended from relationship girls live longer than those descended from criminals. Females who have sexual intercourse with someone they don't love or like strongly, when they're not prostitutes are criminals if they turn down a worthy male in need, or possibly otherwise. Some are more criminal than others. Having sex due to alcohol, weakness and giving in, confusion, this or that being fashionable, because it was her boss, because of an agreement, because of lies, hypocrisy, money, shallowness, arrogance when you don't have the right to be arrogant being a criminal...anything that hurts a male...these are all crimes, making those girls criminals. Anyone descended from them will not live as long as others, as they can never be as good as innocent females. There is a person's blood in their DNA. It's shameful to be such a person. And of course where the female loves a male, and also where a male loves a female, it can lead to severe consequences if certain things happen unless healing begins as soon as possible. The more love a female has for a male she has sexual intercourse with, unless she owes another male when love is concerned, the better,

as her body is of greater value. A number of the men in this country are weak and will put up with anything from females, leading them to think that criminal behaviour is ok, further harming her value. In many cases if a female has sexual intercourse with a guy that she only likes a little, easily, and then spends a long time and is difficult before she has sexual intercourse with another guy, that second guy is going to be harmed when he finds out that she was easy with this other guy...he'll think "Is that other guy better than me?" Whether he is or isn't, harm is done. Sexual things are not fun for females...you harm the male who loves you, yourself, the male you don't love, and many others every time you "dish out" your body to anyone else. Every human female's body has A value, as does the human female. It is enormously easy if a female has sexual intercourse easily and/or with a male that she has no real love or strong desire for to harm others and herself; for crimes such as hypocrisy to occur. It is also possible in such cases that such cases LEAD to some sort of prostitution somehow; that in a normal world they would either end up as a relationship girl or some kind of prostitute; but of course hypocrisy, lies, arrogance when she has no right to be arrogant having committed crime...these things are all very frequent in england.

Situation With Regard To This Female Human(1*)
When the primary institution I used closed for a while I went to a secondary one. I saw this girl working there, and thought she was beautiful. We chatted a tiny bit. I asked slightly awkwardly whether she had a boyfriend or partner, and she said "Yes." Then another time I was talking to her, although she ignoring me somewhat, and she often would ignore me, and I asked her how things were going with him. She paused for about a full five seconds or so, and then blinking and shaking her head a little said "Yes, fine." One day I walked in and she smiled in my direction and made some comment to her fellow workers about me. However, when I approached and began talking to her while making a transaction, she cast her eyes down, knowing I was flirting, and clenched her fist. And one time I didn't do anything at all but she became paranoid and ran off and didn't come out again. I went back to the central institution, which had reopened. After A period I came down the stairs from activities upstairs. I turned and saw that she had come out. I thought, her again. I carried on with my usual routine, but I noticed that she was quite often there. I thought, she's checking me out! However, I knew that one or two girls had ALMOST formed strong desire for me, and had sat upstairs in order to talk to me. I thought, if this girl ALMOST loves me or SOMETHING, she'll do the same. There would be no point talking to her downstairs, especially after her past behaviour towards me. By 30/12/2010 I had noticed that a lot of the time that I had gone downstairs she had been coming out. Plus my feelings for her had grown somewhat. It'd be an insult to her if I'd ask out any other girl. 30/12/2010. I entered the institution thinking that. I saw this young man who worked there standing with her, and this other girl. This young man I'm fairly sure had had sex with two of the girls who work there(it's a slightly creepy place as those two girls, and possibly more, have had sex with probably more of the guys who work there) and possibly more; the young man was skinny, looked about 19(but I'm rubbish with ages so it's probably older or younger). I saw that she paused in front of him in a flirtatious manner when they were using the till. I went downstairs later, hoping that he would be gone but he was still there. I paused by some items. Her head came up, very quickly looking right at me and then down, and then she did this again about 5 minutes later. I thought "She's more into me than I thought earlier." She also turned to front(face) me when I walked a bit. Now this other girl who felt strongly towards me was acting somewhat hostilely towards this girl that I was into; jealously, because of me. This girl who felt strongly towards me actually came up towards me...she had also dropped hints before, although it had taken her a full year to summon up the courage due to paranoia, being a mess, arrogance etc. I thought: "Why couldn't this girl I'm into do that? Hmm, she's not as much into me as the other girl." I walked towards the exit. I would never forgive myself if I had talked to the girl then, I thought. I could imagine the bast**d going "Do you know him?" then them talking and then him asking her out or something. A lot of guys from my past have used my initial conversation or approaching a girl to their advantage. I thought he wouldn't dare ask her anything on his own, if I didn't say anything to her. I thought I'll come back tomorrow and ask this girl out, when you're gone, definitely. Anyway I was walking towards the exit. This girl turned, shaking a little, and ran downstairs fast, upset. I thought, she's upset that I didn't talk to her. As I was walking I saw the young man start to follow after her, then he looked at me. I saw this look of sheer disgust and hatred, jealousy. I had seen that look before, on the guy who was having sex with this habitual liar and guilt lover that I had fallen for. This guy is insulted that she loves me, someone it's "shameful" to love, or something to that extent, and not him. I looked back and he was still glaring at me. Finally as I got to the street he was still glaring at me. Then I was off. I saw how she didn't even notice him at all when I walked into the room. 31/01/2010. I came in specifically to ask this girl out, although I did my usual things as an excuse of course...in topsy turvy England there are rules AGAINST lovers instead of FOR lovers. It is necessary for a male to go up to a female in order to talk to her. Anyway, she wasn't there that day. Over the next few days I began thinking. I thought, this girl has been downstairs when I've come out a great deal of the time. I think I searched my mind. I remembered how she always fronted(faced) me, always watching me, with this "yeah, yeah it's true" look on her visage(face). Then I remembered her behaviour on 30/01/2010. Then I went back in my mind to when she had come out. I realised then that it had been every time. Every time I had gone to that institution, and come downstairs, she had come out for me. All this time she had been in love with me, but hiding it, not sitting upstairs because she didn't want anyone to know. She had perhaps or perhaps not been ashamed to be in love with me. By 06/01/2011 I believe(almost 100% sure it wasn't 1 or 2 days afterwards)...I had fallen in love with her as well. I began to have all sorts of thoughts, and felt truly alive once for the first time in a long time. 06/01/2010. I walk in and she's sitting down, downstairs. She made some comment to her colleagues about me, smiling. I came up to her. She immediately ran off, going to place some items on a shelf, watching me once or twice. I wandered over there to talk to her, which caused her to run off to the other side of the room...she had tears in her eyes and appeared to be very flustered...happy? Several strong emotions definitely. I walked and carried out a transaction with her colleagues, who had stayed put. Out of the corner of my eye I saw her watching me, then when I turned she ducked out of sight. I left. 07/01/2011. She was there again, sitting down, with a bald guy standing next to her. I carried out a transaction, with her not looking at me at all. The bald guy was listening very intently. I thought is this guy the manager? She's probably done something stupid like reporting me. There was this strange emotion that passed through her,

a sort of joy like she was thinking "He LOVES me!" or something. Also she fronted(faced) me directly in a sexual manner, flirtatiously, and I did too. I thought I'll try to chat to her anyway, somehow, despite the guy intently listening. I said "How are you?" She ignored me. The way she said, after the transaction, "Anything else?" was enormously disrespectful, arrogant. I knew though that she was hiding IT, of course. I was going to do another transaction but I then said "I'll do it later." Upstairs I was somewhat paranoid inside as I think I overheard someone say: "He's using it", referring to me. Also, when I got down there was this girl standing by the door...when I went to leave she walked past me. I think I was being checked up on. And just to make me extra paranoid someone stood smoking a cigarette in the doorway, watching me...but that was probably a coincidence. I AM paranoid! 08/01/2011. She was sitting down at first. However when I approached she ran off, avoiding me. She looked guilty...or perhaps not. I looked at an item on the shelf, but she still refused to sit down so that I could talk to her. She went off to talk to this other girl about me, from a distance. She calmed down as I carried out the transaction with the staff who were sitting down. I left. 09/01/2011. I was unable to enter the institution as I had to visit my parents, who do not live in my current town. 10/01/2011. The young man was there, with two girls. His head was bobbing up and down somewhat, probably because of what he realised on 30/12/2011. When I came down the two girls had left...he looked somewhat lonely. I thought feel free to talk to those girls...there's a girl that I love who loves me and who doesn't love you...leave us alone. 11/01/2011. The young man was there, and his head bobbing up and down once or twice. When I went downstairs he was still there. I carried out a transaction. He looked at me somewhat smiling, lovingly, which he had never done before(I had carried out transactions there for a long time with different people often). I thought: GUILT. 12/01/2011. There was a new bald fellow walking around animatedly that I had never seen before. No sign of the young man. 13/01/2011. She was standing there with the young man when I came in. She seemed somewhat weak. He looked smug and I realised that it was probable that they had had sex. I had this pain, this creeping feeling. It creeped me out, looked awkward. It hurt. "What?...I don't understand. You love me and I love you. So how can you...You were perfect. Perfect. But now...How can you be having sex with him? Ruined. What kind of a girl can do this with her own body, when she loves me? All this time you've been in love with me and then you had sex with this guy? And you're carrying on having sex with this guy? Sick, this is sick. You're disgusting. You didn't even see him that time when I walked in. Slut, you're a whore. How can you do this with your body? How can you do this to me? You're hurting me. Stop it, oh God. Get away from her. Don't go near her. I love her. You sick assh***s. Sick. Oh God." Those were my thoughts regarding that instant, at the time and later and the next day. "Why me? I see lovers everywhere. What have I done to deserve this? Being born?" "It's exactly the same thing my whole life, illegal reasons talking my lover out of being with me, lies and excuses hammering her love for me. Disasters that I've fallen in love with, who have always due to weakness, confusion etc given their bodies to someone else when they love me. Then as I suffer, continuing to lash out at me when I have done nothing, and when it is their fault. But this one sought me out, I didn't ask her to come out and stand there all the time...and seemed different. SEEMED different..." And on occassion(not on this day I didn't think it though) I think: "YOU F**K:STOP F***ING THE GIRL I LOVE WHO LOVES ME. WHO COULD DO SUCH A THING? I COULD NEVER DO SUCH A THING, GET IN BETWEEN A GUY WHO LOVES A GIRL WHO LOVES HIM, AND KEEP RUINING IT." But then I get tired thinking things to that extent and worse; even thinking that drains me now...and death calls me. As I approached, this guy came up the stairs...a guy who didn't like me. He was watching me and as I came he told her to go downstairs. He did it deliberately so that I would not talk to her. She seemed really weak when she responded. As she went down she cast me this apologetic, fearful look. The young man was listening to me intently, as though I had some trick or something, when I carried out the transaction. From around that point on things got bad for me. I began regularly experiencing what I described to you in the introductory section. And at night I think about if they're having sex now, and nothing else, unable to sleep. I knew that, whatever the case was, there had been a promise called love between myself and her before 13/01/2011, which she had broken by 13/01/2011 by having sex with this guy, due to weakness, confusion, what other people think, or other illegal things. 14/01/2011. When I walked in she was not there. When I came downstairs she was there, standing with the young man, who looked smug again. She walked up fearfully to the young man, which sent more pain to me. She smiled at me somewhat sadly when I came to carry out a transaction. She still fronted(faced) me in a flirtatious manner, and I responded. I delayed a little as she was on the phone. Then she said to another colleague "I'm just going to put this downstairs." just as I was about to talk to her. I realised that she didn't like me delaying a little, and that she would probably complain about me or something to hurt me downstairs. Girls have said something like that often out loud, and have gone and hurt me. It's sort of a pattern. 15/01/2011. She was not there now. The young man had lines under his eyes, and looked tired. The man who told her to go downstairs had come out. 16/01/2011. Completely different people at the institution today. 17/01/2011. The young man was there. When I walked in he went behind a bookshelf and looked at me. I thought is this the guilt again? 18/01/2011. When I came downstairs the young man and the man who told her to go downstairs came out. 19/01/2011. When I came downstairs the young man and the man who told her to go downstairs came out. But also the bald guy who had been listening was there, and at the start. At this stage I've given up thinking that she'll sit down where I do certain things upstairs, or even come in. 20/01/2011. Today the young man was downstairs at first. Then when I came down he had gone, and the man who had told her to go downstairs was there. 21/01/2011 Today the young man was standing with a girl downstairs. The guy who told her to go downstairs, was upstairs today, and that bald guy I had never seen before was wandering around upstairs again...watching me? I think so. The guy who told her to go downstairs said to the bald guy: "I saw your cousin today." Cousin? What? Downstairs the bald guy who had eavesdropped on me and the young man were there, and an older woman.22/01/2011 Today downstairs were an older woman, a girl, and a new girl I had never seen before. Then after I had been upstairs two girls were downstairs, and the new girl. I hate going to the place...I always see them standing together. Although it hurts I keep coming in in the hope that I can talk to her and be with her before it's too late for me. The worst thing now is not knowing. Are they together frequently? Has she left even...is she back at her original institution(I doubt it...but she could have left). Why isn't she coming out...I've only tried to talk to her, but she keeps avoiding me. It could be that she'll never admit her mistake or mistakes or her criminal behaviour, and is remaining with this guy...or not. I don't know...the unknown can plague one. 23/01/2011 Today there was a girl downstairs, with two old persons. Upstairs after a while a girl-different-sat down. When I came downstairs the girl who had been there had gone, although the two old persons were still there. I know that she had put above love this sense of not wanting to be seen talking to me, believing herself better than me, hiding the fact that she loves me, and perhaps other shallow, incorrect things, what other people think. But how does someone who is very strongly in love with me but has gone and submitted to someone she absolutely does not love and does not deserve her or belong with her...how does someone like that compare to others, if she does not make amends by being with me soon and only me, so that I can to one extent or another love her again, maybe? Well there exist many individuals who do not have the blood of any innocent person in their DNA. There exist many females who could never do what this girl is doing to me, and many males who could never do what this guy has done to me. So she at present to one extent or another is declining in value compared to them. If someone commits a crime the individual has to in this case repair the damage done to the victim, in this case by her being with me. So here I am, thinking about her 24/7, too weak to work, no enjoyment out of anything, feeling like my life's slowly slipping away from me, like someone stuck in the middle of the ocean watching the boat get further and further away...all the way into the distance.

Story of My Life With Regard To Females And Other Things(1)
I would like you to know that I have received enormous amounts of suffering from females my entire life. First some statistics. The only thing that I have cared about, my number one priority, has been trying to find a girlfriend, and I have been trying to obtain one for the last
12 years. I have never had a girlfriend or had sexual intercourse with anyone that I love. I have been rejected, in terms of chatting up, by at least 1500 females, possibly more than 1700 or 1800. I would go out every night, frequently, and "chat up" and get rejected by 8 or so females, for a while. I have never had sexual intercourse more than once a day, I think, but I don't really care. First time I had sexual intercourse was at 24. I have had sexual intercourse with 3 "standard" females and a large number of prostitutes. I have never loved the 3 females or the prostitutes, and have forgotten most of the time I spent with them, rightly so I think, although prostitutes are no doubt necessary for certain people. The 3 females were a woman who was 9 years older than me(with whom I had two "sessions" of sexual intercourse with), one session with a girl who was somewhat obese(I don't judge obese people though, just that I didn't love her), and one session with another girl that I could never love for reasons I will not disclose. In my quest for a girlfriend I have been to about 8 different towns and cities, and have been to many more from there. When I have been in love I have always stood faithfully by the girl's side. I have learned now that one must be VERY VERY careful when flirting with girls for the purposes of sexual intercourse; I have learned things like this the hard way, like many other things. Close relationships with females for me number or have numbered at least 35/40, some more serious than others.
I came to Sixth Form at 16 or so without any understanding of females or how they are. I spoke to this girl for two years, walking towards the end once or twice with another and chatting once or twice at the end to other girls. She had a string of boyfriends. I asked her out seven or eight times, but she declined: I remember crying on the bus as I spoke to her. However I don't hate her. However that is no excuse for her behaviour. There were two others that I spoke to at Sixth Form. They are good human beings. They are not English. Those 2 non-English girls from Sixth Form, although one of them lied to me once, were distinctly different, and were excellent girls and excellent human beings. One of them, both actually but one especially, NEVER disrespected me or treated me different, was paranoid, confused...and they both had RELATIONSHIPS, most unlike many of the English girls I've run into. After that I spent much time running around. I joined an introduction agency and fell in love with a girl who fell in love with me. She was somewhat unstable though at one point: I won't describe it, or what we talked about. We met up for several weekends and chatted. Then we went back to her flat. We were kissing and we were about to have sex; I was enormously excited. She then stopped and said: "I want to hear you say something" or some strange question which I can't remember. I sort of froze in confusion. She then said, since I didn't say whatever it was that she wanted to hear "You have to go" or something to that extent. We might have met up once after that but that was it. I sent her one or two texts saying something like she was being unfair and that I needed to talk to her, and possibly an explanation. I don't think she replied at all; but what she did was complain to the "introduction agency"; I was expelled from it and not allowed in. I remember crying afterwards. There was an incident with regard to someone who fell in love with me whom I was in love with, during 2001-2004 which I shall go into more detail with below. After I left I chatted to girls here and there, and I remember that I could have had sexual intercourse with one or two of them in their flats. I chose not to however, as I wanted to get to know someone first. Later there was more flirting from me. Then I fell in love with a girl who was in love with me, who betrayed me twice, and this also drained me. I shall also describe this. Then I fell in love with a girl who fell in love with me. I shall also describe this. Now, finally, the thing which shall make up the bulk of this letter, which is severely damaging me at a rapid rate. I shall now describe some aspects of certain things.
Around 2001 I came across this girl from Sixth Form. I thought that fate had brought us together, at the time. We fell in love at some stage. However, she told me that she had a boyfriend. I remember that this guy came up, and she had generated this false "chit-chatty" thing with him. I gave off an unpleasant "vibe" and he left. She became angry with me then. Then my next door neighbour whom I had become friends with earlier and some other people were standing across the room a short distance. He came over and said hello to me, and she said "come and join us". I thought, ok, I guess we'll form this group. I would talk with her, and everyone else generally left us alone apart from occasional brief talks here and there. One day we all went out, and I

became slightly tipsy. I once or twice tried to put my arm around her which she shrugged off. I saw my next door neighbour notice something on her expression. A number of days later my next door neighbour began to flirt with her, coming on very strong and getting very close. One or two people in the "group" were now very hostile towards me, and were trying to encourage my next door neighbour to be with her. It was not what I had with her. They at some point began having sex. I was severely affected, crying every day, especially when these things were happening next door to me. I said that at one point that she sneaked in and she shouted "I didn't sneak I WALKED", proud. I said something about her boyfriend once and she said "Damn(or some word like that) I have to sort that out as WELL?" Her attitude was a complete shock to me, she seemed completely different before. My former friend now mocked and insulted me, and at one point threatened me, and went forward as if to hit me. I told her that I loved her, and she said "no you don't love me" and that I only "thought" that I loved her. She then generated a false romantic dialogue with this guy. I sneered and the act fell apart. As I was unstable and at one point saw that my next door neighbour was imitating one or so aspects of me to try and get her to love him, I left. I thought that I would contact her by mobile. I texted her once or twice but she didn't reply, although my former next door neighbour did, saying that she has "just finished getting over you". I saw them once in a nightclub but we didn't say very much. I sent a large number of texts to her, because I thought that it was impossible that someone, after what I had had with her, could not reply. As I gradually sent more and more texts, I realised that she was never going to respond to these. I kept sending because I just couldn't believe it, couldn't think it possible somehow you know? But one day the mobile was discontinued. I had been severely affected by the whole thing, and if you compare two photographs of me, one from before 2001 and one after the incident, you will see that I aged. I look like a different person, with this upside-down smile and dead unhappy eyes. The incident occurred over the period of a few months, maybe. This was 10 years ago, but I still remember everything, my suffering. I was crying every day. While escapism in the form of friendship, work and other things clouded matters after I had left, it is still there now significantly. Nothing hurts more than someone having sex with your lover.

  Many years later I met this other girl. I ran around flirting though, but one day I realised that I had fallen in love with her. She had fallen in love with me earlier. We flirted but she was avoiding me. I thought that I would ask her out soon, I think, but she was avoiding me on occasion, and so it was difficult, although I knew that she loved me. She said all sorts of things, like "I'm very choosy"(when it comes to guys). She seemed normal, at the time. One day suddenly this guy showed up, she introduced him. They were now going to live together with one or two other girls. This was someone that her friends had picked out. We were talking outside and she told me that she had a boyfriend in another city. However she was flirting with this guy. Afterwards, alarm bells started ringing in my head: I remembered the lies, pride in crime and treachery about the girl from 2001. I said that she should be careful of this guy, and also of one of her friends. She said that she was with him because he was her roommate. We met up at the place we had got together at, an institution, and I saw that they were enormously friendly. He left. I walked up to her and she ran away, talking to other people here and there. I asked her what this was. Her poor friend next to her told me to stop bothering her. I heard her mention something about calling the police. It turns out that she had told her friend that I was harassing her and doubtless something on the lines of that she had no interest in me. I know now that she was getting "kicks" out of the fact that she had this secret love, and that she was enjoying running around lying to people, especially to her poor friend, about someone she evidently believed that she was not "supposed" to fall in love with. I said that I wanted to know if they had had sex. I said I would leave if that was the case. She said: "You would leave just because of THAT?", that being the girl I was in love with who was in love with me having sex with some guy. I asked again if they had had sex, raising my voice. Without turning around she nodded her head, ashamed. She then got up and started to run again, a sign of guilt. I said that I was leaving the institution(and I won't describe what they teach at this institution but I will say that it is a REALLY BAD place, an enormous number of creepy things are here)because of this and I left. I came back after several months though, hopeful that she would be with me. I remember seeing her poor friend who looked like she had aged and was perhaps suffering from depression; this was because of the elaborate lies this girl who loved me had told her friend, who had trusted her completely, in order to hide the fact that she loved me: that was a real crime. She had obviously gotten upset when I had left, which had caused the whole charade to collapse. This girl who loved me frequently appeared to get "kicks" out of guilt on occasion. She was also hiding some enormous crime that she had committed in her past. I was told by the leader of the institution that she had reported me and that I was not to speak to her. She was still with this guy who had come out of the blue. One day I came in. The guy she was with turned around, and there was this look of disgust and real hatred. This was because he knew that she loved me and not him, and I was a "socially unacceptable", different guy. This was the exact same look I received from the guy involved in this latest thing, this realisation. I had also gotten to know this different guy, who had become a friend, a different fellow obviously. I had seen him put his arm around this girl that I loved. He said "I know that you have some sort of thing going on with this girl" or something similar. We spoke and I said something like "would you have sexual intercourse with this girl that I really like if you had the chance" and he said "that'll never happen…" Later myself, this girl, who had been lying about me(I remember her saying bad things and then running off if I came near), and this guy were talking to the man in charge of this institution. I realised that this girl was very false, very concerned with "social" things and other false, shallow things which don't exist or are harmful, above real things. This guy had now turned against me. He said "I have other friends who don't act like you," and made some accusations along with this girl. I realised that this girl that I loved, who had fallen in love with me a long time ago, had either had sexual intercourse with this friend of mine, or had made a promise to do so if he made her look good, and made me look bad; an "agreement". She said "I could leave this place" and I said "*I*, could leave this place," and she said "I wouldn't care" or something. At one point I saw the two guys who had(likely in one case) had sexual intercourse with her sort of surrounding her as she giggled. I couldn't take any more of this, being unhappy, and left. This thing had gone on for a year maybe? This also caused tears. After this incident, filled with hatred and despairing of ever having a first girlfriend, I began having sexual intercourse with prostitutes.

  In the middle of this thing, and I felt I had the right to form another connection because of what this girl did to me, I formed another connection. I chose someone, and began flirting. She seemed interested in me to one extent or another, and we agreed to talk the next day. The next day she was completely different, and ran away from me. I was going to talk to her when the individual in charge of the organisation came up and told me that I was not allowed to talk to her. I fell in love with her. I realised though that she had fallen in love with me at some point during the month for which this lasted. I was crying continuously. I was never really permitted to talk to her. I noticed that a number of guys were flirting with her after I had initially approached her. She had just sat there on her own before. I left because I felt drained and upset, I couldn't stay…but I managed to give her my mobile number(I think she refused to "swap" numbers and refused to meet up), even though she never contacted me.

As well as this a female hit me on the side of the head suddenly, I've been stood up about 100 times or more, lied to, had someone invite me in for sex then when I came out of the toilet she changed her mind, another girl possibly would have stuck a lit cigarette into my eye: it was quite close. With regard to males I've gotten on enormously well. However I've been randomly attacked, bullied at school, had various opportunists take girls I've chatted up away from me, threatened with a knife. Also in my life have been injuries, the odd illness, and much else. I have a list of at least 25/30/40 criminals who have committed crimes of varying degrees against me.

Suicide(1)
Suicide is legal in this country right? I wish it to remain so as it is vital with regard to suffering. You should perhaps have someone listen to a person's story and decide if what the person has been through is simply too much, which it will be in my case if she is not with me soon. I would like people to easily be able to purchase poison from somewhere easily. Other methods of "self" suicide should also be considered. The faster and less painful the poison the better. I have read a little about Cyanide which seems good. There are also pesticides and agricultural things, which could prove good. Please provide easy access to the best poison. I would also like people to be able to commit suicide on the bed in crematoriums which goes into the cremating oven. It is a horrible thought that some "awareness" or nerve cells could linger after death. Once dead, people are meant to GO completely. Cremation is an instantaneous release. Imagine if someone is dead but still aware or still senses, seeing people he does not want to see or be near him looking at him, suffering. Instantaneous cremation after suicide. I would say now that it is impossible for me to take the law into my own hands with regard to killing anyone as I simply don't have the energy to make the effort, I would in all likelihood fail to kill anyone, and the current laws would put me away probably for life. However, although I hope and beg that (1*) and others shall be done, if having refused that you then refuse the three things above labelled "possible…", I MUST take the law into my own hands with regard to committing suicide. It is not possible for me to exist in a universe where this girl has had sex with this guy a certain number of times, or for so and so long, and one in which she will not be with me. Animals often commit suicide when their lover dies, it is how things must be in some cases.
SUICIDE. The name is beautiful, and what it means always holds a lure for certain people in certain situations. It is instant access to a universe in which the cause or causes of your continuing suffering, your agony as you cry and sob, no longer exist, even if the universe is nothingness. Suicide is a vital right, a release from suffering and agony, such as my agony right now. Imagine if someone feels like I do or worse, rotting in a prison cell, knowing what is still happening yet powerless to do anything about it because of liars in government who are cowards and will do anything to prevent this beautiful thing, even harming and causing suffering to the innocent. Imagine that person in a cell, or somewhere which is the same as a cell, numb, not looking up, murmuring "Please…let me die…let me die." England is a FALSE HELL, piling crime and other burdens upon the innocent, forcing them to work, forcing them to conform to things which don't exist, while those who conform to the bulls**t are rewarded with girls which BELONG TO THE INNOCENT. Escape from such a HELL is vital, for some people, although I hope and beg for (1*) and (1), etc. Every second that I'm not with her, ESPECIALLY knowing that she's had sex with this guy to degrees, feels like something's being drained out of me, like blood running out, which I can never get back. But one way or another I'll be happy, I have that right. There will come a point, Deputy Prime Minister, and I beg with my life that I am helped with regard to this girl before then, when too much time will have passed without me having been with her, when they will have had sexual intercourse one too many times, and I will say that it is not possible for this girl to pay her debt to me and for me, to one extent or another, to be happy with her as is necessary. It will not be possible for me to exist at that stage, and I will need suicide. Lack of movement causes suffering: there is no suffering if someone moves towards death. At a certain stage it will be the case that this girl, but also this bast**d that she has had sex with, will have caused me so much damage, and will have taken so much from me mentally, that it is not possible for me to live anymore, since she cannot make up for it as too much time etc has passed. This girl was meant to be with me, and would be with me right now in a normal country.

Theft(1)
A male taking another male's lover is theft. Theft is a crime. But of course there are various degrees of theft, like many other things. You trust in something…and it is taken from you by someone who is feeding off of things that YOU have created and that YOU deserve. As a victim you have this VACANT feeling of something that has slipped away from you, you feel betrayed.

Tory Party(1) or (2)
I must mention this, as I would never forgive myself if they interfered and my saying this could have removed their obstructions and made me happy with this girl, that is all. If this Tory Party harms or delays etc my only salvation with this girl, I would like action to be taken against it, or it threatened. The Tory Party(but only a number of people in it) is illegal. It

has always deregulated. These have been liars, adding "-ization" to things that are illegal or just plain don't exist, for instance "Indianization" and "privatization". Those laws existed to protect. As a result of this people have died, with regard to rail for instance rail accidents, and things have gone backwards, why do we have different versions of the same thing? Two different versions of the same thing is a contradiction, and all contradictions are crimes, especially the contradictions committed by this girl. They created "private television channels", they pushed for it. They have encouraged or developed any fashion blindly, and without understanding or responsibility. They took England into the EU/EEC. And this is a "party"(no such thing as parties) which believes in DOING NOTHING. Suicide/death is what will happen to people if they don't do anything, or run. I think that at A point you should make this organisation illegal, and instead make a number of Tories "Independent M.P.s". Competition is to be limited to sports, as in a competition you have a loser; a competition is a crime against the loser, who feels destroyed. It is not meant to be. The government is the central body which has control and responsibility of everything in a country. So there is no "private sector". Most, it appears to me after a brief glance at it, of the tory party is made up of the "less developed" adult "type" described below. They only have the wealth because the person's parent, and the parent's grandparent passed it on to them. But to pass on money to a child, especially enormous amounts of it, is illegal. Every person is an individual, and sons often do the opposite that fathers do. They WILL turn out different than the father. It could be that long ago the great-great grandparent DESERVED to have more money than everyone else, and to pass it on to his son. But his son is not him. Many generations have passed, with many people in existence being BETTER than a number of those with money that has been passed on. His son, and his sons, have not behaved as legally as the original who obtained the money, or have even committed serious crimes. By contrast, what was perhaps a person who has done nothing, or perhaps committed a tiny crime...that person's sons and grandsons have now achieved much, and deserve more money than the hoarders. But they are not rewarded. A contradiction, a lie, crime. And how do people feel when they're born in the gutter when some are born with wealth? Many people end up suffering like I do, because of England, when it has not been my fault. But (1*) and 1 are vital for me.

Types Of People(1) or (2)
I must mention this, as I would never forgive myself if they interfered and my saying this could have removed their obstructions and made me happy with this girl, that is all. If the types of people who are not fully developed adults, and others, in Parliament interfere harm or delay my only salvation with this girl, I would like their choices not to count, as their choices are not as good as those of fully developed adults. Also if their votes harm my salvation they are to be taken from them. Or they are to be threatened with such things. For the best. When people are born, they have these moist eyes, as children. Those who are children behave in a less developed manner, with tantrums, random uncontrolled behaviour. When children hate, which is the natural way to respond to England, their eyes change to different degrees, and they develop into properly developed human beings. They are mature and responsible adults. Responsible adults are supposed to be in charge, while adults who are in fact mentally similar to children commit mild crimes because of their nature. Those adults who are less developed also have less awareness. Sometimes people with guilt look similar, but they have a sort of "thing" about the eyes, and they smile lovingly at the individual they committed crime against. But the children-adult mental development is a scale, and there are different degrees. Examples of responsible adults in Parliament: most, perhaps. Examples of less developed adults in Parliament: Ian Duncan Smith, Andy Burnham, Michael Gove. Examples of less developed adults in English music include John Bull and Henry Purcell. We all have eyes like this at birth, and it's possible that unless you change before, say 20, you might be "stuck" like this, mentally. What about a Y Dna Level J individual like Ed Milliband? I'm not sure how he compares to those I've described as less developed adults, but he would not take into account certain things that properly developed adults would take into account. He's ok though. The less developed adults have basically grown up sealed off from many things, in a bubble, that is why I think they're like that. At my current location I estimate that at least 66/75% of the population are poorly developed adults, particularly among the upper and middle classes perhaps; perhaps they have the money to seal themselves off. They're ok though. It is also possible that certain things early in development cause an individual to develop or not. On the other hand everyone has the same curriculum don't they, yet they end up different. But 1* etc are vital for me.

Why Destruction Occurs(1)
Destruction occurs with regard to organisms because the organism does something WRONG, something INCORRECT, where there is a PROBLEM with the organism. It comes from a failure to evolve. There are forces in the universe which destroy organisms if certain things happen or don't happen. Regardless of the situation with regard to non-human organisms, human beings are indeed 100% destroyed if the organism does something WRONG, something INCORRECT, where there is a PROBLEM with the organism. Some of the forces which act upon organisms in order to make them accept TRUTH, are GUILT, telling the organism to be killed, and HATRED, telling the organism to kill. However many human beings live in false, incorrect worlds. Normally they would feel such things, but they believe that through lies they can evade the one way that things are meant to be. Shallowness is an especially disgusting lie which has been forced upon this country. When love is concerned two individuals stick by each other, ESPECIALLY that is, the female sticking by the man(is my current belief...not sure about male sticking by the female, if it hurts the female as much if broken). Nothing stops the forces. If someone is meant to be destroyed, they will be destroyed. The truth is that every time a crime is committed that human being's life span is shortened: that human being will either die, die off, or be killed at some point. In addition to this we can talk about IDENTITIES. You have the identity of humanity. If a crime is committed, in this case by this girl against me, it harms first

females of our race, then females as a whole or possibly males of our race or both, (then the other one), then the rest of humanity, then mammals, then animals are harmed. After all these are all distinct identities.
I can give some evidence of this, for human beings. You have how the Earth has had an enormous amount of crime committed against it by human beings; in response the Earth is creating extreme weather and so on("global warming") either so that humans repair the crime or so that the criminals(humans) are destroyed. Saint Barbara was a VIRGIN, and also someone who didn't harm anyone else. When she was tortured and killed by Dioscorus he was struck by lightning and reduced to ashes when he got home.
Therefore the value of a human being is judged first and foremost by crimes that that human being has committed. If someone has committed a crime(using a hypothetical world in which everyone is equal until someone commits a crime) then that person can never again attain the value of other human beings, to different extents.
In a more direct manner you have family trees. How would someone feel if a person who has committed a serious crime against someone like me was your father or mother? You would feel that you had no right to be born, would feel dirty. You might think about throwing yourself off the nearest tall building. In addition they take up space-for by existing in the world you use up space, by living-which could be taken up by those who act in the correct manner. There is also influence. If I had a choice to be influenced by someone who had done the sort of things which certain people had done to me, and someone innocent, I would choose the innocent one. I would not want to think that I have accomplished this or that thanks to a murderer, like this guy. Everything, including influence, is coded in a person's DNA, and subject to the forces.

MATTERS

Crimes Committed Against Me By This Girl(1*)
The greater the "sexual activities" the harsher the punishment, unless perhaps she makes amends sexually. Not all of the following are true for this girl, but have been added for completeness and other reasons. The FAITHFULNESS LAWS are among or ARE the most important, and the LOVE HANDOVER LAW also. It must be understood that she owes me, and that this guy she has had sex with approached her after she had fallen in love with me, or rather BECAUSE she had fallen in love with me, because of the "vibes" she had given out. If a female owes a male like she does me, all else in the world doesn't matter.
SEX HONESTY LAW It is illegal for a female to lie about her sexual status a number of times to [() a male () a male who is flirting with her].
RESPONSE LAW It is illegal for a female to ignore [() a male () a male who is flirting with her () a male who she is in love with () a male who is in love with her () a male who she is in love with who is in love with her () a male she has displayed signs of her love for him ()a male she has displayed signs of her love for him the knowledge of which has entered into the male's brain].
TALKING LAW 1 It is illegal for a female to avoid talking to [() a male () a male who is flirting with her () a male who she is in love with () a male who is in love with her () a male who she is in love with who is in love with her () a male she has displayed signs of her love for () a male she has displayed signs of her love for the knowledge of which has entered into the male's brain] when that male is attempting to talk to her, especially when she has broken a number of other laws a number of times.
TALKING LAW 2 It is illegal for a female to avoid spending 5 minutes every day talking to [() a male who she is in love with () a male who she is in love with who is in love with her () a male she has displayed signs of her love for him the knowledge of which has entered into the male's brain] when the male who she is in love with has been attempting to talk to her.
STEPS LAW It is illegal for a female who is in love with a male to take insufficient steps to make her love known to him when the male lover has entered into a certain radius of the female a number of times, especially when she has broken a number of other laws a number of times.
PRESENCE LAW It is illegal for a female to be suddenly absent from a male who she loves who loves her when she was present frequently one extent or another before, especially when she has broken a number of other laws a number of times.

===

FAITHFULNESS LAW 1 It is illegal for a female to engage in sexual activities with a male that she has [() had such with before () never had such with before] when she is in love with a different male when the male that she is in love with has displayed an interest in her at some point and when she has displayed signs of her love for him the knowledge of which has entered into the male's brain, especially when she has broken STEPS LAW and/or SEX HONESTY LAW and/or TALKING LAW 1 and/or RESPONSE LAW a number of times.
FAITHFULNESS LAW 2 It is illegal for a female to engage in sexual activities a number of times with a male that she has [() had such with before () never had such with before] when both she and a different male are in love and when the male she is in love with is aware of this and has been attempting to talk to her, especially that the male loves her and/or especially when she has broken a number of other laws a number of times.
LOVE HANDOVER LAW It is illegal for a female who has broken FAITHFULNESS LAW 1 and/or FAITHFULNESS LAW 2 not to be immediately handed over to the male she fell in love with(described as such in the 2 FAITHFULNESS LAWS) as his girlfriend.

LOVERS HANDOVER LAW It is illegal for a female who is in love with a male who is in love with her when the male she is in love with is aware of her love for him and when the male has entered into a certain radius of the female a number of times not to be handed over at some point in future to the male as his girlfriend, should the male wish it, especially when she is aware that the male loves her and/or especially when a number of the above laws have been broken by the female.

SILENT PROMISE LAW It is illegal for a female who is in love with a male who is in love with her when the male she is in love with is aware of her love for him and when the male has been attempting to talk with her to break a silent promise to her male lover by engaging in sexual activities a number of times with a different male that she has [() had such with before () never had such with before], especially when a number of the above laws have been broken by the female a number of times.

Crimes Committed Against Me By This Guy and/or Another Guy(2) or (3)

NO INTERFERING LAW It is illegal for a male to engage in sexual activities with a female that he has [() had such with before () never had such with before] when she is in love with a different male when the male that she is in love with has displayed an interest in her at some point and when she has displayed signs of her love for him the knowledge of which has entered into the male lover's brain, especially when she has broken a number of other laws a number of times.

NO INTERFERING LAW 2 It is illegal for a male to engage in sexual activities a number of times with a female that he has [() had such with before () never had such with before] when she is in love with a different male when both she and a different male are in love and when the male she is in love with is aware of this and has been attempting to talk to her, especially when she is aware that the male loves her and/or especially when she has broken a number of the above laws a number of times, and especially when the male that she is not in love with is aware of her love for the other male and that she does not love him.

SILENT PROMISE NO INTERFERING LAW It is illegal for a male to be to one extent or another responsible for a female who is in love with a different male who is in love with her when the male she is in love with is aware of her love for him and when the male has been attempting to talk with her to break a silent promise to her male lover by engaging in sexual activities a number of times with the male that she is not in love with who has, with the female, [() had such with before () never had such with before].

Epilation Replacing Shaving(2)

I use an epilator. However because of my current state I was barely able to epilate the last time. It will get harder and harder as the epilator that I use has too fast a speed which causes too much pain. I would like you to gradually replace all shaving with epilation, for men. Shaving causes the hair to go back thicker and faster. With epilation however hair does not grow back for about two weeks. Since pulling out hair doesn't cause pain it should eventually be simple to emulate it perfectly with an epilation machine.

Evidence of Love(1)

Although I will mention this I want the world to get rapidly away from this whole "Evidence" nonsense with regard to crime(and possibly other things too). If people lie, they get hurt. It is simple.

FEMALE-MALE LOVE

Basically, a number of things from my main story give evidence of her being in love with me, although it's not necessary. EVIDENCE Presence of female when the male is at the location for a number of times and fronting(facing) the male. EVIDENCE Presence of female when the male is at the location for a number of times and fronting(facing) the male and watching the male for a number of times. EVIDENCE Presence of female when the male is at the location and fronting(facing) the male and watching the male for a number of times and downcast eyes with a "yeah yeah I love you" look a number of times. EVIDENCE Turning to front(face) male when the male enters the room, turning to front him as he walks around. EVIDENCE Direct fronting(facing) a male in a sexual manner a number of times. EVIDENCE Looking up a number of times at the male in an animated manner. EVIDENCE Display of weakness, panic, and stress in certain situations. EVIDENCE Fronting(facing) someone in a sexual manner when within a certain radius of the male a number of times. EVIDENCE "Joyous" emotion because she knows that a male loves her. EVIDENCE Smiling at male in a happy manner. EVIDENCE Submissive apologetic look at the male, in certain situations. EVIDENCE Certain signs in certain situations. EVIDENCE Hatred from another male who has flirted with her towards the male she is in love with. EVIDENCE Instability in another male who has flirted with her.

MALE-FEMALE LOVE

Basically, a number of things from my main story give evidence of my being in love with her, although it's not necessary. She picked up that I loved her pretty quickly. She has not been behaving in the correct manner however, never giving me a chance to speak, running, ignoring, being disrespectful, therefore the following is really unnecessary, as she is a mess, and owes me, and I need her.

EVIDENCE Following female across the room once when she ran off after male approached the desk, to try to talk to her. EVIDENCE Presence every day at a locality, when presence was never as strong before. EVIDENCE Pretending to look at items when female runs off after male approaches in order to get a chance to talk to the female again. EVIDENCE Loitering when female is on the phone in order to attempt to speak to her. EVIDENCE Fronting(facing) female in a sexual manner. EVIDENCE Approaching desk when female is there, but not otherwise. EVIDENCE Smiling at female as part of flirtation. EVIDENCE Speaking in a certain tone.

Explanation Of Crimes Committed Against Me By This Girl(1*)

SEX HONESTY LAW is mentioned because finding a girlfriend has always been the most important issue to me; and to many men sexual issues come uppermost...they are very important. Lying is always a crime of course. RESPONSE LAW is important because ignoring someone is a crime if the person does not deserve it...and possibly if the person does deserve it, an insult. Many laws which I've mentioned show a lack of recognition for the male as a human being. FAITHFULNESS LAWS 1 and 2 and LOVE HANDOVER LAW are enormously important because breaking it causes enormous damage to everyone concerned, especially the male lover. LOVERS HANDOVER LAW is also important, as is SILENT PROMISE LAW.

Explanation of Crimes Committed Against Me By This Guy And/Or Another Guy(2) or (3)
His, and/or another guy, breaking of a number of those laws are all THEFT, stealing what belongs, and was promised to me. It's also saying that I've low value as a human being, an insult. That I deserve to suffer pain of theft and disgracing etc of my lover, as I'm inferior to him.

Females And Homosexuals In Parliament, Voting, And The Queen Issues(1) or (2)
I must mention this, as I would never forgive myself if they interfered and my saying this could have removed their obstructions and made me happy with this girl, that is all. I would like you to think about the issue of females and homosexuals in Parliament with regard to the issues in "Science and Female Humans". I will also think about it, if I recover from this incident in the manner I've described. Does the Queen have any power? If so I think that you should make an assessment, in light of this letter, of certain things. Moving on to Parliament, I would like all females removed from Parliament, and not allowed to vote except above an age like 35, except for non-English females who behave correctly I hope. I would like to be with this girl as soon as possible, but if any of these will obstruct my only salvation I think you should do this soon, that's all. Why? Please read "Female Humans and Behaviour". Also read the contents of this letter. It is the case that female human beings in England have developed INCORRECTLY, and that when confronted with certain things will commit crimes, will lie, they will do things which harm themselves and others. They will lash out, especially at men. Rather than seek understanding they will do this, in the manner in which I've suffered my entire life. Females have come across someone they do not understand, ME, have committed crimes against me, against their own selves harming their value, and also against others. There is a nationwide problem. And I know that to a very very large extent this is a WESTERN particularly ENGLISH thing. Look at all the things that females have done to me, and various other things. Do you think such people are fit to decide Parliamentary things, or can judge as well as men can who should be in charge? They don't understand many things which will lead to, in the case of voting, someone suitable being turned down and worse. Let's look at some examples. Margaret Thatcher is an extreme criminal, she has committed very serious crimes against many during her premiership. Harriet Harman has committed a random mild crime out of the blue against an innocent, referring to one of your Liberal Democrats as a "ginger rodent". What if he has been bullied somehow about how he looks in the past? After people stupidly appointed a 10 year old boy as monarch, Jane Grey became the first queen of England, then Mary I after her. It had been a rule for 1500 years not to have a female monarch. In fact in all countries you only now, in a weakened world begin to hear about the "first female this" and the "first female that".

Government Self-Publishing Industry(3)
I would like you to create a government self-publishing printer so that people can create books. I could write these sort of things directly into ISBN books for a job; that's creating a worthy job isn't it?

Guilty Until Proved Innocent
People must be assumed guilty when accused. Only the most disgusting people would concoct something out of the blue and then accuse someone in court. I have included a law which may prevent that. There is always SOMETHING for the majority of the time when one person takes another to court.

Internet Control
The internet may be the next big thing to go caput like the banks did. England had that problem because England is tied to the hip with america. The internet is supposed to be a national network for Britain, but perhaps for Ireland too, yes…make it for Britain and Ireland. The internet can cause extreme harm. Documents, stealing, photographs, videos, pornography(as you can see things which can scar you possibly for life)… these are all easily found on the internet. Good countries are countries where the government has complete control…Bad countries are countries where the government has no control: most obviously that is the case with america. I would like you to buy, or something, all necessary websites, and then cut all of it off from the rest of the world completely, so that it becomes a network for Britain and Ireland. There must be no connection whatsoever with any other country.

Leaving Britain(2)
There have been too many crimes committed. Could you please change things so that noone can leave this country for more than 6 months, unless they have their roots in another country AND submit to a police interrogation and possibly truth drugs.

Legal Cheapness(2)
EVERYONE needs to go to court at some stage of their lives. It is more important than health. Please make it free and easy to

take people to court.
Legal Glossary(1*)
ILLEGAL REASONS=What other people say, what other people think, paranoia, selfishness, arrogance, hypocrisy, anything that can be easily changed.
INSUFFICIENT STEPS=The female not sitting down within a certain radius of the male when given a chance to do so. The female not approaching the male.
LEGAL REASONS=Love.
LOVE(FEMALE-MALE)=Strong desire that a female feels towards a male.
LOVE(MALE-FEMALE)=Strong desire that a male feels towards a female.
LOVE=Both Female-Male and Male-Female Love.
NUMBER=Anything between 1 and Infinity.
SEXUAL ACTIVITIES=(In order of lesser-greater consequences) Significant manipulation of genital region through clothing, french kissing, significant manipulation of unclothed genital region, oral stimulation of unclothed genital region, sexual intercourse.
Legal System Changes(2)
Expulsion of any member of the jury which acts incorrectly…that jury member must never serve on the jury again. Also for judges. Cap on the prices of lawyers, and less reliance on them. Cheaper lawyers. No such thing as a criminal lawyer. In every town, all legal areas covered, and one lawyer specialising in each legal area, so that people don't have to travel to get a lawyer. Expansion of the court system. If a criminal tells 15 DISTINCT lies in court it is automatically assumed that that person is guilty, in a number of cases, or all perhaps, not sure. If a victim tells 15 DISTINCT lies in court the criminal shall be automatically assumed innocent, in a number of cases, or all perhaps, not sure. Also please merge all police systems in England into one NATIONAL POLICE SYSTEM.
M.P. Letter Reader(1)
I would like there to be only one individual who reads the letters sent to an M.P., apart from the M.P. himself. Or perhaps the M.P. could read it straight away, or not. Anyway if there is a letter reader there must be only one.
M.P. Response(1)
I would like a response sent personally by the M.P. who reads every letter sent to them. I would like a voice message on the mobile phone and also a text message, from an "official mobile phone of the M.P." sent from the M.P. himself. This is because the 1471 service no longer works on some phones, and also there is the case of fraud. I would like the messages to include whether a written response will be sent, and also how soon certain things can be done and the entry date into the Hansard, although right now what I need is speedy achievement of (1*), (1), and later (2). In my case with this letter could a letter be sent in addition to 2 messages. People need to know when this or that can be done…waiting for anything now without knowing might kill me, after this theft of the girl who loves me, who I love.
Myself Remaining Unemployed Provided I Take Steps Such As Writing To Someone To Bring My Criminals To Justice(1)
After this incident I have enormous difficulty in doing many things. I have described how I feel. I know how work can drain you. Isn't work meant for people who haven't suffered as I have, and who are not in the situation that I am in? Work would immediately kill me. But isn't writing to you like this or doing something equivalent, once I am with the girl I love who loves me, also a job? Would it be too much to ask to let me remain unemployed and get enough to survive? Or remain unemployed provided I do something like writing letters to you, Deputy Prime Minister? That is what I ask. Everything has just piled up now, with the enormous impact of this "girl issue". EMPLOYMENT. Please cancel ian duncan smith's forced labour program, force all jobs to be on jobcentre plus and nowhere else for easy access and less waste, jobseekers only need to search jobcentreplus, cancel the criminal "New Deal"(I told them at the time that I wanted to become Councillor or M.P. …they tried to force me to do other things. In addition to what jobcentreplus demands they now said apply for 4 vacancies, send 10 cvs to companies, 8 job related phonecalls + photocopies within a 2 week period. I am a HUMAN BEING for goodness sake). You could create a job right now "Occasional Letter-Writer To The Deputy Prime Minister." or what I have suggested in "Government self-publishing industry." Or I could write things directly into the Hansard somehow(does the Hansard have an ISBN?) for a job, by mail or something.
Police Technique Interrogation of Anyone Who Has Committed A Crime(1*)
People are not supposed to RELY on witnesses. Crime is the most important thing, infinitely more real and pressing than some of the escapist things that are talked about on occasion(rarely though) in Parliament. It is horrible to be a victim, and all victims need the criminal to accept the truth, after the criminal tells the truth, as soon as possible. Therefore anyone accused of any crime is subject to official measures. It will not kill them to spend some time being interrogated. Also research into things like "microexpressions". You should also use analyses of WHO PEOPLE ARE in order to estimate how likely they are to tell the truth.

Royal Mail
If you just wash your hands of Royal Mail it will be harmed, a crime. Could you please at least keep the Special Delivery and Recorded Signed For things, not let any other country get it, ensure that it remains ONE organisation, assess the capability of the boss to do the job, have reliable postmen who don't open letters. Also please ban any other mail system in this country as it

threatens Royal Mail. Royal Mail is a vital service; for me now this letter is vital. Could you have it open and running, with postmen as well, on Sundays? If it had been running on Sundays this would have arrived on Monday as opposed to Tuesday. Why don't you take the money directly from someone/somewhere to fund Royal Mail?

Taking Someone To Court For Something That Doesn't Exist
This results in execution, exceptions lovers, and parents and children. Who'd create an elaborate lie like this? No one worth any trouble.
Television Conversion(3)
The laws governing the BBC, but there are nowhere near enough, are not present for "private channels"(term doesn't exist). This means that people can commit crimes deserving execution easily in the case of "private channels" . I would like everything converted into BBC channels or shut down, and more laws governing the BBC. There have frequently been programmes based on real members of the public, including myself a number of times, without their permission, often harmful, illegal things, on "private channels".
Truth Drugs(1)
People are not meant to RELY on witnesses. Crime is the most important thing, infinitely more real and pressing than some of the escapist things that are talked about on occasion(RARE occasion though) in Parliament. It's horrible to be a victim, and all victims need the criminal to accept the truth, after the criminal tells the truth, as soon as possible. Therefore anyone accused of crime is subject to official measures. It won't kill them to be given a pill so that the truth is found, and a victim's suffering ends, or lessens. Please choose one or more of the following, or others: 3-Quinuclidinyl benzilate; Amobarbital; various barbiturates; Ethanol; Scopolamine; Sodium thiopental; Temazepam.

Washing Machine. Laundrette Ban(3)
I would like you to force all rented properties to provide a washing machine. I would then like you to ban all laundrettes, except for 1 in every hotel. Laundrettes would then be nothing but a waste of time, money, effort, resources, and manpower. To me, if I need to use the laundrette now, the path to it seems to stretch all the way into the distance, and other tasks associated with it are too difficult. Everything would be so much easier...and everyone needs to wash their clothes sometime, otherwise the clothes disintegrate etc.

DANIEL PICKFORD-GORDON

Human Brazilian Sexualess Visage Frozen Mouth Open Eyes Quite Wide Typing.
Date And Time
Wednesday 22/08/2012. Definitely finished before 1800, as i was on the train back and thought: "There are only 10,15, Etcetera minutes left until Library F. closes at 1800. I won't make it in time." It was about 1800 when i arrived back in F."
Description
I was kissing her, and telling her how attractive she was. She smiled, slightly red-faced, with her eyes glittering.
     She went on top of me: she started talking while inserting my penis into her vagina. Then she was moving up and down, occasionally leaning in and lying somewhat against me, kissing. Her kisses were brief, but with a lot of tongue. She propped herself up on her hands, and was moving her lower body up and down on my penis. She was leaning forward a lot. I had my hands and upper arms on her back, and along her arms. Buildup was excellent, perfect. I said "stop" as i was coming. She stopped, then i came, then she moved a tiny bit, then i said "stop" and/or held her, and then i came fully. She smiled in that bright way of her's. I hugged her, then we kissed. Buildup perfect, climax perfect.
     Midway through, she put her hand on my testicles, stroking and holding them. Her head went back in pleasure, and i think that mine did too, mine on the pillow, and i let out a moan. As i was coming her visage was frozen, with her mouth open and her eyes quite wide.

Human Brazilian Sexualess Visage Frozen Mouth Open Eyes Quite Wide Typing.
Clan

If her Clan is not the Clan of Human USA Musician Amy Lee, then her Clan is the Cousin Clan of Human USA Musician Amy Lee.
Description Of Her
Long hair. Nose goes down, leans down. She has her origins in Spain, she said, but is Brazilian. Brunette hair. Doesn't have too much of a neck. Not that curvy, more stocky. Looks early/mid 20s or so.

Human Czech Sexualess What Do You Vont Me To Do You Too Heavy!
Typing.
Date And Time
Thursday 21/06/2012.
Description
1.
She greeted me in the hallway, with a smile. She looked fabulous. Things were a tiny bit awkward until after i had given her the money and she had come back in. We kissed on the lips, and i stroked her body. She insisted on using Durex Extra Strong Condoms, when i can't feel very much with those condoms. I told her to go on top. She didn't know how to go back and forwards, but went up and down. She was leaning forward with her arms, one of which looked awesome with her small grey watch on it, either side of my head, but then pressed with both her hands on my chest. The buildup was good, but she didn't stop, so the climax wasn't very good, the climax was mostly if not wholly unnoticeable by me. She got somewhat hateful when

i was coming. She went: "Are you coming? Huh!? Huh!?" while glaring at me.
2.
We lay together. I stroked her hair.
3.
I paid for another half an hour, ie one hour total. It felt good with my arm around her neck from the side, it was like she was MINE, like i owned her: she smiled and looked down when i did this "arm round her neck" thing. She started on top. She moved my body with her own, with my hands on her legs, with a cocky little smile with regard to my slight or more than slight submissiveness. It was difficult for me to come, as i hadn't recharged my batteries. We finished with doggystyle: it worked well. I thrusted in short strokes as she said that she didn't like me doing long strokes in and out with the length of my penis. I thrusted in short strokes, feeling dominant and manlike, like she was MINE, i was "owning" her. She was moaning "Uuuuh" in a human-female-like way. She was twisted to the left to one extent or another though, with her head and arms "down", which spoilt it a little. The buildup was probably perfect, and i came excellently if not perfectly, with her gasping in a flustered manner somewhat afterwards. I realised then that i was sweating horribly.

Human Czech Sexualess What Do You Vont Me To Do You Too Heavy! 2
Date And Time
Thursday 28/06/2012. That is all: there is no written record, by me, of what happened.

Human Czech Sexualess What Do You Vont Me To Do You Too Heavy!3
Date And Time
Thursday 12/07/2012.
Description
      Her: "Hi!" I think that she said something like "Long time!" but i'm not sure. Her: "How long do you vont to stay for?" Me: "I'll see how much i can afford." Me: "I need food and drink. £60. I'll put that away." She told me the prices. Me: "I'll have one hour without a condom and then half an hour with a condom." Her: "Are you sure? It's a lot of money." Me: "What, you don't want to be with me that long!?" She said something or other in response to this.
I Asked About The Prices
I Think That It Was Today She Sucked My Penis With No Condom On
She was between my legs, with her head above my erect penis. Her: "Are you SCARED?" Me: "No i'm not. I trust you." Her: "I have good TEETH." She made a "biting" motion with her teeth. I laughed softly. I stroked her hair.

Human Czech Sexualess What Do You Vont Me To Do You Too Heavy! Miscellaneous
Her: "Love-Condoms"
Her: "Shall i leave your condoms here?" Me: "Yes." Her: "Okay i'll leave your condoms here." She took them. Me: "They're OUR condoms." "Oh yes, LOVE-CONDOMS," she sneered, sarcastically, but in a sexy way. She often attacked me, but she really likes me.
Sexual: Me On Top
I was on top of her: i was about to come, looking at her as she looked at me. I came. Immediately after i had come she went: "Blablabla aging," I hugged and kissed her.
Me: "You're Amazingly Attractive"
I was above her at the end: i was stroking her body, and her hair, and her arms. She said something like "what are you doing?" I said "I'm stroking the body of this amazingly attractive, beautiful girl." She saw how much i was attracted to her, and she smiled faintly at me, her eyes glittering with happiness.
Outside Of The Building
The time before Sunday 29/07/2012, as i was at a certain place, i saw someone who looked like her from a distance: she saw me, and we approached each other: it was HER. She was dressed smart. She smiled at me. "Hi" she said to me. Me: "Hi. Are you blablaBLA?" i asked. Her: "No i'm not," she responded. Me: "Okay." Her: "Okay, bye darling." She leaned in towards me and we kissed for about 1 or 2 seconds-briefly-before i left.
Her: "Have You Been GOOD!? Huh!?"
She once or twice stood with one of her arms bent, with her hand in a fist on her waist: "Have you been GOOD!? Huh!?" she went, teacher-like, bossily.
Her Attacking Me And Then Leaning In And Kissing Me On My Lips!
She would often punch and slap me, playfully, humourously, on my stomach and arms, and then lean in and snog me, sometimes putting her arms around my neck.
Me: "You Can't Attack Me Now!"
I grabbed her by both of her attractive lower arms. Me: "You can't attack me now! Can you!" She put one or both of her knees up, as if to kick me and i released her!
Lying Next To Me
For 2 or more of the days she would often lie next to me with her head on the side, with her left ear on the pillow, looking at me and speaking in that high-pitched voice of hers.
Doggystyle
I had sexual intercourse with her, doggystyle, for a second time. She again didn't put her hands on the bed, she didn't get herself into that position, instead resting upon her lower arms, with her hands and lower arms under the pillows. I felt amazing,

with someone like this sort of "mine" again, her large, white, well-formed body in front of me submissively, with my penis inside her. Around the start i leaned forward, with my body fully over her's, with my hands and arms over her hands and arms, the hands and lower arms of which were under the pillow. I think it was then, or perhaps later, that she mumbled something in a submissive womanlike way, of course, in that nasal high pitched voice of her's. I then, later, moved my body up. I think that i came very well, with her hands and lower arms still under the pillow. Her head often went down. She had been, before the climax, moaning as usual, womanlike of course. It felt nice when i had put my body, arms and hands over hers. Her hands were closed, i think.

Human Czech Sexualess What Do You Vont Me To Do You Too Heavy! 4
Typing.
Date And Time
Thursday 02/08/2012.
Giving The Money To Her
Her: "Hiiii!" I said hello! Her: "How long do you vont to stay for?" Me: "I'm not sure, i'll have to see." Her: "It's £60 half an hour, £120 one hour." Later, me: "Yeah, i'll stay for one hour." I counted out the money on the bed. Her: "You don't have to give me each vone vone by vone!" "Okay," i said, smiling.
Sexual
1.
Her: "Did you miss me!?" She started out on top. She had her left leg bent, with the right leg kneeling. Me: "I'LL put it in." Her: "NO, I'll do it." She put it in. She squatted on my penis, leaning back: that stretched my penis back somewhat: she was going up and down: her legs, waist, back, arms, and hair felt good as i ran my hands and arms over them when she did this. Her: "What do you vont me to do?" "You can do whatever you want to me," i murmured. She then knelt down, instead of squatting, and then leaned forward and snogged me on the lips: i put my arms around her as she did this. Then she was moving up and down.
3.
Me: "I'll go on top." Her: "Okay." She put it in again, as she lay fronting me on her back. I moved forwards so that i was lying on top of her: i put my weight on her. Her: "UUUURRRR! You too heavy!" Me: "Oh sorry." I supported my weight on my hands/arms. She put her fingers on my nipples, but i moved her hands away from them after she had started doing this. I think that she said "sorry" after i had moved her hands away from my nipples. I lay down on her, with my arms and hands around her arms and shoulders, and my head on her forehead. Then i moved up, supporting myself. She was looking down, and we fronted each other directly as my penis went in and out of her. Her arms and hands were around my waist, they were on my back. I reached Buildup, and she was saying something like "come on". I could see her head downwards. Her hands went onto my buttocks. I said "I'm coming: look at me." I think that she moved her head to the side, but then, possibly after i had moved her head, she moved her head so that her visage was opposite mine, and so that she was looking at me. We looked at each other as i came. Buildup had been excellent. I came well. She smiled and her eyes glittered about 5 seconds after i had started coming. She said something to me. I lay against her, with my penis still inside her, before pulling out. There was a tiny amount of her blood on the outside of the condom, just a tiny tiny bit, it had been difficult to see it.
Sexual 2
Her: "Only ten minutes left." Me: "Yeah, we'll go again: we'll do doggystyle." Her: "Okay." I asked her to turn her head while i was having sexual intercourse with her. She insisted on putting it in again, which she did. I was in between her legs. I said "talk to me", as i was having sexual intercourse with her. She said, "Come on let me feel that spunk," quietly. It was difficult for me

to reach Buildup, but i managed it, with my hands on the bed either side of her, and my arms holding her body in place either side of her waist. Another thing that helped me to reach Buildup was the sensation of my penis going into her vagina, feeling her vagina. She started gasping, and moaning, and saying "Oh yes, come on." I let out a somewhat feminine moan as i tried to force the semen out, and hold Buildup, which was difficult. But Buildup was excellent. I came excellently. She said "You did it. Vell done." I was sweating horribly, and panting. There was no blood whatsoever on the condom.

Her Behind Me With Her Arms Around My Neck
Me: "I'm going to lie back against you." I started to lie back against her, with her behind me. Her: "UUURRRR! You too heavy!" Me: "Oh sorry. I'll do like THIS then." After much shuffling around i was lying back against her, with her arms around my neck. I stroked her arms as she had me like this. Me: "You've got me right where you want me now, don't you!" I made some comment about strangulation. She sort of held her left wrist with her right hand and squeezed my neck somewhat. "That's RIGHT!" she went. "Now you tell me your NAME: Vot's your NAME!!?? Huh!!?? Huh!!??" I laughed.

Her: "Look Vot You Did To My Knee"
I had my right arm around her neck, as she was lying to my right, on her side, on her left side, with my right hand on her right shoulder. My left arm and left hand were going on her right arm and right hand, with my left hand often grabbing her forearm. Her right leg was all the way across my legs and my penis. I was stroking her right leg with my left hand, and it felt fantastic: as i moved my left hand over her right knee, i noticed that it felt "grainy", uneven, unshaved possibly, or bruised. She looked at me, and i sort of made an enquiring "look" with my expression, to which she responded: "Look vot you did to my knee."

She Shook Her Hair
I was moving her hair around, to try and get her hair long on both sides of her head: her hair was sort of behind her head on one side. She shook her head. Her hair went all over her visage and eyes. I moved it away. She did it again. I moved it away. I said something like it was slightly psychotic, or mad-looking. I said: "Look what you've done, your hair's gone onto your eyes." I moved her hair away from her eyes, especially her right one.

She Tickled Me
She Slapped Me
She Stared Humourously With Her Eyes
She Made Her Eyes Briefly Crosseyed, Humourously
She Put Her Fingers In My Nostrils, About 1cm In
Me: "DON'T DO THAT!" Her: "It's just a hole!"
She Put Her Hands Over My Mouth
Her: "You Look Like HAIRY MARY"
Her: "I'll Stick Something Up Your BUM!"
Her: "(Next time?) I'll stick something up your BUM!" Me: "No." Her: "You would love it!" Me: "Shut up." I think i slapped her bum then, with her probably responding by attacking me, as she often did.

Her: "Next Time I'll Tie You Up!"
Her: "Next time i'll tie you up!" Me: "No." Her: "It's okay, you can trust me." Me: "I definitely CAN'T trust you and let you tie me up!"

Her: "Let's Wrestle!" We Didn't Wrestle Though
End
I had my right arm round her neck, and i felt like i owned her somehow, it felt nice, as i stood next to her, with her on my right. As i did this she pursed her lips into a "kissing" posture. Her: "What am i going to do, keep you prisoner?" Me: "Yes keep me prisoner!" We kissed and then i left.

Human Czech Sexualess What Do You Vont Me To Do You Too Heavy! 5
Typing.
Date And Time
2012/08/16 Thursday, before Library Folkestone closed at 2000. My hour finished before 1859, probably at 17XX. 1700 i think. So it was probably 1600-1700.
Description Of Her
Visage is "blocky" in the sense that mine is "blocky", i wrote.
Description
She was on top, for the sexual intercourse. Buildup was excellent, probably perfect buildup. She kept going after i had ejaculated, she didn't stop, which made it not as good as other sessions of sexual intercourse, i suppose.
Her: "one by one"
She complained to me that i was giving her the money "one by one".
Her: "You're SCARY MARY."
Her: "Father Christmas"
Her: "You look like Father Christmas, with the beard you know. Make it white and then you vould be like Father Christmas."
She was lying with her head on the side on my chest
She looked at me a little hatefully at times, but that's just her, really
Her: "Pussyhole"
Her: "(You're a) Pussyhole!"
Her: "You SCARED."
Her: "What do you vont?"
I had my arm around her neck, possessively, standing side by side, like she was mine
She was looking up at me with an "open grin", and amused eyes.

Human Czech Sexualess What Do You Vont Me To Do You Too Heavy!
Typing.
Clan
In profile she looks like "Meryl Streep", i think, or was it the woman from "Taxi Driver", with her nose slightly bent in an attractive way. She looks like Human USA Actress Uma Thurman. She perhaps looks a little like Human UK Television Presenter Kate Humble.
Description Of Her
Tall, very pale pink-white, fabulous body, well built not skinny and not obese, long dark hair, SLIGHTLY East European looking visage. Faint lines by the corners of her eyes when her mouth moves, but for the vast majority of the time she looks very young. Large natural breasts. She looks to be in her mid-20s maybe? I asked her to take off her makeup recently, which she did before we had sexual intercourse, and she looked significantly different without it: it's somewhat sunken around her eyes.
Description Of Her
Long dark brown hair. Head shape is quite unsmooth, and angular. Eyes are well developed. Nose bend, a bump. White-pink skin. Nice, fantastic legs, i wrote. A little curvy about the waist. Slightly small hands, proportionately. Nice arms. Slight crow's-eyes, but only from certain angles, i wrote.

Human English A. Sexualess You Take Yours Off And I'll Take Mine Off Sort Of Bouncing Heasytyoai'lltmosob
Typing.
Date And Time
2012/08/23 Thursday. It was between 1000-2000. It was before 1840. It was probably after 1400.
Clan
If the Clan of the "Sporty" one out of the Human UK Musician Group, called Melanie(i can't remember if it's Melanie B or Melanie C), isn't her Clan, then that Clan must be her Cousin Clan. Probably not the Clan or Cousin Clan though. This Sex Worker has the same "playfullness" and slight narrowness about the visage. However, the nose of this Sex Worker is longer. I think that her Clan, though, is the Clan of this Spanish Sex Worker from elsewhere, who has been there for a long time, from

before 2011/03/07 Monday.
Description Of Her
Skin is not too white-pink, but still very much white in the skin. Mid height. She has quite nice legs. She sounded eloquent, well-spoken. She has long brunette hair, thin, straight. She looked young, maybe early 20s.
Condom And Lubricant
Her condom was used.
Description

Her: "How long do you want to stay for?" Me: "However long £60 gives me!" Her: "You're big!" Her: "You'll have to take your's off as well! You take yours off and i'll take mine off." After i had said that i didn't want a massage, in response to her asking me if i wanted a massage....after i had said that, she said: "Give me a massage first!" I gave her a massage. She was on her back while i massaged her, i think. Her: "Oooh that's nice, ooh and my neck....and my back."

She went on top. She didn't seem too keen on my penis going in the whole way into her. I moved it in and out a little. She put both of her hands on my chest and she was moving her vagina up and down on my penis, "bouncing". It wasn't going all of the way down, but it was "stroking" my penis. Me: "Oh i'm going to come soon." My head was on the pillow, probably leaning back. I was occasionally putting my arms around, or on, her arms, and on her back. And also along her legs, which were bent(not squatting), kneeling. She liked (it), and moaned as my hands and arms were along her legs. I told her to look at me as i was coming. She stopped when i said "stop". Buildup was excellent, climax was excellent, but she pulled out three quarters of the way through my ejaculation process. She smiled when i came, i think, flirtatiously.

Human English E. With Scottish Accent Sexualess My Hair's Bipolar
Typing.
Date And Time
Tuesday 28/08/2012, after 1559, but before Tesco Superstore Folkestone. Before darkness had fallen. Half an hour with her.
Condom And Lubricant
Condom was her Durex Orange/Yellow Condom.
Description

She got on top of me, fronting me. She was moving medium pace but steadily, sort of "squashing" my penis, with her hands and arms either side of me, with her leaning forward only at a slightly or more than slightly higher angle than horizontal, 45 degrees maybe. I probably said "I'm coming". I had said something like "That's good, keep control of me." The buildup was perfect for me. She was looking at me with a "pleading" look as i was building up towards ejaculation, with the "pleading" look almost making it seem as though she was crying, or upset or something: it's because she didn't want me to let go of the buildup, so to speak. The climax was perfect for me. After the sexual intercourse she relaxed, "submitted", so to speak, lying flat on me: then i put my arms around her. There was no blood on the condom. I had said "keep going", and then i had said "stop": it had been perfect. We had been looking at each other as i came.

She lay in my arms. Then i tried to lie in between her legs, with my head back against her, but i didn't get my head all of the way up to her head: she had her legs on me, and her arms were around my neck from behind me. She was probably looking in the mirror(s) on the ceiling, at me/us. I tried, and i think managed, to turn my head back and managed to look at her visage, probably upside down.

She told me that she had been born in England, and had lived there more than 7.5 years, before moving to Scotland.

I'm almost 100% certain that i said: "You're my girlfriend for half an hour."

Human English E. With Scottish Accent Sexualess My Hair's Bipolar 2
Typing.
Date And Time
Thursday 30/08/2012, before 1911, and probably(according to my computer) before 1734, and after 1200(my alarm went off at 1200). Half an hour with her.
Condom And Lubricant
Condom was my Purple Durex Condom. Lubricant was my Durex Play Blue Lubricant, which she agreed she was putting in her; i put it on my condomed p+nis.
Description
She started off making the bed. I gave her the money. Me: "Shall i put it here?"(i indicated her breasts, the middle of them). She sort of moved so that i could put the money in between her breasts, which i didn't do. Her: "Do you need a glass of water again?" Me: "I didn't/don't NEED a glass of water." Me: "I'm okay, it's okay."(Something like that). We started off hugging, front to front, while she was getting undressed, with me fondling her nice buttock(s?) and her back, with us kissing in the only way that she allowed me to kiss her: short, without tongues, kisses on the lips, quite long-ish or not. Then i moved back: she took all of her clothes off. Then we were hugging and kissing: i put my arms along her arms, from the front, with us standing up, and i stroked her arms, and had my arms around her back, and was stroking her back. She was putting her hands on my p+nis and my testi+les: i put her hand(s) on my testicles.
       Then she lay down on the bed: i put my condom and my lubricant on the bed. I sort of straddled her, above her groin area, so my legs were kneeling around either side of her waist: in that position i leaned in, bending down, to kiss her, and stroke her, probably stroking her nice relatively large fantastic breasts. Our bodies were pressed against each other. I lifted and kissed her left leg, running my hand(s) along it. Her: "Are you going to go on top this time?" Me: "No!" There was a pause for a number of seconds. Then i said: "I want to make the most of this position, of you. No one has sex like you!" She laughed softly i think.
       I lay down in the middle of the area. She was moving towards my p+nis, with her legs either side of me, kneeling, but i didn't feel ready. Me: "Wait wait a second." Her, smiling: "It's okay, i'm just (getting in position)"(she said something like that). Then i was ready. She started off using the same "technique" as last time, steady "squashing" of my p+nis. This felt good. This time i moved my legs further apart, and it felt even better for me. The pleasure went up here and there for me, and i thought that i would be starting to come, but i didn't, not yet. I was moving down on the bed, so i grabbed the wooden ledge behind me with one of my hands, and held it, keeping me up instead of us sliding down and off the bed: i would often do this today, with my hand(s?) on that ledge, as she was on top of me, front to front.

Then she sat up, and was moving back and forth with her hands on my chest, with her back straight up in the air. She was moving really quickly, and really strongly-she moved really strongly when she was on top LAST TIME as well-like this. I still didn't start coming, even though i thought that i was going to. She was incredibly vocal, loud! which was okay, fine! nice perhaps. Her: "Uuuuuuh i'm coming, oh yes i'm coming." And she was panting. Then she sort of lay at a 45 degree angle on me, or against me, and she was panting significantly: she had come. Then she relaxed against me, and i started thrusting upwards, with my hands on her legs, stroking her upper legs, and lower legs, and my arms against her legs, and then with my hands on her buttocks, spreading her buttock cheeks, and i think touching my p+nis as it was going into her upwards as i lay there. Her: "Uuuuh that's good oh that's fantastic keep doing that." I did that for a while.

During the period that she was on top of me, with either me thrusting upwards or her doing the work moving her body up and down or something on my p+nis, i looked up at her visage, with my arms around her, my hands around her, stroking her. She was looking straight ahead and panting: she looked very attractive to me. I saw that her lips, from where i was lying below her, looked really pressed together, from the side, as though she was pushing inwards with both of her cheeks to make her lips look "squashed", except she wasn't doing that. It made her look really attractive and somewhat unique, with her visage like that, and with her lips like that.

Her hair got in her visage: i moved it away, as we were having sexual intercourse.

I had looked up at the mirror on the ceiling as we were having sexual intercourse: it looked very human-female-dominant, i thought. I also looked in the mirror to my right, as i was stroking her left leg. I also turned my head to my right, and kissed her left arm as we were having sexual intercourse.

I stopped thrusting upwards after a while, and then she started moving again, on my p+nis. We were hugging, and she put her arms around my neck. She started stroking my hair, with her arms around my neck. She was "humping", moving her body up and down on my p+nis, with us more or less hugging, although i moved her up somewhat so that it was more of a 45 degree angle, so i could look at her as i was coming, which i couldn't do with us hugging completely. She was going really rapidly: i realised that i was going to start coming, and my arms sort of flopped down either side of her: then my arms started stroking her legs, and went around her back, and her waist. She kept moving up and down on my p+nis, just moving her lower body. Me: "Keep going i'm coming." She kept going. Buildup for me was perfect. Me: "Stop." She surprised me by sitting up after i said "Stop," which caused a little bit of pain in my p+nis. After that brief pain though, it was a warm release, ejaculation, with her "higher up" than she had been just now. We had been looking at each other as i came. Then we hugged, and kissed etcetera.

There was no blood on the condom. Me: "There's sometimes blood on the condom with other girls, because i'm so big. Well, you KNOW i'm big don't you!" Her: "Yeah I KNOW."

Description 2

She lay in my arms: i think that she was stroking my chest. She had put her leg across me, above my p+nis, her left one. My arm was around her neck, and i was stroking her. Then i sort of moved her, so that she had her right cheek on my chest, and her left leg also across my p+nis. I put her hair, on her left, so that it wasn't behind her, but was along the side of her head, it looked better.

Me: "I'm going to try that lying against you thing, you know like last time." Her: "(My breasts) are like pillows (anyway)"(she had said something like that). Me: "Are you okay? You're not squashed or anything?" Her: "It's okay: i can take it." I sort of looked moved my head back and looked up at her. Me: "HELLO!" Me: "I'm going to try to kiss your cheek!" I didn't quite manage it on the first attempt, but i did on the second one. We laughed softly after i had managed to kiss her cheek while lying like that. Her legs were around my legs, as i was lying on her, and i was stroking them, with my arms probably on them; her arms were around my neck. I sort of moved her arms tighter around my neck, and she gave my neck somewhat of a squeeze! Her: "It's okay i won't strangle you!" She did give my neck quite a hard squeeze, making me verrry! briefly short of breath, and with a slightly compressed neck....which i enjoyed! I felt as though i woke up even more then, after she had squeezed my neck! Her: "I'm very (somethingorother)." Me: "(Somethingorother) or MURDEROUS!!?" Her: "(Somethingorother)."

Her: "Are you a writer? Do you write?" Me: "You mean type? No one writes nowadays." She said something like "You know what i mean." Her: "You come across like you're a writer. Want to set your opinions down."(She said something like that).

She had all of these cute catchphrases.

I looked into her blue eyes, which looked a little bit cold once or twice....but she definitely perked up mostly, when with me. Mostly they weren't cold. Not that it matters, she's fantastic.

Her: "(Something about) mystery." I sort of paused, a little caught by surprise! I probably made some comment.

Her: "What's that expression?" Me: "It's not the size that matters?" Her: "No...." Me: "Good things come in small packages?" She beamed, her visage brightening in a somewhat happy way. Her: "That's it, that's the one: good things come in small packages."

Me: "My girlfriend for half an hour."

Her: "(Nah?) I don't think you're a dodgy type." Me: "I think i'm too submissive." She laughed softly. Then i started saying things like "i AM a man,", and, "I say to myself every day in the morning "I'm a MAN,". Just kidding." Me: "I was a man for a bit in the middle there, wasn't i! See! I was a man! I was thrusting upwards!" Her: "Yeah! Yeah you were!"

She was sitting up, as i was in front on the steps of the bedroom. I turned around, and put my arms around her, stroking her legs, and leaning in to kiss her on the lips, as she watched me, looking very attractive as always. She pushed me with her lips, as we kissed, as she leaned in to kiss me. Me: "You sort of attack me with your lips!" I did a similar thing to her. She did it again to me. It was nice, everything was nice.

Me, as she was standing to my left, and i was sitting down on the bedroom steps: "You have these cute catchphrases. But i mean, YOU'RE not cute as such, just incredibly SEXUAL, very very sexual(ly overwhelming? Did i say that? Probably not.) as opposed to cute, you know! When you were sorting me out!" She laughed softly, probably quite red, probably "glowing" somewhat.

Me, at the end, by the door: "My girlfriend." I leaned in to kiss her on the lips, with one of my arms around her neck, before i left. Her: "Bye!"

Human English E. With Scottish Accent Sexualess My Hair's Bipolar 3
Typing.
Date And Time
2012/09/03 Monday.
Condom And Lubricant
Condom was my Purple Durex Condom. Lubricant was my Durex Play Blue Lubricant, which she agreed she was putting in her; i put it on my condomed p+nis.
Description
She was on top. She was doing that thing again, "squashing" my penis. I grabbed the wooden thing behind me again, as i had started moving down the bed. Then she lay flat on me, and i thrusted upwards somewhat, with my arms around her. Then she was lying flat on me, and "humping". I had my hands on both sides of her waist, one on each side of her waist, with my fingers spread somewhat, which looked fantastic in the mirror(s) on the ceiling. I started coming, and i told her so. Me: "Stop." She sat up again like last time, contracting slightly, which caused me a little pain, but i came excellently, in a (few bursts?). I think that we were looking at each others' visages as i came. Buildup perfect, climax perfect, after a little pain. The sexual intercourse had been better than last time, when she also sat up when i said "stop". Her: "Beat you to the post again."

Her: "My hair's bipolar."

After the sexual intercourse i was straddling her, with one leg each side of her waist, looking down at her, sitting there.

First i lay back, using her breasts as pillows, with her legs either side of me(briefly). I managed to turn my head to kiss her right cheek.

Her: "(Her i am,) Your part-time girlfriend."

Her: "Hit with an iron." Her: "Nose looks like it's been hit with an iron." [Her] [Her nose].

Her, about her hair: "It's straight today: i was playing with (curlers?)."

Her: "....Ay."

Human English E. With Scottish Accent Sexualess My Hair's Bipolar
Typing.
Description Of Her
Curly red hair, very pale pink-white, blue eyes, Scottish accent, body somewhat stocky but not curvy but still fantastic, medium height, legs don't have too much flesh on them but they're very nice, visage is attractive, visage is slightly broad a "puffy" visage, breasts medium-large and very nice fantastic, nice arms, nice back. Very comely, "country girl" like, somehow. Chin doesn't jut out too much. Small nose, quite flat against the skull. Quite a short neck. "Vague" expression. "Soft" expression. Her: "My dad has straight hair." Her: "Both men and women on my dad's side have more curly hair." Penetrating blue eyes.
Description Of Her
Curly red hair, very pale, Scottish Accent, body a little stocky as opposed to curvy but great, only one or two crows' eyes-eye corners-when smiling like most human beings have. Hair is perhaps more wavy than curly. Hair is not as straight and flat as the hair of a number of other Human Females, in any case, whether wavy or curly. She looks young, in her mid 20s perhaps?
Clan
I'm fairly sure that her Clan is the Clan of Human USA Actress Nancy Allen, of the "Robocop" series of Human USA films. Superficially, and significantly at times, she resembles "phone hacking" Rebekah Brooks, born Rebekah Wade: however, the noses of the two appear significantly different. I think that her Cousin Clan is Mercedes McNab. She said something like: "I looked her(Mercedes McNab) up: my friend said we have the same nose." I thought at times that she looked a little like Adele, the Human UK Singer, but i perhaps doubt it.

Human English F. Sexualess No I'm Not Deceptively Innocent Looking!
Typing.
Sexual
She was on top. She moved very quickly, she was quite shy, looking away occassionally. At the end i was moving her body up and down on my penis, with her gasping and moaning: it got quite quick and frantic. I came well i think.

Human English F. Sexualess No I'm Not Deceptively Innocent Looking! 2
Sexual
She was on top. This time i noticed that i could move her body over mine in certain ways. As she leaned back, and at other points, i was stimulating a certain thing, which felt nice for me, and also gave her a lot of pleasure, she appeared to lose control in a womanish way, moaning. I think that she was squatting over me at the end. I moved her body up and down over mine. It was very frantic: it became very automatic and fast paced towards the end, with a large buildup. There was no going back! I kept moving her body up and down over mine, this time, unlike the first i believe, with her vagina going "higher" over my penis, instead of being all the way down: it felt "better", or something like that. I let her go, and she moved up and down in the same way that II had been moving her: it felt extremely good. Then she surprised me: she started going back and forth over my penis with her vagina quite high over it, not all of the way down: she took control completely. I gasped. The buildup was excellent. I came with her moving back and forward quickly in that way, although i think that i might have told her to stop, but i think that she knew when. My ejaculation was delayed, but it was perfect when it came, about 2 or 3 warm releases, with both of us looking at each others' expressions as we had done it: she looked slightly hateful and slightly cold, but in a very sexy way, when i was coming. I doubt that anyone has taken control of me during buildup, leading to ejaculation, so well, so successfully.
Her Lying On My Chest
She put her hands together, with the palms flat down on my chest, and placed her chin in between them on my chest, looking up at me, fronting me, with her naked body over my naked body: it was so cute. Then she removed her hands and just put her chin on my chest, looking up at me, and then she put her head on the side briefly, on my chest.
Me: "You're My GIRL"
I had my arm around her neck from the side, possessively: i believe that it was my right arm: it was like she was MINE, like THATs. Me: "You're My GIRL". Her: "No i'm not." Me: "Yes you are, for the time that we've agreed to be together you're my girl."
Her: "You Got Rid Of Your Beard Like I Told You Not To"
"You got rid of your beard like i told you not to," she said, scolding me, telling me off. I said something like: "It's typical of girls to attack men, it's just a matter of time before they start." She smiled/laughed.

Human English F. Sexualess No I'm Not Deceptively Innocent Looking! IS THIS DAY 1/2?
Date
On 2012/07/21 Saturday i wrote her times, and also "Lindsay Lohan", and "Blonde one from Mean Girls Karen". I must have had sexual intercourse with her on this day: i had sexual intercourse with her on this day. I would have to look at a number of receipts to try and estimate, or get, the time. Was it Day 1 or Day 2? It must have been Day 1, since i wrote that i booked with her at 1900 on Monday 23/07/2012.

Human English F. Sexualess No I'm Not Deceptively Innocent Looking!
Clan
Her Cousin Clan is Human USA Actress Lindsay Lohan, i think. I was looking at her at one point, and at that point she looked very much like Lindsay Lohan, extremely like her. However, this Sex Worker has a "beak" nose, and Lindsay Lohan does not. Some photographs of Lindsay Lohan look very much like her. Superficially she looks like Human USA Actress Amanda Seyfried, but apart from the shape of the nose in profile-which is very similar if not the same for both of the two Human Females-there isn't that much that's similar between the two.
Description
Long blonde hair. A little thin, not as much flesh upon the body as a number of other Human Females. As tall as me. She looks like she's in her late teens. I think that she told me that she's in her late teens.

Human English F. Sexualess If You'd Like To Come With Me It Hurts
Hefsiy'dltcwmih
Typing.
Date And Time
This occurred after 2009/11/29: after some research i have found that this is a Sunday. This occurred before 2011/03/07 Monday.
Clan
She looks somewhat like the Human USA Actress Sean Young. That could be her Cousin Clan. I swear that i saw a member of her clan in F., around Junction 12 on the M20, before then on the bus route: the Human Female had been shorter than her, though....i'm almost certain that that Human Female had been shorter than her. This Human Female had dark hair, and the same hair format, along with pink skin....i don't think that she looked as pale as the Sex Worker.
Description Of Her
She is as tall or a little bit taller than me. She has long black hair, down to her shoulders but not below the shoulders, thin, straight, it sort of always stays just above the shoulders, AT the shoulderss. Some hair falls over her forehead, concealing it, i

think. Skin is white-pink, very pale, there is much white to the pink of her skin. She is quite curved, and there is a significant amount of flesh upon the body, but she was not thin and not obese. Her voice is light, feminine, somewhat playful. She is attractive about the visage. Her eyes seem somewhat broad and slightly narrow. She has something of a lisp, sort of. She looked very youthful, and looked to be 20 or in her early 20s.

Condom And Lubricant

I wore condoms during sexual intercourse with her; i can't remember if lubricant was used or not.

Description

One day when i had sexual intercourse with her she was on top. She moved very energetically on my penis, straddling me. When i came, her eyes closed, and her mouth opened with pleasure: she often did this when i came.

One day when i had sexual intercourse with her i was on top. Her long legs were against my chest, together, and they were bent back somewhat closer to her head, with our visages close to each other, looking at each other while we had sexual intercourse. Both of my hands were pinning her arms to the bed, with my hands being placed around her arms, at some point along the area from the middle of the lower arm to the middle of the upper arm. She was moaning with pleasure, and her mouth was open again with her eyes closed, and her head moving back somewhat as i moved my penis into and out of her vagina. I realised that i was going to come soon. The feel of her arms in my hands, and also my thrusts etcetera, and also her attractiveness all combined to get me to buildup. I was moving my penis and moving my penis, getting more and more and more turned on. I think that i must have told her to look at me. We looked each other in the eyes when i was close to ejaculation. Everything else in the room seemed to vanish as we looked each other in our visages, it was strange, somehow. I was moaning with pleasure. I was building up and building up and then i came, with us still looking at each other. Immediately after i ejaculated she made this gesture with her lips, with her mouth, a sort of "disappointed" expression, i think, moving the corners of her mouth. We looked at each other somewhat for a number of seconds after i had ejaculated before i took my penis out of her body.

One day i had sexual intercourse with her with both of us standing up, with me standing behind her, with my arms around her waist and body from behind. This was "cheating", ie my penis was all the way inside her, but instead of moving my penis in and out, our bodies were moved, like that, back and forth together, with the penis not actually seeming to move at all: in what i have just labelled "cheating" it's the movement of the body, or bodies, that causes ejaculation, and it's a sort of "non-standard" method of sexual intercourse. We were both standing up, with our bodies moving together, with my penis all the way inside her body, full vaginal penetration. She started saying "it hurts", with the odd tear in her eyes, some time after i had started the sexual intercourse; this was perhaps because she has a somewhat tight vagina, and my penis is large....but she also felt ill, and said "it hurts" one time when i first came in, when it wasn't because of me, so i think that it was mostly something else that was causing this. In any case she went "it HURTS!" and there was the odd tear in her eyes....but it was too late, because i was in buildup, and i would be ejaculating soon. For some reason her tears, her crying a little bit, was a turn on for me. My hands and arms were around her waist and around her breasts and gripping her arms and gripping her wrists hard and i kept moving our bodies together and i extremely frantic as i was in buildup, getting more and more and more turned on, and i was gripping her waist very hard as it felt like my penis was going incredibly deep into her....she had tears on her visage but she had submitted completely to her sexual feelings, and her eyes were closed and she was moaning in pleasure together with me, through the tears. I came, and we hung together, standing up, with me holding her, appreciating how tall she was, as tall as me. Buildup perfect, ejaculation perfect.

I had sexual intercourse with her on more days than that, but i don't remember very much, if anything, of it, just that i always enjoyed being with her.

On some day, or days, when she was on top of me, having sexual intercourse with me, straddling me, i told her to use the "bone": she knew what i was talking about and did....but it hurt if she used it too much. At times, on one day when she used the "bone" on top of me, and possibly on other days too, there was blood on the condom when i pulled my penis out of her. With a number of Sex Workers, for me, there has, on a number of times, been blood on the condom, to different amounts, when i pull out, because i have a large penis. In THIS Sex Worker's case, though, it might not have been because of the size of my penis, or it could have been only partly due to the size of my penis.

Her, sitting down: "It HURTS!"

I was sitting next to her, with both of us sitting on that funny bed, on the side of it, with our feet on the floor. She had tears in her eyes. She was looking down, or straight ahead, but not at me at that time. "It HURTS!" she wailed, complaining. I had put, or i put, my arm around her, with my hand on the top of one of her shoulders, or just below it on the upper arm, stroking her there, rubbing her. We sat together like that in silence for a period of time. I felt at that point that i cared enormously for her, very very much, that i liked her very very much, that she meant an enormous amount to me. We sat like that in silence, with me looking at her somewhat from the side, and my hand probably going around her waist, and perhaps on one or more of her upper legs at times. We must have sat like that for at least a good few minutes, probably more than five minutes.

Me almost falling asleep on one of her shoulders

I was sitting next to her, with both of us sitting on that funny bed, on the side of it, with our feet on the floor. She had tears in her eyes. She was looking down, or straight ahead, but not at me at that time. I had put, or i put, my arm around her, with my hand on the top of one of her shoulders, or just below it on the upper arm, stroking her there, rubbing her. I had my hand there. My hand possibly went around her waist. Then i put my head on its side, onto her shoulder. I closed my eyes, happy, with my head on her shoulder. We stayed like that for some time. Then i heard her voice go "I think your time's almost up," or something like that....in any case it was something about my time being up.

She told me that she liked being with me

Her, at the start: "If you'd like to come with ME!"
      A number of times, when she would first walk through the door, i would think that she looked fabulous. She would walk in on her high heels, with her right hand holding the frame of the open doorway to her right, and leaning in so that her body was all of the way across the open doorway, standing there looking tall and attractive. Then she would smile, and say in a light girlish voice, with her somewhat of a lisp, somewhat playfully: "If you'd like to come with ME!"
She told me that she was saving up(money)
She couldn't have sexual intercourse with me one time
      She had been to see a doctor for whatever it was that was causing her pain. I suggested that it was perhaps the hours that she was doing this, i said maybe it's too much sexual intercourse or something. In any case, one time when i went into the bedroom with her, she told me that she was in pain, and that she couldn't have sexual intercourse with me that day.
Her eyes widened and then she smiled
      My visage was very close to her's. I had difficulty seeing her eyes, since they seemed to narrow often. I said something like "I can't see your eyes: open your eyes wider." She opened her eyes very wide, staring out at me with somewhat bulging eyes, before reducing the opening of her eyes to a normal amount. Then she smiled at me, knowingly somehow, that sort of smile.

Human English F. Sexualess Looking Down At Me While Covering Her Breasts Cheating Hefsldamwchbc
Typing.
Date And Time
This occurred after 2009/11/29: after some research i have found that this is a Sunday. This occurred before 2011/03/07 Monday.
Clan
Description Of Her
She is attractive about the visage. She is of medium-tall height. Maybe, i don't know, 10 centimetres shorter than me? She has brunette hair, down to her shoulders but not below the shoulders, thin, straight, it sort of always stays just above the shoulders, AT the shoulders. She has some flesh on her body. She is a tiny tiny bit obese. She is stocky, and not that curvy. Her skin is white-pink, and she is quite pale, there is a little white to the pink of her skin. She looked to be in her late 20s or so, or perhaps 30, or in her early 30s: i still found her very attractive though.
Condom And Lubricant
I wore a condom during sexual intercourse with her; i can't remember if lubricant was used or not, but it probably was used.
Description
      I had sexual intercourse with her on her hands and knees, from behind her, at least one time.
      I had sexual intercourse with her on her back, with both of us fronting each other, at least one time.
      One time i had sexual intercourse with her from the side. Her hand went back to hold me about my waist or about my chest after i had told her to do this, with one or both of my hands holding her, and perhaps one or both of my hands holding one of her legs up. I had entered, or entered, her vagina, with my penis, from behind, with me fronting her back. I moved my erect penis back and forth inside her. I'm fairly certain that one of my hands was holding her leg up, by the flesh of her lower leg, which felt good in my hand. I kept f+cking her and f+cking her and f+cking her and then i came: it was a warm release into her, into the condom. She felt it. Her head moved. Her head went back, i think, or perhaps it went down. Buildup perfect, climax perfect. She had kept her hand around my waist or about my chest the whole time.
      One time i had sexual intercourse with her with her on top of me. She straddled me, and "cheated". She moved our bodies up and down quickly, with our bodies locked together and my penis fully penetrating her, the whole length of my penis. The bed was, i think, creaking horribly. I came.
She had her hands covering her breasts, and then looked down at me
      At least one time when she was on top of me, during sexual intercourse, she had her hands covering her breasts, and seemed a tiny bit worried, looking straight ahead. Then i said something and she looked down at me, moving only her eyes down.
I see her sometimes
I see her sometimes, in F., here and there. She always looks like she has woken up on the wrong side of the bed, with slightly

scruffy looking hair a little!
She was not very talkative
She was generally not very talkative, but i enjoyed having sexual intercourse with her. She was bossy at times, though.
Her legs looked somewhat slender
Her legs looked somewhat slender, as she would strut around on her high heels before we would have sexual intercourse. They weren't thin, but they weren't obese either....they had some flesh upon them.

Human English Ma. Sexualess Interrupted With My Ejaculation
Hemfsiwme
Typing.
Date And Time
This occurred when i was in L. This surely occurred after i had finished living in P. This occurred before 2009/11/29: after some research i have found that this is a Sunday. This occurred after the year 2006.
Clan
The clan is the clan of a Human English F. Female Non-Sexualess who works in HMV F., who was working in HMV F. when or before i had first started going there and obtaining items, before 2011/01/01. I think that this was a Saturday. 2011/01/01 Saturday.
Description Of Her
She is attractive about the visage. She has vague eyes. She is of medium height. Maybe, i don't know, 20 centimetres shorter than me? She has dark hair. I'm fairly certain that her hair is brunette, although it might not be, it might be black hair. Her hair definitely wasn't "red hair", or "blond hair". She's curvy. She doesn't have very much flesh on her body, being a little thin.
Condom And Lubricant
I wore a condom during sexual intercourse with her; i can't remember if lubricant was used or not, but it probably wasn't used.
Description

   She looked to be in her early 20s or so: she looked significantly youthful....not too "bright and sparkly", but significantly youthful nonetheless. She was quite sparkly, but not too much, quite animated, but not too much. She wore a grey or silver watch on her left wrist during the one session of sexual intercourse i had with her, which made her arm look fantastic somehow, i thought at the time. Now, though, i think that watches are an unwanted, by me, addition to the Human Female body, with regard to sexual matters, for me. But it seemed fantastic at the time, and perhaps there is a certain attractiveness about a bare Human Female arm, and from there on a bare Human Female body, which has a watch or some other item around the wrist....but perhaps not.

   I hadn't seen her before she was there, as a Sex Worker, that day. I was on top at times, and she was on top at times: i felt that she moved well on top of me. However, i hadn't had enough sexual intercourse to know enough about sexual intercourse....i was having trouble building up for the purpose of ejaculation, as i was having sexual intercourse with her, because i had had sexual intercourse recently before that day....during that period of my life, i left a period of at least one day, probably two days, between each session of sexual intercourse, otherwise i just couldn't really achieve ejaculation, achieve climax.

   Time was running out, the time that i had paid for to be with her. She was saying a number of things like "You have to hurry up and come now," and "Time's running out." I was on top of her and she was saying a number of such things. I was thrusting into her, with my visage relatively close to mine: i realised that i had to hurry up. I started rubbing my erect penis, inside her body, against her "bone", some thing inside her body that can be rubbed against a man's erect penis. This helped turn me on more and more during the sexual intercourse that i was engaging with her in. Still on top of her, i was rubbing my penis against her "bone" and i was rubbing my penis against her "bone", building up and building up and she said something like "You're going to have to hurry up and-" and then i rubbed my penis against her "bone" one last time and my penis "broke": i ejaculated, came, interrupting her: as i came her head moved back against the pillow, still with her head close to me, with her eyes closed....and her mouth opened in pleasure: i thought, at the time, it is as if she just died, it was that sort of expression process that she went through. I think that her eyelids might have fluttered during this expression process. I probably smiled then.

   I saw her again at least one day after that, but not as a Sex Worker: this time she took me into the main room to wait, to wait for whichever Sex Worker i was going to have sexual intercourse with. I told her that i had had sexual intercourse with her, as one of the girls, and she denied this, but it WAS her, so she was lying. She still had vague eyes that day. That, or a similar day after that, with her taking me into the main room to wait, was the last time that i saw her. I can't remember if i saw her on one day after that "sexual intercourse day," or on two days, or on three days after that, but it couldn't have been as many as on four days after the "sexual intercourse day".

Human English Ma. Sexualess Tanned Tall Head Down
Hemfstthd
Typing.
Date And Time
This occurred when i was in L. This surely occurred after i had finished living in P. This occurred before 2009/11/29: after some research i have found that this is a Sunday. This occurred after the year 2006.
Clan
Description Of Her
She is as tall or a little bit taller than me. She has long black hair, down to below her shoulders. She is extremely tanned, all over, although i don't remember if the breast area and/or vaginal area is tanned. She is incredibly curved, and there is a significant amount of flesh upon the body, but she was not thin and not obese. Her voice was soft, and calm. She is attractive about the visage, i remember THAT.
Condom And Lubricant
I wore a condom during sexual intercourse with her; i can't remember if lubricant was used or not, but it probably wasn't used.
Description
     She looked to be in her mid 20s or so: she looked significantly youthful....not "bright and sparkly", but significantly youthful nonetheless. She behaved in a calm manner. I probably did some foreplay or something with her, stroking her, and we probably kissed, with tongues perhaps, somewhat. She knelt down on the bed, with her hands flat on the bed, completely on the bed. I knelt down in a similar position behind her. I inserted my erect penis into her vagina, or she might have put my erect penis into her vagina. I might have started moving my body, thrusting into her, or not. At some point i put both of my arms around her waist, and started moving her body up and down on my penis, as if i was masturbating, in a way. I had my arms holding her body firmly around her waist, and moved her body back and forth over my erect penis. Her head was down, looking at the bed/pillow(s), at times....at other times her head probably looked straight forward, at the wall(s). I moved her body and moved her body....i can't remember if i was squatting, with my feet flat, or whether i was kneeling....but i think that i was kneeling. I'm fairly sure that her legs were in between mine, with my legs touching her legs, with her legs in between my legs. I moved her body and moved her body, and felt the upcoming ejaculation begin to build up. I started moaning with pleasure. This was somewhat(slightly?) tough on my arms. Then i came: it was a warm release, very warm. Her head went down after i came. Buildup had been perfect, and ejaculation had been perfect. Buildup perfect, ejaculation perfect. I hugged and kissed her afterwards. I was only with her for 1 day....i never saw her again after the 1 day that i had been with her. I had never seen her before she was there on that day. At least not as a Sex Worker. I thought right after i had had sexual intercourse with her, that that was the best buildup and the best ejaculation that i had ever had during sexual intercourse.

Human English N. Sexualess Tanned I Think Squatted Smiled

Henstitss
Typing.
Date And Time
This occurred when i was in L. This surely occurred after i had finished living in P. This occurred before 2009/11/29: after some research i have found that this is a Sunday. This occurred after the year 2006.
Clan
She looks somewhat like the actress who plays a female android-not the character played by Daryl Hannah, the other one-in the Human USA Film Blade Runner.
Description Of Her
She is attractive about the visage. She is of medium-tall height. Maybe, i don't know, 10 centimetres shorter than me? I think that she has brunette hair. Her hair definitely wasn't "red hair", or "black hair". She has some flesh on her body, a medium amount, being not obese and not thin. She is, or was, tanned. She has a sexual smile.
Condom And Lubricant
I wore a condom during sexual intercourse with her; i can't remember if lubricant was used or not, but it probably wasn't used.
Description
She looked to be in her mid-20s, late 20s or so, significantly youthful. On one day that i had sexual intercourse with her, she was on top. I was lying down, and she squatted down on my erect penis, lowering her vagina down onto it. She probably put her hands either side of my chest, around the middle of my chest, on the sides of my chest, while she did this. I came relatively soon after she had done this, but it must have lasted more than a minute. Buildup probably very good. Ejaculation excellent. She smiled in a highly sexual way-and i think that she had quite penetrating eyes-when and/or after she had sexual intercourse with me that day.

On another day that i had sexual intercourse with her i remember her standing by the door. I don't remember if i had sexual intercourse with her more than those two days. She didn't stay very long there, as a Sex Worker, and must have left at some point.

Human English P. Female Non-Sexualess Wet Kisses Fell Asleep In My Arms Looked Back
Hepfn-swkfaimalb
Typing.
Date And Time
This occurred when i was in P. This occurred before 2009/11/29: after some research i have found that this is a Sunday. This occurred after the year 2006.
Clan
The clan is the clan of the Human Female depicted on the front cover of the CD by "A Sei Voci" of Josquin Desprez, called, i believe, "Missa de Beata Virgine" with "Motets a la Vierge" also on the front cover of the CD. This CD was released in 1995- although this could be a rerelease of an old recording-, and the label is "Astree", with the CD having been assigned the number "8560". AMG(AllMusic Group) Album ID is W 1956.

Description Of Her
Hair is long. Hair is dark: dark brown, if i remember correctly. It's possible that the hair is "medium brown"; it's unlikely, though, that the hair is black. Hair is long, and goes down to at or below the shoulders; hair is straight. Skin is white-pink. Skin is extremely pale: there is much white to the pink of her skin. Height is slightly shorter than me: she is about 10 centimetres shorter than me, medium-tall. She is mostly stocky, but slightly curvy: i don't, though, at present, and didn't in the past, place much importance on "curves" in Human Females, when it comes to Sexual matters for me. She isn't thin, and isn't obese: medium amount of flesh upon the body. Voice is light.

Condom And Lubricant
I wore a condom during sexual intercourse with her; no lubricant was used.

Description
The first time that i saw her, in a "night bar" that i went to at times in P., she was flanked by two of her "girl friends". She looked about 20 or so....in any case she looked beautiful, and attractive, young. Her arms were bare: i think that she wore some sort of vest that night. There was that place, and the place next door: i at times, when i went out at night, went from one to the other, and that was the case this night: she also went from one place to the other next door that night. That night she walked off, linking arms, with a certain Human Male. I didn't like what i saw, and it was beCAUSE i found her attractive that she had caused, at that time, an amount of suffering to me. I don't think that i spoke to her that night, or i might have spoken a tiny bit with her.

    The second time that i saw her, also at night, we spoke, and i walked with her part of the way to where she was going, before i left. I think that she had permitted me to stroke her back, and put my arm around her, that time, which i think that i did, that time. I think that i saw, and also spoke with her at least one other time, at night, before the night that we had sexual intercourse, but of this i am uncertain.

    Now for the night that we had sexual intercourse. I was in a "night bar", the one that i went to at times in P., the "main" one, wearing my contact lenses and my sunglasses. I had just entered. I might have sensed something. In any case, i turned around: she was standing right behind me: she smiled at me. I said something like: "Let's get out of here, okay?" and she nodded. Outside, i asked something like "Is it okay if we go back to your place now?" She said yes. In any case, although one or both of us didn't say "We're going to have sex", it was sort of unsaid that we were going to go back to her home and do a number of sexual things together, sexual intercourse together i think. I think that she had permitted me to stroke her back, and put my arm around her, kissing her cheek(s), at that time, which i think that i did, at that time. I must have done that sort of thing then, i think. We reached her front door. Her friend opened it: after her friend saw me she seemed to "wobble" somewhat, and, after she had said something like "come in" to both of us, walked quickly over to the sink, and started humming loudly in a somewhat disturbed manner, with her back to me. It was, i thought at the time, as if her Human Female "housemate" had thought: "Oh no she's brought someone back to have sex with AGAIN i don't like it," or something like that. Her room was on the right, downstairs: the two of us went in, and the door was closed behind us.

    She went immediately and lay down on her bed. I paused for a small number of seconds by the door, where we had first entered, before moving and lying down next to her on the bed. At least much of one side of her wall was full of photographs of her with her friends, with photographs of her laughing, joking, and smiling with them....she didn't seem as happy now as she seemed in the photographs, i realised, at all....i had felt a slight sense of horror and sadness when i had looked at the photographs. I was stroking her body, kissing her cheek(s), murmuring to her in a sexual manner. We started kissing on the lips, each kiss being for a few seconds, and a number of them involving our tongues. I was enormously turned on, and had a serious erection. I started taking her clothes off. She took her jumper or t-shirt or whatever off, when she was lying on top of me, i think. I put a condom on, or had put a condom on shortly before this. At this point we were groping each other heavily, and there were more kisses on our lips. Her visage was all wet, since she was sweating, and the kisses felt "wet". I think that i pushed her panties to the side, with her still wearing them, before she moved herself onto my penis. She moved herself onto my penis, straddling me, with her panties still on. I was completely naked. After she had put her vagina over my penis, she started moving from side to side, on top of me. Then, however, she seemed to not like that position or something. I was enormously turned on, and actually felt a little bit like i was going to come soon: i put a number of my arms around her waist, and moved her onto her back. I was thrusting into her, with my visage very close to her's: she had locked her legs around my back, sort of putting her ankles together. I was frantic. Buildup was perfect, i think, and climax was perfect. Buildup perfect, climax perfect. Around the time that i came, or ejaculated, her head had gone back, with her eyes closed, and she had gone: "AH!" I'm not sure if she had actually come though....i think that she had, perhaps. I still had my sunglasses on at this point. Less than a minute had elapsed from when she had lowered her vagina onto my penis to when i had put her onto her back. When she had been on her back, the sexual intercourse had not lasted more than a minute.

    I took my sunglasses off and placed them on some wooden thing to my left, and told her that i had contact lenses on, or something like that. I then told her that i was taking them out. I took my contact lenses out and placed them in my canister, which i then placed on the aforementioned wooden thing to my left. I lay down on my back, on the bed. Only a small number of seconds, perhaps 2 or 3 even, after i had laid down on my back, on the bed....only a few seconds after that and she, from my right, moved onto me, lying on my chest and closing her eyes, or perhaps she had closed her eyes shortly before she had moved onto me, from my right. Her right arm was bent, and went onto my chest with her head, and her head was on one side. We fell asleep together like that. I had never felt so calm, and so at peace with the world, as at that point, i thought at the time, although i think that i had also felt calm and at peace when i had experienced a number of things regarding Natural Science Identities. In any case, i felt incredibly calm, and incredibly at peace with the world, and relaxed, and happy.

    In the morning she went upstairs, and came back down. She told me that she had to go, and therefore that I had to go. I asked if we could have sexual intercourse again, now, before she went, and she said no. I had an enormous erection, another one. She made some promise that she would text me back, or something....in any case i remember her breaking a promise that she made, via texting. I think that she didn't answer her phone when i called a number of times, at a number of points, after i had left. I definitely sent her at least one text, which she didn't respond to: i didn't receive any texts or voicemails on my mobile telephone from her. I no longer have her mobile telephone number on my telephone, and although i remember roughly where she lives, the homes in that area look very very similar to each other, and it's impossible now for me to know exactly which of the homes in that area she lives in.

After this, one day I was in the main Shopping Mall in P., standing still, when i saw her walk past me with a girl friend of her's: she ignored me, and walked straight past, despite me looking at her. However, when she neared the corner, she turned back to look at me: i was standing there looking at her. Me standing there looking at her seemed to upset her somewhat, for some reason or other, and she turned away, and had then, after a number of seconds, gone around the corner, to the right, and out of sight. That was the last time that i saw her.

Despite her breaking at least one promise to me, with regard to myself and her meeting up again, and despite a serious motivation-but i surely would have gone after her and surely ended up having sexual intercourse with her anyway had she not gone off with that guy the first night i saw her-for myself having sexual intercourse with her being her walking off with that guy-i assumed, at the time after i had seen them go off together, that they had had sexual intercourse that night-........despite those things i really like her, and i think of her in a positive manner. Those things did cause me an amount of suffering, but she is one of the only three Human Female Non-Sexualesses that i've had sexual intercourse with, and she's the one out of the three that i like the best, by a long way, and the pleasure and happiness that she has given me, the memories that i have with her, outweigh the suffering that she has caused me by a significant way. I thought back then, at a number of points after she broke at least one promise to me, that i didn't like her, but my current view is that i like her, and i like her very much.

Correctness And Incorrectness Clothing Destruction Typing. Identity's Image:
CLOTHING CUT WITH SCISSORS
Sunday 08/07/2012. Time is now 19:40.
CLOTHING PLACED IN RECYCLING BIN

Correctness And Incorrectness HMV Folkestone
Typing. Identity's Image:
HMV Folkestone. J.D.P. This Order Took More Than 1 Year, And It Never Came, I Had To Refund It. It was probably in March 2011.......it was definitely before Monday 07/03/2011. Type Dates From Receipt(s).

Correctness And Incorrectness Noise
Typing. Identity's Image:
Motorcyclists, Especially One, Speeding Motorcycles Illegal Saturday 09/06/2012 16:32 Lot Of Motorcycles Going Back And Forth. Probably The Usual Individual As Well, Who Did It Earlier.

Motorcyclist, probably the usual one today, 10/06/2012, also part of it.

"The speeding of the motorcycles begins when they read certain parts of my Internet posts. The ones are the type of criminals that are eager to jump to conclusions: they saw "It doesn't matter if you lie to a criminal, or if you cause more than the maximum amount of suffering to a criminal. What matters is that they suffer and DIE." (SUFFERING EXTREME: INCORRECTNESS SEXUAL OF HUMAN ENGLISH FEMALES NON-SEXULAESSES TYPING 127, which i was reading on my computer at the time) and then started speeding. Motorcyclists: Short Memories? Motorcyclists: Poorly Mentally Developed/Evolved? Realised at 2012/07/28, 22:46. Motorcyclists often start and/or speed up when i bring up THIS on my computer or bring up THAT on my computer, the timing is exactish."

Human East European: "Kajoh" shouted.

The human being next door to me in the other whatever(i can work out the address). Loud music blasted on Tuesday 14/08/2012 during my "breakfast". This address often blasts loud music, including having blasted it after 2300, but not too much recently: it was worse before i started posting again, under Pickford-Gordon. It has blasted loud music at least 5 times after 2300.

CORRECTNESS AND INCORRECTNESS NOTES
Typing. Identity's Image:
I entered Debenhams Folkestone at about 17:20, Thursday 03/05/2012. "f+++k". 3 schoolgirls: Human English Folkestone Incorrectess Sexual Litter F+++k, or HEFISLF(Yvette Cooper clan i think); Human English Folkestone Incorrectess Sexual F+++k Song, or HEFISFS(tall blonde perhaps unattractive); Human English Folkestone Incorrectess Sexual Bit Of A F+++k, or HEFISBOAF(round, dark hair, pierced tongue). I wrote "after spat on shirt incident".

HEFISBOAF threw, or spat, some liquid thing at me when i was outside a church: i don't THINK that it hit my shirt or anything like that because i heard a "splat" on the steps behind me, and saw her running off. HEFISFS was also there.

I have somewhat lost count of the number of times that HEFISFS and a number of other schoolgirls from that school have called, or sometimes shouted at the top of their voices, "f+++k" at me: a number of them always do it as they walk past me, or are near me.

NOTE: Thursday 05/04/2012=> Just Got Back. Time Is Now 20:14.

Human English Folkestone Incorrecter. M. P. put an extra standing order in. £410 was taken on 2012/07/24 and on 2012/07/27. He said "Yes i deleted the 27th one, it's all gone," or something like that. I think that it automatically went onto the 27th, but then i put it in on the 24th, since it was late from the 21st.

MONDAY 09/07/2012
Bin And Recycle Various Clothing Etcetera. Did That.
Bags That The Clothing Were In Destroy. Did That.

FRIDAY 13/07/2012
Natural Science Volumes: I Was Almost Attacked, Type Up
Human English Folkestone Incorrectess Sexual "Hi Sexy" And Kept Looking At Me, Or, Hefis"hs"aklam
MONDAY 16/04/2012: 1925-1945 Human English Folkestone Incorrectess Sexual "Hi Sexy" And Kept Looking At Me, Or, Hefis"hs"aklam. Hefis"hs"aklam asked me, "Why are you sitting here?" Hefis"hs"aklam said to me, "Uuhhhh don't sit next-to/near me you fr++k." Me: "What did you just call me?" "A fr++k," she replied calmly. A number of her Human English Folkestone Incorrectess Sexual friends, wearing the same school uniform, have also called me "fr++k". Her school is a different school than the school of HEFISBOAF.

20101108 was probably the date when i reported a guy who looked somewhat like Philip Sidney, i thought at the time, accompanied by a long blond-haired guy and a group of other young men....when i reported him doing something to me. A police receptionist gave me a kp number that contained this date etcetera, which i spoke to her about before, so it was probably on that day that i reported it. He threw what was probably a firecracker at me, after he had walked past me, at Walmer, near Walmer castle. Him and this group of guys had been sitting on benches throwing firecrackers onto the Shingle. After he had walked past me i think that i heard or sensed something. I turned. They were running off i think. I saw what to me looked like a small stick of dynamite. It was hissing i think. I started running forward but then it went off: my vision went white for a large number of seconds and my ears rang loudly despite the fact that i tried to cover one or both of them with my hand(s) as i had been running away from the explosive device. I saw a doctor afterwards. An older blonde-i'm significantly sure with high probability that the woman was blonde-woman had witnessed this incorrectness, or crime, and i spoke to her about what had just happened to me for a short period of time.

YES the above was indeed on Monday 08/11/2010 that i reported the above. I came in at 1355. I came in 1 or 2 days after the crime occurred, i think that the police receptionist said to me. In any case it was definitely very very close to when the crime occurred. I do indeed vaguely, i think, remember that it was exactly that....ONE....or TWO days ago: ie the crime either, i think, occurred on the Saturday or the Sunday, ie Saturday 06/11/2010, or Sunday 07/11/2010. I'm leaning towards the Sunday, but i'm not 100% sure at the moment.

A number of police receptionists had complained, i was told on Saturday 22/09/2012, about me spending too much time coming into Folkestone Police Station.

HUMAN ENGLISH FOLKESTONE INCORRECTESS NON-SEXUALESS SEXUAL BABY, THEN WE'LL HAVE FUN, OR HEFIN-SSB,TWHF

TUESDAY 04/09/2012. I first met her on this day. We swapped mobile telephone numbers. She started off by saying "hi!" to me. She was talking to me a lot, smiling at me a lot, making a lot of eye contact, her eyes fluttered after i kissed her cheek. Her: "Are you ready?" in a sexual manner. She said "I'm single." She said something that was probably "What are you doing NOW!?" while looking in my eyes and smiling at me. She was disrespectful at the end and walked away from me, not letting me say anything more since she went off. At some point, not necessarily on Tuesday 04/09/2012 she explained that she had run off "That's (be)cause they were calling me to come." referring to her friends.

WEDNESDAY 05/09/2012. Today i booked a date with her via mobile telephone, for tomorrow(Thursday 06/09/2012). Her: "Haven't you planned it? Our first date, haven't you planned it?" Her: "I thought you were gonna ask me out on a date?" Her: "Baby." Her: "I'm busy during the daytime but at night(time) i'm all yours." Her: "All of the first dates that i've been on, they always bring a gift."

THURSDAY 06/09/2012. She was not there, where we agreed to meet up. I telephoned her mobile telephone at/after 8 minutes past the "meeting/appointment time". First it was engaged, but then the second time it rang, and she answered. Her: "I forgot." Her: "I can't tonight, i'm babysitting for a friend." Her: "I've been really busy, i've had lots of m++++++s." We agreed to meet tommorrow instead, at the same time, at the same place....except not the same day obviously. I had been standing there waiting for her, on Thursday 06/09/2012, holding the "gift".

FRIDAY 07/09/2012. She was not there again. I had checked my mobile telephone earlier and there had been no messages: however, after the time when we were supposed to meet up i received a text message from her which, i think, should have been received by my mobile telephone before. The text message, which says "Received: 19:16:13", says: "Hello I can't make it tonight I'm so sorry, we're do it next week ?x" . I telephoned her mobile telephone and she said "Hello" and hung up. I telephoned again and she told me that she was in Hythe. She said that her "nan" was "ill". I said that she wasn't there(where we were supposed to meet) yesterday either, to which she replied "I was BUSY." We then agreed that i was to ring back an hour from "now", with now being the time at which we were speaking via mobile telephone, shortly after the "meeting/appointment time". Her: "Then we can have FUN! Okay!?" I replied "OKAY!" She at first said something like that her "nan" was seriously ill, but then i think there was something about a cold....i'm not sure, i don't really remember. There was laughing in the background when i called: she said "telly", "dog". I said something like "who's there", or "is it just you and your nan?" to which she replied: "Me, and my nan," ie her and her "nan" are the only ones who were there, when i was talking to her on her mobile telephone. We agreed to meet up, when we spoke about an hour from "now", outside the Prince Of Wales Pub, in Hythe. I began to make my way to the Prince Of Wales Pub, in Hythe, bringing with me the "gift".

Correctness And Incorrectness To Do
Typing. Identity's Image:
Freedom Of Information Act Ask, Human English F. Male Council Noise Guy????
Human English F. Male Council Noise Guy Noise Etcetera
Human English F. Male Police Community Support Officer?? Protection From Harrassment Out Of Building Police Community Support Type Officer Guy???? Check Magazine That Was In Library Folkestone Wood Avenue
Recycling Create Log
Sainsbury's Manager Search Internet Dover Website Type In Full Name Verify
Sainsbury's Deputy Manager Search Internet
Printed Record From Police Station Of All Crimes
Human Deal Or Walmer Incorrecter Was Throwing Firecrackers On A Bench. Threw Firecracker/Dynamite At Me. Download Philip Sidney Pictures. Cousin Clan.
Motorcyclists, Especially One, Criminal Speeding Motorcycles Illegal Stupid Saturday 09/06/2012 16:32 Lot Of Motorcycles Going Back And Forth. Probably The Usual Individual As Well, Who Did It Earlier.
"Kajoh" Was Often Shouted Loudly.
Human Scottish Incorrecter(Carved Abusive Names On My Desk), Human English L. E. Incorrecter(Punched And Kicked Me, Many Days)[John Howard], Human English L. E. Incorrecter(Punched Me Many Days, Said To Me "Don't Stand Like That, It Looks Gay: Stand Like This(With Your Arms Folded)")[Christopher Moss], Human YDNA Level O Incorrecter Get Up(Fingers On My Neck, Squeezed, Pain, Quite A Lot Of Days)[Errol Hui][It Could Be Hoi, But Probably Not], Human English L. E. Incorrecter (Punched Me Most Days, Called Me Names Most Days "Cripple", Karate Chopped The Back Of My Neck One Day)[Christopher Pawley]
Folkestone Sports Centre, Gymnasium Receipt (Thursday) 08/03/2012 1908; Human YDNA Level E Incorrecter; Human

French Incorrectess Sexual Julia Roberts Cousin Clan.
Folkestone Sports Centre, Gymnasium Receipt (Thursday) 15/03/2012 1929; Human YDNA Level E Incorrecter; Human French Incorrectess Sexual Julia Roberts Cousin Clan.
Stagecoach Bus Ticket Adult Explorer(A Percentage Of Kent) (Thursday) 10/05/2012 1608; I Had Written, On The Back Of It, "Spat On Shirt".
Stagecoach Bus Ticket Adult Explorer(A Percentage Of Kent) (Tuesday) 29/05/2012 1533.

HUMAN BELGIAN INCORRECTESS NON-SEXUAL
Typing. Identity's Image:

CRIME: EXTREME, SATURDAY 26/11/2011, DESCRIPTION
I was wearing 1 green chequered shirt, 1 dark trousers, 2 white socks, 1 white underwear, 1 white vest. I s i v of HBIN-S. HBIN-S spat b. Spit in my visage 2? times in total.

Human Belgian Incorrectess Non-Sexual, labelled HBIN-S, blocked the front door as I was about to leave. She said something like "Put a coat on. You're not leaving until you put a coat on." I told her to get out of my way and stop imprisoning me. He came out. "You need to put a coat on," he said. She threw my 2 trainers out of window.

SUFFERING HISTORY: CRIME: EXTREME: HUMAN BELGIAN FEMALE: SPAT ON MYSELF 2? TIMES: CLOTHING WORN
Socks, Donnay, 1 pair, white, green stripe, black stripe
Underwear, 1, white, non-crossed, Marks and Spencer, 3 part set, 1180 053, T14 00041/6654C
Vest, 1, Crossed, Marks and Spencer, 2 part set, 6440 497, T14 00236/7216N
Coat, 1, grey, put on after crime occurred,
Trousers, 1, brown
Shirt, 1, green blue red

SUFFERING HISTORY: CRIME: EXTREME: HUMAN BELGIAN FEMALE: SPAT ON MYSELF 2? TIMES: CLOTHING WASHED
Shirt, Trousers, given to be washed, Friday 23/11/2011, before 1600

CRIME: EXTREME, SATURDAY 26/11/2011, HEALING
Shower and Dettol Soap 1
Visage Extra Dettol Soap 2
Glasses Dettol Soap 1, except between glass and metal frame

CRIME: EXTREME: HEALING: F: SHOWERED, WASH AND GO SHAMPOO, AND DETTOL SOAP
The day before I first went to the gym. Thursday/Friday. THURSDAY, I'm fairly certain.
Saturday 31/12/2011. 0 hair on visage. I had (just?) shaved. I had (just?) epilated.
Wednesday 04/01/2012. 0 hair on upper visage. Faint stubble on shaving area.
Monday 09/01/2012. 0 hair on shaving area, as had (just?) shaved.

CRIME: EXTREME: HEALING: L: SHOWERED, SHAMPOO, AND SOAP
1, Friday 23/12/2011, before 1600

CRIME: EXTREME,
Body, parts of, rain on 1
Visage rain on 1
Glasses rain on 1, while in L
Glasses rain on 1, while in F

HAIR TUESDAY

TUESDAY 27/12/2011, L.
Grey Coat was on the left side of the wardrobe. It was taken out. These things occurred after 1600.
The trousers and the shirt had been washed by today. These things occurred after 1600.

IMMERSION IN WATER, F.
Bath. Thursday 05/01/2012. 0 soap. I rinsed my body with hot, or warm, water. I dunked my head so that it was at the bottom of the bathtub, opened my eyes underwater, and put 1 hand in front of my visage.
Bath. Saturday 07/01/2012. Made to have a bath before I had sexual intercourse, in R., with Prostitute. I dunked my head 1 time, 2 times, or more, with my eyes closed. I used shampoo, and then conditioner. I used 1 kind of soap thing. Everything was rinsed away.

Human Belgian Incorrectess Non-Sexual
Punishments
Typing. Identity's Image:
TYPING
Ripped Up Book
Punched Arm At Least 5 Times
Called Piece Of Shit
Bent Fingers Back At The Time Of Crime
Sp I H V First, Then A Second Time After She Had Spat At Me, Then A Third Time Near The Other Room, Possibly Also More Times
Put Apron On The Floor

Human English C. Incorrectess Sexual What Can I Getu Maluv
Typing. Identity's Image:
DAY 1: TUESDAY 17/01/2012-TUESDAY 06/03/2012.
I was in the building, for X. Human English C. Female What Can I Get You My Love, or HECFWCIGYML, showed up, presumably having recently arrived to work there. She looked fantastic, i thought.
DAY 2: TUESDAY 17/01/2012-TUESDAY 06/03/2012.
HECFWCIGYML showed up, after i had been in the building for X minutes. "Hi! Darling!" went HECFWCIGYML to this Human English C. Male, a Human YDNA Level R Male. M. She kissed him on the lips for approximately 2.5 seconds, and then repeated this procedure 2, 3 times. Then she turned to D.M., a Human YDNA Level I, J, or K Male. "Darling!" she went to him. She did the same thing with him, kissing him on the lips repeatedly, for 5 seconds this time. Now she was to the

NorthWest of me. She turned to a Human English C. Female, an MTDNA Level H individual(or whatever most English girls are). A. "Darling!" she went to her. She kissed her repeatedly on the lips, for 5 seconds this time. They then had their arms around each other, and turned towards D.M. and the Human English C. Male. After that, though, i thought at the time, that she was having sexual intercourse with the Human English C. Male. It had begun at some point between Day 1 and Day 2, i thought at the time.
DAY 3: TUESDAY 17/01/2012-TUESDAY 06/03/2012.
HECFWCIGYML was sitting to my SouthWest with the Human English C. Male that i thought that she was having sexual intercourse with. They were both observing me, frequently.
DAY 4: TUESDAY 07/02/2012-TUESDAY 06/03/2012.
   Human English C. Female Non-Sexualess It's Good To Be Honest, or HECFN-SI'sGTBH, had walked over to HECFWCIGYML, who was sitting down with the Human English C. Male that i thought that she was having sexual intercourse with, far to the West of me, in order to complain to her about me, when i hadn't done anything to deserve it. I was about to leave. HECFN-SI'sGTBH said something to HECFWCIGYML. "Huh?" said HECFWCIGYML to HECFN-SI'sGTBH. She walked directly at me as i was on my way out, demandingly, aggressively, and probably angrily.
   I was at C. Bus Station. There are subtle ways, that i will not describe at this Event in SpaceTime, that a Human English Male can make a Human English Female aware that he's sexually attracted to her, and also the reverse for a Human English Female making a Human English Male aware that she's sexually attracted to him. I had attempted, prior to Day 4, to transmit this information to HECFWCIGYML in such ways. I had been thinking about her a lot. I thought that she wasn't going to have sexual intercourse with that guy forever, and that they could talk about it, etcetera. As i was waiting for his bus home, HECFWCIGYML approached C. Bus Station. This had only been 10 minutes, if not less, or perhaps more, after i had left the building. She sat down, with me way to her East. She was staring at me as i got on my bus, staring for about 2.5 minutes. I looked up from the Map that i was looking at, i glanced at her from a distance. I looked at her in a certain subtle way, related to the mating ritual. Her eyes went wide and she took a breath. She yanked her head down angrily. It had been a command: "How DARE you look at me in a sexual manner! LOOK DOWN RIGHT NOW! Like this." I put my head down and looked at my Map again; then the bus drove off. I thought that it was likely that HECFWCIGYML and the Human English C. Male might have complained with HECFN-SI'sGTBH against me, to D.M. after the bus had driven off, and before the next week, or next 2,3,4 weeks.
1 DAY, AROUND TUESDAY 07/02/2012.
A Human YDNA Level I, J, or K Male had started working there; i estimated with 95% certainty that it is a Human YDNA Level J individual. In profile he had a strong "Jewish nose". His skin colour was relatively brownish. He had a shaved head, was built, was stocky, medium height, about 10, 15, 20 or more centimetres shorter than Anon. His clan was unfamiliar to Anon. His visage was somewhat "worried" looking, with a sort of peculiar arrangement of the eyes in the visage position-wise, that sort of clan. His head was not wide, not tall, just standard shaped, somewhat rounded. He did afternoon-night shifts. I labelled him Human YDNA Level J Male Shavedhead, or HSAYDNALJMSC.
TUESDAY 17/04/2012.
I walked into the building for X, around 20:00? 21:00? 10 seconds after i had entered the building HECFWCIGYML rushed downstairs in a hurry. Later i asked for something from someone who worked there. "I'll do it," said HECFWCIGYML quickly. She walked over to me. "What can I get you my love?" she asked me, in an educated voice. She had said it as if we had been lovers, confidently and assuredly, as if we ALREADY WERE boyfriend and girlfriend. My mouth probably went open in surprise; i emitted a surprised, embarrased, but happy, and excited, expression on his visage at HECFWCIGYML. HECFWCIGYML smiled at me in response: her eyes glittered with excitement, pleasure, happiness, and amusement, in a sexual manner as she looked at me. I looked in the direction of D.M. and then HSAYDNALJMSC; perhaps they were outside, i thought. D.M. and HSAYDNALJMSC had been INside, and watching me. They both looked away from me when i looked in their direction, with pity probably. It was as if they were going, "How sad that he's so affected by her." I then looked back at her, and told her what she could get me, the standard customer-worker "talk". She then walked back afterwards. She said something to D.M. and HSAYDNALJMSC about me. First D.M. looked directly at me, and then HSAYDNALJMSC looked directly at me; both stared somewhat. It's possible that she had Unnecessarily Lied to both D. M. and HSAYDNALJMSC. I estimated with 95% likelihood that she had either said something to the extent of "[My First Name] fancies me," or had Unnecessarily Lied to D.M. and HSAYDNALJMSC, perhaps saying something to the extent of "[My First Name] called me "my love"" when i hadn't referred to her as that. She came back later, after i had asked her for something, since she worked there. She said again, in the same manner: "What can I get you my love?" At the end, after D.M. had told me that the place was closing, and as i was leaving, she came to the door towards me, also leaving at that time. She, but also D.M., said goodbye to me, who said goodbye in return. The conversation that she had been having with D.M. as they both had approached the door, had been somewhat staged, like a play or a film. It's possible, or even likely, that they had done that so that she would leave at the same time as me...or in any case it was something to do with me.
TUESDAY 24/04/2012.
I arrived around 15:00? 16:00? this time. HSAYDNALJMSC walked in for the afternoon-evening shift, from my SouthWest. "How have you been?" asked the Human English C. Male that she had had sexual intercourse with in the past; he asked it to her, so to speak, in a happy, flirtatious manner. She walked past him, not looking at him, as if he had done something to make her angry prior to this day. She answered him in a standard manner without looking at him, just keeping on walking straight ahead. She went NorthWest. She stood fronting HSAYDNALJMSC, the Human YDNA Level J Male, behind a pillar or something, out of eyeshot of me, since the pillar was in my way...i couldn't see them, or couldn't see much of them. However, the pillar wasn't very thick: they were standing very close, within arms distance of each other, fronting each other in a sexual

manner, about 60, 70, 75 centimetres away from each other, or less. They were talking quietly...and probably intimately. I glanced in their direction: D.M. saw me looking at them and started to sort of wobble around, in a slight panic. After that, HSAYDNALJMSC spent the day working on the LEFT of the room. SHE spent the day working on the RIGHT of the room. IE on opposite sides of the room. They avoided each other, and didn't speak at all. I knew that they had had sexual intercourse with 100% certainty, i thought at the time.
TUESDAY 24/04/2012.
HECFWCIGYML had caused an amount of suffering to me before this, and an amount of suffering to me when i realised that they had had sexual intercourse: the total amount of suffering of the 2 amounts is enormous. I don't have any negative feelings(dislike, hatred) for D.M., i thought at the time. For HSAYDNALJMSC and his clan, however, i DO with no doubt whatsoever have negative feelings(dislike, hatred) for HSAYDNALJMSC and his clan, i thought at the time. Later, HECFWCIGYML was a short distance to the NorthWest of me. She was angrily doing something. I was about to ask her to get something for me, since i am a customer. She stormed off hatefully when she realised that i was about to talk to her: she did this SO THAT i would be unable to talk to her...it had been a refusal to talk to me at that Event in SpaceTime.
TUESDAY 01/05/2012.
Human English C. Female What Can I Get You My Love, or HECFWCIGYML, showed up for the afternoon-evening shift.[1] She said "Ok" when i asked if she would bring it over, and then didn't.[2] After my transaction, she said, "I'll bring it over," and then didn't.[3] After my transaction, she said, "I'll bring it over," and then didn't.[4] After my transaction she said "I'll bring it over," and then she said, "Not a problem". Then she didn't bring it over.[5] After my transaction, she said, "I'll bring it over," and then didn't.[6] After my transaction, she said, "I'll bring it over," and then didn't.[7] After my transaction, she said, "I'll bring it over," and then she commanded: "Over there." Then she didn't bring it over. SEVEN TIMES.
TUESDAY 01/05/2012.
HECFWCIGYML was standing with Human YDNA Level J Male Shavedhead, or HSAYDNALJMSC, a lot; they leaned over towards each other very close on occasion; they often stood together like a couple; they whispered together a lot; HSAYDNALJMSC was somewhat jealous when i spoke to her, and was walking around in a worried, or disturbed, manner; they whispered together in a conspiratory manner a lot, probably about me, i thought at the time. HSAYDNALJMSC, as i was doing a transaction, said to me: "Do you have a problem with that?" since it was 1 time when HECFWCIGYML had said that she would bring it over, except HSAYDNALJMSC had brought it over instead. At the end a different guy, probably a YDNA Level R individual, although i didn't get much of a good look at him, was leaning over very close to her. They were talking as lovers...A LOT: she seemed to ignore many other things, and no longer said anything to HSAYDNALJMSC from that point onwards. I estimate that they had sexual intercourse that night with 100% certainty, i thought at the time. I had spoken with her a lot that day. I said to her, after i had given her something: "If you don't understand something about me just ask." After i had said this she nodded as if she already knew that she needed to think about things more, or something like that. It was a sort of "Yes I know" nod, or perhaps a "Yes i'll do it" nod.
TUESDAY 08/05/2012.
HECFWCIGYML was already there when i showed up, at 16:00 maybe: that means that she had done the early afternoon-morning shift, and also that she would do the afternoon-evening shift as usual. HSAYDNALJMSC was speaking intensely to a different girl, Anon DOES remember which one, and left at the start of the afternoon-evening shift. It does NOT look like they are doing anything sexual anymore(HECFWCIGYML with HSAYDNALJMSC), which is good.[1] After my transaction, she said that she would bring it over, but she didn't.[2] At 18:52 she agreed with me that she would come over in 5 minutes time so that i could do a transaction with her. She didn't come over: i waited for her to come over for 10/15 minutes.[3] Again, after another of my transactions, she said that she would bring it over, but she didn't. I saw her with this somewhat slightly unattractive-looking, pink-skinned, quite tall, brunette/black-haired guy, YDNA unknown as i didn't get much of a look at him, to the North. It looked personal, whatever they were talking about: i estimate with 100% certainty that they had had sexual intercourse, i thought at the time. She came up to me and fronted me in a sexual manner after that...it was as if she was trying to communicate the information: "I sexually like YOU now" or perhaps "I haven't sexually been with him because I'm sort of with YOU now", or "I'm faithful to YOU", although she had not had sexual intercourse with me. I saw D.M. hug her from behind, with her smiling, with his arms around her waist. It's possible that they had had sexual intercourse...DM sort of blocked my way when i was going towards her once...but i don't know whether they HAVE or HAVEN'T had sexual intercourse, i thought at the time. The embrace was highly sexual, and hurt me. She often laughed at my humourous comments.
HECFWCIGYML often fronted me in a sexual manner. She often laughed at my humourous comments. I was saying: "[Human English C. Female Non-Sexualess It's Good To Be Honest's, or HECFN-SI'sGTBH's, First Name] complained about me. However I trust the staff here. Not HER! Just everyone else." I paused veeery briefly after saying the word "trust", or perhaps i didn't. In any case after i had said the word "trust", her eyes glittered flirtatiously, happily, sexually, and she smiled knowingly at me. She knew that i had wanted to say "I trust you" but couldn't, and she liked that i was thinking such a thing, she enjoyed it. I had, of course, been thinking "I trust you", but i said "I trust the staff here." There was another occasion when she had looked at me flirtatiously, sexually, when i had been talking to her. On a third occasion i started saying: "So anyway, my full name's [My Full Name], and I..." i had started talking. As i was saying these things she was looking at me as though she was impressed, flirtatiously, sexually, happily. I gave her some w+++++n information etcetera about myself. A new guy who had started working there that day, or at least he wasn't there last Tuesday, after i had given her the "information etcetera", some time after that, he walked around as though he was alarmed, or disturbed...as though he knew that she sexually liked me to a great extent, and that knowledge shocked, alarmed, or disturbed him. This new guy might have YDNA less than R, but i'm not sure, i thought at the time. If he doesn't then he's poorly mentally developed, i thought at the time. She did come over a few times though, with it, for me, when she said that she would bring it over.

She told me that she had worked there since [1/2/3/4 Months Before 01/01/2012]: she had just changed her shift. Her: "I just changed my shift-" After she had said "shift" she paused; she sort of leaned back somewhat, studying me; it had been an abrupt termination of her sentence by her. It had been because she feared to complete what she had been about to say. The whole sentence, cut short by her, was probably something like: "I just changed my shift to Tuesdays in order to speak etcetera to you." She told me that she was s. t. b. a n. She said to me: "[About c. me m. l.]I do it to a lot of m. p. as well."

TUESDAY 15/05/2012
TUESDAY 22/05/2012
I arrived about 18:10, or more.
TUESDAY 29/05/2012
I arrived at 1629. I wrote 1630-1700. I wrote time now 1636. I saw HECFWCIGYML today, in red, not in her work-clothes, in the building. I then saw her in a grey top, in the building. She left at the 1800 shift. She said: "Where are you?" on her mobile telephone, and stormed out past me, ignoring me. D. M. still here, i wrote. I wrote "She wasn't talking to him on the thing."
TUESDAY 05/06/2012
HECFWCIGYML seemed hateful towards D. M. today. She said to me: "I'll get someone to bring it over for you." A Human USA Male went up to her and started talking to her today, as she was sitting with a number of human beings; he kissed her cheek; i watched him leave some time afterwards. She turned her head back to watch me today.
TUESDAY 12/06/2012
This day could have been TUESDAY 19/06/2012, but it's unlikely. The paper that i have placed, by me, behind Monday 18/06/2012, so it's extremely likely that it WAS indeed Tuesday 12/06/2012. HECFWCIGYML said to me: "You're going to have to ask someone else sweetheart because i'm a BIT, BUSY." She said goodbye to everyone except me today, before leaving. I asked if it was okay if i sit next to her at the whatever and she said "yes". We spoke. Her: "It's not wrong, so...." Her: "My boyfriend lives in [County's Name]: i go to see him on Thursdays." I asked her about the Human YDNA Level R Male that she had spent a lot of time sitting with a long time ago, at the very start, near the time when i first saw her: she told me that she had never had sexual intercourse with him. It's possible that i in fact asked her if she had done anything sexual with him, with her saying no, that she had never done anything sexual with him. I said something like "I saw you two together so i assumed that you were dating." I asked her if she had read my Internet Posts. She said: "I haven't read them." She said: "I'll read your Internet Posts when i have time." I told her that i might not be in on this day or on that day because i had had a crime happen to me. She asked about it, and i told her about it. After i had kissed her on the cheek-which she had permitted-i left. I looked back: although she looked up at me once, for a number of seconds, she mostly had her head down. When her head was down she was smiling, and looked incredibly happy, content, somewhat dreamy-looking.
TUESDAY 26/06/2012 She was not there.
TUESDAY 03/07/2012
Hecfwcigyml had come back. Human English C. Incorrecter Huh Him But Everyone Likes Money, or Hecihhbelm, was all over her etcetera. She had her h. in a p.(he has a p.) when i don't remember her ever having her h. in a p.. She was acting as if she had had sexual intercourse with him. Her, to Hecihhbelm: "Who, my boyfriend?". After she said that, her and Hecihhbelm were smiling at each other in a "playful" way, in a "fun" way. Her and Hecihhbelm were hugging in a highly sexual manner, and he kissed her cheek. At the start they were talking to each other from sort of opposite sides of the room.
TUESDAY 10/07/2012
Hecfwcigyml stood next to that young-looking guy, 19, 20? perhaps as if they were a couple. She could have just been
    thinking it, though, as if it was nothing. Around that point a girl who worked there walked away and up the stairs: she was disturbed, as if she couldn't believe something, and was upset. It's possible that such walking behaviour from the staff happened more than once, though, and that it was a coincidence. The young-looking guy went upstairs and perhaps looked at my c. s. or at a c. s. that contained what i was looking at or something like that. Suffering Extreme: Incorrectness Sexual of HEFN-Ses Typings. When he served me he nodded solemnly as if i had asked him if he could give me some cyanide. He behaved somewhat differently towards me after he had perhaps looked at my c.s.. But he also appeared not to notice her that much, apart from that one time, or not.
I was talking to her near the till. Then that YDNA Level (J?) individual, D.M., interrupted, and took my order instead, acting
    extremely jealous. Her head bobbed up and down when he had done this, as if his gestures had revealed something, some truth. He was highly irritable during the process, jealously.
That YDNA Level (J?) individual, D.M., looked tired when he approached her.
That YDNA Level (J?) individual, D.M., and her, they sort of went up to each other when i was making these notes.
When that YDNA Level (J?) individual almost "banned" me from the building, he said something like: "You can't chat to girls
    here, it's a business." I said: "It's not girls, just [Hecfwcigyml's First Name]." After i had said "just [Hecfwcigyml's First Name]." he started crying, and came across as unbalanced and somewhat unstable during the "crying" process, but it was not proper crying.
She also, when i was talking to her today, mentioned that she had a "boyfriend": she said: "....my boyfriend....".
TUESDAY 17/07/2012
She was acting in a sexual manner towards HSAYDNALJMSC today. Her, to HSAYDNAJMSC: "What? My boyfriend?" HSAYDNAJMSC then said, to her: "TELL HIM." We spoke today. Her: "I ALWAYS take a taxi home by myself after work." Her: "I AM okay talking to you...." she continued saying somethingorother after that phrase.

I wrote that i arrived at 1808 on TUESDAY 01/05/2012.

HUMAN ENGLISH F. INCORRECTESS SEXUAL STICK WITH ME TONIGHT YOU WON'T REGRET IT
Typing. Identity's Image:
[BEHAVIOUR]
She often walks and runs around, not still too much.
[FRIDAY 06/01/2011 ~ 22:00/23:00-SATURDAY 07/01/2011 BEFORE 01:07]
1.
Was outside Mexican Restaurant to the right of Remembrance Road, with my Sainsbury's F. shopping. Human English F. Incorrectess Sexual Stick With Me Tonight You Won't Regret It, or HEFISSWMTYW'tRI, approached me from the direction of the bar on the corner, at the top of Remembrance Road. I turned my eyes in her direction: she was looking at me, and approaching. "Hi (sexy?)", she said. We snogged for 3 seconds, the first of about 15/20/or whatever such snogs that night. She was very flirtatious. "Come and join us tonight," she said. Then, when we got into the bar she said in a "singing" tune to me "Stick with me tonight, you won't regret it."
2.
We had had about 5 such snogs. We were also holding hands. I must have said something about her being single. "Mmmmm...I don't know. I sort of...well...sort of have a boyfriend...I don't know." "What do you mean, sort of? You don't have one, do you. Come on." "Okay," she said, lowering her head. We sat down together with the rest of her group thing, holding hands and having such snogs. "We're going to spend tonight together aren't we," I murmured to her. She (said yes and?) nodded distinctly without looking at me, looking down like she often did. "I'm worth it," she said to me later, while we were sitting down.
3.
I started walking towards her later. She was watching me as I walked towards her, and dropped her glass, which shattered. She had been dancing. She might have, but probably didn't, kissed this shaved head light brown skinned Human Male who was standing by the entrance. She was talking to him, and they slightly held hands briefly. I told her my full name, as we were walking towards the bar all the way at the end of the coastal road. In the bar this Italian looking Human Male came in. "Is this fellow your sort of boyfriend," I asked her. She nodded. "You should take [Her first name] out for a (drink/meal) sometime," he said to me, smiling. I said to her somthing like, "Lets swap mobile telephone numbers so that we can talk later as well." "Mmmmm I can't," she murmured tunefully. But she was squirming towards me in a highly sexual manner and sort of leaning her head back a little bit and looking at me, as she said this. "As friends so that we can talk," was something vaguely akin to what I said. "Okay," she said. We did, with difficulty, because of her mostly, almost wholly.
[MOBILE TELEPHONE CALL]
"Babe," she said to me. "Babe!" I said back.
[SHE DIDN'T SHOW UP ETCETERA] I was "stood up" by her: i waited some time. We agreed to meet up but then she wasn't there. She didn't answer her mobile telephone when i rang to find out what was going on, and she didn't reply to the text message(s?) that i sent to find out what was going on.
[THURSDAY 26/04/2012 AFTER 21:19. UNTIL BEFORE 23:55.]
1.
I met a Human English Male outside the bar at the top of Remembrance Road, on my way back from Tesco F. with my shopping. I looked in the bar. I spoke to him, said hello. "You left your job in countdown," he went. I said something like, "[Her first name] stood me up." "Ahh! You're that guy! Come here come into the bar mate." HEFISSWMTYW'tRI was sitting down, and her friend from Day 1 who had told me where she works(although she doesn't work there any more), was there too, along with a number of others. After both of us being unsure of whether to shake hands, because of the timing, we shook hands.
2.
"I have a boyfriend now. We're in love," she said to me. "Do you mean that, you know, that Italian-looking guy?" "No we split up. I'm with someone else now. It's kind of serious." "She's cute, she's got (flat?) curly hair." "Who?" I asked her. "My niece," she said. "[Her first name]," I said to her. After about 2 seconds she looked at me. "We agreed to meet up. What happened." "I was with my boyfriend." "The new guy? You were with him on that day?" "Yes," she said. "Is that why you didn't meet up with me?" I might have said then. She might have said "yes". "You-didn't-respond-to-my-text/you-didn't-answer-when-I-called." I SAID one of those 2 things. "I'm sorry," she said to me. Later, the aforementioned Human English Male said to me, jealously perhaps, "Listen mate you're making everyone uncomfortable so-" HEFISSWMTYW'tRI interrupted him then: "No. YOU'RE making everyone uncomfortable!" The group chat thing continued. To this slightly older "landlord" "joint tenancy" guy, I asked, as he came back from the car, "What are they doing in the car?" "You tell me," he said to me, somewhat as if I had been talked about. Or not. She had spent a lot of time talking to the "aforementioned Human English Male". Her friend pulled my hand towards her and kissed me firmly on my cheek before she left. "Er...oh!" I went as it happened.
3.
The bar would be closing soon. "[Her first name]," I said. After about 2 seconds she looked at me. I asked what time it was, or what time the bar closed or something. She told me. "What are you doing now?" The others had told me that they were going to someone's house. She looked down, and stayed looking down the whole time. "I'm going home to be with my boyfriend," she said to me. "Is it okay if I walk with you a section of the way, you know when you're going to the boyfriend you're with at the moment(I emphasised "moment" slightly)? As friends, so that we can talk." "I...I have to see my boyfriend." "Does that mean no, that you're not okay with me walking with you today, okay." "Where are you going, Dan?" said "diabetic guy", a Human English Male, to me, interrupting us. I paused. "I'm going home to be with my boyfriend," she said somewhat snappily. "Okay well we have each others' numbers so we'll talk later." "Actually I don't (think) I have your number anymore: I think I

deleted it," she stammered at me. "Well I have your number." "I...there's...I...there's a problem with my phone," she stammered. "Well we shouldn't talk about things like this in a group." I snapped angrily at her. There was a silence for 5 seconds or so. Then she chit chatted with the group thing.

4.

Everyone said goodbye. "Say goodbye to Daniel, [Her first name]," said "diabetic guy", a Human English Male. "You do have my number though don't you," I said to HEFISSWMTYW'tRI. "Yes," she said. "Okay we'll talk later then," I said to her. "Okay," she said to me. We shook hands and kissed on the lips briefly, not full on, but somewhat to the side of my lips, only slightly on the side though. "Bye," I said to her. "(Bye) darling," she said to me. We left.

HUMAN ENGLISH FOLKESTONE AND HYTHE INCORRECTER YOU REMIND ME OF MY OLDER BROTHER YOU WANNA SMOKE, or HEFAHIYRMOMOBYWS?
Typing. Identity's Image:
Name
"Tommy". She went: "Tommy! Tommy!" Thomas.
Description
About 6 Foot Tall, short straight brown hair, skinny, pink skin, dead eyes. A little bit taller than me, it appeared, i think, when i saw him on [the CCTV Bouverie Place Shopping Centre] Wednesday 12/09/2012 1248(Ordered Item At HMV)- 1254(Telephoned 999).
Has an older brother.
Him: "I was banned from Maidstone." I looked at him. "Really?" He nodded at me in a somewhat serious manner: "Yeah". He paused for a number of seconds. "Some small theft," he went after a number of seconds had passed.
Clan looks a little bit like the tall, slightly vague-eyed, glasses, short-brown-haired guy at Waterstones Folkestone.
He looks somewhat like an incorrecter, somehow. Features of the visage are lean. Features of the visage don't really leap out. Standard skull shape, not "broad" features of the visage or anything.
Had a white "3" on the side of his dark (t-shirt probably). On Wednesday 12/09/2012 i saw that he had a large white "3", on the back of his dark (t-shirt probably).
I think that he said that he hasn't live in Folkestone And Hythe that long. I think that he said that he's originally from somewhere else.
He asked if i wanted to buy some drugs.
Age at time of incorrectness definitely 16(only 25% certain that it could have been 16), 17(88% certain), or 18(only 50% certain that it could have been 18) (only 2% certain that it could have been 19). I think that he said that he was 17.
He was drinking alcohol: flavoured vodka.
Migration(Delete When He's Found)

Him: "I live on London Road." I think that he said that twice, if not more than twice.
Him: "I live in Folkestone." I think that he said that twice, if not more than twice. Her: "He's gone back to Folkestone."
Him: "Let's go to C. (beach). (Nah?)"
Did he say that he used to live in L.?

What Happened: Date And Time
2012/09/07 Friday. I met him at 2235. I dialled 999, probably for the second time or more, at 2346. It probably happened at 2330 maybe?

What Happened: Location
Near The Prince Of Wales Pub, Hythe.

What Happened: Description
HEFAHIYRMOMOBYWS? shouted threats and obscenities at at least 2 other passers by, as we were sitting there. One of the obscenities, repeated by him, sounded like a racial obscenity.
The guy who looked like John Squire was walking along a street, towards my right as i was sitting down.
  HEFAHIYRMOMOBYWS?: "Yeah keep walking you (obscenities) walk on boy." The Non-Incorrecter stopped.
  HEFAHIYRMOMOBYWS?: "I said walk on, you f+cking (obscenities)." Non-Incorrecter wasn't walking away.
  HEFAHIYRMOMOBYWS?: "Why you stoppin huh?" Non-Incorrecter said something like: "You insulted me. It's not nice to insult people (who walk past you?)." HEFAHIYRMOMOBYWS?: "Yeah? You wanna go yeah? Yeah? Alright let's go then come on." Incorrecter got up and walked towards where Non-Incorrecter was standing. They stared each other in the eyes, fronting each other. Me and the 2 girls went up. Her: "He's sorry, aren't you? Say you're sorry." They continued staring each other in the eyes for a number of seconds. He said he was sorry. HEFAHIYRMOMOBYWS?: "Here mate nice one let me shake your hand". The Non-Incorrecter went to shake his hand, but HEFAHIYRMOMOBYWS? moved his hand away before the Non-Incorrecter could shake it.
  HEFAHIYRMOMOBYWS?: "Ooooh! Gotcha! Hahaha!" HEFAHIYRMOMOBYWS? walked off laughing. The Non-Incorrecter walked off.
Him: "Okay. Now get lost. Go. F+ck off." Me: "(Her name) do you want me to go?" Him: "I said GO! I'll knock you out. (Probable Obscenities)." Me: "(Her name) do you want me to go?" Him: "I said GO! I'll knock you out. (Probable Obscenities)." I started walking away, then took out my Nokia 2610 Mobile Telephone. I dialled 999. Me: "Police." He suddenly just ran up to me, sprinting very fast. I shouted for help while running away from him towards the Prince Of Wales Pub. I don't know whether i shouted "Oh GOD," after or before he hit me, on the lower left jaw, causing my head to go to the right. He hit me, on the lower left jaw, causing my head to go to the right. I ran into the Prince Of Wales pub and he walked off in the opposite direction with her and her friend.
In the taxi i saw that i had blood on the edges of my teeth, the bottom ones, where he hit me. Not too much though, but an amount of blood. A check before 2354 on 2012/09/09 showed that all of my lower teeth are in the same spots that they were before he hit me. The bottom central ones are crooked, but they were exactly like that before he hit me. The police officer dealing with my case, as of before 2012/09/10, or his colleague as of before 2012/09/10, said that there were no marks, or bruises or something, at the spot where i was hit.

Victim Description
About 6 Foot Tall, long thin brown hair that falls down, not as skinny as the incorrecter but quite skinny
Looked like a tall John Squire, possibly even of the same Clan. If not, then surely Cousin Clan.
Probably lives in Hythe

Police Officer Assigned To My Case(As Of 2012/09/09 SUNDAY)
Police Officer: "Common Assault."
Police Officer's Colleague was very reluctant for me to bring this to court: he was trying to have me perhaps let go of the crime. "He could have meant this or that," "You don't know."
Police Officer/Colleague: "Nobody matches the description on our Databases, been through all of the Tommys in Hythe as well and negative as well, I've asked Our Media Office Release This Information into the Newspapers see anyone come by."

Human English Folkestone Incorrecter Banging Door Open Up You C+nt Yeah, or HEFIBDOUYCY
Typing. Identity's Image:
Name: Matthew

Has been imprisoned.

Description: short straight brown hair, sideburn type things, visage didn't stand out, not a familiar clan, dead eyes, beak nose slightly, pink skin, tall, older than a teenager but not middle-aged(as of 11/06/2012).

The police apparently used my testimony to imprison him, he was "out on good behaviour" or something like that. Incident with regard to him started on Sunday 10/06/2012 19:00.

Sunday 10/06/2012 19:00 There was hard, loud banging on my door. "I know you're in there, all right open up," a Human English Male voice shouted. Me: "Hold on a second." Name: Matthew. "Open up I know you're in there." Me: "You're not allowed to bang my door." "Why did you

On Monday 25/06/2012 I spoke to the "new" Police Officer-not the two from before-who was now dealing with this. He said that HEFIBDOUYCY is(was) now in prison until December 2012.

Him, to me: "Weirdo! You're a WEIRDO! Isn't he [Human English Folkestone Incorrectess Non-Sexual Noise 100 Times She Complained's, or HEFIN-SN100TSC's first name]?" HEFIN-SN100TSC, to him about me, quite loudly, outside my door, as they were talking to me: "Yeah he's a FR+AK."
Him, to me: "The next time i see you in the street, i'm gonna kill you: you got THAT hanging over your head now."
Him, to Human English Folkestone Incorrectess Non-Sexual Noise 100 Times She Complained, or HEFIN-SN100TSC, about the door of my home: "Do you want me to break the door down [her first name]? SHALL I?" He moved back a small number of steps.
Him, to me: "C+NT! You STUPID C+NT!"
Him, to Human English Folkestone Incorrectess Non-Sexual Noise 100 Times She Complained, or HEFIN-SN100TSC, about me: "I bet he's standing there with his little thing hanging down." He then opened my mailbox, sticking his hand/fingers through a short distance.
Him, to me: "You're DEAD!"
Rammed his shoulder against my door a number of times, not as much as the standard heavy banging with his fists from him, though.
Him, to me: "C+NT! I can do whatever i WANT!"

HUMAN ENGLISH FOLKESTONE INCORRECTER OPPORTUNIST GRINNED, SPAT ON MY SHIRT FOR FUN, AND RAN OFF
HEFIOG,SOMSFF,ARO
Typing. Identity's Image:
SPACETIME EVENT OF ACT OF INCORRECTNESS
Tuesday 01/05/2012. The time was before16:17. I believe that it was not long before that time. It was sort of "at" 16:17. It was after i had paid a bill at WHSmith Folkestone. I might have purchased a deodorant at Boots Folkestone....i think that i did, but i'm not sure.
POLICE
Neighbourhood PCSO Number 56192. I gave my name to this man. He said that an Intelligence Report would be created. I wrote "Speak to you, official crime". I wrote "INTEL". I wrote "Year's". I wrote "Will not get number": that probably refers to when i might have asked for the mobile telephone numbers of a number of the three incorrectesses. He said that this report stays on forever. He took down the names of Human English Folkestone Incorrectess Sexual F+++k Song, or HEFISFS; Human English Folkestone Incorrectess Sexual Bit Of A F+++k, or HEFISBOAF; and Human English Folkestone Incorrectess Sexual Why Can't She Call You A F+++k?, or HEFISWC'tSCYAF, who told me her name: her name is Williams. ("Pent Valley High School"). This Police Officer saw the spit on the back of my shirt.
WITNESSES
European accent short haired woman driving that bus. This bus driver, i think the guy who looks like the guy who was the father of the guy filming the plastic bag blowing in the wind in the Human USA Film American Beauty(possibly the same Clan), was one of the individuals who pursued the incorrecter, i think, but the incorrecter escaped that day.
DESCRIPTION
DESCRIPTION WRITTEN DOWN ETCETERA ON THE DAY, AROUND THE TIME OF THE ACT OF
   INCORRECTNESS. Brunette hair, thin "bowl" hair in a bob, hair in a "bowl", like the Jim Carrey character haircut from Dumb And Dumber, vague-eyed. Pink shirt, blue jeans, grinning, (i wrote) 10 centimetres shorter than me. I thought at the time when i first saw him that there was an "aspect" of him that was like Human English Folkestone Male Private Company It's Theirs We Disagree, or HEFMPCI'sTWD(DAMIAN COLLINS), when he grinned.
When he grinned the first time, i thought that this incorrecter looks just like Hefmpci'stwd when the incorrecter grinned: in certain photographs of Hefmpci'stwd his mouth opens in a certain manner when grinning with open mouth, and THAT pose is the similarity.
Clan looks a little like the George Sterling Clan. Clan also might have a connection to Ben Affleck, or Matthew Lillard, especially Matthew Lillard out of the two.
Somewhat dull, drugged-looking eyes. Standard build. Build is not skinny: has more flesh on body than "skinny" human beings. Head looked somewhat large in comparison to the body, i think, or not. Freckles on visage? I think that i saw freckles on the visage. Forehead is relatively tall, or large, and extends upwards in a certain manner.
This Clan might very be the Sam Anderson Clan: the shape of the upper skull-with the high forehead and with the forehead extending in a certain way-looks possibly identical to Sam Anderson. Sam Anderson is a Human USA Actor who has acted in the Human USA Television Series "Friends"; Sam Anderson notably played the role of "Holland Manners" in the Human USA Television Series "Friends". This Clan also appears to have the "bowl" hair, quite long, but the hair doesn't go down to the shoulders or anything like that.
RECOVERY PARTIAL
The "same night". Night of Tuesday 01/05/2012. Dark blue shirt 1 was bagged; fancy black trousers 1 were bagged; underwear 1 was bagged; vest 1 was bagged.
SUNDAY 01/07/2012. The shirt was cut in two with a scissors, and then my hands were rinsed, the time is now 18:30. The trousers were cut in two with a scissors, the time is now 18:34. The underwear was cut in two with a scissors, and the vest was cut in two with a scissors, and then my hands were rinsed, and then the scissors was rinsed, and then my hands were rinsed, the time is now 18:41. They are now in a Tesco bag.
MONDAY 02/07/2012. I will dispose of the contents of the relevant Tesco bag on Monday 02/07/2012.

Also, i believe, seen on Friday 01/06/2012, see written notes. Also add MORE to this, from my memories. I did dispose of the relevant Tesco bag, probably on that day, although i will have to check my notes.

Human English Folkestone Incorrectess Non-Sexual Noise 100 Times She Complained
Typing. Identity's Image:
Human English Folkestone Incorrectess Non-Sexual Noise 100 Times She Complained, or HEFIN-SN100TSC. Name: H. Mc.
       i've got it typed on one of my papers + noise log. The noise was officially witnessed by someone from the council in at least 1 occassion, breaking a number of Acts. HEFIN-SN100TSC is guilty of hiding in her home, possibly more than that one time, Human English Folkestone Incorrecter Banging Door Open Up You C+nt Yeah, or HEFIBDOUYCY(Name: Matthew Green), guilty of some crime(s) or something BEFORE he did the things that he did to me. [i had called the police to say that i know where HEFIBDOUYCY is] She ignored the police when they demanded, 10 shouted sentences or so, that she open up: it was only after a battering ram or something had been used on the door and it had probably come off somewhat that she spoke, no longer staying silent. HEFIBDOUYCY was in there, and was arrested. After he was gone, HEFIN-SN100TSC, who came across as somewhat intoxicated, shouted obscenities, possibly "wankers!" etcetera out of her window, at a number

of human beings on the street outside; it was dark outside. She did this for at least 10 minutes. She had been unable to get back in and i had let her back in. She also banged my door one time relatively hard, saying something like "It's YOUR fault." after HEFIBDOUYCY had been arrested.

When She Had First Arrived
HEFIN-SN100TSC or some girl with her, probably her, outside my door, in the direction of my door: "Do you know what it smells like around here? KeBAB."

Before Sunday 06/03/2011.
When I was watching the episode of Naruto, Season 6, where Sasuke "stabs" Naruto, in my Lounge/Kitchen, a young girl upstairs started crying. Then she stopped crying. Then when I saw the "stab scene" again, she started crying again.

Saturday 09/06/2012.

Sunday 10/06/2012.
05:30 Loud Continuous Music.
16:30 Approx. After I Had Typed This: HEFIN-SN100TSC: "Shitshit": HEFIN-SN100TSC: "Go away"?: HEFIN-SN100TSC: "I swear".
16:40 Movement of HEFIN-SN100TSC heard after I had typed Mobile Telephone: Now a door slams: HEFIN-SN100TSC. "Oh dear".
19:00 There was hard, loud banging on my door. "I know you're in there, all right open up," a Human English Male voice(HEFIBDOUYCY) shouted. Me: "Hold on a second." (HEFIBDOUYCY): "Open up I know you're in there." Me: "You're not allowed to bang my door." "Why did you

"HEFIN-SN100TSC is aware of one or more human beings filming me while in my rooms in Folkestone. Video. Mobile Telephone? Yes Mobile Telephone. + What is on the sheets." is something that i typed on or around Sunday 10/06/2012....it was probably typed by me ON Sunday 10/06/2012 as above.

2012/06/30. PM.
HEFIN-SN100TSC Moved when i clicked "Euthanasia in Canada" Wikipedia.
HEFIN-SN100TSC Moved when i clicked "T4 Programme" Wikipedia.

My computer has been moved to my bedroom.

HEFIN-SN100TSC, to HEFIBDOUYCY about me, quite loudly, outside my door, as they were talking to me: "Yeah he's a FR+AK."
HEFIN-SN100TSC to me: "Dickhead, you're a DICKHEAD." I was called a "dickhead" by HEFIN-SN100TSC at least 3 times. When HEFIBDOUYCY was also outside my door.
HEFIN-SN100TSC to me: "You were banging on my DOOR."(noise issue ages ago). When HEFIBDOUYCY was also outside my door.

NOISE
2012/08/16 THURSDAY
Probably Surely Blasted Music Before 1105, Thursday 16/08/2012.
2012/08/24 FRIDAY
Music/tv. Before my Alarm went off at 1130.
2012/08/25 SATURDAY
Music/tv. Before my Alarm went off, Alarm went off probably before 1200.
2012/08/26 SUNDAY
Music/tv. Before my Alarm went off, Alarm went off before 1200.

"Often pauses directly above me in my bedroom(at least 10 times), and also in my toilet(at least 5 times). Pauses directly above me, following me above as i move around, very frequently."
"Motor vehicles often speed after i TYPE certain things, and/or READ certain things, when certain things COME UP on my computer screen: the timing of them is always in time."
"The individual(s) immediately downstairs of me was/were not here before Sunday 06/03/2012: someone else lived there at and before that time."
"must be"
"on the Internet"
"It is "extremely likely" that she has filmed me through her floor, and it is very likely that it is JUST a number of human beings from her home and no one else who have filmed me while in my home." was something that i typed.
"Scottish guy who lived opposite me, who has gone now; possibly, probably, couple upstairs; the individual(s) immediately downstairs of me....these often, after i type certain things on my non-Internet connected computer, walk out of their homes

at those exact points, especially when certain things are typed and/or looked at on my computer screen."
"C. and the other girl often with her when i asked C. "What's your name then, if not C.?" she said "[Sex Worker's first name/code name]" when i had typed about this Sex Worker in my bedroom only, how could she know about [Sex Worker's first name/code name]?"

I just typed HUMAN ENGLISH FOLKESTONE INCORRECTESS NON-SEXUALESS SEXUAL BABY, THEN WE'LL HAVE FUN, OR HEFIN-SSB,TWHF in Correctness And Incorrectness Notes and immediately after i had typed it a number of human beings from HEFIN-SN100TSC's home-more than one human being-left her home and went outside to the street: it is now 2012/09/23 Sunday 1033, so i typed this from 1015-1033, or rather very much closer to 1033.

Human English Folkestone Incorrectess Sexual Aaaah! Waiting Outside School, or HEFISA!WOS
Typing. Identity's Image:
1
2
3: 2012/07/26 THURSDAY
Human English2 Male H?, or He2mh?. Hefisa!wos: "I'm staying at He2mh?'s tonight."
Me: "You gave me the wrong number, you gave me your friend's number." Hefisa!wos: "(Some name)? I HATE her."
Me: "You stood me up. I went really quickly to meet you." Hefisa!wos: "My dad died of cancer (some timeorotherago)." Me: "That's why you couldn't come?" I asked something like "Was it ON THAT DAY?". Hefisa!wos: "My dad died of cancer."
Hefisa!wos: "I don't have my mobile telephone on me. I know my number off by heart." Me: "Isn't there supposed to be another digit?" She realised that she'd missed out the last digit, the 11th digit. Hefisa!wos: "Okay....X," where X is a number from 0-9. Me: "Should i bother to write this down? Are you being honest now?" Hefisa!wos: "Nonono, that's right, that's it."
Hefisa!wos: "We're going to be at X tomorrow, at One PM. (Come down)." Me: "Okay." The meeting had been set.
Hefisa!wos: "Can i have some money? Please. I just need a pound or so." Me: "How much do you want/need?" Hefisa!wos said something like "How much do i GET?" I gave her a £5.

Human English Folkestone Incorrectess Sexual Aww That's Not Very Good Now Is It, or HEFISAT'sNVGNII Typing. Identity's Image:
BEFORE SHE READ A NUMBER OF MY TOPIX INTERNET POSTS
ONE DAY
She rushed over to help me with my transaction, to the side till, from the centre till.
GENERAL
Blushing while i was talking to her, always there on the Wednesday that i used to go in there on, laughing at my humourous comments, smiling at me a lot,
ONE DAY
She looked up at me as i entered, "noticed" me. She became incredibly animated after she had looked up at me. The "vibe" was that of happiness and/or excitement, from her.
ONE DAY

AFTER SHE READ A NUMBER OF MY TOPIX INTERNET POSTS
2012/08/01 WEDNESDAY
She came out after i entered and. She was highly disturbed and alarmed.
2012/08/02 THURSDAY
She came out after i entered and. Me: "[Her first name]! Long time no see!" She smiled, and laughed softly in response to this. Me: "Do you live in F.?" Her: "Hmm, yes, in F."(something like that). Me: "Oh okay."
2012/08/03 FRIDAY
She came out after i entered. Me: "It is okay for us to speak a little, while i'm doing this, isn't (it)." Her, saying the following in a "i want to but i'm not allowed to" way: "There are customers waiting though". Me: "Yeah but it's okay to chat a little isn't it (while we're doing this)." Her, a quiet: "Yeah". She then immediately grinned and then the grin led on to that cute "quirky" "playful" grin, that she has done in response to something or other that i've said, before. A certain woman came up and stood next to her.
2012/08/04 SATURDAY
She came out after i entered and. Me: "Hi! Long time no see!" Her, seriously(she used to be flirtatious with me): "Okay what can i do for you today"
2012/08/06 MONDAY
The certain woman went to get her when i came in. HEFISAT'sNVGNII entered the room from the side. HEFISAT'sNVGNII went to that place round the corner. HEFISAT'sNVGNII walked around, waited a while, and then drew down the blind. Then, as i did a transaction, HEFISAT'sNVGNII went and started talking to a line of customers at the side till. Earlier, the certain woman wanted me to stop whatevering, and tried to hurry me.
2012/08/07 TUESDAY
HEFISAT'sNVGNII was walking towards the main till when i entered. She waited a while, then went and drew down the blind again. The "vibe" was "i hate you", from her.

ONE DAY 2012/08/01 WEDNESDAY-2012/08/04 SATURDAY INCLUSIVE
A "new that i'd never seen before" guy came out and was unbalanced, he hated that i was talking to HEFISAT'sNVGNII, i could see that.

HUMAN ENGLISH FOLKESTONE INCORRECTESS NON-SEXUALESS SEXUAL BABY, THEN WE'LL HAVE

FUN, OR HEFIN-SSB,TWHF
Typing. Identity's Image:
Will, if necessary, be a witness against him, she saw the whole thing.
2012/09/07 FRIDAY, TELEPHONED MY NOKIA 2610 AT 2359, ALTHOUGH NOKIA 2610 SAYS 2012/09/08 SATURDAY 0000
I don't think that she asked whether i was okay or not. Her: "Did you really call the police?" I didn't answer that directly. Her: "Okay but did you really call the police?" Me: "Where is he now?" Her: "He's gone back to Folkestone."
AGE
Going to be 17 soon(she said on 2012/09/07 Friday). 16.
SEXUAL HISTORY
Her: "I've had sex with 6-8 guys. About that. Roughly." Her: "My (ex?) tried to put his dick up my a++ but i wouldn't let him. He put the lube all the way up there and all. There was a lot of lube. It wouldn't go in (properly?) so we stopped."
DESCRIPTION
Hair colour brown, somewhat reddish brown, but not red-haired.
Chin juts out slightly.
Very whitish-pink skin, but not too whitish, not as much whitish as a number of Human Females that i've seen.
Very large breasts.
Eyes quite deadish.
High mental development, high mental evolution.
MIGRATION
Her: "I used to live in L."
Lives in F. itself.

Human English Incorrecter Harrasment Act 1997 Pretended That He Wanted To Make Things Better
Typing. Identity's Image:
This incorrecter is responsible for Letter To Nicholas Clegg 2, or a copy of it, having been given to the incorrect, or illegal, "Fixated Threat" or whatever organisation, who then gave the letter, or the copy of it, to the police. An incorrect, or illegal, law was then used against me. Monday 07/03/2011. I had sent a copy of Letter To Nicholas Clegg 2, to this incorrecter. Copies had also been sent to a number of other mps. This incorrecter is the leader of a certain 100% incorrect, or illegal, political group, political "party", and has been leader of it since 12/2005, December 2005. He is mp for Witney.

DEPRESSION
I must start doing things, launch into things, as quickly as possible. Every day I must have a sense of progress. I must have entertainment when necessary. If necessary, think about all the people of my group who've spent 500 days or more imprisoned, people with Motor Neuron Disease and other such diseases, and certain other disabled people. See myself doing the things, in my head.
"Girlfriend" is just a label.
I HAVE girlfriends: half an hour every few days, or whatever.
Other people only APPEAR happy/happiER.
Think about how most human beings in existence have worse lives than me.
Think about the awful lives that the human beings of the past have lived, including my ancestors? No homes like this, no razors even, probably, no soap.

OTITIS
NON-CONTAGIOUS. EAR CONDITION.
KEEP HEAD STILL Turn body, which also results in turning head, all or most of the time instead of turning head.
FOCUS WITH BOTH EYES UPON A TARGET
DO NOT GET WATER INTO EARS
PERHAPS SIGNIFICANT EXERCISE HELPS
SENSE IT GETTING WEAKER AND WEAKER. NOSE BECOMES LESS AND LESS BLOCKED, AND BREATHING BECOMES EASIER

NATURAL SCIENCE IDENTITIES
NATURAL SCIENCE VOLUME TR ROUTINE
2. NATURAL SCIENCE VOLUME TR NEAR HOME URBANISED AREA ASH, HART'S-TONGUE FERN
Ash at least 8 extremely tall trees; Hart's-tongue fern at least 4 ferns; Hawthorn at least 2 tall trees; Lords And Ladies Species(possibly now gone); Garlic Mustard(possibly now gone); Holly at least 1 plant.

POSSESSIONS
CLOTHING
Shirt Grey. Obtained in the USA.

www.ingramcontent.com/pod-product-compliance
Lightning Source LLC
Chambersburg PA
CBHW041202230426
43673CB00035B/498